Books in the series 'The Colonial Economy of NSW 1788-1835'

A Brief Economic History of NSW

The Colonial Economy of NSW 1788-1835–A retrospective

The Government Store is Open for business–the commissariat operations in NSW 1788-1835

The Enterprising Colonial Economy of NSW 1800-1830–Government Business Enterprises in operation

Guiding the Colonial Economy–Public Funding in NSW 1800-1835

Financing the Colonial Economy of NSW 1800-1835

Essays on the colonial Economy of NSW 1788-1835

Industries that Formed a Colonial Economy

Two studies on the role of funding and servicing the Colonial Finances of NSW

GORDON BECKETT

For book orders, email orders@traffordpublishing.com.sg

Most Trafford Singapore titles are also available at major online book retailers.

Printed in Singapore.

ISBN: 978-1-4669-2771-1 (sc)
ISBN: 978-1-4669-2772-8 (hc)
ISBN: 978-1-4669-2773-5 (e)

Trafford rev. 08/14/2012

www.traffordpublishing.com.sg

Singapore
toll-free: 800 101 2656 (Singapore)
Fax: 800 101 2656 (Singapore)

A LIFE AND TIMES OF WILLIAM LITHGOW
and
COUNTING THE PENNIES–THE PUBLIC FINANCE OF COLONIAL NSW

William Lithgow–'The Man with Zeal'

Gov Darling, writing to Earl Bathurst on 12th April 1827, and referring to Lithgow states 'As to zeal, I can assure you from long experience that no one has a stronger claim to, nor is better qualified to serve in, the post of Colonial Auditor'. Gov. Brisbane also wrote to Earl Bathurst one year later, on 28th July 1828, commending Lithgow's services "I express my high sense of zeal and talents of the commissary of accounts, Mr Lithgow, on this as on every other occasion for the furtherance of the public service".

CONTENTS

WILLIAM LITHGOW

'A MAN WITH ZEAL'

Synopsis and introduction

The life of William Lithgow paralleled the most interesting period of colonial history between 1824 and 1852. From the Macquarie residue to the strains of self-government approaching fast. Born in Scotland in 1784, his life tracked closely the growth of the Colony of New South Wales, however, his contribution to the colony did not commence until his transfer from Mauritius in 1823.

As characterized by Governor Darling in 1827, Lithgow was a man with great quantities of devotion and dedication, but mostly he was 'full of zeal'.

This then, is the story of Lithgow's contribution through his work and advice to the five Governors he so ably served during 28 years in the New South Wales colonial public service. Lithgow's contribution has not been demonstrated sufficiently previously, as we will see, and in economic history terms his gift to the people of the colony was unsurpassed in 'value'.

His life was as varied as the times in which he lived. A more interesting and varied Colonial would be hard to find. A lifetime of Public Service was rare for the 1800s, but Lithgow successfully divided his time between his salaried position and numerous Boards and Committees, many of which he sat on by request of the governor of the day, as a community service. He was selected for these tasks and assignments because of his broad experience, insight and loyal government service.

His mantle was broader than that offered through Commissariat accounting, to which he devoted the first 10 years of his working life (he had risen to the position of assistant deputy-commissary of accounts in Mauritius) before turning to the arduous and demanding task of auditing the Colonial Accounts under the umbrella of the Colonial Secretary's office. This experience of dealing effectively with British Commissary and Treasury bureaucracy was invaluable in the new settlement, and his know-how was called upon frequently in the struggling colony. Although he eventually became second in command under the Colonial Secretary, his activities were never fully recognised, at least publicly. He was just another Public Servant trying to set down the financial affairs of the Colony in the format demanded by the British Treasury. By today's auditing standards Lithgow's tasks were mundane, regimented and routine; however, his title of Colonial Auditor-General may well have been too generous as his real and more exacting role was as financial advisor to the colonial governors, and the implementer of practical solutions to keeping the colony on an even economic keel. The procedures of fiscal governance were demanding and bureaucratic–vouchers, vouchers and more vouchers. Each one having to be verified, firstly for authorisation within the appropriation of public funds, and then approved for payment with supporting paper work of 'receipt of goods', matched against Purchase Orders, and finally 'passed for payment' by a supervisor, within each government department. But even that wasn't the end of the process. Lithgow, as Auditor, had to confirm the trail of paperwork, and to finitely confirm that all the paperwork was in order. Each piece had to bear the correct number of signatures, carry the correct supporting vouchers and then be authorised, appropriately, for payment. Bureaucracy was rampant, but even so we find as Lithgow carried out his onerous tasks that even he was capable of making simple arithmetic errors. The Accounts forwarded over Lithgow's signature to the British Treasury contain some arithmetic errors, but any notation of weakness in this regard was more than compensated by his insatiable contribution to other aspects of the Colony.

Lithgow was a Magistrate, a Board member of the Female Factory in Parramatta and a Board Member of the newly created 'Board of General Purposes' whose role, as defined and laid down by Governor Ralph Darling, was to oversee the Colonial Planning Operations on behalf of the Governor.

From 1824 and until October 1825, Lithgow held the senior post within the Commissary System of being both Assistant Commissary General and also of being in charge of the Accounting Records and Returns. A second position was created after the British Treasury released in 1826 the revised 'Recording and Reporting Procedures'. These updated guidelines for Colonial Accounting were partly in response to the relatively unprofessional (and essentially 'privatised') accounting system invoked by Macquarie who, from 1810 to 1821 relied on amateur 'treasurers' to collect, record, disburse and report on Colonial funding. Some responsibility for this temporary clerical assistance is due to the fact that the Colony had no Treasury. Nevertheless the two 'treasurers', being Rev'd Samuel Marsden and Mr (Surgeon) Darcy Wentworth, handled all the locally raised revenue and expenditures.

After Macquarie left the Colony, Brisbane and then Darling had been instructed to install the 'Blue Book' system of recording and reporting, and so from 1822 the British Treasury received two copies of the hand compiled reports whilst the Governor kept the third copy. These records were only compiled at the end of each year and rather than assist in reducing the work load of the Colonial Secretary's office, this procedure increased it substantially, since the Blue Books were summaries taken from other summaries but then recompiled into the format required by the British Treasury. The 'Blue Book' process was a marked improvement ob the Orphan Fun, the Police Fund, the Land Fund and the many other 'funds' that were really an extension of have a separate bank account for each process of government.

Lithgow fulfilled the duties of Commissary of Accounts and Colonial Auditor admirably and impressed Governor Darling to the extent that when the Governor was given approval to form an 'Executive Council', Lithgow was offered the role of 'acting' secretary to the Council. It did not take long for Lithgow to move from mere scribe to active participant and he later filled a vacancy on the Executive Council itself.

Brisbane saw the need to create the position of Auditor of government accounts, having seen first-hand the benefits of having Lithgow fill the extra role of Auditor of Commissary accounts. Brisbane thought nothing of the potential conflict of interest of the one officer acting as both accountant (preparer) and Auditor (reviewer) of Commissary accounts, nor did he see the potential for conflict having the one officer fill the roles of commissary accountant and government auditor. Today these roles would be arms length and very independent. However Brisbane's problems were of a more practical nature than considering conflicts of interest. Brisbane found a dearth of experienced public servants in the colony and having an officer of Lithgow's experience was like a godsend. Likewise Brisbane desperately wanted and needed some 'financial' advice to assist his economic planning for the economy. Again Lithgow filled that role in terms of experience and background.

Soon, however, the dual roles of Commissary Accountant and Colonial Auditor were growing too much for one man to handle, and it was Brisbane's successor, Ralph Darling who sought the approval of The Secretary of State in London to make Lithgow a full-time Auditor (in 1825) at an increased salary. Governor Darling's salary recommendation was not accepted and Secretary of State Huskisson imposed his own limits on the Lithgow remuneration.

Even after Lithgow settled into his new restricted position (as Colonial Auditor-General) he continued to take an active role in economic analysis and future planning for the Colony, by becoming an active participant in the Governor's exclusive but unofficial 'executive council'.

Four interlinking roles (which will be explored more fully in the main text) included:

Lithgow working with Major Ovens, before Oven's premature death, on assessing the organisation of and work practices for the convicts. The idea for and organisation of the work gangs used at the dockyard, the Lumber Yard, the timber yard, the land clearing, road making gangs was that jointly of Ovens and Lithgow, although Ovens placed his name alone on the final report, lest it be thought by Governor Bourke that Lithgow had surplus time on his hands.

Working on and with the Board of the Female Work Factory to develop outputs that were worthwhile and meaningful. As a former Commissary principal, Lithgow was in a good position to gauge what could be produced within the colony by the growing 'army' of female prisoners. The numbers for the Female Factory are interesting, as the private placement of 381 of the 573 women meant that the government was denied the working output of these people, although on the other hand the government was saved the direct cost of clothing, defending the morals, housing and feeding of these women.

The Land Board prepared a detailed series of reports (they were authored and assembled by Lithgow) for the governor, that established the role and needs of land sales, land clearing, surveying and set aside land for townships, schools, churches and the need for town planning including communications and transportation.

His association with the Bank of New South Wales was long and successful. Lithgow was a Director, initially representing the Government, but was re-elected in his own right, an association that lasted almost 20 years. He became a trustee of the Australian Society for Deposits and Loans. Lithgow also became an initial shareholder (nominal value 100 pound) in the Bank of Australia.

Lithgow filled his position for 19 years as a member of the Legislative Council admirably and used his participation to assist in interpreting the all-important Appropriation Bills for the benefit of the other members.

The Lithgow committee work would have brought him in touch with most, if not all, of the notable and significant members of the Colonial community. is voluntary associations and community interests included those already mentioned, as well as the Southern Cattle Association and the Railway Association and the Steam Navigation Company. These committees were then extended to the Board of Trustees of the Clergy and School Lands; the New South Wales Legislative Council; The Bank of NSW and the Savings Bank of NSW; Magistrate and J.P; nomination to the Executive Council in December 1835, and membership of the Coal Board in October 1847.

Lithgow served under five governors, one of which he also served as acting Private Secretary. He liaised with eight British Secretaries of State and five British Prime Ministers. He was threatened with termination by Sir George

Gipps, who was being chastised for failing to deliver the 'Blue Books' for 5 years past the due date. Gipps blamed Lithgow; Lithgow blamed the down the line record-keepers, but in the end Lithgow delivered six years of audited annual records (the Blue Books) in less than six months.

We have yet to learn very much about his early life, except that he was born and raised in the Scotland of the late 1700s. It is most likely, that the Lithgow family home was in the Lanark district in the Clyde River region of south-central Scotland. He graduated from the University of Edinburgh as a licentiate of the Church of Scotland, but shortly after graduating chose instead to join the Commissary Operations of the British Military abroad. Another conjecture, by this author, as yet unverified, is that Lithgow was a second son, expected by tradition to enter the 'church', but as the Church of Scotland was, at that time in turmoil and undergoing major change, it is likely that young clerics were paid very little and Lithgow saw a larger benefit in a secure, government position. Scottish Home Office records do not include references to the early Lithgow family, and so we are left wondering if William was a descendent of the famous Scottish explorer from the early 1600s who bore the same name We could attribute, in yet another giant leap of imagination that Lithgow's decision to remain an unmarried loner all his life could have been due to a family tragedy before he joined the army, or possibly he had the predilection of this forebear, William Lithgow (1583-1637) to roam, adventure and travel. The British Military had headquartered their commissary operation for Europe in Edinburgh, and after two years of pounding the streets following his graduation, earning a small pittance as a stipend and feeling he was going nowhere, Lithgow decided to join the military in as non-military field as he could find. He spent the next two years in the original quartermaster's stores in Edinburgh and found he had a flair for numbers, clerical organisation and a good judgment for forward planning. The military decided, following the initial training period that his commission should be made permanent and his knowledge and instruction extended. Thus commenced a lifelong period of public service.

His first appointment was to Heligoland, a small piece of British Territory–an island in the North Sea. When the British were relieved of control over Heligoland and it was handed back to the Germans, he was transferred (July 1812) to Mauritius, still with the Commissary division of the British Military, where he rose through the ranks to become assistant commissary. He was in Mauritius at the same time as Ralph. Darling, who, upon his appointment (in April 1823) as Governor of New South Wales, requested the transfer of Lithgow as Assistant Commissary-General for 'Accounts' at the same destination. Lithgow had sailed directly to Sydney, via Hobart, arriving May 1824, whilst Darling took himself and family back to England for twelve months before sailing for Sydney. Whilst in London he received two commissions–one as Governor of the colony of New South Wales and the other as Governor-in-Chief of Van Diemen's Land, with a lieutenant governor, resident in Hobart responsible for day–to-day operations. Thus Lithgow's journey into Colonial Australia began in Sydney in 1824, but he was serving Governor Brisbane until Darling arrived in 1826.

Lithgow had grown up in a Scotland that had unified in 1707 with England to form a creative and beneficial union as Great Britain, and he chose to contribute to the growth of the British Colony in New South Wales. Lithgow's participation in just about every aspect of the future government of the colony made him a potentially formidable force in Colonial public affairs, and he was an influential adviser to each successive governor of the day. Darling anticipated this potential and Lithgow was the first of a number Darling had worked with prior to 1825 who he selected to gather around him in Colonial New South Wales. This 'team' included Major Ovens, his son in law, William Dumaresq, and the other Dumaresq brother–Henry.

The post Macquarie colony was a rapidly changing place–the colony had matured remarkably since Macquarie had generated unparalleled growth in the land, through his building program and his placement of the swelling ranks of male and female convicts into productive, both private and public, work. Macquarie's encouragement of new colonial industry sustained the growing levels of British investment and speculation in the colony. Decentralisation and the need to open up new settlements including Van Dieman's Land, Port Phillip and Morton Bay continued to grow the local revenue and de-emphasise the need for British Treasury funding. However the Commissary operations grew increasingly important, as they were the sole support programs for both the convicts and the military remaining in the colony.

Lithgow received at least two land grants: a rural grant of two thousand acres in the Hunter district, and a residential site in Sydney town (on the North Shore at St. Leonard's), on which he built a cottage. He also held a 'grazing' licence in the then Riverina District, but in an area we know today as Gundagai. His 'run' was on the eastern bank of the Murrumbidgee River, where the township of Gundagai now stands. This property was managed on his behalf and records show that he only visited this area once in the 8 years he operated the 'lease;' but this pastoral activity made him think a great deal about the agricultural planning in the colony and its potential, and he then spent many years in the two agricultural societies that became so influential during the rise of the pastoral and squatting industries.

Lithgow retired in the Colony in 1852 on a pension of £339/3/4 per annum, and relocated from Sydney to his cottage on the rural property in the Hunter region. He retired also from the Legislative Council in 1848 (after 19 years of service), and from his position of Auditor-General in 1852. Lithgow died in 1864 (11June) at the age of 80. Lithgow's was a remarkable career, stretching 50 years in the service of his country and leaving a legacy of contribution to the colony, and such a contribution would be difficult to ever match again. His memorials are few, other than a town that retained his name and became an established settlement in the area known originally as 'Lithgow's Valley' (the name was given by Lithgow's friend and colleague (Surveyor-General John Oxley). We learn from newspaper reports of his land-sales (first at Kissing Point and then Lithgow Valley) and of his sheep 'run' at present day Gundagai in the Monaro Region of southern New South Wales.

CHAPTER 1

THE SOURCES

William Lithgow was and is an enigma. We know so little about him, but can interpolate quite a lot from his times, his work, his colleagues and his more public moments. Because we glean so little from the secondary sources (we have no primary sources of information), we are left in the dark about any direct assessment of his character, or any direct information on his career, family or living arrangements. We do however, have a portrait of William (Lithgow), sketched in 1903, no doubt from an earlier portrait, since he died some 40 years previously. The original sketch would have been made not long before his retirement since he appears to be an older man, not the distinguished looking 'executive' type one would expect, slim, tall, moustached and in a bowler hat. The sketcher saw him as slightly chubby, a man of short stature, without the normal facial hair of the day, seated with his books about him and looking thoughtful. For headgear, the sketcher gave him a 'cap', which makes Lithgow look like a railway porter. The source of the original sketch was the NSW Government Printer–their collection of negatives 1870-1988–being portraits of government servants, with Lithgow being identified as the 'former Auditor-General'. The few copies of hand-written Lithgow letters to the Governor and the Colonial Secretary, are in neat readable copperplate showing care in their writing with plenty of thought, since there are no scratching or erasures.

> The secondary sources are surprisingly few. The writer has observed elsewhere in the text that the authors dealing with events and personalities of the times, including Lithgow's immediate colleagues barely mention his name let alone

say anything about his work or life. The biography of Ralph Darling, the governor that recruited Lithgow to his post as Assistant Commissary of Accounts for New South Wales, and who had previously known him in Mauritius does not even mention Lithgow. And as surprising as this omission is by Brian Fletcher, the biographer, even more surprising is that Butlin in his excellent work on the Development of Monetary Policy in the Colony does not mention Lithgow more than once, which was a minor reference to Lithgow being the first auditor. Why are these omissions surprising? For a start Lithgow, as the first Commissary of Accounts–a new position set up by Governor Darling in 1824, was responsible for returning the Commissary to a practical and legitimate operating basis. The post-Macquarie years had not brought the necessary changes to the Commissary that had been desired by Commissioner Bigge. The succession of Governors since 1788 had brought only minimal changes to Commissary operations as the demand for food, tools and materials had grown with the colony. The various arms of Commissary operations such as the Government Farms, the 'manufacturing' locations, the dockyards and a variety of storage facilities, had grown unwieldy in their accounting and control aspects. Governor Darling wanted to implement the latest inventory control, budgeting, purchasing and bookkeeping systems in order to make decisions as to how to cut costs and improve Commissary performance. For this reason and to implement new directives from the Commissary-General in London, Darling decided to recruit an experienced and useful officer. Lithgow was that choice and in 1823 was assigned to the new post in Sydney town. Darling's choice to find a creative, personable Commissary Accountant was warmly received according to another new recruit to the Commissary–Lieutenant Boyes, who, in writing to his wife in London, explained that there was 'great anticipation' for the arrival of Lithgow in Sydney.

Few letters exist in Lithgow's meticulous handwriting, but the first to be found from the archives of the Mitchell Library in Sydney is one signed by both Lithgow and Colonial-Secretary Goulburn, later discharged in disgrace, but who in January 1825, joined with Lithgow to persuade Governor Darling to impose a duty on foreign imported spirits. Lithgow wrote 'we are of the opinion that whilst duties on imported spirits continue at present rates, the interests of the home distillers would be sufficiently protected, should a duty of five shillings per gallon be laid (imposed) on spirits distilled within the colony'. The other two signatures appended to this letter to 'Governor Darling, The Governor in Chief' were Darcy Wentworth and John Piper. Darling acted positively and promptly on this recommendation. The political strength behind the signatories was overwhelming.

Piper was the first Naval Officer in the Colony (appointed by Macquarie in 1813), with the duties including collection of customs duties and excise on spirits and harbour charges, the control of all lighthouses and water policing generally. His remuneration was based on his collections and his income rose to over £4,000 per annum. Macquarie made him a magistrate in 1819 and in 1825 he was elected Chairman of the Board of the Bank of New South Wales (Lithgow had been appointed a director, representing the government, in 1824). He was suspended from the post of Naval Officer in 1827 when Darling, acting on an audit report by Lithgow, recognised a deficiency in the public naval officer's funds of over £12,000.

Darcy Wentworth was also well qualified to advise Darling with respect to customs and excise collections. Wentworth, the father of W.C. Wentworth, had been the 'Treasurer' of the Police Fund from 1802 until 1818. The Police Fund, a successor to the failed 'Gaol Fund', was in receipt of 7/8ths of the local revenues from customs and excise collections, and expended its collections on public property maintenance, road and bridge maintenance, gaol maintenance and the recovery of absconding convicts. The other 1/8th of the local revenue was directed to the Orphan Fund, whose treasurer was the Rev'd Samuel Marsden. Wentworth had become the police magistrate in the colony, and had been very successful as a property owner and trader, after an inauspicious start as an assistant surgeon in the early Colony. Darling was to be persuaded, by the weight of this public opinion, to the view of Lithgow (his Commissary of Accounts and part-time auditor) and his co-signers. Mostly he was persuaded because of Lithgow's expertise in Government Financing but somewhat by Frederick Goulburn, as his Colonial Secretary, whose appointment had been imposed on his administration but by direction of Lord Bathurst, he was advised to co-operate with Goulburn; and by Darcy Wentworth who in addition to his wealth and influence, had twenty years of treasury experience in the colony; and by Captain John Piper, whose distinguished military career was only usurped by his distinguished role as the colony's Naval Officer.

Amongst other correspondence to and by Lithgow, we find the official announcement of his appointment as Commissary of Accounts, together with instructions to Assistant Commissary General Lithgow (they came via Major Goulburn–Colonial Secretary) from the Lord Commissary and the Lords of the Treasury on the duties for the Commissariat of Accounts at this station. This correspondence was dated 18 February 1824, shortly after Lithgow had arrived in January of that year.

For purposes of historical accuracy, the instructions are reported below. The instructions for filling this new posting contain an insight into the times, the reporting needs of the day and the elementary conditions of accounting standards within the British Government and financial system. Even though hundreds of millions of pounds were being expended in all quarters of the globe, the standard of bookkeeping was extremely basic.

'You are already in possession of the Instructions & Regulations under which the examination of the accounts of the Military expenditure is to be conducted, but your duties will not be confined to this expenditure only, but will extend to the examination of the accounts of the Commissariat by whom rations are provided and issued to the convicts, and to various other persons as well as to the military. The rations and extent of the rations issued are from time to time settled by the governor of the colony, and in the examination of the accounts of the Commissariat, you will take care that the officer in charge conducts the duties of the department in strict conformity to the Instructions communicated to him by this Board, or to the directions which he may from time to time receive from the Governor.

From the distance of the station from the Mother Country and from various other causes, the accounts and periodical returns required and received from other stations have not been received from this station with any regularity. I am particularly to call your attention to this point and to acquaint you that the officer in charge of the Department will be instructed to deliver his accounts to you, in duplicate, monthly, and also the accounts of this sub-accountant at Van Dieman's Land monthly as they may be received. My Lords trust that you will complete the examination of the Cash Accounts within a month, and the other accounts within two months after they may be delivered to you; and that you will transmit them to this office by the first opportunity which may occur, and that a duplicate of the accounts may be transmitted by the first opportunity, which may offer after the first have been dispatched and that by the next succeeding opportunity their Lordships may be advised of the particulars of the accounts and of the conveyance by which they have been forwarded.

The names of the officers who may be directed to act under you will be communicated by you as soon as they are selected, and you will, upon your arrival at New South Wales, report yourself to the Governor and submit to him a copy of your instructions and his Excellency will be required, to direct a proper office be provided to you. It is their Lordship's intentions that the officer in charge of the Commissariat at Van Dieman's Land should be subordinate to, and act as a sub-accountant to the Officer at Sydney–but it will probably much facilitate the examination and settlement of the accounts, if they are made up for each station separately; the officer at Sydney taking credit in one item for the whole expenditure by the officer at VDL in whose accounts the particulars of the expenditures will be, of course, detailed.'

(Signed) Geo. Harrison

The remaining secondary sources relating to Lithgow come to us from the newspapers of the day, the reporting of land grants and official proclamations by the Governor, all of which are recorded in Historical Records of Australia.

The newspapers of the day, the 'Australian' and the 'Sydney Herald' seemed to have had a grudging respect for

Lithgow. He was reported frequently in small snippets of 'news'. No major expressions of opinion were ever sought, or if they were sought, were never published. The general news items involving Lithgow related to his general work activities.

Newspaper Headlines

A modest selection of headlines from the newspapers of the day will offer a chance to see a sampling of Lithgow's life. These 'headlines' are taken from the Australian newspaper published between 1824 and 1842. Robert Wardell was the publisher of the newspaper at that time and became the nemesis of Governor Darling, especially when Darling took steps to, firstly, impose a duty on all newspapers sold, and then proclaim severe libel laws relating to text in the newspapers. Chief Justice Forbes refused to certify the first move by Darling but allowed the second, much to his regret. Darling immediately sued Wardell for seditious libel, as did Marsden, Macarthur, Lord and Wentworth. These lawsuits clogged the Forbes Court docket for many months and imposed great delays on justice as well as hardship on the Magistrates trying to keep urgent cases moving through the system.

Signs regulations for estimates as Asst Comm General (14.10.1824)
Attends agricultural society dinner (14.10.1824)
Appointed to audit colonial revenue accounts (18.11.1824)
Subscribes to Busby's culture of the vines (9.12.1824)
Elected member of agricultural society (20.1.1825)
Confirmed as auditor of accounts (25.1.1825)
Appointed auditor of Male, Female Orphan and Church Accounts (24.11.1825)

In addition to many of his official work appointments, as auditor of numerous government supported funds, we read of his appointment to the bank boards of the Bank of Sydney (20.5.1826) and the Bank of

NSW (6.1.1827), his appointment to government Committees, such as the Harbour Dues Board (2.5.1827), and the Immigration Committee (6.6.1837) and his elevation as a J.P and Magistrate (27.1.1827). We can read about his property purchases–a house in Elizabeth Street for 1200 pound (30.8.1836), and his first land grant (13.4.1832). Probably the appointment he appreciated most was to the board of the Southern Cattle Association in 1836. At this time Lithgow was very active in getting around the colony, and his first land grant had been a sheep run of several thousand acres on the banks of the Murrumbidgee River on the site where the town of Gundagai now stands. We learn from the newspapers that Lithgow was opposed to transportation and signed a petition to the Governor seeking to terminate transportation (20.12.1838).

Despite a civil rank second only to the Colonial Secretary, and with a seat in the Executive and Legislative Councils, he appears to have escaped most of the unpopularity of Darling, Goulburn and the 'Darling creatures' (Australian 26.5.1826). Darling's successor, Richard Bourke, thought Lithgow to be distinguished for his liberal principles (*An Epitome of History of NSW*–p185), and employed him sometimes as private secretary and even hoped to make him Colonial Treasurer (by elevating that post to number one financial officer in the colony). Lithgow's health suffered together with his reputation when his normally punctual transmission of audited accounts to London, began to slip further and further behind. They were five years in arrears when a threat of dismissal by George Gipps brought swift resolution to the problem and in six months Lithgow had caught up all overdue accounts. This effort was at great expense to his health and his career commenced a downhill trek from that time. He considered himself affronted by being overlooked, once again, for the position of colonial secretary, a position he aspired to as being on the top of the public service ladder. His one time mentor and close friend, Edward Deas Thompson, received the call and shortly thereafter Lithgow decided to retire, right at the time that he could have made a gargantuan contribution. Lithgow had been thwarted by an early example of nepotism. The Governor of the day, Sir Richard Bourke, had approved of his second daughter marrying the son of Deas Thompson, Edward, thus giving the fiercely competitive situation a boost towards Deas Thompson.

Lithgow's retirement at such a critical time was at once an evidence of his peevishness at being overworked and overlooked, but mostly it was evidence of his deteriorating health. We can only be distant witnesses to a public servant who devoted his whole life to a cause he deeply believed in, but having worked so long and so hard, did not life to enjoy his memories. The crisis of timing is simply explained. Lithgow was an important member of the Legislative Council, representing both the ultimate financial knowledge available in the colony and the governor. W.C. Wentworth was at his most peacockish and was leading the debate on the new constitution for the colony. It needed Lithgow's temperate language and thinking to keep the debate on an even keel. The major unresolved questions in the constitution debate were financial. The British Government did not want to maintain the civil list, but the colony could not reasonably or rationally support the growing civil list without additional revenue sources. However the British Government wanted to retain the revenue stream from the sale of crown lands, as a means of defraying its previous expenses of supporting the colony from 1788. Lithgow accepted both arguments but made his contribution on the side of the colony by drawing attention to the gains and benefits the home government had already received from the colony–trade, insurance, shipping, direct investment in property, wool and branch manufacturing. Lithgow strongly put the case for these major benefits filling the 'payback' needs of Great Britain, but his contribution was still needed between 1852, when he retired, until 1856 when the self-government constitution was brought down. His continuing role would have been significant and worthy, but for those four years, instead of being an adviser to the new government in waiting, he retired to his Hunter Valley property and his sheep. We should not think that Lithgow took his sheep lightly. He applied to them the same economic and financial rationale as he did to his professional duties. In 1833 he wrote to his friend Terry Hogan:

The getting up of the wool clean and well is an object of the first importance, as it makes a difference of two or three pence (per pound) in the price, and too much attention cannot, therefore, be given to the washing. (William Lithgow to Terry Hogan, 8 January 1833, Hogan Papers 1830-36 ML A663)

Hogan befriended Lithgow whilst he was working in the accounts section of the Commissary's head office in London, before being transferred to the Colony with another of Lithgow's friends, David Allen, who became the Chief Commissary-General in the Colony of New South Wales. Lithgow, whilst working in Mauritius took to tutoring David Allen's children, so he developed a strong bond with Hogan and Allen and even more so when the two arrived in the Colony.

In spite of the vast amount of knowledge on the Lithgow times and colleagues, we are left with an unwholesome ponderance on some important questions. We do not know of Lithgow's early years, at least through his first 20 years. We know not where he was born nor of his parents. We learn that he was educated at Edinburgh University for four years and became a licentiate for the Church of Scotland but we cannot begin to understand the circumstances of his original intention to join the church, nor of his change of mind to turn to government service. The choices are broad and compelling. Was it family, economic, running away from a lost love, or simply a failure to grasp the religious intolerance of the day? Could he have been persuaded that the Church was not his bailiwick? Was he related to the great adventurer, William Lithgow, a hundred years before him? Was he born and raised in the traditional Lithgow region of Lanark, halfway between Glasgow and Edinburgh? Did he have family? No records exist of his family tree or lineage, and no mention is ever made of a family in Sydney. Can we raise with any degree of honesty the question of his celibacy? Was he a colonial homosexual, or was work his first love so that he never found time to settle down with a wife and family? Fact or fantasy? Answers would be persuasive in understanding Lithgow's temperament, philosophy and skills base.

However this is not all of the missing information we seek. There are other gaps in the current knowledge. For instance, we cannot rely on the newspapers of the day to provide reporting of the Lithgow speeches in the Legislative Council. During those early years and before self-government, 'Hansard' reporting was limited and *Votes and Proceedings of the NSW Legislative Counci*l did not commence until the 1850s. This is an unknown: how did Lithgow present himself and his practical politics to the Council and the settlers of the colony. We must rely on the reporting of the times and the general political expediencies pursued by the Governor of the day. We will be left wondering how Lithgow coped (or did he?) with his colleagues and friends becoming successful and wealthy away from public life, whilst Lithgow himself restricted his activities to a little land speculation, which was in the end result to no avail, since he left neither issue nor family.

The final question is, how has history treated or assessed William Lithgow? One can only be disappointed that the word Lithgow does not appear more ardently in the texts of history. The fact that he is largely overlooked, if not completely ignored, should not influence our own assessment of the man and his life and times. His (Lithgow's) was a remarkable contribution, or was it mediocre and passé. Surely the answer is more than merely being in the eye of the beholder or individual reader: it can be documented, assessed, classified and graded. We can be thankful that, like so many other mortals, Lithgow was in the right place at the right time. The fact that he was not a Churchill or a Menzies does not diminish his stature or standing. His was a behind the scenes contribution: he kept the public service cogs greased, and working smoothly;. he advised five governors, fearlessly and honourably; he wrote many reports that changed and improved the life of his fellow free settlers. He changed the colony in a way that Macquarie could never do. His was the contribution to good governance, which comes from persuasion and analysis, driven by that fine sense of political nous.

Out knowledge of the life of Lithgow is a challenge still to be met in full but our understanding of the times of Lithgow are one that is substantially complete. We know that he served with five Governors and 10 Secretaries of State during the time he was in the Colony, and no less than another six whilst he worked with the Commissariat Department of the British Treasury in Heligoland and Mauritius. He colleagues in the colony included four Colonial Secretaries and four Colonial Treasurers. He saw the Colonial economy grow in so many ways: the population grew from 30,000 in 1824 to 230,000 at the time of his retirement; imports and exports grew from a combined 460,000 in 1824 to 2,360,000 in 1852; wool production was only 324,000 lb when Lithgow arrived but grew to over 41 million pounds weight by 1852. Lithgow contributed to much of this economic growth as a grazier and who sold his woolclip overseas and by buying goods in London and entering into a number of trading joint ventures with his colleagues and friends. He lived to see the first of the railways being developed, which would open up greater decentralisation and new farming communities and he lived to see, but not directly benefit from, the gold rush. He would have felt partially vindicated by these two major economic steps in the Colony, especially since he had petitioned to end transportation and allow the Colony to development as a completely free and self-governing society, increasingly independent of Great Britain.

Lithgow's contribution is worthy of noting in a detailed study.

CHAPTER 2

ASSEMBLING THE SOURCES

Sources for information about William Lithgow are scarce but his is such an interesting career and life that the search is ample reward in itself. Primary sources are essentially restricted to the records from the State Records Office (SRO) of NSW. As Auditor-General, his official papers have been kept for nearly 180 years, and we are able to determine quite a lot about his official role in various colonial administrations. The history of Public Finance, auditing and treasurership in Australia is essentially the story of William Lithgow.

Instructions on Colonial financial practice

In 1826, Lithgow (Colonial Auditor), Balcombe (Colonial Treasurer) and the Governor were all supplied with more detailed instructions on financial matters. Governor Phillip's instructions included no reference to the keeping of accounts during the early settlement of the colony of New South Wales, but Governor King did receive additional instructions for record keeping. The new governor, Ralph Darling, had carried these up-dated instructions to the Colony with him, arriving in 1825.

The **Governor** was requested to ensure that:

All public accounts were to be kept in British currency
Collectors of public revenue paid over their gross collections at least twice a month to the Treasurer

Collectors of public revenues submitted monthly accounts
A schedule of fixed establishment was prepared i.e. a full civil list together with salaries and allowances
This schedule was to be updated monthly
A schedule of contingent charges were to be furnished to the Auditor monthly
Details of all stores received and issued to be prepared monthly
Abstract of expenditures to be submitted to the governor, as well as a full year detailed summary of all revenues and expenditures
Statements of all public buildings including occupancy and rents were to be prepared annually
An annual report of all dues and tolls levied was also to be prepared
All warrants for the issue of public monies to be counter signed by the governor
All documents of accounts to be prepared in duplicate, with one set being retained in the colony and one set sent to London

The **Auditor** was required to transmit to England:

One set of certified monthly accounts
Copies of all surcharges made by the auditor
Detailed statements of all advances outstanding at the end of each year
A complete set of government gazettes for the year along with orders and regulations

The **Treasurer** was requested to send to the Auditor:

Monthly Accounts, current, of all received or issued by the Treasury, specifying the individual transactions
Monthly statements of all monies temporarily deposited in the Treasury, subject to orders of the Court of Judicature, or of any other Public Department or Officer but not available for the general service of the colony, specifying each transaction.
Monthly abstracts of the negotiation and disposal of all Bills of Exchange and
Specie other than the currency in which his accounts were kept.

At the close of the year the Treasurer was to make out on account current of the whole of the receipts and disbursements (Source: *Instructions to the Treasurer of NSW for keeping the accounts of the colony* 13h June 1826*).*

Lithgow later drafted a set of notes for Sir George Gipps to send to Lord Stanley in London regarding the onerous provisions in the 1826 instructions. His objections to these instructions were:

'The instructions . . . . issued in 1826 . . . apply to a very different state of things from that which exists at present; they apply, or seem at least to apply, to a chest constantly opened to the Treasurer, in fact chest out of which he makes his daily armaments; but, in this colony, he has no such chest, his daily payments being made by drafts on the different banks, the government keeping a balance in and a current account with each of the principal Banks in the colony.' (7 February 1843)

This 'chest' may well be the result of Lord Bathurst's instructions in 1826 to Darling for the safe-keeping of colonial funds, i.e. a sealed room, to be opened by two keys and two senior officers to be present. This 'system' had long been abandoned due to the dramatic growth of Government financial transactions in the colony and by 1843, when Gipps was trying to bring Lithgow into line with his 'Blue Books'–those being up to five years in arrears–the instructions of 17 years previously were no longer relevant or applicable.

However, back in 1826, Lithgow became responsible, with the complete support of Darling, for a 'review' of the offices attached to the Treasury function and he recommended a reallocation of duties and some new titles. A Collector of Internal Revenue was first appointed in 1827. The holder of this office (the successor to the Naval Officer) was to be responsible for the collection of quit-rents, fees for licences, rents from turnpikes and ferries, market dues etc. He also took over the issuing of licences and the auctioning of tolls. A separate Collector of Customs was also appointed, this duty previously having been performed by a Naval Officer. The offices of the ***Colonial Treasurer*** and the collector of Internal Revenue were later consolidated in 1837, the change being accomplished by the creation of a Revenue Branch of the Treasury.

Throughout his service as Auditor General and Assistant Commissary-General of Accounts, Lithgow had held many other responsible positions, which may well have contributed to the many complaints his department received about arrears in his accounts, and serve to illustrate his situation in the colony. He was made a Justice of the Peace in November 1825, and on the 25 November 1825 he was appointed Auditor of the Male and Female Orphanage and of the Church Accounts. (Source: The *Australian* 17 and 24 November 1825). He became a member of the Land Board on 10 January 1826 (*The Australian).* This Board was existed for the purpose of assisting the Governor to investigate applications for Land Grants and purchases and for convict servants, together with other general duties (Source: *Blue Books* 1826).

Darling praised Lithgow's assistance in a Despatch (*Governor's Despatches* 1826 p327-9) to Viscount Goderich:

Mr Lithgow is invaluable from his perfect knowledge of business and information on all points connected with Official Details–I have only to regret that his services in the Land Board cannot at present be dispensed with; as they are much required in the general arrangements of the departments.'

However, Lithgow ceased his Land Board position on 12 April 1827, according to the Blue Book of that year.

In 1826, he had become a member of the Board required to investigate the state of the Bank of NSW. The Bank, which was in a precarious position due to a shortage of liquidity, applied to the Government for a loan. Governor Darling insisted as a condition of a loan that several directors of his own choosing be nominated and Lithgow was one. He retired from this position in January 1827 (*Sydney Gazette* 5 January 1827), as a requirement set by Lord Bathurst. On 3 February 1829 the Treasurer was instructed not to deposit any more money in the Bank of NSW (*Colonial Secretary to Colonial Treasurer,* 3 February 1829).

In another crisis, the Bank again accepted Lithgow as a Governor's nominee director but, when the Government loan was repaid in May 1829, he ceased to act in this capacity. He was then elected a Director in his own right in December 1829, and was a member of the Stockholders' Committee in June 1830. Lithgow's association with the Bank remained, even after the Bank was reinstated as a depository for Government funds. His knowledge of banking was invaluable and he was appointed a trustee of the Savings Bank of NSW in January 1844.

In May 1827, Lithgow was nominated as a member of the Harbour Dues Board. Lithgow had been private secretary to Sir Thomas Brisbane during the fatal illness of Major Ovens; with whom Lithgow had collaborated on a study of Convict Work practices finally presented to Brisbane's successor, Governor Darling. In June 1827 he was temporarily returned to that office during the absence overseas of Colonel Dumaresq. Stewart Ryrie was chosen to act as interim Auditor of Colonial Accounts. Lithgow also acted as Clerk of the Executive Council until 8 September 1827. He returned to his duties as Auditor on 24 November 1827 and in October 1827 he was a member of a Board to investigate the state of the office of Colonial Secretary. Throughout his career Lithgow had similar assignments in his official capacity of colonial Auditor-General. Acknowledgement is made of the assistance of official records relating to the office of the early Auditor-General by the Archives Authority (now the State Records Office) of NSW (1964)

During a dispute in 1827 over the election as a director of the Bank of NSW of J.T. Campbell (then Collector of Customs and later to become the Colonial Secretary), the *Sydney Gazette* enthusiastically supported giving this office to Lithgow:

'The public have long been anxiously looking for the appointment of Mr Lithgow–a gentleman universally regarded by all classes of inhabitants–to the important, responsible and arduous situation of Collector of Customs.' (Sydney Gazette 12 November 1827)

However, Campbell resigned from the Bank, and the matter was closed.

On 12 April 1830, the announcement was made of Lithgow's appointment as Commissioner for managing the affairs of the Church and Schools Estates in NSW.

As Auditor-General, Lithgow was appointed an ex-officio member of the Legislative Council on 30 January 1829 and held the office until January 1843. When Riddell, the Colonial Treasurer, was suspended from membership of the Executive Council on 1 December 1835, Governor Bourke proposed Lithgow as his successor. He was renominated on three occasions to the Council (21 July 1843, 8 December 1848, and 13 October 1851). He finally resigned from the Legislative Council on 5 May 1852, shortly before his resignation as Auditor-General on 31 May 1852.

Lithgow was at one time or another, a member of the semi-Circular Wharf Committee (renamed Circular Quay), Immigration Committee, Provisional Committee of the Australian Steam Navigation Co., Central Immigration Committee, a trustee of the Australian Society for Deposits and Loans, a member of the committee to consider erection of Lighthouses in Bass Strait, the Southern Cattle Association, and the Legislative Committee to consider Immigration Debentures.

It is interesting to review these secondary sources of information about Lithgow–The Governors' Despatches, the newspapers (*Sydney Gazette*, *Sydney Herald* and *The Australian*), the SRO files, the HRA and the NSW Parliament Records (of Petitions). They offer us a further insight into the great public service followed by Lithgow and in spite of his murmurings to the contrary immediately following his arrival in the colony, his obvious commitment to and love of his adopted country. His early distress in the colony was due to the promise of a house to be shared with a friend Lieutenant Boyes, but Brisbane reneged on this arrangement and gave the house to Balcombe and his family. This was not the last disappointment Lithgow would face at the hands of a 'flexible' governor. The location of his audit office changed three times within six years due to pressure of demand for office space in the town. He never seemed to grumble officially but kept about his heavy work schedule and kept his office staff happy.

The biggest newspaper story concerned the growing official (London) complaints over arrears in accounts. These had begun in 1827 and were to continue through most of his career. In April 1827, Darling separated the Office of Deputy Commissary-General of Accompts, which was a military appointment, from that of Auditor-General. In theory, this reduced Lithgow's workload but still the story of the late Blue Books persisted. The three newspapers of the day (*Sydney Gazette*, *Sydney Herald* and *The Australian*) made much of the arrears and the ensuing criticism of Lithgow and the governor, and recited Darling's written explanation to Lord Bathurst of 12 April 1827).

'The fact that no steps had been taken, previous to my arrival, to establish regulations for the conduct of any of the Departments, either civil or Military, and the trouble in endeavouring to correct the evils, which existed, had been commensurate with the confusion and disorder which prevailed. It is only justice to Mr Lithgow, the Auditor, to inform your Lordship that he has been indefatigable, and has afforded me every possible assistance in preparing the general arrangements. But the duties of the auditor in a government like this, where a new system of accounts is to be established under the Lords of the Treasury, which have been regularly received, are as much as any person, however zealous, can properly discharge. By attempting too much, something must be neglected, which has, in effect, been experienced; and the only remedy is to make a more just distribution of the business, which I find will be best accomplished by separating the civil and military branches of this Department'. (Darling to Bathurst 12.4.1827 HRA 1:13.249)

Darling also requested a more suitable salary for Lithgow '. . . as there is perhaps hardly an officer of more real importance under the government. In Mauritius, the Auditor ranks next to the Colonial Secretary'. The British Treasury agreed to the separation of offices and to Lithgow's appointment at a salary of £650. Mr Spurrier, formerly of the Commissary at Mauritius, succeeded Lithgow as Commissary of Accounts in the colony of NSW. However, in spite of these changes, the audit office continued to be behind in its operations but, at this point. Lithgow does not appear to have been blamed for this result. It was Governor Gipps who threatened him with dismissal unless the problem was fixed but, it should be pointed out that the lateness of the Blue Books was intrinsic in the system of preparing and assembling the formal records. As explained previously, the Blue Books were merely a summary of the various detailed ledgers and accounts kept by various departments and 'bureaus'. Supposedly the audited audits were the basis of the compilation for the Blue books and Lithgow stated that he felt constrained from making any changes to the existing system, which was obviously slow, archaic and unworkable. The existing system had been laid down by the British Treasury and it would have been a major move for changes to take place, including convincing the governor, the Treasury, the Colonial Office and probably more local officers and a great deal of retraining of local officials. Thus it was essentially within Lithgow's capacity as Colonial Auditor to correct the problem but it would have been a lot of work, and he felt the system should be made to cope. It was not laziness on his part but a calculated decision not to rock the boat.

The *Sydney Gazette* appears to have considered Lithgow worthy of considerable public respect, when it wrote: 'Mr Lithgow, the indefatigable Commissary of Accounts, has now been two years engaged in the production of the public accounts for 1826. The time of this gentleman has been elaborately taken up with a thousand other multifarious departments, and we often wonder that he wears it out so well'. (*Sydney Gazette* 11 February 1828). Darling lent his general support to Lithgow and his high opinion of him apparently did not diminish.

Lithgow did try to correct the situation, but continuing staff problems and budget cuts weakened his capacity to recruit skilled clerical assistants. By July 1828, Lithgow's staff of four clerks was obviously inadequate to meet the volume of work being created. The numerous new departments within government had increased Lithgow's workload, but Darling could only afford one new assistant. Accompanying this increase of one extra clerk, Lithgow was required to undertake preparation of not only the Blue Book but also the Official Statistical Tables, now required by the Colonial Office in London. This work had originally been completed by the Colonial Secretary's office, but Darling agreed with the transfer of the preparation to Lithgow's office. Upon Lithgow's appeal to Darling and on the request of the British Secretary of State, the work was transferred back to the Colonial Secretary's office.

The next problem undermining Lithgow's completion of the audit work was the death of William Balcombe, the Colonial Treasurer, in March 1829. Campbell Riddell was subsequently appointed to this post in 1830 but this circumstance further delayed Lithgow because, as there was no successor within the Treasurer's department, he was forced to train Riddell in the office of Treasurer.

A government order dated 1 September 1829 required that all communications about accounts should be first addressed to the Auditor-General, who was to make his preliminary examination but not a final determination. He was then to forward the documents to the Governor with a report as to whether there were any considerations which may affect the governor's decision.

In 1828 the whole of the expenditure connected with the convict and police establishments, including the medical and agricultural branches and the penal settlements, as well as disbursements on account of the Colonial Marine, were transferred to the Commissariat. The Commissary of Accounts, instead of the Auditor-General, was later placed in charge of the examination of all accounts and preparation of the warrants for all expenses incurred for the civil government or the convict establishment payable from the military chest. (*Colonial Secretary to Auditor-General,* 7 September 1828*)*.

Once again in 1830 Governor Darling defended Lithgow's lateness in the accounts to Secretary Hay:

'. . . It would be impossible to point out the extent of the arrears in business generally: but it may be useful to instance the auditor's office, and there cannot be a more indefatigable public servant that Mr Lithgow, but who, to this day, has not been able to do more than commence the examination of the store accounts and they are consequently years in arrears.' (Darling to Hay, 30 September 1830 HRA 1: 15:745)

Lithgow tried valiantly to explain his problems to Darling in a letter dated 31 December 1829:

'. . . The entire want of any specific rules for determining the nature of many vouchers . . . difficulty in obtaining from departments amended accounts . . . as well as vouchers and documents . . . owing to the want of clerks, qualified or experienced to a satisfactory state, and the number of the articles to be accounted for. These are the underlying causes of my delays.' (SRO Letter File No. 127)

The problems swelled until the Commissioners of Audit suggested (Governor's Despatches Vol 38 1842) that Lithgow be suspended. In January 1842 Governor Gipps threatened Lithgow with suspension if he did not soon produce his accounts. Later that month, Lithgow reported that the 1836 accounts had been shipped to London, those for 1837 were ready and he hoped that accounts for 1839-41 would be ready within 90 days. He mentioned reasons for the delay including the establishment of the border police, the extension of older Establishments, and the great expenditure for Immigration. On receipt of these accounts the Lords of the Treasury dropped their suspension request and hoped that Lithgow would not again allow transmission of the accounts to be delayed for a period as long as five years 'My Lords however trust that the warning Mr. Lithgow has received will induce him to attend regularly hereafter to this important part of his duty.' (Governor's despatches May-July 1842)

In November 1845, the Legislative Council in, willed along by Lithgow, passed an 'Act for Auditing and Regulating the Accounts of the Ordinary Revenue of NSW'. The Bill prescribed that a select committee of the Legislative Council audit the Accounts of Revenue derived from taxes, duties, rates and imports. However the British Treasury, prompted by this independent move of the colony, issued instructions to the colonial governors in 1847 supplying details of how accounts were to be kept and requesting further details on proposed/forward expenditure, a comparison statement and more minute details in the cash book. This request resulted in a cumbersome system that commenced on 1 January 1850.

Due to the gradual decline of convicts transported after 1840, the Commissariat Accounts Department in NSW was abolished in 1846, although until 1855 the NSW Commissariat continued to pay for all convict establishments, including hospitable and medical expenses for convicts. It continued to pay for the British military establishment although in 1850, all barracks and military buildings were handed over to the colonial government. This military responsibility continued until 1870 when all Imperial forces were withdrawn from the Australian colonies. Lithgow retired as the Auditor-General on 30 April 1852 (Blue Books, 1852*)*. The Auditor General's office records show that Lithgow's tenure was longer than any of his successors, whose tenure in office averaged only one year.

We are fortunate to have a central source with the necessary records to learn about Lithgow's career. The Mitchell Library in Sydney holds copies of the original Blue Books, the Auditor-General's Office Reports, Governor's despatches and the inter-departmental Letter file. These records also offer an insight into the struggles between Lithgow and his superior, the Colonial Secretary, whose office he obviously coveted.

We learn also from these records that the Auditor's office changed location on numerous occasions. The first 'Treasury' building was on the corner of Bent and O'Connell Streets. It was originally to serve as Lithgow's residence but Balcombe (Colonial Treasurer) manipulated Darling, and his 'home' was transferred to this prestigious location. *The Sydney Gazette* of 29 July 1826 records a move to the northeast corner of Barrack Square of the Treasurer, the Auditor, and the Commissariat Cash office so that 'all the monied Public Gentlemen will be brought under one roof'. Bourke wrote to Lord Glenelg in January 1837 'the Auditor and Collector of Internal Revenue had for some years occupied a house as an office, belonging to the Chaplain of St. James Church'. This house stood on the western corner of Macquarie Street and Queen's Square. Later that year it was decided to rent premises belonging to Mrs Reiby in Macquarie Place, but in 1839, Lithgow was moved once again to the former residence of Colonial Secretary McLeay in Bridge Street (near Macquarie Place). Lithgow moved again in 1849, in 1850 and again in 1851 not long before his retirement. The new Treasury, situated in Macquarie Street on the corner of Bridge Street was opened on 27 October 1851 and has remained there ever since.

What we do not learn from the records is what manner of man was Lithgow or his colleagues. We are left to interpolate from other secondary sources about life in the early colony and Lithgow's contribution thereto. The records of the State Records Office of NSW relating to the role and history of the Office of Auditor-General are invaluable to understanding the bureaucratic side of the office. SRO files numbers NAU/1to NAU/29 contain a great deal of valuable research information and these were made available through the Mitchell Library.

In the course of reviewing Mitchell Library references, an Appendix D to an SRO file was located and this contains the listing of Colonial

Secretaries during the Lithgow era of public service. For our purposes of understanding a little more about Lithgow these may be useful, especially as Lithgow continually aspired to this rank but was overlooked in favour of 'a governor's man'.

Early Colonial Secretaries

Major John Ovens	1824-1825
William Lithgow, Acting	1825
Henry Dumaresq	1825-1827
William Lithgow, Acting	1827
Thomas De Condamine	1827-1829
Henry Dumaresq	1829-1831
Richard Bourke	1831-1833
G.K. Holden	1833-1837
H.F. Gisborne	1837
John Snodgrass	1837-1838
Henry Parker	1836-1846

We should ask whether Lithgow would have been a suitable candidate for Colonial Secretary. This writer thinks the ultimate Lithgow role was as number 2 man in the colonial public service and number 1 man in the finance section of the service. Lithgow's contribution from the post of chief financial officer of the Colony was exemplary and his advice to the Governor of the day from this specialist position must have been greater than it would have been as Colonial Secretary, speaking on financial matters, of which he had lost daily and 'hands on' contact.

Lithgow's Historical Setting

Lithgow had been born into a burgeoning British Empire (surely the greatest empire ever witnessed in the history of the world), fast becoming the envy of the rest of the world. Britain itself was being healed after the Cromwell revolution, and England and Scotland were being united, for economic, social as well as historical reasons. It was a time of great change, and Lithgow, in line with his forbear bearing the same name) entered the adventurous world with his eye on travel and learning. The British

Military offered such a challenging career, whilst the commissary offered a peaceful haven within a rapidly changing and dangerous Empire. This career moves was at definite odds from his ecclesiastic life in the Church of Scotland, but he had, it seems, at last found his true calling.

At the other end of the Lithgow spectrum, his retirement in 1852 came at a surprising time. The Empire was at its supremacy. The Indian Revolution had lost Britain the support of much of that sub-continent. Queen Victoria was in the depth of depression following the death of her Prince Albert; many of the colonies in the New World were preparing for self-government. A new draft constitution for each colony had been released for discussion. New South Wales needed every ounce of strength and experience to accommodate all these changes, but Lithgow retired on 8th June 1852, right in the middle of the gold rush (a period of great imposition on government services) and whilst W.C. Wentworth was leading the Legislative Council in constitutional reform. This would have been an exciting time to be a senior bureaucrat in the government ranks as well as in the Legislative Council, but work pressures from within the public service as well as the failure of Governor Gipps to keep his salary in line with other senior heads of departments and the fact that he was overlooked for the plum post of colonial secretary when it had become available in late 1851, all contributed to Lithgow's decision to retire at 68, albeit with a relatively small pension.

Lithgow survived by being professional, flexible and most co-operative with his governors. He had made a very positive impression with Lord Bathurst during the Bank of NSW crisis in 1827, but there were other endeavours he was involved in that brought his name into influential colonial circles. These other endeavours are more explained later in the text but Lithgow's activities, both work and professional are much of the history of the colony, during its first fifty years. Lithgow's life was a blessing for the rich interest it creates in the colonial economy and the financial institutions that created the foundation of entrepreneurship and the strength of purpose to grow the economy at as fast a rate as it did.

The publicity-shy William Lithgow

We seem to know very little about the private William Lithgow from the Australian records. As we have already seen, few Australian historians have included Lithgow in their writings. The official records available from the State Library of New South Wales and the National Library of Australia contain only references to the original documents signed by Lithgow in his official capacities and most of these are reproduced in the HRA. The HRA and the Colonial newspapers of the day cite Lithgow frequently but they are mostly about the role of the man with little about the man. These summaries of the public record are worthy of citation.

Lithgow from the HRA

Lithgow's importance in the colony, on so many fronts, made him an active name in the Historical Records of Australia A summary of the various events that brought Lithgow to the prominence that he achieved between 1824 and 1842 follows:

Appointed as Auditor-general	2. 1. 1825
Committee on convict work practices	16.6.1825
Brisbane commends Lithgow to Bathurst	23.7.1825
Committee on colonial coinage	22.5.1826
Committee of enquiry into BNSW	20.5.1826
Appointed Colonial Land Board	30.5.1826
1st Land Board Report	22.7.1826
2nd Land Board Report	22.8.1826
Report separating Commissary in NSW from VDL	22.7.1826
3rd Land Board Report	25.12.1826
Appointed Magistrate	31.1.1827
Report on Expenses of Convict	6. 3.1827
4th Land Board Report	11.3.1827
Rpt on value of convict labour	14.3.1827
Separation of Commissary accts from colonial audit	12.4.1827
Director Bank of NSW	24.9.1827
Receives detailed instns to Treasurer	24.9.1827
Board of Female Factory	15.5.1828

Appointed to Legislative Council	1. 2.1829
Report #2 on Female Factory operations	18.2.1829
Acting Private Secretary to governor	23.11.1829
Trustee on Clergy & Land Board	10.2.1830
Trustee for will of Major John Ovens	28.10.1831
Questions of the Colonial-Agent in London	8. 2.1832
Nomination as Executive Councillor	2.12.1825
Report by Emigration Commissioners	30.1.1842
Report on Commissary & water police	12.12.1842
Report on gov't printing office	20.8.1842

Dates of Transmission of Blue Books from Sydney to London

Since the arrears of the 'Blue Books' in being transmitted to London were the sole responsibility of Lithgow, the lateness of their transmission may be of interest.

1832	24.7.1834
1833	5.10.1836
1834	8.6.1839
1835	31.12.1840
1836	26.6.1841
1837	31.1.1842
1838	6. 2.1843
1839	12.4.1842
1840	12.4.1842
1841	16.5.1842
1842	2.10.1842

We could ask why the Blue Books were so late in being completed and presented. The reason is quite simple and even halfway plausible. The British Treasury had issued instructions on the treatment various accounting conventions arising in the preparation of colonial accounts, in order to maintain comparability and routine of preparation. One such matter is relating to the treatment of fixed and variable expenses in the colonial accounting system, as well as for current and accrued expenses. The effect of following the strict accounting system requirements was not only enormous delays in completion but also an inability to 'close' the set of books at an early date after the end of the fiscal year. The fiscal year under British Treasury regulations was the calendar year, ending on the 31st December. Using 'accrual' accounting of the day, expenditure was accounted for by expenditure code. So, as an example, if a bridge was to be constructed, and the allocation of funds, in 1831,was for 5,000 pound, then that account could not be closed or settled until the work was completed. That means that if the bridge took three years to complete, then the accounts of 1831, 1832 and 1833 remained open and incomplete until the work was completed. It was this problem that confronted Lithgow and brought the wrath of the Lords of the Treasury, as well as the Lords of the Audit (within the Treasury) down on him relentlessly, because they, the Treasury officials, did not use this archaic system in England. Lithgow changed the system unilaterally in 1838 so that from that time the blue books could be closed, completed, audited and transmitted to the Treasury officials as per their timetable.

In hindsight, and with today's knowledge, the books could have been closed at the end of each year, prior to the completion of any incomplete public works by simply 'accruing' the expenditure to-date, and carrying this forward until individual projects were completed.

Such revision to the system would have caused an equal amount of contretemps in London and Whitehall, and so Lithgow stayed with the system until his own career was on the line and then the choice became a simpler one. Change career or change system.

Lithgow through the newspapers

Lithgow's position in the colony, together with his background and education, made him quite newsworthy, and the *Sydney Gazette* and the *Australian* newspaper of the day, offered many snippets of news about Lithgow and his work. Here are some of the highlights from the headlines of each report. It is these reports that place a human face on his work, dedication and public service.

Sydney Gazette

Signs regulations for estimates	4.10.1824
Attends agricultural dinner	14.10.1824
Appointed to audit colonial revenue accounts	18.11.1824
Subscribes to Busby's culture of the vine	9.12.1824
Member of the Agriculture Society	20.01.1825
Confirmed as auditor of accounts	21. 01.1825
Subscribes to Benevolent Society	21.04.1825
Sign civil officers address	3.11.1825
Made a J.P.	17.11.1825
Appointed auditor of orphans & church accounts	24.11.1825
Signs address to Gov. Darling	29.12.1825
Requires claims against female orphan school	1.04.1826
Appointed by Gov. Darling as director of BNSW	20.05.1826
Witness in Oakes case	2.08.1826
On agricultural Society committee	13.09.1826
Elected to board of Bank of NSW	6.01.1827
Sits on bench in Sydney	27.01.1827
Member of Harbour dues board	2.05.1827
Appointed private sec to gov. and clerk to exec cncl	8.06.1827
Returns to Audit Office	30.11.1827
Resigns from commissary office	19.09.1828
Member of Agriculture society	21.09.1828
Appointed to act as colonial treasurer	17.03.1829
Appointed to legislative council	17.07.1829
Elected a director of BNSW	12.12.1829
Member stockholder's committee B of NSW	6.08.1830
Appointed trustee of Clergy & School Estates	1.07.1831
Buys shares in Bank of Australia	13.05.1831
Receives land Grant	13.01.1832
Subscribes to Hibernia fund	23.08.1833
Subscribes to Edward Lombe Fund	9.09.1834
Explains to L C his views on Police and Gaol exps	11.09.1835
Committee of Southern Association	11.03.1836
Signs Address to Governor	31.05.1836
Member Southern Cattle Association	17.06.1836
Buys house in Elizabeth St.	30.08.1836

On Circular Wharf Committee	13.09.1836
On immigration committee	6.06.1837
Outlines census plans	6.08.1840
Comments on Municipal Corporations Bill in L Council	8.08.1840
Speech in Legislative Council	6.08.1840
Committee on purchase of land in Macquarie Place	4.08.1840
Speech in Legislative Council	13.08.1840
Calls meeting to support Immigration Fund	15.08.1840
Speech in Legislative Council	20.8.1840
Member Immigration Committee	22.9.1840
Member committee to establish library for L C	27.10.1840
Subscribes to Christ Church Building fund	2.02.1841
Lithgow's farm at Kissing Point for sale	15.04.1841
Trustee of Australian Society for Deposits and Loans	6.08.1841
Committee of Australian Immigration Association	12.10.1841
Supports Land Fund remaining in the Col Treasury	11.05.1841
Says government should place immigrants where it likes	6.02.1841
Committee on Dr. Lang's finances for church & college	15.06.1841
Committee to consider lighthouse in Bass Strait	24.06.1841
Subscriber to Gould's Birds of Australia	10.07.1841
Retired as Director of Bank of NSW	1 8.11.1841
Appointed Trustee of State Bank of NSW	18.11.1841
Committee on Immigration Debentures	2.12.1841
Re-appointed director of B of NSW	12.07.1841
Resident Gipps Ward	26.09.1842
Lithgow's Valley 100 acres to be sold	7.04.1842

Sydney Herald 1842-1845

House in Cumberland Street (Gipps Ward)	14.09.1842
Votes for dissolution Nth Sydney Ferry Co.	24.12.1843
Robbed in Parramatta Road	11.03.1844
Claim against J.H. Potts	20.09.1844
Retires director BNSW	29.11.1844

The Australian 1824-1842

Signs regulations for Estimates	14.10.1824
Attends Agricultural Dinner	14.10.1824
Appointed to audit Colonial Revenue Accts	18.11.1824
Subscribes to Busby's Culture of the Vines	9.12.1824
Member of Agricultural Society	20.01.1824
Confirmed as Auditor of Accounts	15.02.1825
Subscribes to Benevolent Society	21.04.1825
Acting Commissary of Civil Accounts	3.11.1825
Made a Justice of the Peace	17.11.1825
Ap'ted Auditor of Male & Fem. Orphan & Church Accts	24.11.1825
Signs Address to Gov. Darling	29.12.1825
Requires claim against Female Orphan School	1.04.1826
Apptd by Gov. as Director of Bank of Sydney	20.05.1826
Witness in Oakes case	2.08.1826
Ap'td to Agric. Committee	23.09.1826
Elected to the Board of Bank of NSW	6.01.1827
Sits on Bench in Sydney	27.01.1827
Member of Harbour Dues Board	2.05.1827
Ap'td private sec to Gov and Clerk of Exec. Cncl	8.06.1827
Returns to Audit Office	30.11.1827
Resigns from Commissariat Department	19.09.1828
Member of Agric. Society	26.09.1828
Ap'td to act as Col. Treasurer	17.03.1829
Ap'td to Legislative Council	17.07.1829
Elected Director of Bank of NSW	12.12.1829
Member Stockholders C'ttee B of NSW	8.06.1830
Ap'td Trustee of Clergy & Schools Estates	7.01.1831
Buys shares in Bank of Australia	13.05.1831
Receives Land Grant in Sydney	13.04.1832
Subscribes to Hibernia Fund	23.08.1833
Subscribes to Edward Lombe Fund	09.09.1834
Explains to Leg. Cncl view on Police & Goal Exps	11.09.1835
Ap'td C'ttee of Southern Cattle Assocn	11.03.1836
Signs address to Governor	31.05.1836
Attended Levee	31.05.1836
M'br Southern Association (Sydney C'ttee)	17.06.1836

Buys Home in Elizabeth St. 1,200 Pnd	30.08.1836
Ap'td Circular Wharf Committee	13.09.1836
Ap'td Immigration Committee	06.06.1837
Re-appointed to Legislative Council	09.03.1838
Pledges not to supply spirits as wages	01.05.1838
Subscribes to Bourke Memorial	05.12.1838
Calls for Immigration meeting	08.05.1838
Subscribes to Bourke Statue	15.05.1838
Signs petition against transportation	20.12.1838
Granted title to land in Murray	25.09.1838
Ap'td committee of BASN Co	26.03.1839
Takes shares in India SS Co	21.05.1839
Mbr C'ttee of LC to consider Maritime Law	30.07.1840
Mbr C'ttee of LC to consider new Banking Law	08.08.1840
M'br C'ttee of LC to consider form of Census	16.08.1840
Recommends purchase of land in Macquarie Place	24.08.1840
Calls meeting to promote immigration	25.08.1840
Ap'td member of Central Immigration C'ttee	22.09.1840
Subscribes to Christ Church Building Fund	02.01.1841
Farm at Kissing Point for sale	13.04.1841
Ap'td Trustee for Austn Deposits & Loans Co.	08.06.1841
C'ttee to consider Lighthouses in Bass Strait	24.06.1841
To retire by rotation from Board of B of NSW	18.11.1842
Ap'td as Trustee of Savings Bank of NSW	18.11.1842
Supports Immigration Debentures	02.12.1842
Calls for Land Fund to support immigration	19.12.1841
Re-elected Director of B of NSW	07.12.1841

These newspaper headlines offer a personal glimpse at the life and business activities of William Lithgow. Each of the five governors he served kept him extremely busy and he led the colony in understanding, regulating and administering governmental business affairs.

Lithgow finds a friend

So little has been written about Lithgow that the discovery of a long forgotten letter in the vaults of the Public Library of New South Wales which makes a number of references to Lithgow in the colony, especially between his arrival in 1824 as Commissary in charge of accounts and his appointment as Auditor-General, means that we can understand a little more about early life in the Colony from the viewpoint and vantage point of a Lithgow colleague. The letter between Assistant Commissary Boyes and his wife in England makes fascinating reading. It is reproduced here in extract form, from the original text, with editing in keeping with removal of spelling errors and certain language intending to portray the Germanic intonations of a key character.

This letter was written by one of his colleagues with whom Lithgow had planned to set up, and share, a house in Sydney. Boyes was to arrive in Sydney, supposedly at the same time as Lithgow, but to take up a posting in the Commissary–operations branch, whereas Lithgow's posting was to the Accounts branch. Their paths failed to cross for some months as Lithgow was delayed in leaving Mauritius (the Isle de France) and by the time of his arrival the Governor had commandeered the original house as a government office for the Treasury, and a residence for the Balcombe family. So Lithgow spent his days in the house instead of his nights and he located alternative accommodation in Sydney Town, without the benefit of Boyes as a sharer of accommodation. The complete text of the Boyes letter to his wife is found in the Appendix to this volume, and make fascinating reading about the times, the people and their doings.

CHAPTER 3

GOVERNANCE OF PUBLIC FINANCE UNDER LITHGOW

Many works (including Brian Fitzpatrick's *The British Empire in Australia* and Butlin's *The Colonial Economy)* offer an interesting study of the Colonial Economy in the Period 1788-1850, and although Lithgow's great industry contributed to the Colonial Economy, his main interest is in just three specialised aspects of the colonial era. His contribution to (a) establishing and upgrading the Public Service over 30 years of concentrated effort is significant; he oversaw the establishment of many new government departments as well as introducing meritocracy into the colonial public service and a pay scale that served his governors and colleagues well: (b) his expertise in the topic of public finance obviously came with the job and it was what his governors sought in recruiting him to higher posts in the Public Service: (c) As Colonial Auditor his main role was in creating transparency within the government service to the community and thus refining accounting procedures, but as the person responsible for compiling the annual *Blue Books* between 1826 and 1852, his ideas of meaningful reporting to his peers in London either made or diminished their understanding of financial events in the colony.

Before reviewing more of the economic and political climate associated with the Lithgow years, we should explore the quintessential Lithgow role in public finance within the colony.

The Governance of Public Finance

Government Accounting and finance changed a great deal between 1802 and 1824 when Lithgow commenced his dual role as Commissary accountant and colonial auditor. The reader will become aware of many of those changes, especially in the recording and reporting roles of the Colonial Treasury, and the Colonial Auditor. In theory, or at least in the mind of the British Treasury officials, there was a clear separation of duties between Colonial Auditor and Colonial Treasurer. In practice, however, there was a great deal of overlapping responsibilities, if the two positions were to make any progress in reaching the ultimate goal of an audited set of accounts. Lithgow endured a number of Colonial Treasurers, commencing with Balcombe and then Ridden followed by Riddell. Each met with an inglorious end, but Lithgow never recorded objection or discontent, with the man or the man's work. It is of interest to trace some of those changes and we find that included in the appendix to the *Financial Statements of NSW–1856-1881* is the record (by the adviser to the Colonial Treasurer–James Thomson) that:

'The Financial System of the Colony of New South Wales is regulated chiefly by the Constitution Act of 1855 and the Audit Act of 1870, and in matters relating to Trust Funds and Loans by special Appropriation Acts of the local legislature.

The Imperial Act granting a constitution to the Colony of New South Wales was assented to on 16th July 1855, and became effective on the 24th November 1855. This Act provides for a Legislative Council (Upper House) and a Legislative Assembly. The Upper House members were to be nominated by the Governor, while the Lower House members were to be elected by inhabitants of the Colony.

Prior to the passing of the Constitution Act, the territorial revenues of the Colony belonged to the Crown, but on that Act coming into operation in 1855, these revenues were all placed at the disposal of the local Parliament, and together with the taxes, imposts, rates and duties, were formed into one fund, under the title of the Consolidated Revenue Fund. In lieu of the Crown Revenues thus given up to the Colony, an annual Civil List of £64,300 was made payable to Her Majesty out of the consolidated revenues of the Colony.

The Constitution Act also provides that the legislature of the Colony shall have power to make laws for regulating the sale, letting, disposal, and occupation of the wastelands of the Crown within the Colony; and also for imposing taxes and levying customs duties. All Money Bills must, in the first place, be recommended to the Legislative Assembly by message from the Governor, and no part of the Public Revenue can be issued except on warrants bearing the Governor's signature, and directed to the Treasurer of the Colony.

The **Audit Act of 1870** was passed to regulate the receipt, custody and issue of public monies, and to provide for the audit of the Public Accounts. The Treasury is the Department entrusted with the collection and disbursement of the revenues and other public monies of the Colony. It is under the control and general management of the Treasurer and Secretary for Finance and Trade. The permanent head of the Department is responsible to the Minister for the efficient conduct of its business.

The revenue of the Colony is now to be classed under the following general headings:

Taxation
Land Revenue
Receipts for services rendered
Miscellaneous receipts

The main elements of the these four categories items consist of:

Taxation
Customs duties
Excise duties
Duty on gold exported
Trade licenses

Land Revenue
Proceeds from land auctions

Sales of improved lands
Rents and assessments on pastoral runs
Quit rents
Leases of mining lands
Miner's rights

Services receipts, include:
Railway & telegraph revenue
Money orders
Mint charges
Gold escort fees
Pilotage & harbour fees
Registration of cattle brands
Other fees of office

Miscellaneous
Rents
Fines
Sale of government property,
Interest on bank deposits
Other general revenues

The revenue and expenditure of the Colony is increasing year by year in proportion to the prosperity of the people and the increase of population. This is naturally to be expected for as new lands are taken up and outlying districts occupied, demands upon the government for all those services which tend to promote the well-being of a community are constantly being made; and although these services when granted create an additional expenditure, there generally follows an augmentation of the revenue both from the sale and occupation of the waste lands of the Colony, and the larger consumption of dutiable articles.

When responsible government was established in 1855, the revenue amounted to £973,178 (or 3.51 pound per head) and the population was then 277,000. In 1875, exactly twenty years after the introduction of responsible government, the population had increased to 606,000 and the revenue to 4,121,996 (or 6.80 pound per head)."

From the *Government Gazette* of 2 January 1879, this condensed statement is taken:

REVENUE, 1878

Taxation
Customs Duties 44,220
Duty on gold 6,898
Licenses 109,851
Land Revenue
Sales 1,915,466
Other 410,254
Services 1,183,582
Miscellaneous 172,907

TOTAL REVENUES for 1878 **£4,991,919**

So revenue was increasing dramatically, mostly by way of Land Revenues spurred on mainly by speculation from absentee landlords in the major towns and in Britain.

Problems with preparing financial statements 1822-1855

A significant problem found whilst comparing the annual revenue and expenses from 1822 to 1855 is that there was no consistent treatment of items for inclusion from year to year nor any explanation as to how each item was to be handled. Thus various records are giving different totals for revenue and expenditure depending on the source of inquiry. For instance even the James Thomson work–'Financial Statements 1855-1881" is giving different figures to those provided in the 'Votes & Proceeding of the NSW Legislative Assembly Vol 2 1858–Page 1153' which records in a summary format the totals by year from 1826 to 1875.

There are some explanations for these differences:

The records for each year were not closed until the committed forward expenditures for say, Public Works, were spent and the work was completed. In practice this meant that a commitment may have been made in 1852 for a bridge construction, and the work was not completed until 1855. Thus the final totals for 1852 would have remained incomplete until 1855. Such practice was complex and misguided and was reviewed and changed in 1856, when annual statements were prepared by a date certain and annual appropriations were made for Public Works. This revision made it a little more cumbersome and difficult for the Treasurer and Audit staff but much easier for the Legislative Assembly to review the performance of the Government on a current or an annual basis.

There was only limited Appropriations made for the Parliament or forward estimates of Ways and Means from 1832 until 1886, when a whole new updated and revised system of Parliamentary Accounts was installed for the post self-government Parliaments.

From self-government a modification to the pre 1855 system was made to include the recording and reporting for all items of both revenue and expenditures, due to the British Government reluctantly agreeing to release control of the revenue from Crown Lands in exchange for the local (NSW) Legislature paying the annual civil list salaries which at that time had grown to about 45,000 pound per annum. This gave the legislature greater flexibility and control over all Colonial revenues, gave them greater revenues but also increased their operating expenses.

The categories of revenue accounting were also streamlined, in 1856, to just four headings for ease of preparation in the Treasury and comparison purposes. Both the Treasury office and the Audit Office prepared estimates and reports from 1832 until 1856 when as part of a major Government cost cutting exercise, the unnecessary duplication between the two offices was removed, the staff trimmed and a significant savings realised. The five headings of revenue in common use became

Indirect taxation
Direct Taxation
Land Revenues (sales and rents)
Receipts for Government Services rendered (railways, postal)
Miscellaneous receipts

Misallocation of Loan Funds or Government debt raising complicated comparisons from year to year. For instance, the railway system was financed mostly by debt but sometimes, in part, by current account revenue. The Parliamentarians wanted to, obviously, see what the total capital cost was and so accounts of expenditure often included the total outlay, and the revenue statements then included the amount of loan funds allocated to the railway project. Likewise a similar treatment occurred with community services such as water and drainage installation. This system was not changed until 1859 when different statements were handed to the Parliament. One being the 'Statements of General Account–Current' and the second being 'Consolidated Revenue Fund'. This was further modified in 1862 when additional statements were provided of capital raising and expenditures, sub-statements of the income and expenses of each service department, and a complete itemisation of Public Works expenditures.

Another minor complication after self-government was the charging of certain operating expenses to the British Treasury. For instance, in 1858, there were still 304 convicts being maintained at British Government expenses. The total cost charged back to Britain was 10, 514 but because the cost per head was 34.11.8 ¾ was considered excessive, the British Treasury refused to make payment and the Colonial Treasurer of the day–Mr Donaldson suggested they either make payment immediately or take the convicts back. Obviously payment was forthcoming promptly.

The Colonial Treasurer's from 1821 to 1851 provided a haphazard approach to informing the Parliament. Annual Statements were made any time between March and December. There was no statutory date for presenting Statements of Actual or Forward Estimates to the Legislative Assembly and such was the instability of the post self-government Political System that only one Treasurer (Elias Carpenter Weekes) ever presented more than one statement. Weekes presented three statements to the Assembly (31.01.1861; 7.08.1861; 7.08.1862). Because of this continual changing of Governments and Treasurers, statements never followed the same format from year to year. The Hon. Charles Cowper was Premier for 5 years (not successive) from 1859 to 1865 and had five different Treasurers. Even Henry Parkes submitted a statement on 21st November 1872 as acting Colonial Treasurer in the Robertson Government, whilst in

1875 John Robertson, once again the Premier, gave the annual statement on 8th December as Acting Treasurer.

The Colony changed dramatically in its fiscal standing between 1856 and 1875. The Government, for the very first time in the history of the Colony, surpassed the one million pound mark for both revenues and expenditures. From 1856 revenues rose from 1125,090 pound to 4191,996 pound in 1875. Likewise expenditures rose from 1067,710 in 1856 to 3336,609 in 1875.

Healthy, end of year cash balances were maintained each year but overseas borrowing increased annually, as well as 'temporary' loan transactions, until in mid 1870s the annual temporary loans were running at 350,000 pound, although the annual surplus at the end of 1875 was over 2 million pound. Obviously cyclical cash flows caused these temporary borrowings.

Although Lithgow retired just prior to self-government, the Lithgow hand can be seen in so many of these changes and even after retirement, and whilst living in St. Leonard's for much of the year, he was continually consulted by legislatures, committees and the bureaucracy.

James Thomson, consultant adviser to the NSW Treasury in the 1870s prepared these notes in order to explain the transition from dependency to free colony and the self-governing colony. The progression was necessary relevant and meaningful. Thomson had offered this overview to governors and treasury officials for their understanding of a little background to the complex treasury scene. However, Lithgow had been given precise written instructions for his numerous financial reporting roles commencing with his tenure as Commissary of Accounts. It is of value to follow some of these instructions provided.

Instructions for the governance of public finance in the Colony

(Lithgow received a variety of instructions in order to fill his roles, firstly as Commissariat accountant, and then as Colonial Auditor. However here are some general instructions on assembling the accounting procedures for the handling of the public finance. These extracts are relevant to our story about William Lithgow and are included as a brief history of Government accounting in the colony.)

General observations . . . on the origin and nature of the New South Wales Colonial Revenue:

'The Revenues collected within the Colony of New South Wales, from its establishment until the commencement of the administration of Governor Macquarie in 1810, were raised in support of the 'Gaol' and 'Orphan' Funds respectively. The Revenue thus levied for, and appropriated to the Gaol Fund consisted of a Duty of 1s. per gallon on Spirits, 6d per gallon on wine, 3d per gallon on beer, together with a wharfage duty of 6d on each cask or package landed. These duties appear to have been first established upon the authority of Governor John Hunter R.N. during his administration in 1795-1800 and were the earliest sources of local revenue in the Colony.

The Revenue raised for the Orphan Fund was derived from fees on the entry and clearance of Vessels, and for permits to land and remove spirits–both were first levied in 1800; from licenses to retail liquor and from a duty of 1.5% on goods sold by auction (first collected in 1801); from a duty of 5% ad valorem on all articles imported, the produce of countries to the eastward of the Cape of Good Hope (first imposed in 1802); from fines levied by the Courts and Magistrates; from fees from grants of lands and leases, and quit rents on crown lands (Quit rents ceased in 1805). Other than quit rents and crown land fees, all revenues were levied upon Colonial authority.'

The followings revenue was raised in 1805 (James Thomson reports that the records from 1805 to 1810 are 'imperfect').

1805 Revenues in Gaol and Orphan Funds:

Duties on Spirits 69.11.3
Fees on Vessels, licenses 595.13.7
Ad valorem duty 531.10.3
Fines by courts 86.5.8
Revenue raised in 1805 £2,783.0.9

In 1810, Governor Macquarie changed the designation of these two funds to 'Police Fund' and Orphan School Fund. The designated revenues were split 3:1 into each fund. The Westminster Act 3 Geo IV c.96 of 1822 gave further powers of taxation to the Governor, as well as validating previous tax raisings in the colony, which were considered to be 'illegal', since they were without legal foundation as a means of raising local revenues.

Lithgow's contribution to public accounting and reporting

Colonial origins of public accounts

One goal of the Governor of the Colony of New South Wales in 1788 was to achieve self-sufficiency for the colony even though it was a penal Colony. By 1823, the British Government had taken the approach it would be limiting its direct expenditure to the transportation of the convicts and their travelling food and supplies. The Colonial Administrators would be responsible for the convict's security, food, clothing and accommodation in the Colony. The proceeds from the sale of Crown land were to be the exclusive reserve of the British authorities, and not that of the colonists. The Governors commenced working the convicts for growing food, extracting minerals (eg coal production), roads, housing and public buildings, and generally paying their own way. By 1796, other non-working convicts had been assigned to landowners on a fully maintained basis, thus saving the British Treasury a great deal of money.

Such a policy, of the Government maintenance of convicts, created the need for an accounting by the Colony to the British Parliament and would commence with the appointment of a Treasurer acting as a Financial Controller, who could prepare monthly and annual despatches to the British Colonial Secretary. Following self-government in 1856, these procedures changed, as the Colony became fully responsible for their own economic planning and fiscal management.

Colonial Accounting in New South Wales

The Colony went through two stages before adopting the standards recommended in the 1823 'Blue Book', which replaced the 'gaol' and orphan funds. These two phases were the Gaol and Orphan Funds pre-1810, and the Macquarie promoted Police and Orphan Funds of 1811-1821, which financial statements were published quarterly in the *Sydney Gazette*. The 'gaol' fund was a record of funds raised by a surcharge on the citizens of Sydney town, as a means to complete the construction of the Sydney 'gaol'. The voluntary collections fell far short of the funds needed and the part-completed gaol required official support. Customs duties were imposed on imports, and the gaol was completed with Government monies, and the fund was renamed the Police fund. The Orphan Fund started shortly thereafter, in 1802, and accepted as its source of funds the customs duties on spirits and tobacco and was later (1810) re-named the Orphan School Fund with the intention of creating a fund to erect the first school building in Sydney town. The advisory Legislative Council was appointed in 1823, and the first Appropriation Act was passed in 1832, even though, in the interim, the Governors were passing 'messages' of the financial condition of the Colony, annually to the members of the Council.

Upon self-government in 1855, the government accounting procedures were again revised, since the Colony was now fully responsible for all its fiscal matters. At this same time, gold was discovered and license fees, duties on exports of gold and duties on the domestic conversion of gold were applied and helped fill the Treasury coffers. This was a major step forward in Government economic planning. A limited deficit budgeting commenced at this time. Deficits were short term and recovered usually within 5 years, although the Colonial debt, mainly to overseas bondholders was kept very much in check after the surge of investment in railways and telegraph services. The check, in practical terms, was two-fold, that the investment (eg railways) had to be self-supporting and the debt extinguished from current revenues within a five-year period.

The governor's need for a 'discretionary' fund from which they could draw funds for 'special' purposes prompted revised fiscal management in the pre-Macquarie era, as well as set the standard for 'local revenue raising'. They wanted to do something other than perform the minimalist functions allowed by the British Treasury. Every official pound had to be pleased for, and the governors needed just a little cushion for the people of the settlement.

From the earliest records (as recorded in HRNSW), certain conclusions can be drawn, on colonial public finance and these can be set out as follows:

There was a wide range of **duties and taxes** imposed on the early settlers, especially on alcoholic beverages. The general rate of duty on spirits was 10 shillings per gallon, and on wine it was 9 pence per gallon. On tobacco the rate was 6 pence per pound, while timber attracted a rate of one shilling per solid foot. General Cargo attracted an ad valorem duty at a flat 5% rate.

There were also **licenses and tolls**. Hawker's Licenses sold for 20 pound, and it cost a settler 2 pence (tuppence) to go from Sydney town to the settlement of Parramatta. A country settler (in the Hawkesbury) paid One penny to cross the Nepean River Bridge at Windsor.

References to **crown land sales** were recorded in the 1825 'Blue Book', and based on the decree by George 3rd in his Proclamation of 25th March, 1825, that there was to be imposed a new charge on crown lands at the rate of One shilling for every 50 acres, to commence 5 years after the date of the original grant. To that date all crown lands had been disposed of by way of grants, and this rent was a form of back door compensation to the crown. In the official grant documents, the receiver of the land grant was given notice that further costs may attach at some future time to the land, and it was this opportunity that provided the Crown to raise this 'rent' charge on the land in 1825.

There was to be a **Land-holder's fee** of Fifteen shillings per 100 acres of crown land reserved for each three years for free settlers, followed by a two shilling fee per 100 hundred acres redeemable after twenty years from purchase.

On the 18 May 1825, the **'rent'** was changed, by order of Governor Sir Thomas Brisbane, to a flat rate of 5% of the estimated value of the grants, without purchase (as opposed to purchased land), to commence 7 years from the date of grant. 'Rents' on any 2nd and subsequent grants were payable immediately, without the benefit of the 7 years grace period.

The Table of Land Grants between 1789 and 1850 shows the substantial number of acres granted to settlers and we can conclude that the revenue sourced from 'rents' on Crown land grants could build into a considerable sum for the Crown in the future.

By Proclamation, also dated 18th May 1825, George III authorised the sale of crown lands at the rate of 10 shillings per acre, to a maximum of 4,000 acres per individual or a maximum of 5,000 acres per family. Payment was by way of a 10% deposit and four equal quarterly instalments.

The title pages to the 1822 Blue Book are entitled 'Abstract of the Net Revenue and Expenditure of the Colony of New South Wales for the Year 1822', which indicates (and as the detailed records also reflect) that all Colonial revenue and expenses were consolidated in the 'Blue Book'.

The table of Civil List Salaries for 1792-1793 sets the Governor's Salary £1,000. But in the 1822 statement of expenditures on the Civil Salaries, the Governor's Salary had increased to £2,000. By 1856 the Governor's 'establishment' was costing £15,000 per annum.

In fact, the total of Civil List salaries in 1792 was only £4,726.0.0, but by 1822 the total had increased to £9,828.15.0, due to both individual salary increases as well as more names being placed on the Civil List.

Observations upon revenue for the Colony in 1828 by James Thomson, a consultant to the Colonial Treasurer of New South Wales makes an interesting point. It observes that the 'net colonial income' of the year 1828, as actually collected, is exclusive of sums in aid of revenue, which cannot be viewed in the character of income. This item is further defined as 'the proceeds of the labour of convicts, and establishments connected with them, being applied to the reduction of the amount of parliamentary grants for their maintenance'. In subsequent reports, 'receipts in aid of revenue' included items such as–'sale of Crown livestock; sale of government farms produce; sale of clothing and cloth made at the Female Factory at Parramatta; sale of wheat, sugar, molasses and tobacco produced by the convicts at new settlements such as Port Macquarie.' Such revenues were reluctantly included in official financial statements on the grounds that livestock had originally been included as an 'expense' whilst convict production was produced by 'prisoners' whose cost of maintenance was not recorded if self-produced.

The total quantity of alcohol imported into and thus consumed in the Colony, even in 1828, and with a population in that year of only 37,000 people, of which adult numbers would be less than 25,000, was 162,167 gallons of spirits and 15,000 gallons of Colonial distilled spirits (distillation from sugar was prohibited in 1828, however, the high price of grain and the higher taxing of locally manufactured spirits became a natural deterrent). A final observation was made in the 'Blue Book' compilation of 1829 that the only duties imposed on spirits in that year was upon spirits imported directly from H. M. Plantations in the West Indies. So the British authorities received the double financial benefit from the trading in spirits and charging duties thereon at their destination.

The quantity of dutiable tobacco in 1828 was £136,748 (compared to £91,893 in 1825). The Government experimented with locally grown tobacco at establishments in Emu Plains and Port Macquarie with the result being £51,306 produced. So the total consumption of tobacco in 1828 was over 4 pounds per head of adult population.

Shipping companies also paid lighthouse charges, along with wharfage. The growth of shipping, into the Port of Sydney, was so great that it meant that by 1828, the revenue from lighthouse dues, harbour dues and wharfage was over £4,000.

In 1828, the postage of letters attracted fees, for the first time, and the official Postmaster collected £598 for general revenue. This revenue grew rapidly so that by 1832 the amount of postage collected was £2,000. Each colony imposed its own postage and printed its own stamps until Federation.

The commencement of sales of both crown lands and crown timbers increased general revenues to the extent that in 1828, the amounts realised were:

Sales of Crown lands	£5004.19.2
Sales of cedar cut on crown land	£744.15.11
Sales of other Timber	£9365.11.4

The Governor imposed a fee of One halfpenny per foot for all cedar cut on crown lands. The Blue Book makes the further observation that this charge 'has checked bushrangers and other lawless depredators by depriving them of ready means of subsistence by the absence of all restraint from cutting Cedar upon unallocated lands'.

There was a major improvement in record keeping and reporting after self-government in 1855. *The Financial Statements of the Colonial Treasurers of New South Wales from Responsible Government in 1855 to 1881* provide a detailed accounting mechanism for recording classifications and compilation of budgets and reporting to the Authorities. They contain 'explanatory memoranda of the financial system of New South Wales, and of the rise, progress and present condition of the public revenue'.

Since Lithgow was the Colonial Auditor-General of not only the colony of New South Wales but also of Port Phillip (subsequently Victoria), it is of value to review colonial accounting in that jurisdiction. The new settlement of Port Phillip adopted the standards set out in the Governor George Gipps Report on Government Accounting and Reporting on Public Finance following the 1836 separation from New South Wales to form the Colony of Victoria. The Blue Book was more accurately kept in the new settlement than in the colony of New South Wales and full records are available concerning the commencement of the settlement and leading to the separation from New South Wales.

The interest in this period (from 1822 to 1881) is that these records, The Blue Books and the printed Financial Statements of 1881, provide the first identification of the items included in the revenue and expenditures for the Colony. This historical data is relevant to understanding the social conditions in the Colony, the application of duties, tariffs, tolls and fees which embraced the essential revenue of a Colony that was designed to be self-sufficient and which was being given minimal economic support by the British Government, even though the opportunity cost of housing 'prisoners' in the Colony was a fraction of the cost of housing them in England.

TABLE 1: ORPHAN, GAOL AND POLICE FUNDS 1802-1821

Year	Revenue			Works Outlay
	Operating Balances	Customs	Total	
1802	490			O
1803	5,200			
1804	3,100			
1806	1,900			
1807	1,200			
1808				
1809				
1810	1,384	3,272	2,194	
1911	769	7,872	10,393	2,965
1821	5,016	5,579	13,949	3,259
1813	4,502	5,228	14,621	4,426
1814	6,016	4,529	13,325	4,993
1815	1,681	13,197	17,994	6,350
1816	3,327	11,200	17,782	5,582
1817	5,453	16,125	24,706	7,048
1818	9,363	17,739	31,008	6,219
1819	18,900	22,579	42,968	17,131
1820	10,725	27,891	44,507	14,700

Commentary on Table 1

In 1876, the Colonial Financial Officer (the Treasurer, James Thomson), consultant to the Colonial Secretary of New South Wales, wrote, in a report to the Imperial Government that 'From the foundation of the Colony in 1788 to 1824, the records of local revenue and expenditure are too imperfect to render them of much value for statistical purpose, or for comparison with subsequent years.' However these figures, from Table 1 above, have been collated in the '*Historical Records of Australia–Statistics*' from reports by the Colonial Governor to the British authorities and go someway to telling a story. The claim made by historian N.G. Butlin in his introduction to the Historical Records of Australia series–*The economy before 1850*–'that the British Colonial Office spent millions of pounds to start up the Colony'–does not seem to be verifiable. In fact it seems the results show exactly the opposite. The discussion of 'benefits' received by Britain from supporting the colony is to be found elsewhere in the text.

The British expected their colonies to pay their way

We know that the British authorities had the choice of building new prisons in Britain and housing, feeding, guarding and clothing these prisoners, or relocate them to a 'penal colony'. The previous penal colony in America was no longer available because of the American Wars of Independence and the British were no longer welcome there. The recommendation of Sir Joseph Banks, after his voyage to the southern oceans with Captain James Cook, was to use the land and resources available in the newly charted East Coast of 'Australia'. The favourable opportunity cost of this arrangement was enormous. Britain was fighting wars in a number of areas and had numerous Colonies to administer, and one more Colony; supposedly rich in potential rewards and able to be converted to self-sufficiency was most attractive. So, the opportunity cost was to become just one form of savings for the British Treasury.

By 1824 the convicts were also paying their way (in opportunity cost terms) by removing coal from the ground in the Maitland area and the extracted coal being used for heating purposes by the military, the convicts, and through the commissary, by the free settlers. No value was ever placed on this work, nor on the use of convicts as builders of roads, housing, barracks, storage sheds, port wharves, churches and government buildings. It would appear that the convicts earned their keep whilst the Colony paid its own way very quickly. The 'Blue Book' of 1828 states that there was revenue from the sale of convict produce such as 'coal, wheat, sugar, molasses and tobacco' but the value of convict labour was to remain unreported. Economic historians recognise the value of the convict work as well as the opportunity cost of having transported the prisoners offshore, when an assessment is made of the 'investment' made, and the benefits gained by Britain in the new Colony of NSW.

The original estimate of direct gains by the British authorities from the original and continuing investment in the Colony of New South Wales was based on five identifiable and quantifiable events, even though the convicts were assigned jobs on the basis of 'full keep'.

The opportunity cost of housing, feeding and guarding the convicts in the Colony compared with the cost of doing the same thing in Britain.

The original estimates, in this category, were based on an estimated differential of ten pound per head–an arbitrary assessment of the differential cost.

However recent and more reliable information has come to hand which gives further validity to a number of £20 per head per annum, compared with the original £10 per head per annum.

A letter to Under Secretary Nepean, dated 23 August 1783, from James Maria Matra of Shropshire and London assists us in this regard.

It was Matra, who first analysed the opportunity of using the new Colony as a Penal Colony; only his estimates at that time were incorrect and ill founded. He had advised the Government that it would cost less than £3,000 to establish the Colony initially, plus transportation cost at £15 per head and annual maintenance of £20 per head.

In fact, transportation contracted for the second fleet was at 13 pound 5 shillings per head and local Colonial revenues from 1802 offset all annual maintenance of convicts as far as food, clothing and housing was concerned. The British Treasury outlay after this period was mainly for the military upkeep and the civil list.

However, Matra made a significant statement in his letter to Nepean, when he pointed out that the prisoners housed, fed and guarded on the rotting hulks on the Thames River were being contracted for in the annual amount of £26.15.10 per head per annum. He also writes that 'the charge to the public for these convicts has been increasing for the last 7 or 8 years' (*Historical Records of NSW*–Vol 1 Part 2 Page 7).

Adopting this alternative cost (of £26.75) as a base for comparison purposes, it means that the benefit to Britain of the Colony over a twenty-year period increases from £140,000,000 pound to £180,000,000. This calculation assesses the Ground 1 benefit at £84,000,000.

The benefit to Britain on Ground Two is put at £70, 000,000 (again over a 20-year period) which places the value of a convict's labour at£ 35 per annum. Matra had assessed the contract value of labour of the hulk prisoners at £35. 85.

The valuation of convict labour in the new Colony should reflect the convicts not only used on building sites, but also on road, bridge and wharf construction. This would add (based on 35 pound per annum) a further £21,000,000. The estimated declared 'cost' of public buildings in 1819 (declared to Commissioner Bigge) is slightly less than £1,000,000.

The Molesworth Committee (a House of Commons Committee investigating transportation) concluded that "the surplus food production by the convicts would feed the Military people and this, over a period of 10 years, would save £7,000,000 for the British Treasury."

The value of 'fringe benefit' grants of land to the Military etc can be estimated (based on One pound per acre) at over £5,000,000 before 1810.

We learn from Governor King's Report to Earl Camden (which due to a change of office holder, should have been addressed to Viscount Castlereagh as Colonial Secretary) dated 15th March 1806 that the Convicts engaged in widely diverse work. The Report itself is entitled

Governor King records in the *Historical Records of NSW*–Vol 6 P43, details of the

'Public Labour of Convicts maintained by the Crown at Sydney, Parramatta, Hawkesbury, Toongabbie and Castle Hill, for the year 1805

Cultivation–Gathering, husking and shelling maize from 200 acre s sowed last year–Breaking up ground and planting 1230 acres of wheat, 100 acre of Barley, 250 acres of Maize, 14 acres of Flax, and 3 acres of potatoes–Hoeing the above maize and threshing wheat.

Stock–Taking care of Government stock as herdsmen, watchmen etc

Buildings–

At Sydney: Building and constructing of stone, a citadel, a stone house, a brick dwelling for the Judge Advocate, a commodious brick house for the main guard, a brick printing office

At Parramatta: Alterations at the Brewery, a brick house as clergyman's residence

At Hawkesbury: completing a public school

A Gaol House with offices, at the expense of the Colony

Boat and Ship Builders: refitting vessels and building row boats

Wheel and Millwrights: making and repairing carts

Manufacturing: sawing, preparing and manufacturing hemp, flax and wool, bricks and tiles

Road Gangs: repairing roads, and building new roads

Other Gangs: loading and unloading boats'

Thus the total benefits from these six items of direct gain to the British comes to well over £174 million, and this is compared to Professor N. G. Butlin's proposal that the British 'invested' £5.6 million, meaning they 'outlaid' this amount without receiving any return.

However, one item of direct cash cost born by the British was the transportation of the prisoners to the Colony, their initial food and general well being during their passage. Although the British chartered the whole boat, some of the expense was offset by authorising private passengers, 'free settlers', to travel in the same fleet. A second saving was the authorities had approved 'back-loading' by these vessels of tea from China.

Only limited stores and provisions, tools and implements were sent with Captain Arthur Phillip, the appointed first Governor, and his efforts to delay the fleet until additional tools were ready was met with an order to 'commence the trip forthwith'. This turned out to be a mistake as the new Colony could only rely on minimal farming practices to grow a supply of vegetables and without the tools to scratch the land, remove the trees and vegetation, little progress was made. A potentially big cost to the fledgling Colony.

The 'Blue Book' accounting records as maintained by Governor Macquarie from 1822 includes a reference to 'net revenue and expenses' which suggests an offset of all revenues against all expenses, and would include as revenue certain convict maintenance charges, to be reimbursed by the British Treasury. Such reimbursement was accounted for and reported only once–in 1825, when it is recorded as a 'receipt in aid of revenue' that an amount of 16,617 pound 'the amount of the parliamentary grant for the charge of defraying the civil establishment'. Prior to and since that date, there are only reports of payments and outgoings to the civil establishment, military and other personnel, without offset from reimbursement.

Other notations in 1825 include revenues from rentals of government assets (Government outsourcing and privatisation obviously started back in 1825) such as:

Ferries	£1,584
Toll gates	£6,554
Gardens	£1,835
Mill	£1,749
Canteen	£910
Church pews	£1,296
Hiring out of convict 'mechanics'	£6,853
Slaughtering dues	£975
Duty on colonial distillation	£4,901
Duty on imported spirits	£178,434
Duty on imported tobacco	£21,817

Even in 1822 the Colony was showing a small operating surplus. This surplus grew through 1828 until, other than for transportation of convicts to the Colony, the charges on account of the British Treasury were less than £100,000 for protecting, feeding and housing nearly 5,000 fully maintained convicts. Against this cost, the charge for housing, feeding and guarding this same number of prisoners in Britain would have been substantially higher, since in addition to the 5,000 fully maintained convicts there were a further 20,000 being paid for by free settlers and used as supervised labour. By 1822 Britain surely had found a cheap source of penal servitude for at least 25,000 of its former prisoners, and found a very worthwhile alternative to the American Colonies as a destination for its prisoners.

Revenue from Crown Land sales and rents was used initially to offset Civil (Crown) salaries and expenses.

It is probably incorrect, at this stage in 1825 to say that it cost Britain nothing or at best, very little, to establish and maintain the Colony, but it can be said that from 1826 the costs were limited to maintaining fewer and fewer convicts. This came about through the reorganisation efforts of Lithgow. The Lithgow-Ovens Report to Governor Darling showed how the convicts could be organised intro work gangs with better supervision and resulting in much greater production and output. This new system would apply to road gangs, land clearing gangs, tree harvesting gangs, the lumberyard, the dockyard, the brickyard, the government farms, and the commissary store workers. But from these convicts great value in terms of agricultural produce, coal and other minerals was derived. Just in terms of coal for lighting, heating and power, the cost to the government of purchasing these items would have been substantial. The Blue Book reflects the use of the coal as a cost rather than a gain as would be the accounting standard today.

A final conclusion could be given that there are many more known records available for this period (the 100 years) than this author originally thought. The reproduction of the Blue Book by the State Archives Office (now renamed State Records Office) is a major step forward in understanding the economic challenges faced by settlers and convicts in the early Colony. The sourcing of material from the Blue Book unveils the financial statements and conditions of these early years. It is still considered that finance records of the period 1788 to 1822 are not re-constructible, but the author feels that a deep search through the microfilms forming the Joint Copying Project will provide information on the two Colonial operating funds of the period–the Police Fund and the Orphan Fund. This challenge is underway with the results held for another time.

An interesting observation is to be found in *The Constitutional History of Australia* by W. G. McMinn (1979), referring to the post 1855 financial arrangements. On P 33 he records 'Subject to the need for a vice-regal message, accepting that any locally (Australian Colony) initiated legislation of a money bill nature requires The Sovereign's ratification, the New South Wales Legislative Council was to have a general right to appropriate revenue from taxation, except for an amount of £81,600, the expenditure of which was to be in accordance with 'three schedules' to the Act; £33,000 for the salaries of those on the civil list eg Governor et al, the superintendent of Port Phillip and its judges and for the expenses of administering justice; £18,600 for the chief civil officers and their departments, for pensions and expenses of the council; and £30,000 for the maintenance of public worship.

The Lithgow approach to practical measures

Corruption in the Colony

The reader may have questioned whether the colony was rife with corruption of one type or another. Public and official corruption, was to be found in the commissary and the public service; banking or private sector corruption, took many forms, not least of which was price gouging under government contracts. Lithgow came across at least three major instances that could have resulted in a huge public scandal, but for reasons of belaying investor confidence were kept under 'wraps' by the government.

a. Bank of NSW and the Balcombe scandal

One of the first real challenges to be met by the fledgling economy was the creation of the Bank of New South Wales in 1817. The British Colonial Office had assigned Commissioner J.T. Bigge to review the colonial operations and he reported in 1823 that 'the establishment of the

Bank has greatly added to the facility of commercial transactions in the Colony', although his secondary comment was that the bank had been formed illegally, was operating illegally and its existence required official legislative ratification. These concerns, following Macquarie's hastened departure from the colony was that the bank, in its illegitimacy, may fail and the government would not bother to step in to rescue its deposit holders. Illiquidity became a real problem and as if further steps were needed to undermine the depositors' confidence in the bank, it became public knowledge that the bank was appealing to the Governor for urgent funds to restore liquidity.

Select Documents in Australia History records (P388) these extracts from the Bigge Report:

'The evils of a paper circulation, issued upon the credit of individuals, had become the subject of universal complaint, and had defied all the measures of restraint or correction that from time to time had been applied to them. Supported by the patronage and influence of the local government several of the inhabitants of the Colony met together, and after agreeing upon the great expediency of establishing a bank, drew up the rules and regulations, that were submitted to Governor Macquarie.

The Bank was declared to be established for the general and customary uses of deposit, loan and discount, with a sanction to charge interest at ten percent for the same, on a fund or capital stock of 20,000 pounds, which was to be raised by shares of 200 pounds each. The charter was granted for a period of seven years; and the subscribers were constituted a body corporate and joint-stock company under the formal name of "President and Company of the Bank of New South Wales", with the stock being transferable as usually granted to chartered incorporations.'

Two significant problems associated with the Bank of New South Wales confronted Lithgow when in 1825 Governor Brisbane asked him firstly to review the letter from the Directors of the Bank which requested a £40,000 advance to underpin its liquidity, but then in reviewing the Bank's operations, Lithgow found a discrepancy in the cash on hand at the bank, and uncovered a fraud on the bank by the government's own treasurer. The treasurer of the day was Balcombe whose reputation for playing loosely with the truth had preceded him, but in contrast, Lord Bathurst sponsored him. The Balcombe scandal was not the first banking scandal that had touched the colony, but it certainly had the most important and potentially damaging impact.

In summary (the event is discussed elsewhere in detail) Balcombe was the Colonial Treasurer, at the time that Brisbane was governor and Lithgow was the Deputy-Commissary–Accounts.

Although Balcombe did not directly cause the scandal, he was the main contributor, and it was in his nature that he could not remain uninvolved from money or greed or impetuous dealings in order to satisfy his greed and his urge to cumulate wealth at others expense. His arrival in the colony was plagued by scandal, as he had previously been the accounting officer on the Island of Saint Helena where Napoleon was temporarily secured under British guard.

The post of Colonial Treasurer was established in October 1823. Balcombe did not apply for nor seek the position, but it-suited Bathurst to place Balcombe into that role and rid himself of a liability–both financially and metaphorically.

Balcombe had been accused of assisting Napoleon to mail correspondence unseen by the senior officers in command and of supplying him money by discounting his bills. Balcombe was returned to England but the charges could not be verified, and he threatened to seek compensation for his treatment from Bathurst.

Bathurst thus appointed him Colonial Treasurer of NSW and solved his problem and in so doing, kept an important ally of the government in the House of Commons on side.

Once in NSW, Balcombe used his position, with the governor, to cancel the housing arrangement made by Brisbane in favour of Lithgow and Boyes (another commissary appointee). Balcombe then proceeded to again engage in 'side' deals between the main colonial bank (the BNSW), its directors and management, in order to fill his personal purse, and enrich himself at the expense of the public coffers.

Balcombe used government funds to 'discount' (i.e. buy and sell) commercial bills. The bank and its controlling directors probably encouraged this mischievous behaviour, because

The Bank was short of liquidity

Three directors were borrowers of the majority of the bank's capital, but still wanted more

Balcombe wanted to engage in commercial trade, but had no personal funds, but had the knowledge of commercial discounting of bills and knew that, even if not a safe practice, it could enrich him quickly and if needed he could return the bills to the bank and account for the funds he was using. He would pocket the profits from his misbehaviour and unless the governor made a surprise audit of the bank, he should never be caught. Even if he was caught he was the 'protégée' (if not the protected appointee) of Lord Bathurst.

The bank directors would not inform the governor of Balcombe's fraud because they needed him involved and were also making money out of his activities. What the directors forgot was that as the bank struggled with its growing liquidity crisis, the only way out was for the governor to loan the bank some short-term funding. For this to be accepted by the governor a full disclosure would have to be made, and there was a likelihood of the government audit.

It is most likely that Balcombe was aware of the liquidity crisis, and of the request to the governor to make a substantial loan in order to stop the bank closing its doors. Balcombe, occupying an office close to that of Lithgow, was also probably aware that a surprise count was being planned. Balcombe, in order to protect himself, would have done two things

Informed the bank directors of the intended count, and

Plan to return the bills and unused cash he was using from the bank, or else the 'cash at bank' balance would never balance with the balance sheet figure.

Lithgow planned the count for 26 May 1824; Balcombe returned over £20,000 in bills and cash the previous day, but the balance was still not in line with the balance sheet figure expected. Nearly £4,000 was still missing. Balcombe went to Darling and admitted his activities but no action was taken against him. Lithgow's complete audit determined that Balcombe had discounted (by using Government Funds) over £76,000 of bills

This was not the only defalcation by Balcombe as with both matters, no action was taken by the governor against him. We can only surmise:

This type and level of 'white collar crime' was not worthy of action, nor unexpected, nor frowned upon.

Bathurst had privately expected Balcombe to engage in such activity and would just ease him out of the position at the right time but in the meantime Balcombe would be watched closely, and the right person to do this was Lithgow, rather than the governor

The more likely explanation is that if the Balcombe scandal had been made public, (and no hint of the scandal was to be fond in the press of the day), then the bank's doors would have been closed and the colony may well have been abandoned. Brisbane informed the Secretary of State fully of the matter, but Bathurst's only response was to issue regulations for future handling of government funds.

Brisbane's successor, Darling, did not take action against the bank; his official position had been that the only established bank in the colony had been caught in a cash drain affecting the whole community. The situation stemmed basically from a balance of payments deficit caused by a high rate of growth, and was accentuated by a currency shortage arising from measures to speed up the switch to a sterling system of payments. That some of the bank's discounting had been unwise and sufficiently spread, and a senior Government employee had been acting illegally, and the bank director's had also been taking liberties, was really not relevant to Darling. The Bank, he said 'had been dragged along by the tide'. (Governors despatches 1826)

b. Lithgow and the Bank of NSW

Lithgow's second challenge, having assisted in settling the Balcombe matter and keeping the scandal out of the Press, was to analyse the Bank's potential and determine if the Bank could repay a £40,000 loan.

Lithgow's appointment as a Director (representing the Governor and Colonial Administration) of the Bank of New South Wales was prompted by and follows the concerns Governor Darling had about the capacity of the larger of the two operating banks to avoid 'Bankruptcy'. (If the Bank had run out of liquidity, it would have had to close its doors–'bankruptcy was the only means recognised by Law of closing up chartered operations) Part of this concern was due to the Colonial Treasurer, Balcombe, using colonial funds as his own money and effectively co-mingling personal and colonial monies. The Directors, when they jointly wrote to Governor Darling acquainting him with the precarious liquidity situation that the bank was in, advised him that one option they were considering was 'closing the doors'. Darling's response was ambiguous. He was reluctant, as he wrote to Lord Bathurst, to have government intervention in a private concern–because it set precedents–but government money was at risk, as was an economic depression, if the bank failed and depositors lost their money and traders were unable to issue bills or have bills discounted–it could have turned into a commercial calamity, of sufficient power and purpose to close down the colony. On 22 May 1826, Darling again wrote to Lord Bathurst saying that he had sent the Deputy Commissary-General and Auditor of Accounts (Lithgow filled both positions), on the 10th May to the premises of the Bank of NSW in order to count 'the money in the Treasury' on that morning. Lithgow reported back on the afternoon of the 11th May that he had counted £22,396.13.2 ½. This total was still at variance with the 'Weekly State of the Colonial Treasury', prepared by William Balcombe, which as at the 13 May, showed a balance of £26,000.7.9¾ sterling. This sum did, however, include funds and other 'paper' securities returned by Balcombe on the morning of the inspection. Balcombe would have been aware of the pending liquidity problem facing the bank and of the formal Bank request to Darling for assistance. Balcombe had already been approached privately (as Colonial Treasurer) for assistance but was unable to raise the level of funds required by the Bank. He would have also (he shared an office with Lithgow) have been aware of the surprise count of Bank funds and so returned what monies he had in his possession and remaining undiscounted bills, to the Bank in order to 'balance' the funds to be counted. The difference of £3,600 was a large and significant error (it meant that this amount of funds had gone missing and was unaccounted for by the Bank), but Balcombe personally explained his actions to Darling who then wrote to Bathurst:

'I attribute this difference to be a result of Balcombe having been in the habit of discounting bills of private individuals, and that he (Balcombe) hoped that the money would be back in the bank at the time of any examination of the Bank's records, and that his previous transactions would not be enquired into or discovered' (Governors' Despatches 1828). This is a remarkably understated assessment of a major fraud and report on the Balcombe activities. What Balcombe had done amounted to fraud on the Government funds as well as a fraud on the bank, and in any other circumstances the perpetrator would have been severely censored, dismissed from public office and possibly gaoled. Even when it was found that Balcombe had 'interfered' with the Naval Officer's funds, no action was taken, against Balcombe but the Naval Officer, John Piper, was dismissed. Obviously Balcombe was known to be owed favours by Lord Bathurst and was essentially untouchable. Straight-laced Lithgow must have found this situation hard to understand, but there is no record of his having tried to persuade the governor to a different course of action. Instead Lithgow agreed to be appointed to the Bank Board (as a representative of the Governor), perhaps thinking he could stop the situation from being repeated or from getting worse. In fact Darling's requirement that the bank accept a government-appointed director in exchange for a loan of £20,000 was opposed by Bathurst and Lithgow was forced to resign from the bank board.

This concern by the governors about the liquidity and the solvency of the Bank was based on a letter from the Directors to the Darling dated prior to Darling's despatch of Lithgow to count the Treasury balance. The four directors (John Piper–Naval Officer and collector of Customs; W.C. Wentworth–a Legislative Councillor and member of the Executive Council; T. Raine and R.Pritchett–two businessmen and traders) advised the Governor 'In consequence of the large exportation of Dollars, which has lately taken place, and the alarm which it has created in the public mind, we request you will give the bank credit on the commissary account of twenty-thousand pounds in Silver currency and take as security any bank assets which your excellency may select' (HRA I:XII P 299). From a review of the Bank's books of account, it was not insolvent, merely illiquid. The bank was not in a negative equity position, which would have made it insolvent, but was with sufficient cash/coinage to meet its expected daily obligations to depositors. So the bank was profitable, and had a surplus of assets over liabilities and if Balcombe had not taken £76,000 of liquidity from the bank, then this crisis would not have arisen, at this time. But the whole operation of the bank, its management and its directors, was flawed and if the damage had not been discovered in May 1828, it would have occurred at another time. The bank was run for the director's benefit and as a personal fiefdom of the large stockholders and the controlling directors. The total assets of the Bank as of the 12 May was £472,412, of which only £5,907 was in coinage, the balance being mortgage balances and bills awaiting collection, whilst the debts and account balances amounted to £407,662 leaving an equity of over £64,730. Of this sum, the subscribed capital amounted to £43,200, so that 'retained profits for eight years since the bank commenced business was only £21,000, and yet for the previous three years the average assets of the bank was in excess of £400,000'. Obviously the directors were skimming off the profits by misusing bank funds to their own benefit whilst knowing that Balcombe was offering privately the services of discounting of bills rather than have the bank make these controlled (the governor was setting the discount rate) services available. On the other hand, from the Bank's viewpoint, Balcombe was shielding them from the underlying risk, provided Balcombe had the means to repay any defaults.

A shareholders' equity of nearly £65,000 left the Bank fairly healthy but illiquid, and if there was a further 'run on the Bank's remaining coinage', the doors would have to be closed. The directors had cause to request the governor's assistance, especially since Balcombe had placed the colonial government funds in some jeopardy (more so if the bank closed its doors) and it was thus necessary for the governor to prop up the Bank's position, in order to protect not only the colonial funds, but the funds of all the depositors. Another problem detected by and reported upon by Lithgow to the Governor was that three depositors held the majority of the indebtedness to the Bank, so that if either, Messrs Robert Campbell (a merchant), Raine (a bank director) or Ramsay (a trader) failed, the Bank would be brought to its knees. These three gentlemen had endorsed bills to the value of nearly two hundred and fifty thousand pound out of the £400,000 of gross assets (or more than half of the assets) of bills receivable owing to the bank. Signature loans amounted to a further £50,000. We read in the Report of the Examination by Lithgow of the Bank's fiscal position that on the 12 May, Balcombe had discounted (by using official funds) over £76,743 in bills, and lodged the bills as collateral with the Bank, as a substitute for the missing cash. Balcombe had obviously directly caused the illiquid situation that the bank was in, but it is hard to believe that Balcombe took all these actions alone. A director must have authorised the bank to accept these bills for discounting. Balcombe obviously enriched himself very substantially (he 'earned' a spread between buying and selling the bills, as well as earning both the interest rate spread and the discount rate spread), as these were not the only bills he discounted–these were the only bills he was caught with, and his discount rate was probably in excess of 12%. Balcombe was also reported by Lithgow to have been fiddling with the Naval Officers funds as £16,995 was missing from Piper's funds due to the Colony.

Obviously the Governor was very correct in being disturbed about the Bank's policies and actions, and especially those of Balcombe. Although it was a privately owned institution, the Bank of New South Wales held the colonial funds on deposit and processed all the cheques used in the colony, as well as holding all the coinage in circulation. The bank had been substituted as a colonial 'treasury'.

Lithgow pointed out that 'It appears that on a real money capital of less than £50,000, the present directors of the bank have thought proper to extend credit of upwards of £500,000 or ten times the equity of the bank.' He concluded that, if the Governor decided to extend credit to the Bank, it should only be done by ensuring 'management of the bank be conducted with much more circumspection than that shown recently'.

The opposition bank, the fledgling Bank of Australia, stepped up to fill the possible void created by a failed BNSW, and offered to assist the BNSW with its problems (the offer was to take over the government deposits and handle the discounting of bills). The Bank of Australia was offering to take over the most profitable areas of the BNSW operations, but the directors of BNSW declined the offer. It appeared, from events shortly thereafter, that the Bank of Australia had more than enough problems of its own and lasted only another few years before tumbling into liquidation in the next negative colonial economic cycle.

Governor Darling, on the 16 May 1826 agreed to advance credit to the BNSW and thereby averted a major calamity, but with conditions–firstly that Balcombe was not to be allowed to use bank or government deposited funds in the future and that Lithgow was to be appointed a Director of the Bank as representing the Governor and colony.

On 1 December 1826, Darling received a response from Bathurst in which Bathurst is approved of Lithgow being appointed a director of the BNSW, but rather recommended Lithgow to have a prudential supervisory role over the three banks (the BNSW, the Bank of Australia, and the new Commercial Banking Company of Sydney) in existence and operation. Since Darling had already made the appointment of Lithgow, he suggested Lithgow remain a director in his own right, rather than on behalf of the government, but in doing so neglected to offer the government's prudential overview of the banks which in a few short years would cause the demise of many new colonial banks and allow the big British banks to seek representation in the colony. The prudential responsibility for banks by government had long been recognised in London, as numerous county banks had failed in the 1775-1825 period by being overextended in bills. The decision in London had been not to artificially support the failed banks with government funds but to more closely supervise their lending activities and other areas of business–'the ordinary banking business of deposit, discount and exchange' (R.F. Holder–*Bank of NSW–A History).* It was this prudential aspect of bank regulation that the colony lacked, and, at this time, lacked the talent because of this conflict of interest by Lithgow. Lithgow could either act as a director of the BNSW or act as a prudential regulator of the banks on behalf of the government. He could not do both, as this was an innate conflict. Lithgow, as Colonial Auditor, paid 'lip-service' to the question of regulating the banks, by calling for their financial statement every six months, for an 'in-office' review, but this was of little value if a bank was about to close its doors.

Bathurst also strongly disapproved of collecting officers accessing or holding/using public funds. Bathurst directed:

All officers collecting revenue pay over their balances on a prescribed day each week.

Officers away from Sydney shall remit funds on a monthly basis.

That a fire-proof vault shall be built in the Treasury offices and hold all colonial coinage, rather than depositing these funds in a bank

Bank accounts shall be held at both banks in the colony with funds distributed equally

Monthly bank statements are to be reviewed by the governor and by the auditor.

Lithgow became responsible for implementing these relatively minor changes in procedures, which were of minimal interest to the banks continuing problems.

Lithgow maintained his close association with BNSW for another 20 years until pressure of work forced his resignation in 1846.

The Bathurst Solution to the Bank (of New South Wales) Problem was as follows:

In December 1826 Bathurst reviewed the bank situation (following the Balcombe crisis) as it affected the colonial treasury and set down some guidelines (HRA 1, xii p702-6). In essence the colonial government was to patronise each local bank equally, but never to have more than £5,000 on deposit in any one. Revenues in excess of this were to be kept in a fire–and theft-proof vault to which there were to be three locks and three keys. When it was necessary to open the vault, the Colonial Treasurer, the Colonial Auditor and the Colonial Secretary or his appointed representative were to meet, unlock the vault, and ceremoniously deposit or withdraw specie. Auditor Lithgow, who had been appointed a director of the Bank of New South Wales by Darling as a condition of the governor 'saving' the bank, was ordered to resign as a director (representing the government), because, as Bathurst states 'his presence there gave a false impression of government responsibility'. Lithgow's resignation was accepted reluctantly because of his past contribution and he was influenced to stand in his own right and was thus reappointed without loss of time. Lithgow's conflict of interest was greater than being the colonial auditor and a director of the Bank of NSW.

Lithgow was also an initial contributor of capital to and a stockholder of the Bank of Australia. However, Lithgow still carried out his official duty as inspector of both banks, and acted, for a further twenty years, as a private, but independent director of the Bank of NSW.

Bathurst's position, as set out in his dispatch # 95 to Governor Darling on 27th September 1827, was in itself a contradiction. On the one hand, Bathurst recognised the need for the Bank of NSW to handle monetary transactions in the colony, and its role to regularise coinage, loans and discounting processes, but on the other hand, Bathurst stated that the bank itself had not had its illegal charter regularised and therefore the settlors in the colony were accepting 'collective and individual responsibility for their deposits' whilst the stockholders, themselves, were accepting joint and several liability for any debts of the bank. The proposed increase of capital for the bank could only be completed if the proprietors of the bank recognised and accepted their individual liability and responsibility. Bathurst states 'such increase in capital should not be permitted to be raised under any false impression that the subscribers were only individually liable for the amount of their subscriptions'. Bathurst had advised Darling in his same memorandum, that "I beg to call your attention to the letter, which I addressed to the late Governor Macquarie on the 29th October 1818, in which it is stated on the opinion of the crown law officers that the governor not being empowered to grant to the bank a charter, it was consequently null and void: its renewal therefore in 1823 by Sir Thomas Brisbane was equally invalid; so that the several subscribers of the stock are liable for the whole amount of the debts and engagements of the company". Much of the pressure Darling was under to solve the Bank liquidity crisis was due to the economic downturn that hit the colony in 1827. Darling was not acting entirely selflessly. His choices were to save the bank and save the people's deposits, or save the bank and save his rich and powerful friends who were the directors and major stockholders of the bank. Darling's solution was to save everybody, including protecting the government deposits. Thus by Darling loaning the bank the sum of forty-thousand pound to underpin the liquidity of the bank during the slump of 1827, and of appointing William Lithgow as a director of the bank, he was placing both the treasury monies and Lithgow at great risk but relieving at the same time the liability of the stockholders. But then Darling's great friend Robert Campbell, together with Macarthur, Wentworth and other colonial 'giants' were those stockholders and he had to return their favours and general support in a practical and helpful manner. Darling's actions could be challenged as being unbalanced but the end result made the bank and the Darling stature much stronger in the eyes of the free settlers.

In the same dispatch (#95), Bathurst is complimentary of the Lithgow enquiry and report. It is surprising that Bathurst was not critical of Balcombe, but as a former protégé Bathurst decided to leave Balcombe to be dealt with by Darling. What is more surprising, is that Bathurst's response did not recognise the potential conflict of interest he was creating by allowing Lithgow to serve the Governor, as a bank regulator, and of serving the bank as a director. "The persons, whom you appointed to investigate the affairs of the bank establishment, seem to have conducted their enquiry in a very able and satisfactory manner; and although the impression caused by this report is that the Directors of the bank had managed their concerns upon very unsafe and improper principles, yet, considering that the whole of the subscribers were individually responsible for the whole amount of the debts, there does not seem to have been any reason to apprehend that they would not ultimately be able to perform the whole of their obligations; and you (Darling), therefore, were justified in granting them the assistance you did". Bathurst's second conflict was that although he insisted that Lithgow resign as a Director ('resign this office'), however, 'whilst there be any debts due to the Public, Lithgow should be appointed to inspect and control the affairs of the bank'. Lithgow had become very valuable to the Bank Board with his inside knowledge: and his being in the governor's confidence; as well as being responsible for keeping the directors clear of any wrongdoing in his report to the Governor; but mainly for his financial and planning skills. So the decision of the bank Board to re-appoint Lithgow in his own right was a masterstroke to uphold the bank's reputation amongst merchants and to underpin future government deposits. The bankers were heavily reliant on the government deposits for their liquidity and future treasurers (Balcombe died in 1828) were being paid (on their personal account) an interest on the money being deposited by their offices into the two banks. Darling, upon learning (from Lithgow's audit of the banks) of this practice, threatened to withhold further deposits unless the banks paid this interest into the treasury funds rather than onto the treasurer's private funds. This was a third ploy be Balcombe, uncovered by Lithgow, to enrich himself at the expense of the colony.

The 1827 recession period was largely encouraged a great influx of British capital, which was accompanied by the establishment of a number of British Banks in the colony. In addition, writes S. J. Butlin (*Foundations of the Australian Monetary System)* 'the banking system was transformed. In place of a few localised unit banks relying on capital for loanable funds, content with restricted business and averse to serious competition, there were a number of large banks–all the colonial banks had greatly expanded, and were engaged in aggressive competition. A scramble for deposits had pushed interest rates to high levels and had established deposit banking as the general practice'.

c. Bank of NSW subscriber's breach the Law

Individuals were not the only one's abusing bank privileges. A group of subscribers were actively breaching the law, as the report by Lithgow on behalf of the Executive Council found. This wide ranging report assessed the general effect on the colony of the suspension of bank operations and the realisation of its assets, and it disclosed the bank's continuing unsatisfactory financial position and poor management. Of the nominal capital of £150,000 only £29,018 was shown as paid up but the amount of actual cash subscribed was £17,583. The remainder represented promissory notes given by shareholders, which had been renewed once and were coming up for renewal again, reducing 25% on each occasion. This procedure was flawed, even if convenient, and distorted the bank's balance sheet. Further, the bill portfolio amounted to £61,590 of which £11,435 was in notes for bank stock. Bills totalling £8,900 were overdue, with some dating back two years. All the overdue holders also had their names on current bills. Were these practices fraud, malfeasance or bad management? Half of the directors admitted to Lithgow that they had personal deposits with the rival Bank of Australia.

d. Balcombe and the Naval Officer's funds

John Piper was the first Naval Officer in the Colony (appointed by Macquarie in 1813), with duties including collection of customs duties and excise on spirits and harbour charges, the control of all lighthouses and water policing generally. His remuneration was based on his collections and his income rose to over £4,000 per annum. Macquarie made Piper a magistrate in 1819 and in 1825 he was elected Chairman of the Board of the Bank of New South Wales (Lithgow had been appointed a director, representing the government, in 1824). He was suspended from the post of Naval Officer in 1827 when Darling, acting on an audit report by Lithgow, recognised a deficiency in the public naval officer's funds of over £12,000.

Again it would appear that Balcombe was using the Naval Officer's funds as the source of funds to discount bills with the BNSW (see above). This flagrant abuse of his position again brought no official reprisal against him.

The naval officer's position was shortly thereafter converted into a salaried one, upon the recommendation of William Lithgow and Piper was suspended.

It seemed that Piper was admonished for the wrongdoing of Balcombe, although Piper was culpable by giving consent to the Balcombe malfeasance.

e. The First defalcation in the Colony

The Bank of NSW in 1821 lost £12,600 when its Chief Clerk apparently misappropriated bank funds. Shann, in *The Economic History of Australia* describes a defalcation of approx. one quarter of the original subscribed capital of the Chartered Bank of New South Wales in 1821. It appears that the sum of about £3,000 (one quarter of the subscribed £12,600) was stolen by the Chief Clerk from the Bank. The Bank had been 'chartered' illegally (according to Lord Bathurst in 1825), but Bathurst suggested to the Governor (Macquarie) that rather than close the Bank, that the capital contributors acknowledge that they were not entitled to the privileges of indemnity that were usually accorded a new Bank, and having done so they should be allowed to continue to operate.

Shann describes the event this way: 'Macquarie had hoped the original offer of limited liability would induce the sound and the cautious to subscribe adequate capital to commence banking operations. Even Commissioner Bigge's report of 1823 bore testimony to the utility of the bank in evolving order out of the commercial chaos of paper based on the honesty of individuals, and to the high credit it enjoyed'.

The Bank had already survived the loss of a quarter of the subscribed capital (£12,600) through defalcations by its chief cashier, discovered in January 1821. That credit, Bigge thought, had grown in part from the belief in its possession of a royal charter, but as he could not be 'insensible to the consequences of insufficient control that a chartered immunity from the ordinary risks of commercial partnership has a tendency to produce' (Bigge Report P67), he did not recommend the charter's renewal". The Charter was in fact renewed later in the year of 1824.

Holder, writing in *Bank of NSW–A History* offers the best description of this event:

"The public confidence in the Bank had been shattered by a series of defalcations by a former cashier Francis Williams. The first scent of trouble came in September 1820, when he was requested to resign for making unauthorised loans to the extent of £2,000, which the directors were obliged to call in. No doubts as to his integrity existed at this stage but in the following January a full count of cash revealed a shortage of over £12,000 in notes, which in itself would throw doubt on the accuracy of the balance sheet at the end of 1820, disclosing notes in circulation as less than £6,000 and showed up the lack of supervision of the note issue. Williams had apparently gained nothing for himself but had obliged his friends by giving credit for payments, which were never made: he was subsequently convicted of embezzlement. This incident was revealed in Bigge: Report on Agriculture and Trade p.66.'

The moral of this story is that only five years later, and again relying on a surprise 'audit' (count of balance sheet assets), a similar deficiency was revealed; again caused by a negligence to 'issue' notes properly. That is really where the similarity ends. On this next occasion, no fraud or embezzlement was thoroughly investigated, and even though grounds could have been found for a criminal prosecution, no charges were laid, and so no convictions were entered. Unlike the Williams situation when there was a minor run on the bank by depositors and the governor withdrew the Police Fund deposit, there was no adverse publicity, no charges and no government action, other than a special deposit by the governor of a further £40,000. We are left wondering whether Darling had something to hide rather than assuming that Bathurst alone wanted to overlook any Balcombe angle.

f. Military Officers, the Rum Trade and corruption

Lithgow did not discover the first incidence of corruption in the colony. In fact corrupt practices probably commenced on the 26 January 1788. However the most common practice of corruption was almost given official standing during the Rum Rebellion of of Governor Bligh's administration

H.V. Evatt in his reference book *The Rum Rebellion* writes of the rise of the power and influence of the Rum Corps (p26-27) in these times:

'The explanation of many, if not most, of the difficulties which overwhelmed the three Naval Governors who succeeded Governor Phillip viz Hunter, King and Bligh, lies in the increasing ascendancy of the officers of the New South Wales Corps. They not only possessed the monopoly of violence, but:

They became an aristocracy. They were allowed to engage in trade and agriculture; but gradually, they obtained control of the imports, particularly spirits; and the consequence was that, within twelve months of Phillip's departure, rum became the recognised medium of exchange. So much so that even labour could only be purchased with spirits. Under this system the officers reaped enormous harvests.

During Hunter's governorship, the officers repeatedly smuggled convicts away from government control so as to use them in private employment, including, of course, that of the officer's themselves. After Phillip's departure (in 1792), the commanding officer of the regiment, Major Grose, administered the Colony for 3 years after which Captain Paterson, the next in command, succeeded him. Under both Grose and Paterson, 'convict servants were lavishly bestowed, not only upon commissioned officers of the Corps but by most other Corp men.')

The general quality of the Marine recruit was pretty low, many buying their commission, or being relatives of convicted criminals. Macarthur participated, like most of his military colleagues, in carrying on trading ventures in and to the Colony, but owes most of his success to his close association with the Marine Commander (Major Grose), who had befriended Macarthur and provided priority access to convict labour, extensive land grants and other government resources. This was a breach of government regulations, but since the very regulators were participants in these trading activities, which was left to exercise the regulatory function? Macarthur also participated in the sale and distribution of liquor that eventually got out of hand and became the source of protest during the Rum Rebellion If Macarthur followed the practice of his fellow officers, he must have charged extremely high prices for the goods he sold. This practice was to the disadvantage of the lower end of the community. But it did assist him, and many of the senior officers, in building up substantial capital by which he was able to buy land and livestock and generally progress his own wealth. Was this official corruption or an oversight of administration?

g. Corruption takes on a religious mantle

The two financial funds that effectively constituted a quasi-treasury between 1802 and 1822, and which were privately operated and accounted for, were only replaced when Balcombe was appointed Colonial Treasurer, and Lithgow was appointed as Deputy-Commissary of Accounts and pro-tem Colonial Auditor. There was ample opportunity for manipulation of the accounts by the two treasurers, and it is a fact that both Treasurers became more and more wealthy as the two funds grew. Opportunity is only one element of criminal activity, and we cannot jump from this accusation to a provable fact without a lot more work. But it must be more than just coincidence that the Treasurers became wealthy at the same time the funds grew and there was complete lack of control by way of internal audit over the accounts.

The Police fund was operated by Darcy Wentworth who was also the Police Magistrate and Superintendent of Police. It was used 'as a kind of consolidated revenue fund out of which payments for construction and maintenance of wharves, roads and bridges, and watch-houses as well as the salaries of many officials were made. In 1821, for example, the Police Fund was charged with an annual salary bill of £9,779 for various government officials and a further £3386 for overseers, constables and watchmen'. (HRA I: X p 579-83).

We cannot use the standards of today to evaluate fraud or misappropriation, but we can identify right and wrong even in a society generally blind to this sort of activity. Opportunity was everywhere. There were no salary records to support the weekly or monthly payments. The amounts were never the same from period to period and the names of recipients were never the same from period to period. Wentworth may well have been padding the payroll, using dummy names for payees and overstating the amounts due. The system did not call for an audit trail, and even if it had, there was none experienced, until Lithgow arrived two years later, that could have tracked irregularities. Bigge did find however that their respective treasurers kept the accounts of the Police and Orphan Funds in 1823 at the bank. Marsden transferred the Orphan Fund balance of £3,000 to the bank in 1818, but no record exists in the BNSW ledger of the Police Funds until 1823. Prior to 1818, Marsden kept his cash on hand, in the drawer of his desk, in his home office, to which his family and servants had access. Marsden is on record as saying; he only counted his 'money once each month and it rarely balanced with his ledgers'. The Bank's ledgers show that Wentworth's large and active personal account reflected 'substantial part of the flow of transactions through the fund (Holder p43). Macquarie had used the William's defalcation as the reason for withdrawing the Police Fund deposit from the Bank. The Governor was rightly concerned for the public Funds, which he had caused to be deposited with the Bank. Possibly Darling's inaction some three years later, in similar circumstances were the result of the Bigge Reports. (They had arrived in the colony in 1824, and supported the role of the banks in financing trade, however, 'some instances of the bank's generosity had led to a degree of over trading and speculation on the part of individual merchants'.

Marsden had a not unsimilar problem, as had Wentworth. He was the number two preacher in the colony after Richard Johnson and was on a civil salary of £150 per annum. From this base, and his activities as treasurer/manager of the female Orphanage, he owned 4,000 acres and many thousands of sheep and cattle. During the days when the 'master' had to furnish, housing, clothes and food for all servants and convict workers, Marsden employed 25 convicts. The meat bill for 90 young orphans grew constantly whilst Marsden arranged with the Orphanage to raise a growing number of sheep on Orphanage lands in Parramatta. Again there were opportunities for Marsden to skim money off the Fund. Why raise sheep but sell them 'on the hoof' to the butcher, and buy back dressed meat from that butcher at top prices? Why did the sheep numbers never balance with the Orphanage books? Why did the money contributed to the Orphan Fund by single parents wanting to place their children with the Orphanage, at £25 per head, never appear on the records of the Fund? The elder children, both male and female, were often 'sold' out to settlers for day work, but the receipts were never logged into the Orphan Fund. The Orphan Fund never balanced its accounts and in 1818 the account was out of balance to the amount of £916. A little bit here and a little bit there. Who would ever have suspected a cleric or a Police Superintendent of padding the books? Corruption, defalcation, or just plain fraud?

This, like the Rum Rebellion, was long before Lithgow's arrival, but these instances laid the precedent for bad practices in the colony. After all, it was a penal colony and criminals know no geographic boundaries. Upon Lithgow's arrival he was to be confronted with 'more of the same', even among government officials.

h. Corruption by the NSW Agent-General in London

It was Lithgow who detected a major 'theft' against the colony by its own appointed representative in London. It is as close to corruption as one can get–be it theft, misappropriation of government funds or just plain stealing, the agent-general in London was receiving money from the British Treasury (on behalf of the Colony) and other sources in London, not declaring in it the books of accounts and misappropriating it to his own use. Its importance was not so much an act of corruption as its discovery, a stroke of luck by Lithgow that was sufficient to restore his credibility with both the governor and Treasury officials in London and turn the tide of negative fortunes gathering against him, in such a way that his good reputation was restored.

As the means of recovering his reputation, he presented the governor with an event that demonstrated the Lithgow diligence. He had located a misappropriated sum of money and those funds had now been returned to the colonial coffers. What had happened was that the agent-general in London, a Mr Barnard, had been accumulating funds in London and not accounting for them to his colonial treasurer.

As Governor, Charles A. Fitz Roy advised Early Grey on 21 December 1848, 'certain sums have been remitted to the Colonial Agent-General by the British Treasury, but which had not been carried to the credit of the colony'. Lithgow had located and tracked these sums over an extended period and had first advised Fitz Roy that the amount was £3410.2.9. However on 16 December 1848 he amended his advice to the Governor and increased the amount he was tracking to £5928.3.2. The size of the missing funds and its discovery made Lithgow something of a hero, and corrected all those negative thoughts that had travelled through government circles for the last few years, due to the lateness of the 'Blue Books' in being transmitted to London.

i. BNSW Directors place Colonial Funds at risk.

The whole operation of the Bank of NSW, its management and its directors, was flawed and if the damage had not been discovered in May

1828, it would surely have occurred at another time. The bank appeared to be run only for the directors' benefit and as a personal fiefdom of the large stockholders and the controlling directors. The total assets of the Bank as of the 12 May, 1828 was £472,412, of which only £5,907 was in coinage, the balance being mortgage balances and bills awaiting collection, whilst the debts and account balances amounted to £407,662 leaving an equity of over £64,730. Of this sum, the subscribed capital amounted to £43,200, so that 'retained profits for eight years since the bank commenced business was only £21,000, and yet for the previous three years the average assets of the bank was in excess of £400,000. Obviously the directors were skimming off the profits by misusing bank funds to their own benefit whilst knowing that Balcombe was offering the services of discounting of bills privately rather than have the bank make these risky services available.

The bank had always been in need of experienced clerical help, and at the board meeting on 12 February 1817, the directors accepted an offer to help in opening the books of the Bank from John Croaker, a "banker's clerk" who had arrived the previous year under a sentence of 14 years transportation for embezzlement, and whom they had declined to employ as principal bookkeeper (Holder p 34). Obviously 'good help is hard to get'. Holder (op cit) states that 'the impact of the Bank's notes on the money instruments of the colony does not 'lend itself to precise analysis'.

However, an estimate made in 1826 gave an idea of the composition of total circulating media other than coin towards the start of the Brisbane administration. Of the total £210,000 'sterling' due to the Bank, drafts on the British Treasury were estimated at £150,000; negotiable store receipts £20,000; notes of the commissary-general £15,000; bank notes £15,000, and notes 'of respectable private individuals £10,000. (Wollstonecraft to Colonial Secretary 15 August 1826 HRA I: XII p 508). These risky practices by the bank directors were in the same vein as allowing Balcombe to manipulate and abuse bank funds. What was so badly needed was a prudential review of bank practices and activities but most of all experienced, honest and honourable officers and employees of the bank.

j. Conclusion and Summary

Writing about 'corruption' in the colony could easily fill a book. In today's terms corruption is very different to the various types of wrongdoing we have shown as taking place in the colony. However, not only has the definition changed, peoples standards and attitudes to wrongdoing have also changed so that in the same way, the convicts arrived in the colony for having stolen a silk handkerchief or for stealing a loaf of bread or some silverware, corruption in the 1800-50 period was regarded in a very different light to how it is regarded today.

So definitions and attitudes have changes but then too the people who were inclined in the direction of wrongdoing have changed. It was not only the convicts that were doing wrong; in the cases referred to above, the common theft by convicts was replaced by a real 'white collar crime' of criminal mischief, malfeasance, fiscal manipulation and financial skulduggery, undertaken by 'free settlers' who were often the 'pillars of society'.

This selection of crimes, few of which resulted in punishment, are a small proportion of what would have gone on in the colony, but they are representative of the type and level of corruption that would have confronted Lithgow during his years in the colony. Of course, as Colonial auditor, Lithgow was not as technically competent or as thorough in his examination of the public records as auditing standards would require today. Much of his work was tedious, and mechanical, rather than technical and corruption seeking. The most demanding challenge facing Lithgow would have been ensuring that purchase orders were in triplicate and that invoices were matched by appropriately signed purchase orders and the purchase orders were within the scope of the parliamentary appropriations.

CHAPTER 4

LITHGOW–A COLONIAL ADVENTURER

Lithgow was born in Scotland on 1 January 1784. He was educated to a university standard, as he commenced at the University of Edinburgh in 1802 at the young age of 18, and graduated in 1806. We know nothing about his life between his birth and the age of 22, when he graduated from the University with a degree in Divinity and accepted the role of a licentiate of the Church of Scotland. He practiced as a Churchman–a licentiate has earned a degree in Divinity and is in effect a trainee preacher–between 1806 and 1808. It is possible that although the personal challenge was there the cash rewards were not forthcoming and he sought a better paying career.

The University, situated in Edinburgh since 1583, was renowned as a liberal arts college and a school of divinity between its founding and the early 18th century. At that time schools of medicine and law were well established and later schools of music, science, arts and social sciences were added. It was known as the Town's College from its original royal charter in 1582 until 1858, when it gradually assumed the name of University. The Faculty of Divinity has always been of singular importance to the university. During the 18th century the University boasts a number of great names as students and graduates–Charles Darwin, Sir Walter Scott, James Mill (philosopher), Thomas Carlyle, Robert Louis Stevenson and Alexander Graham Bell.

During the latter part of the 18th century the Scottish economy became weaker relative to that of England. Edinburgh at that time was becoming a head office for entrepreneurs, in particular the establishment of a free port at Darien on the Isthmus of Panama, manned by Scots colonists. At the time of the project's failure, many Scotsmen lost their life savings and the political and economic union in 1707 between England and Scotland was hastened with the guarantee of a return of capital to those who lost their money in this venture. The Scottish Australian Investment Company of 1825 was an investor of significant size in the Colony. It would appear that the Scots were more eager to take a gamble in investing than some of their colleagues south of the border.

The Church of Scotland–the national church in Scotland–was the precursor to the Presbyterian Church during the 16th century reformation. Moderates became influential in the church and separated from the Evangelicals. The church supported a strong missionary organisation and many of the best divinity students from the teaching establishment joined the Free Church. This career path must not have appealed to Lithgow as he moved away from the Church organisation and instead pursued a commercial career. As previously conjectured, a family or personal calamity may have influenced this decision.

In 1808 Lithgow was accepted as a Clerk in the Army Commissary Service and was assigned to his first posting in Heligoland–a British base in northern Germany. Although the dates do not show this, Lithgow must actually received some local training before being sent abroad, but any such training must only have been in terms of months and not years. Edinburgh at this time was a military stronghold, the seat of the Scottish Parliament and a centre of intellectual activity. Helgoland was originally spelt Heligoland, an island in the State of Schleswig-Holstein, in northwestern Germany. It lies in the Deutsche Bucht (German Bay) of the North Sea. The Island has an area of 520 acres, and consists of a level cliff-girded, red sandstone plateau. But historical evidence suggests in 800AD the island had a periphery of about 120 miles. Continuous wave attack on the cliff and a rise in sea level reduced the Island's periphery to about 8 miles by 1649. The area was seized by the British Navy in 1807, and was formally ceded to Britain in 1814 at the Peace of Kiel following the Napoleonic defeat and King Frederick of Denmark's indifferent diplomacy. The area was returned to Germany in 1952. Lithgow, assigned in 1808 to the Commissary station in that new possession, was with the first group of British military officers to occupy the area. This experience of establishing a new accounting system would serve him well upon his transfer to the new Colony of NSW.

After four years as a clerk in Heligoland, Lithgow's second transfer within the British Commissary system was to Mauritius where he was appointed the deputy assistant commissary of accounts. He worked with Ralph Darling, who was the head of military operations in Mauritius. With strong leadership support, Lithgow rose further up the ranks until he was recommended by Darling to the position of Assistant Commissary of Accounts in the Colony of which Darling was to be the Governor, Commander in Chief of the military and head of the Commissary. Lithgow's 11 years in Mauritius between July 1812 and April 1823 gave him extensive experience in organising Commissary accounts and understanding the British system of commissary accounting. His was the experience so very badly needed in the new colony of Botany Bay. He was able to bring change and simplification to the all important accounts system in the Colonial Commissary, commencing upon his arrival in January 1824.

Lithgow's historical etting

So many plans and theories can be observed in outlining an historical setting for Lithgow. Without appearing trite, the scenario should open with the reasons for the settlement in Botany Bay. The First Fleet was despatched to create a strategic location in the south Pacific. The east coast of NSW would also serve as a stopping/resting place for trading ships moving between England and China or India. In theory, ships could take on fresh supplies of food, fresh water, carry out running repairs and provide a respite from the heavy seas and bad weather for the crews and any passengers. Of course, a permanent operation could be established and the opportunity for gathering suitable and appropriate raw materials taken advantage of. The east coast of the great southland was also a strategic place to launch any naval attacks and confront the French and Dutch who were gathering strength in the East Indies. In addition there was potential for creating a settlement and generating trade for English merchants and ship owners. Now, who could be the first settlers and workers in the new land? Having just lost the resources of North America as a depository for mid-term prisoners, it was immediately considered that the new land in the South Pacific could be used as the strategic hub for commerce and new world domination, and be settled by English prisoners. How could they escape? Where would they go? These men and women would become fodder for developing the new land.

However, NSW was to be that little bit different to the norm. Most new English settlements or colonies were begun by trading companies or settlement associations and were expected to be self-sufficient from the start or very soon after. The British Government was usually prepared to provide a civil administration and military protection, but wherever possible these were to be funded from local revenues. In this case, the Colonial Office thought the prisoners, with British military supervisors, would clear the land, build the barracks and store facilities, cultivate the land, grow their own food, and be the basis for providing raw materials (such as cotton) for British Industry. In less than a year, considered James Matra, and with less than £3,000 of expenditure, we (the British Government) will have a huge 'free' prison, without walls and at no further cost to the British taxpayer!

With this in mind Captain Arthur Phillip, the first Governor was instructed to create a new settlement, transport sufficient food, materials and tools for a year, until the second transfer of prisoners could follow, and 'economise rigidly'. He was also instructed to keep statistics on the convict, military and civil establishments. The Commissariat was responsible for providing supplies, rations, tools and accounting for the needs of developing the settlement. It was also responsible for harvesting and gathering the timber for building, making bricks and tiles so that precious stores could be housed safely and away from the risk of fire and theft. Because the only coinage or means of exchange that came with the First Fleet consisted of a few odd coins in the pockets of officers, the Commissary was responsible for the early financial arrangements. Exchange items became a matter of convenience, arising from opportunity and common practice. Circulating in the early colonial economy were government Bills, promissory notes, commissary store receipts, bartering, spirits (the rum trafficking) and infrequent shipments of coins from Britain. The colony had no treasury but it had the best alternatives, although it created instability, corruption and scandal.

The first local revenues were raised in 1800 and like most taxes in most societies, it continued to grow and broaden as an impost on the colonists. Macquarie's arrival in 1810 turned revenue raising into a fine art, but this was more than balanced with a growing free market economy. New buildings, a sense of community pride, a rapidly growing population and economy turned the penal colony, 'barely emerging from infantile imbecility' (wrote Macquarie in a letter to the Secretary of State) into a functioning society. The treasury problems were to be solved by the introduction of a local bank–the Bank of New South Wales. Although it would seem that the Governors from King, through Hunter, Bligh and Macquarie did not have legal authority to raise taxes in the way they were so doing, the Imperial Parliament ratified these actions retrospectively in 1819. Macquarie's successor, Thomas Brisbane, was authorised by an 1823 British Statute to establish a Legislative Council in NSW. Such a body was intended to provide advice to the Governor and guide his political and economic endeavours. Some Governors were determined to be more trusting than others, but it took a further 3 years for the autocratic powers to be whittled away whilst an Executive Council was put in place to both give advice and consent to the governors actions.

R.F. Holder in his two volume history of the Bank of New South Wales claims:

'. . . not the least of the achievements of Macquarie's decade in office from the end of 1809 to 1822 were his monetary reforms, so necessary to release production and trade from the shackles and circumscription of a limited currency and a chaotic expediency in financial transactions. The reforms were not final and their significance could not be assessed at the time, but they marked the beginning of the end of earlier makeshifts and pointed the way to more settled principles of monetary operation'.

Holder also makes the point that the contributions of Governors Phillip and Macquarie were most valuable, whilst the period of King and Hunter barely maintained the status quo and the contribution of Bligh and the pro-tem military administrators were merely self-serving. The post–Macquarie Governors (Brisbane, Darling, Bourke and Gipps) were preoccupied with presiding over a transition from a penal settlement to a free-market capitalist economy, and this step required a conjunction of public service reform, new government departments, people with appropriate skills, and a banking and finance sector appropriate to the needs of an emerging Colony.

Holder identifies the immature operation of the early colonial economy and its dependency on Britain. With this dependency came responsibilities to effectively uphold the rules of British justice and economic laws. Britain expected obedience, conformity and a solid economic return from 'investing' in the colony, and if that meant imposing suitable public servants in high positions, then the governors would just have to accept this imposition.

The Macquarie monetary reforms were in the nature of introducing coinage and currency, trading in Bills and Notes and commencing a quasi-treasury through the medium of a local bank. That the Bank charter was both illegal and opposed by the British Government was not of great concern to Macquarie who decided that the end justified the means and moved ahead with the policy, in any case. The challenge was not to British policy but more so towards seeing whether Britain would unravel what Macquarie had completed. It was Commissioner Bigge who accepted this proposition and persuaded Lord Bathurst to ratify the illegal action. It took some years to complete but Bathurst found rectification when, during the Balcombe affair, he was able to pass full liability for the bank's potential failure to the shareholders and Directors and none to the depositors or 'regulators', the latter in fact being the government itself. The Balcombe scandal will be discussed in full a little later on.

Both Brisbane and Darling tried to follow through with the Macquarie reforms but found the going difficult. Macquarie had built a certain social structure and pride within the colony and, when he returned to England, the admonition and instruction to the next governor and then his successors (Brisbane and Darling) was to trim colonial expenditures, implement the Bigge report and bring the colony into line as a subservient dependent. Thus Macquarie's economic gains and growth was whittled away by lack of creative energy from his successors and other distracters and want of funds.

Macquarie's monetary chaos was reformed in a convenient but illegal way, and was symptomatic of his refusal to bow to the impractical ways of the Home Government, which in so many respects was ignorant of local conditions. Most post-Macquarie governors, especially Brisbane and Darling were aggrieved that Lord Bathurst had picked, as being more suitable that anyone picked by the governor, senior public servants and civil list appointee at pay levels that were not ungenerous, but out of alignment with colonial conditions. Darling was particularly concerned with the intent of Lord Bathurst to demonstrate that wisdom could only come from England in the form of appointees to the civil service in the colony, not all of whom were admirable. In fact, it was a Bathurst appointee that brought about an end to Brisbane's period as governor–Frederick Goulburn took the position, as did Bathurst, that as Colonial Secretary, he should both hold, and exercise the power of monitoring the governor and his relationship to the outside world, especially the colonial subalterns and Bathurst himself. Bathurst used this internal wrangling to recall both Brisbane and Goulburn and transfer Darling from a sleepy situation in Mauritius to a more mainstream posting in the newer colony of NSW. Bathurst had a good opinion of Darling and his broad range of administrative experience, and allowed him to bring to the colony a range of close associates in the form of a new team. It was Darling's recommendation of Lithgow that brought him to the colony, although Lithgow arrived in the previous year to his new Governor.

Macquarie was confronted with the circumstance that:

'. . . no currency had been supplied for the convict settlement; its food and material needs were to be met from the communal store (the government commissary) and replenished from the produce of the colony. Soldiers and the civil servants (those on the civil list) were paid with bills drawn in London. Bills drawn on the Treasury met administrative expenses incurred by the Governor. Foreign coins trickled in through the pockets of convicts, seamen, soldiers and new free settlers, but the more reputable currencies soon left again in payment for occasional cargoes'. (Holder Vol 1 p4)

Holder also reflects on the expanding role of the Commissariat.

'The Commissary Store was originally intended to supply the basic needs of the population and become the market for the grain and livestock produced in the settlement. It paid for local produce by issuing store receipts, which generally circulated as a kind of official note issue but were eventually withdrawn in exchange for bills drawn on the British Treasury; bills drawn on the British Treasury were the only means of paying for imports, apart from the small amount of available coin.' (Holder I: p16).

Store receipts were an important component of monetary arrangements in the colony for at least the first thirty years of existence.

Lithgow's initial role as Commissary for Accounts kept him busy with the overall accounting functions of the large Sydney commissary store plus those 'remote' stores at Parramatta, Liverpool, the Hawkesbury (Windsor), the government agriculture farms (whose accounting work was handled by the central Commissary in Sydney). The Dockyard, the Brickyard, the Female Factory and the Lumber Yard were jointly controlled by the Commissary and the Superintendent of Convicts. Lithgow's skills were used successfully in remodelling the accounting functions within the Commissary and with making the Dockyard, Lumber Yard and Female Factory more efficient. Its isolation meant that shipping, storage and distribution were important to the colony and the Dockyard served these roles. It was also important that production of regularly needed and important items such as tools and clothing should be completed locally. But most importantly these three commissary/convict operations kept over 4,000 convicts in gainful employment.

Conflicts between Governor & Colonial Secretary during the early Lithgow Days

Brisbane faced a difficult and challenging role, in order to follow the policies and successes of Macquarie. Brisbane's despatch to Lord Bathurst dated 1 May 1824 was a direct affront to the Secretary of State whose appointment of Frederick Goulburn, as Colonial Secretary in Sydney, was of such distress to Brisbane. The disagreements between Goulburn and Brisbane and their respective tests of strength in the public arena were distressing to those around them and led both being recalled to Britain in 1825. The root cause of the disputes was that Bathurst, as Secretary of State for the Colonies, felt empowered to hand pick and appoint senior public servants wherever he decided and at whatever pay-rate he saw to be convenient. Most of his selections were personal or pressure group candidates and not necessarily the most appropriate person to fill a vacancy. For instance, his selection of Balcombe as Colonial Treasurer in 1825 was a result of pressure from a House of Commons colleague whose vote the government needed. Balcombe was a ticking time bomb and 'exploded' in 1826. More details of the Bathurst interference are discussed in the Rise of the Public Service section a little later.

By 1823 Brisbane had become enmeshed in a struggle to rearrange the government departments and appoint new permanent heads. The unannounced arrival of Frederick Goulburn brought no solace to Governor Brisbane, whose appointment of a clergyman, Reverend Thomas Riddell, as Director-General of Government Public Schools, was questioned by Goulburn. Goulburn was Bathurst's appointee to the role of Colonial Secretary and Brisbane's action, upon written complaint by Goulburn to Bathurst, was consequently disallowed. The civil service was changing and the steps initiated by Macquarie of not victualling settlers who had the capability to feed and clothe themselves was now extended to public servants located in the main towns (but not those located in remote settlements). Nor were officials any longer allowed the use of government houses, except in special circumstances, and the judge of those circumstances was to be Lord Bathurst and not the governor. The exceptions were to be the Colonial Treasurer and the Colonial Auditor.

Barnard writes (*History of Australia* P330)

'One of Brisbane's difficulties was that now a civil service was taking shape, he had no control over the appointments. A properly regulated service was at last possible because the colony had sufficient revenue to pay for one. Men had been chosen in England for various posts, Oxley as Surveyor-General, Captain Rossi as Chief of Police, James Bowman as Principal Surgeon, Balcombe as Colonial Treasurer and Lithgow as Colonial Auditor".

Such appointments were made without consultation and the results were out of Brisbane's hands. The assumption in London was that there would not be men on the spot with proper qualifications or, if there were, they would be tied to one or the other faction. One result was that some of those selected considered themselves far superior to the inhabitants of the colony (which was still largely penal) and allied themselves to the local 'aristocrats'.

Brisbane's successor, Ralph Darling also encountered trouble with his administration, and in particular, salaries were the source of concern and conflict. The underlying problem, it appeared was that the 'Home' Government did not understand how expensive living was in the colony or the explosive effect it had when a government clerk earned £250 per year but a botanist, who was the curator of the Botanic Gardens, could earn only 7s per day, and as well must pay his own travelling expenses when collecting specimens. Darling's efforts on behalf of Lithgow resulted in an annual salary of only £600 instead of the £850 recommended but much better than the £100 first proposed.

Darling tired of these constant conflicts and established a Board of enquiry to establish multi-tiered pay rates for the civil service, which would recognise parity within the service and with outside employment. Lithgow was included in this special committee.

Lithgow as Colonial Auditor

On 12 April 1827 Governor Darling wrote to Earl Bathurst concerning the separation (of the roles of preparing and auditing accounts) of Colonial Treasurer and Colonial Auditor, but before the letter arrived in London, Bathurst had died and Rt. Hon W. Huskisson responded to the submission. Darling wrote:

'The public business is increasing to such an extent that I have been under the necessity of separating the office of Accompts, which is a military appointment, from that of colonial auditor and placing the two in distinct hands. The fact that no steps had been taken, previous to my arrival, to establish regulations for the conduct of any of the departments, either civil or military, and the trouble in endeavouring to correct the evils, which existed, has been commensurate with the confusion and disorder which prevailed.

It is only justice to Mr Lithgow, the auditor, to confirm that he has been indefatigable, and has afforded me every possible assistance in preparing the general arrangements. But the duties of an auditor in a government like this, where a new system of accounts is to be established by the Lords of the Treasury, is as much as any person, however zealous, can properly discharge. The separation of the civil and military branches will best accomplish the need to handle more government accounting business. Mr Lithgow holds the present appointment at the salary of 442.3.9, and I recommend his salary be adjusted to 800 pound per annum instead of the double salary amounting to 542.3.9. In Mauritius, the auditor ranks next to the colonial secretary.' (HRA I: XIII P250)

Lithgow's next appointment came in May 1827 when he was appointed the Acting Clerk of the Executive Council. Lithgow certified the minutes of the 25 May Executive Council meeting in which were recorded that the plans by Mr Busby, Surveyor-General for a new source of water for Sydney and its distribution, were approved.

As Auditor, Lithgow assisted in drafting the new regulations for 'Controlling the Public Treasure". These regulations followed the recommendation of Bathurst after the Bank of NSW crisis and the Balcombe scandal in 1825. On 4 September 1827, the regulations were released and declared

All officers employed in the collection of revenue in Sydney were to hand over the amount collected by them every Saturday, 'furnishing half monthly statements of their collections to the Treasurer'.

'The Treasurer will cause the door of the money vault of the colonial treasury to be secured by three separate locks and keys. One key is to be kept by the Treasurer (Balcombe), one to be kept by the colonial auditor (Lithgow) and the third by the asst colonial secretary. The door is never to be opened except in the presence of the three key holders. The money in the safe was only to be British coin.

Secretary of State Huskisson responded to Darling's request for separation of duties on 30[h] April 1828, and agreed to the appointment of Lithgow but at a salary of only £650. A replacement commissary officer was being despatched from Mauritius to fill that side of the Lithgow job. Darling was quite miffed at Huskisson's intervention in internal Colonial affairs, but the Secretary's action just followed the long adopted practice that London knew best about what the Colony required and both Lithgow and Darling had to live with the decision.

At the other end of the spectrum, and after 28 years of colonial public service, Lithgow's retirement was as confusing in its timing as was his initial appointment.

Lithgow retires at the peak of excitement in the colony

Lithgow retired from the Legislative Council on 8 June 1852, and this brought to an end an era of substantive public service and contribution to the colony, as well as 28 years of colonial service. Lithgow left no correspondence detailing his reasons but we can make a number of valid assumptions concerning his decision to retire

He was now 68 years of age (past the official retirement age)

His was in growing ill-health

He was still feeling unwanted after Gipps had threatened him with dismissal for allowing the 'Blue Books' to fall behind, and never received credit when he caught up 4 years of Blue Books in under a year

He had accumulated extensive property and would retire on a government pension as well as living off his investments

He was overlooked for the post of colonial-secretary and this was upsetting to him

He was very overworked and growing tired from the constant pressure

He could see that the movement towards self-government and the discovery of gold would further increase his workload

As we get to know Lithgow, we learn of his means and motivations, outlook and troubles. He was a generous man, with his time and his money, and the potential to rest and enjoy his agricultural pursuits must have held great attraction too him.

The changing public service

The Sydney Gazette of 16 November 1827 offers an insight into an aspect of a changing public role, when Governor Darling decided to thwart a financial crisis in the making, by loaning liquidity to the Bank of NSW and appointing a senior government representative (William Lithgow) to the Bank Board to ensure the Bank could meet its obligations to the community. The *Gazette* wrote:

'The Governor has submitted the nomination of Mr Lithgow as Director. This temporary appointment of that gentleman was solely with the view of ensuring the fulfilment of the engagements entered into by the Bank with the Government, and to prevent any loss to the public, in consequence of its monies, which had been deposited in the bank, by the Treasurer and the Naval Officer. As soon as these had been secured, Mr Lithgow will retire from the Board.'

The Governor Darling despatch to Viscount Goderich of 24 September 1827 explained the Lithgow involvement in a slightly less manipulative way to that set down in the newspaper. Darling wrote:

'Such we believe to be the true state of the case, and the country was in such a condition at that era, as to render it necessary that Mr Lithgow should view his attendance at the Bank, in the character of Director, as a very important branch of his public duty; and whilst Mr. Lithgow continues in that post, like every other in which he has had the honour to move, he will attend to the interests of the people as if they were his own. Mr Lithgow, therefore, did not voluntarily enter into the Direction of the Bank–he was, as it were, pressed into office–and it was one of that nature, with which he would gladly have dispensed, could he have conveniently declined with a compliance of His Excellency's wishes.' (Governor's Despatches Vol II 1827 A1200 p.300)

The same newspaper, at the time of the public conflict over the Collector of Customs (Mr Campbell) accepting a Board position as Director of the Bank of NSW reported: 'Due to the over-issue of paper, and the sudden export of Spanish Dollars, the Bank became so unpleasantly situate, as to render it imperative to apply to the government for an adequate loan.' (*Sydney Gazette* 5 January 1827).

The support staff for the governors was initially a part-time role for the more literate convicts. However, as the colony grew and the clerical requirements swelled, the appointment of full-time persons (other than convicts) commenced. The office of Colonial (or Chief) Secretary had effectively begun with the foundation of the colony in 1788. From 1788 to 1820, the secretary to the governor acted as secretary to the colony, and clerical assistance was provided through casual employment–paid or otherwise. The duties of this position gradually increased to those described by Governor King in 1804:

The Secretary has the custody of all official papers and records belonging to the colony; transcribes the public despatches; he is charged with making out all grants, leases and other colonial instruments; also the care of numerous indents or lists sent with convicts of their terms of conviction, and every other official transaction relating to the colony and government; and is a situation of much responsibility and confidence" (Governors Despatches 1804-5: P358)

Macquarie himself only employed casual staff to assist him with his workload but also relied on his wife as a support person.

In 1821 Frederick Goulburn was the first officer to be officially appointed to the position of Colonial Secretary. The offices of Secretary to the governor and colonial secretary were not separated until 1824 when Major Ovens was officially appointed Governor Brisbane's Private Secretary, although he had been acting in this capacity since mid-1823.

The role grew from that point and we find that Lithgow got involved in the changing public service in a number of ways. He was requested by Brisbane and then Darling to review the public service structure for manning and a structured, competitive pay scale

He acted as Colonial secretary on two occasions in the absence of the official in that position. Lithgow set down job descriptions, minimum skill levels for new occupants and a comparable pay scale for each position.

The Governors become involved

Brisbane undertook the first wave of administrative change in the Colony, after Macquarie's departure and the handing down of the Bigge Reports to the House of Commons between 1822 and 1823. The administrative structure had undergone change following strains because of the expansion and growth of the colonial economy and its continuing conversion from a penal to a free colony. Commissioner Bigge had included administrative matters among the subject of his enquiries and recommended many reforms.

Between 1820 and 1825 efforts were made to bring the system into line with British bureaucratic operations, and allow heads of departments' greater scope for initiative. The Secretary of State rather than the governor was increasingly sponsoring and appointing these officials. Personnel fitting this category included Major Frederick Goulburn as Colonial Secretary; William Balcombe who was appointed to the newly created post of Colonial Treasurer in October 1823 and Frederick Hely who was appointed superintendent of convicts in place of William Hutchison in 1823 who, as an emancipist and a Macquarie appointee, had been criticised by Bigge. Others included William Lithgow, who was brought from Mauritius where he had served with Darling, in 1823, and given charge of the commissary accounts and Francis Rossi who also arrived from Mauritius to take charge of the reformed Police Service in 1825. John Piper, the naval Officer, and John Oxley, the Surveyor-general, were also hand-picked by Bathurst.

The Brisbane appointment of his aide, John Ovens, as his private secretary was made permanent by Lord Bathurst when he permitted Darling to bring Henry Dumaresq as his private secretary and appointed Alexander Macleay as Colonial Secretary. Between mid-1827 and 1829, while Dumsaresq was overseas, he was replaced, first by Lithgow and then by Captain Condamine. The Colonial Secretary's Office was reformed during the Darling Administration. Both Colonial Secretary Dumeresq and the Governor reported on the changes:

'Lithgow, assisted by two clerks, one a lad of 14 years old, both sons of a deceased officer of the garrison, placed the private secretary's office on a new basis' (Letters of Henry Dumaresq ML).

'They formed the instrument through which the governor conveyed his instructions to the colonial secretary'. Darling enjoyed a close working relationship with his colonial-secretary and observed to Bathurst "There are few as competent as Mr Macleay, his official experience enabling me to get through business with greater facility than almost any person I have met with.' (Governor's Despatches 1826 p.691)

Chief Justice Forbes notes in his private letters (to Wilmot-Horton in London–ML) 'Macleay and Dumaresq formed a close friendship and in fact inter-married' (Macleay's daughter married Henry Dumaresq's brother), and these two, together with Lithgow and the Commissary-General, formed a close-knit group 'being the real cabinet of the colony'.

Darling notified the colonists on 5 January 1826 that all Heads of departments and Commandants of Stations are to address their applications and reports through the Colonial-Secretary's Office (SRO papers). Brisbane observed, prior to his changes to the Public Service 'Every department appears to act for itself, without check or control, and indeed without apparent responsibility' (Governor's Despatches 1825)

Darling endorsed these changes but went one step further:

'The chief engineer's department must be taken entirely to pieces and be subdivided. It engrosses the whole of the executive and everything done in the Lumber Yard. This department comprises everything–over public works and prisoners–road-making and clearing gangs–the Dockyard and Telegraph' (Governor's despatches 1826)

Lithgow's contribution to this stand by Darling is to be found in his joint report with Ovens, and his second, independent report to Darling, submitted after the sickness and retirement of Ovens, and just prior to Oven's death in 1826. Lithgow endorsed the Lang opinion (J.D. Lang author of *Historical and Statistical Account of NSW*) that 'before Darling's arrival the colonial state machine was frequently out of order, and it was often a matter of difficulty to ascertain which of its wheels should be touched, to set it a-going in a particular direction'. Darling had anticipated the need to reorganise the colonial administration and only a week after his arrival stated 'I shall begin and reorganise the whole of my administration. He appointed a Board (Lithgow sat on and advised this board) to advise on ways to 'rearrange Public Departments, according to the nature and institution of each' (SRO papers) Its report was followed in January 1826 by an Order defining the new functions of each department and its principal officials, specifying how financial transactions were to be conducted and stipulating procedures under which settlers could obtain land grants and convict labour. (Government & General Order 5th January 1826–HRA XII p151).

The Australian newspaper of 12 January 1826 observed:

'Throughout the various regulations which the general order promulgated, there is one principle visible–that the Governor must be looked up to as the controlling power and that the Heads of Departments, however high they may be, must not consider themselves as so many heads of the colony.'.

The board appointed by Darling to consider the Administration reforms was formalised on 7 February 1826 (after its initial report was delivered and because Darling wanted to maintain its expertise) and was named the Board of General Purposes. It was originally composed of the Lt-Governor, the colonial secretary (Macleay) and private secretary (Dumaresq) and Colonial Auditor/Chief Financial Officer (Lithgow). Darling's closest confidants were Macleay, Lithgow and Dumaresq. Subsequent to the Administrative Reorganisation, the committee was appointed to report on 'any particular points, which may require investigation'. At least twenty-seven matters were investigated by the Committee between 1826 and 1831, one of the earliest being the decision to stop employing convicts as public servants. (Governor's Despatches 1833).

Although Lithgow lost some clerical assistants in this latest change, Darling observed in an 1826 despatch to London 'hardly a Clerk in any of the Public Offices, even those of the greatest trust and confidence, was not a convict'. He considered that such a practice could not be justified now that free colonists were available and pointed out that 'the use of convicts was a very serious evil'. 'It degraded the offices, by placing individuals in them who had forfeited every claim to character' (Darling's minute 7 February 1826–SRO). In June 1826, the Board determined a public servants pay scale and annual increases based on ability not seniority became the criteria.

The colonial secretary's office worked six days each week, from nine to six (nine hours), with the Public Boards (those chaired by the Colonial-secretary) meeting at six AM. A further study in 1827 instituted by Darling, determined to equate salaries with those paid by private enterprise and agreed that the minimum level of pay scale should rise by 50 pound per annum. As a means of reducing his office's work load, Darling transferred the correspondence section associated with 'supplying the penal establishment' to the Commissary and responsibility for the Lumber Yard, originally under the Civil Engineer's charge was transferred to the responsibility of the Superintendent of Convicts. Responsibility for assigning convicts was transferred from the Colonial Secretary to the Land Board, and ticket-of-leave applications remained with the Colonial Secretary's office until 1828, when they were again transferred to the Superintendent of Convict's Office. (Source: Government Orders)

Besides reallocating duties to the departments, Darling extended the role of the Post Office and established a separate Customs office. Darling gave the postmaster a salary, instead of leaving him dependent on fees. With this step the post office was converted into a government establishment, which resulted in more regular services and the opening of eleven branch offices. Further reform encouraged the establishment of an office of Chief Officer of the Customs Department and instead of Captain John Piper, who was charged with neglect of duty and misuse of funds, J.T. Campbell was appointed. Campbell changed the fee remuneration for his agents with salaries and removed a source of temptation.

Obviously Lithgow's contribution, as a member of this Board of General Purposes brought him into contact with many aspects of the colonial economy and administration, and he was later to have his role extended to numerous other government review boards.

CHAPTER 5

LITHGOW AT WORK

Having reviewed a little more of Lithgow's work and support role in the colony, it is timely to again review his audit role in uncovering the first major scandal within the government ranks.

The Balcombe Dilemma

The first colonial treasurer, William Balcombe, was appointed on 28 October 1823 (prior to Lithgow's arrival in the Colony), and became the first of the new additions to the civil list to be paid from the growing Colonial Revenues. The role of colonial treasurer was one recommended by Brisbane, and greatly anticipated as a means of improving the mechanism of accounting and reporting within government administration, functions that were increasingly in demand, as Britain needed to know where all the funds were being expended in the colony. Bathurst had ulterior motives for both recommending and approving the appointment. Balcombe had been transferred from government service in St. Helena, having been accused (falsely–as it turned out after an enquiry) by the governor of the island (Sir Hudson Lowe) of being an agent of Napoleon Bonaparte. Under great pressure from Jane Balcombe, a member of the House of Commons and a Balcombe family member, Bathurst decided to reappoint William Balcombe to government service in the capacity of Colonial Treasurer of New South Wales. (Sourced from the State Records Office–Concise Guide to the State Archives: Treasury).

Before the appointment of a colonial treasurer, the Commissariat accountant, the treasurers of the Police Fund, the Land Fund, and the Orphan Fund, administered the colony's finances. From 27 May 1824 all payments were now made through the new Colonial Treasurer's Office. Shortly after Lithgow's arrival and he received instructions to fill the dual role of Commissary Accountant and Auditor, Balcombe's role was expanded: He took over control of finance (acting as the Chief Financial Officer, rather than merely accountant) from Lithgow at the Commissary, and also replaced the Naval Officer, whose role (since 1801) had been harbour-master and collector of customs, but who was paid for half the time on a commission basis and so the appointee (John William Piper) earned more than the governor in many years. Balcombe, at this same time, also took over from the honorary treasurers of the police and orphan funds (that is, from Samuel Marsden and Darcy Wentworth).

Only then could Lithgow be appointed as the full-time Colonial Auditor in 1825 and with the result, it seems, that public finance in the Colony was, at least for a short time, regularised. Darling, who accepted this rearrangement was heartily glad to be relieved of such responsibility and wrote to Lord Bathurst (HRA 1,viii, 123) 'I have never for my own part considered that a discretionary power in the expenditure or disposal of the public money was at all desirable'.

Balcombe, from his centralised position of financial power began to co-mingle private and official funds and before, he was caught, he was using government funds to discount bills from settlers and local merchants and pocket the proceeds and profits. Innocently, and without being officially forewarned of the forthcoming surprise 'audit' he restored the 'borrowed' money to the Bank of NSW on the day before the count took place, and averted both a banking and official government crisis.

It was in his new dual roles of Colonial Auditor and Commissariat accountant that William Lithgow carried out the official count for Brisbane at the Bank of New South Wales main office in Macquarie Place, as a step towards verifying the 'weak' cash position of the Bank as portrayed in a letter from the Directors to the Governor. Lithgow could scarcely have known that he would uncover a fraud, if not a deceit on the Bank, by a senior government official.

Governor Darling, arriving the following year in 1825, brought with him detailed instructions for keeping a full account of revenue and expenditure (as set down by the Lords of the Treasury) and realised the need for a second tier 'watchdog'. The Treasury had also released further instructions for the auditor and treasurer and Darling, knowing Lithgow from their days in Mauritius, appointed him to the new post of Colonial Auditor. The burden of the implementing new regulations fell largely on the auditor, as did the need for financial advice to the Governor. It was not long before Lithgow accepted the role of Auditor-General, being replaced by another commissary officer also from Mauritius. The separation of colonial funds and the military chest accounting and reporting in 1827 closely followed the appointment of Lithgow as the Colonial Auditor in 1826. This was a significant move, as it turned out, because the British Treasury was forced to pay its full and fair share of convict expenses rather than have them subsidised from locally raised revenue.

Balcombe's appointment as Colonial Treasurer in 1823 was induced by Lord Bathurst, no doubt as a means of rewarding the man for his loss of income since he had left Helena following a scandal. Although Balcombe had been officially exonerated over supposedly transporting mail written by Napoleon Bonaparte and his treatment as a traitor, he failed to find another posting within the British Army or The East India Company and sought to recoup his lost back pay by threatening to expose his plight through his cousin who was a member of the House of Commons. Bathurst became aware of the Balcombe plan and thwarted it by appointing him to the Colony of NSW and hurriedly arranging transport for Balcombe and his large family.

Lithgow's appointment in 1824 as the first Colonial Auditor meant he was to hold the dual post in conjunction with his role as Commissary for Accounts. The post of Colonial Treasurer had first been planned in 1823, following Commissioner Bigge's Report to Lord Bathurst on the operations within the Colony, specifically to stop any repeat of Macquarie's apparent rampant overspending. Bigge criticised the system of privatised accounting/recording and reporting of all funds flowing through the colony. These roles had been approved by Macquarie with the appointment of Samuel Marsden, Darcy Wentworth and the Commissary, as the general 'treasurers' of colonial revenue and expenditure. Macquarie had little choice in his actions. There was no treasury in the colony, the Commissary had the sole official access to Treasury Funds, and the local (discretionary) revenue was rapidly growing in volume and in need of some organised recording and reporting. Macquarie, having assumed responsibility for the already active Police and Orphan Funds, merely reorganised the sharing of local taxes between the two funds, ordered a more logical usage of those revenues through the funds and continued on with the existing treasurers, Marsden and Wentworth.

William Balcombe's appointment was not widely welcomed; he was just another 'import' on a high salary. Balcombe was born in England and at the usually young age for recruits into the Royal Navy of just 10 years, joined the senior service. At the still comparatively young age of 28 he transferred to the service of the East India Company and was based at St. Helena, where he dealt with Napoleon during his exile. In 1818, at the age of 39, he returned to England under a cloud, having been accused of secretly transmitting Napoleon's letters from the Island and of negotiating Napoleon's bills.

He was soon forgiven when Bathurst appointed Balcombe in 1823 (aged 44) as Colonial Treasurer of New South Wales. It was considered that his appointment was in settlement of his potential claim against the East India Company for loss of earnings and unjust termination in 1818. The *Australian Encyclopaedia* writes:

'. . . as treasurer his career was for the most part uneventful, although in 1826 he was accused by Governor Darling with having paid public moneys into the Bank of New South Wales at a time when it was unsafe to do so. Bathurst agreed that Balcombe had acted wrongly, but his only admonition was to require future government deposits be shared equally between the two major banks in the colony.' (The Bank of NSW and the Bank of Australia).

It is interesting that Balcombe was not chastised for acting improperly, if not illegally.

This was the first major colonial banking scandal and Lithgow was caught in its web, being required by Darling to be appointed to the Bank Board

(27 January 1826) as a condition of the colony making a cash loan to the Bank in order to underpin their liquidity. The Bank of New South Wales had had a short but chequered history. Brisbane's first Colonial Secretary, John Thomas Campbell, was appointed the bank president in 1817, when it opened in Mary Reiby's house in Macquarie Place, in response to a perceived currency crisis (at Macquarie's instigation)

Lithgow was confronted with a constantly changing scene in the colony. The creation of a Legislative Council in 1823, just prior to his arrival, and then its extension in 1828 (at which time he was first appointed to the Council); freedom of the press; large volumes of free immigration; the emergence of a coherent organised opposition to the local government; the separation of VDL, and under Governor Arthur, the growing concentration of VDL as the primary penal settlement. All of these factors, comments S. J. Butlin in *Foundations of the Australian Monetary System* 'marked the decline of the gaol as the primary purpose of British settlement'. Lithgow was in the centre of most of these changes, both as a policy maker and numbers man for the governors. However, in addition to general policy advice, Lithgow acted for Darling and his successors as 'point' man in a number of specific areas. Discussed now are some of the most significant events of Lithgow's public service in his 28 years in the colony before his retirement in 1852.

The Female Factory at Parramatta

When Darling appointed Lithgow to the Board of the Female Factory he was far from confident in the outcome of the Factory's activities. Darling was suspicious of the Macquarie reasoning behind the expensive construction and 'high wall' attitude of the Factory. He was also concerned about the proximity of the Parramatta military personnel to the Factory and the failure to assimilate the vast majority of women convicts into the community, not only so the government could avoid a heavy financial burden but so that there were more workers available in the colony. Both policies had been frequently repeated government goals.

The Lithgow appointment was not made in ideal circumstances. Brisbane had directed his brother-in-law, confident and friend, Major John Ovens, together with Lithgow, to review convict work organisation and practices, and he would have preferred to receive the Ovens' Report on restructuring the Factory before making any appointments to the Factory Board. However the timing was not right and although Lithgow was the best choice, the Board failed to make the appropriate changes, or rather the changes that Darling considered appropriate. It will be remembered that Lithgow became acquainted with Darling during the time they were both located in Mauritius, and Darling had requested the transfer of Lithgow from that colony to NSW to improve the Commissary accounting programs.

Darling's generally low opinion of the Female Factory can be seen in this extract from the Report into the enquiry into the State of the Female Factory, April 1826 (HRA I; XI P294)

'Despite the new building and improved regulations, conditions (in the Factory) left much to be desired. The inmates were employed in knitting socks and manufacturing slops, sheets and nightcaps for the commissariat. Since the Matron and her principal assistants received a percentage payment it was in their interest to keep the women working as hard as possible. The emphasis was more on profit than on welfare as was made clear in a report by the Grand Jury, which made an inspection in August 1825, and drew attention to the inadequacy of the water supply, the quality of the bread and the shortage of iron bedsteads, clothing and shoes. A coroner found that a woman prisoner had died of hunger and ill-treatment, shortly after Darling had arrived in the colony.'

Darling's hand was forced; the outcome of this episode was the appointment of a new Board of Management that included Lithgow. It was required to submit half-yearly reports and two of these reports are set out below.

Report of the Board of Management of the Female Factory for the half-year ended 31 December 1828

'1st. The number of convict women in the different classes of the Establishment is:

First Class 208

Second Class	107
Third Class	173
Hospital	49
Total	537

Crown prisoners, who together with 36 free persons committed as to House of Correction, make 573 women and 71 children–Total 644 persons showing an increase during the period of 63 crown prisoners, 19 free persons, and 12 children.'

Fletcher (Ralph Darling–A Governor Maligned) reports (P117):

'. . . the classification of the females was now prescribed with a degree of detail that had previously been lacking. Provision was made for three classes. The first comprised prisoners eligible for immediate assignment; the second, probationers who had conducted themselves improperly, either as assignees, or whole residents of the factory; the third was 'strictly penal' and included those who had broken the law after reaching the colony. Each group was subject to different treatment. For the first, the factory was 'considered as an asylum and not as a place of punishment'. Those in this category were allowed to receive visitors once a week, and to dress in a 'superior style', attend the local church, earn money from extra work, and use this money to purchase 'personal comforts'. The second group was not eligible for any concessions unless they behaved for three months. The third class was allowed no communication with the other two classes and received only minimal benefits. These were not removed from that list until they were released, which release was further delayed if they misbehaved.'

'2nd. The number of crown prisoners received into the Establishment and discharged from it during the half year is:

From Ship *Competitor* not being assigned	19
From Ship City of Edinburgh	39
Private Service to First Class	210
To Second Class	5

To Third Class	275
Total Receipts	548
Assigned to Service	381
Returned to Service	38
Returned to Husbands	33
Sentences expired	10
Married	12
Dead	9
Absconded	2
Total Discharged	485
Net increase of Crown prisoners	63'

(Source: HRA I; XI P307)

These two reports, which were constructed by Lithgow under the Darling requirement that the Board report each half-year on its activities tell us that indeed assimilation of these women was slow, and that the suggestion by Board Member Murray (he wanted Darling to allocate so many women assignees with each group of males assignees–this would reduce expenditures and 'produce a great moral improvement of the unfortunate females) *Murray to Darling (*HRA 1: XV p 795) would have been a practical one. Darling rejected the suggestion as being 'temporary relief, but whereby in the long term the women could be returned to the factory in a state of destitution and disease' *Darling to Murray.* Instead Darling wanted the female transportation program suspended for 12 months. A compromise of sorts was reached with the Home Office, whereby more women convicts were sent to VDL. The reports also show that the number of female transportees was still well below the number of male arrivals, indicating that England was keeping more women prisoners in British gaols because they were less trouble, less expensive and able to be put to work more easily.

We do not know a great deal about the Francis Greenway design of the Female Factory at Parramatta, but from the *Greenway Papers* (SLNSW), we find a brief account of the design. As a 'manager' of the factory who oversaw daily operations and a member of both the Management Advisory Committee and the Board of Management, Lithgow's interest was, amongst other things, in the design and practical operations of the Factory as, together with Ovens, he was trying to generally improve convict work practices and productivity.

Darling recorded that the Female Factory was:

'Founded in 1804 by Governor King, it occupied increasingly overcrowded and unsatisfactory premises on the upper floor of the Parramatta Gaol and adjacent buildings. On 9 July 1818 Macquarie laid the foundation stone for a new structure that was not to be completed before February 1821. Designed by Greenway, it was situated on four acres of land.' (Darling to Viscount Goderich–Governor's Despatches 1828)

Greenway also noted that the Female Factory was located:

'At the extremity of a large, unenclosed tract of sterile ground . . . separated by the Parramatta River from the town: and from the pleasure-ground lately attached to the residence of the Governor.'

The main building had a basement and two storeys and was intended to accommodate up to 300 inmates. The factory was designed as a place of confinement for women convicts who were not in private employment. There were various work activities located within the high brick wall surrounding the Factory–wool scouring, wool weaving and numerous other working organisations.

We learn a little about Lithgow's work on the management committee of the Female Factory from reports within the HRA (Historical Records of Australia). A *Report of the Board of Management of the Female Factory* and dated 12 August 1826 was released over Lithgow's signature and it showed some interesting improvements in the Factory operations. The report noted:

'The number of women prisoners admitted rose to 513, whilst those discharged rose to 437 leaving a population of 366 women at 31 December 1828, being an increase of 80 prisoners during the preceding 6 months

A number of women had escaped following a disturbance at the nearby penitentiary but as of the end of the period only three remained at large

'The discipline of the establishment is considered to have been improved and improving and the regulations enforced. Prayers are read each morning and evening'. 300 punishments were administered which the Board did not think to be excessive.

Lithgow's colleagues on the Board included: the colonial secretary; G.T. Palmer the son of the earliest Commissary-General and a large land owner (Commissary-General John Palmer); the Rev'd Samuel Marsden and William Dumaresq.'

The next half-yearly report for the period to 31 December 1828 again showed an increase in women prisoners. The gross gain was only 35 prisoners, but the net gain rose to 63 convict women.

Other Female Factories were in operation in Hobart and Launceston, and continued in existence in Parramatta until the end of transportation in the early 1840s.

Lithgow appointed to Board of Church and School Establishment.

Another crisis for Darling followed immediately on the heals of the Bank crisis. T.H. Scott, representing the recently created Church and School Establishment (the successor to the School and Church Land Corporation) had written to the Governor on 1 May 1826 pleading for a grant of £20,000 to defray the proposed expenses of the Establishment, which included:

An Infant School in Sydney
A School of Industry
Subsidy of the salary costs of educating 1,035 children, being over 1,457 pound per annum
A teachers' college for training future teachers
Expansion of the school system so that more of the 5,042 children under 14, in the colony, can be educated
Improving the operation of the Female Orphan School in Parramatta (Marsden had retired from its supervision)
Appointing additional chaplains

As a means of raising this amount, Archdeacon Scott suggested to Darling that the extensive land holdings be either subjected to grazing revenue (which could pay the interest on the loan requested) or sold to cover the full amount. Darling agreed to this request but added the provisos that the carrying out the indicated work be supervised and Lithgow be appointed to the Committee to ensure the Establishment was operating correctly. The outcome, once again, was in Darling's favour. The Board survived financially; Lithgow was cloaked in success and the Governor had acted wisely, at least in the eyes of the British bureaucrats.

That the *Sydney Gazette* was quite proud of its editorial policy is noted in the biography of Howes, its first owner, publisher, editor and journalist. This policy was that the Gazette would be positive and objective in its analysis and criticism. The *Gazette* dated the 30 May 1831 published on its front page (it was a four page broadsheet newspaper, published each Monday at the cost of 7p each 'number' or 6s 3p per quarter for a subscription–postage included). On this occasion, over the signature of Charles Cowper, a Board member of the Church and School Corporation, an Abstract of the Receipts and Disbursements for the year 1829 (the calendar year was also the fiscal year) was published 'for general information'. The abstract showed receipts of £23,566 for the year derived from colonial revenue of £20,500; pew rents of £416; and sale and lease of lands at £2,401. Expenditure came to £22,895, and the surplus for the year was £700. Expenditure categories included: Management expenses (of the Trust) £2,157, improvement and building of new churches £11,005; parochial schools operations including new school buildings £3,330. The male orphan school cost £1,739 to operate and the female orphan school cost £2,772 while the aboriginal school cost all of £165.

The Abstract for the year 1830 was published the next Monday (6 June 1831) and showed that both revenue and expenses had declined (revenue from the colonial fund was only £17,000; whilst the operating deficit was only £300 mainly because there was no expenditure on the aboriginal school at all. We can learn a little about the operation of the Church Corporation office from these financial records:

1,759 children were being educated by the corporation

The church establishment received far more than the school establishment did
The archdeacon with an annual stipend of £2,500 was, after the governor, the most highly paid civil servant in the colony.
The Church Corporation had assumed responsibility (from the Police Fund) of fencing and maintaining public burial grounds
The female orphan schools (in Sydney and Parramatta) were being operated by the corporation at a cost much, much less than operations during the time of Samuel Marsden and processing more children. The male orphanage held 118 boys and the female orphanage held 145 girls
The only expenditures that increased between 1829 and 1830 was that of the management committee, on which Lithgow sat
The corporation employed a full-time surveyor and assistant even though land grants to the corporation were incomplete and without specific locations.

The *Sydney Gazette* had prepared an editorial for the second publication date (6 June) in which they opined:

'A very general feeling of surprise and we may add of regret, was excited by the publication of the official receipts and disbursements of the colony, when it was announced that £17,000 or 1/7th of the whole government revenue, had been devoted to the trustees of the Church and School Corporation. It had been assumed that their peculiar and extensive privileges and the absolute grant of 1/7th of the territory, had relieved the country forever from frequent and heavy appeals to the colonial revenue, for assistance; it is now the duty of the community at large to enquire into the propriety of the appropriation of a sum that would, in a common year. Amount to the value of 100,000 bushels of grain, or 1/4th of all duties derived on foreign or homemade spirits. The amount of cash drawn in this last year from Colonial revenue by the Church Corporation was 1/5th of the total. We want to show the perfect fallacy of the supposition that the Corporation can manage the affairs of the churches and schools better than the colonial government. The pew rents and collections in the churches were less than £340 (which is less than 1/–per annum for each of the 7,000 persons) whilst the church establishment as a whole cost £10,000. The government pays not only to support the churches but to manage them as well, and the management cost over £2,300 per annum; this is a fact unprecedented in the history of public institutions. We contend that the system is radically bad and can never be efficient.

The education system is costing £1.10.0 per child per annum, whilst the male orphan school is costing £13.10.0 per annum and the female school is operating at £12.10.0 per child per annum. Much has been done for the rising youth by the establishment of elementary schools.'

'A corporation endowed with land and revenue, for the support of teachers and religious instructors is so laudable in the abstract that it meets with general approbation, and if economically conducted may be made highly useful. From the abstracts of 1827-8-9-30, the corporation has expended £87,78 for churches and schools, of which £42,262 was spent on churches and of the remaining £33,232, the sum of £18,086 was spent on the two orphanages leaving but £15,000 as a contribution for public education.' (Sydney Gazette of 13 June 1831)

Lithgow accepts extra-curricular work

As the second most senior public servant in the Colony, Lithgow was naturally appointed to numerous investigating committees and expected to offer fair and unfettered advice to the Governor of the day. As we will see, probably the most intransigent dilemma resulting from this capacity to be involved in so many committees and investigations was that his regular day work fell behind. Lithgow was condemned by the very hand that encouraged him to be involved with this 'other' work, especially when Sir George Gipps threatened him with dismissal, unless the audit was completed on the overdue Blue Books and in future they were kept up to date. These 'controversies' covered a broad range of events and in many ways reflected the major events in the Colonial economy:

Lithgow's involvement with the two Banks in the colony and the apparent disagreement on policy between the Bank's board and the Governor;

His involvement as a Trustee of the Female Factory at Parramatta, at times put him at odds with Government policy towards convicts, their employment and rehabilitation;

Lithgow acted for the Governor and colonial community in first challenging, and then defending (by answering) the charges raised by a House of Commons member, Charles Hume, that the colony was out of control, was too expensive to the public purse and not showing any return to Britain;

Actions of the Land Board, on which he sat, were often under challenge and disputes arose between the Board and its clientele. Lithgow soon found himself in the middle of the dispute between pastoralists and squatters;

Likewise, the Clergy and School board faced regular community challenge, which Lithgow was left to defend. One such regular and major challenge came from the robust Dr. John Dunmore Lang, who was also a member of the Legislative Council.

He was once again in the midst of a furore when he delayed settling the estate of the late Major John Ovens, and got Ovens' family members off side. Ovens, Darling's brother-in-law, was brought to the Colony by Darling as his aide, private secretary and Chief Engineer of the Colony. When he died, Lithgow was asked by Darling to settle his estate. However, Lithgow was busy with affairs of state and allowed the estate to go unsettled for nearly two years. Darling received some of the blame for the effect this had on Ovens' widow and other family members, before he reminded them that it was Lithgow's problem not his.

As a member of the Legislative Council and the secretary of the Executive Council, Lithgow was involved with the dispute over the reimbursement of Police and Gaol services by the British authorities. He wanted to keep both the Governor and his Legislative Council allies as supporters so he left the Governor to vigorously defend the British line, but in reality the argument was strongly in favour of the colonists. However the British decision prevailed, and the Colony claimed it lost nearly £1 million in funding. In other words, the Colony (and therefore the colonists) funded British operations to this extent.

Obviously Lithgow's financial acumen was invaluable to the functioning, discussion and report recommendations of these committees, but they took valuable time from his attentions to the Audit Office. The Coal

Board had to deal with major challenges; the Female Work Factory Board was dealing with constant disputes, whilst the Land Board and the School and Clergy Board were facing mounting complaints from pastoralists, squatters, Legislative Council members and foreign investors. By 1845 Lithgow had caught up and delivered five years of back audit reports on the Colony, and returned himself to favour, at least with Governor Gipps (if not with the British Treasury), by uncovering a 'fraud' being committed by the Colonial Agent-General in London, right under the noses of Treasury officials and no doubt with their knowledge. Lithgow's discovery returned over £5,000 to the Colonial coffers, but not before the British Treasury officials tried to recover that amount for themselves. It was Earl Grey's intervention that Gipps relied upon to see the funds returned to the Colony.

Lithgow contradicted the Governor when he publicly disagreed with Sir George Gipps over the Colonial Treasury making unsecured loans to both the Military Chest and the Commissariat Chest. Lithgow's concerns were valid–the loans were not properly documented, no interest was applied to them and they had no firm repayment date. However the Governor prevailed and we are left wondering whether the loans were ever repaid in full. We must assume that, since there was no further dispute over them, they were eventually repaid.

Lithgow was asked to report by Gipps on the cost effectiveness of the Colonial Government printing arrangements. The Governor wanted to change the status quo but had been directed by London to determine whether owning the two printing presses required to carry out the government printing work was less expensive that sub-contracting through the office of the *Sydney Gazette*. Gipps was 'empire building' by wanting to have a separate Government Printing Office, whilst Lithgow found in favour of the sub-contracting arrangement. This was the last evaluation Gipps asked of Lithgow, and the GPO went ahead regardless.

Each successive Governor had become increasingly involved with the work and activities of the Legislative Council, and, in our analysis of Lithgow during each Governor's era, the interests and knowledge of the Governors is demonstrated. It should not be thought that Lithgow was always in trouble with the Governors or the British Treasury Officials, or that he could be considered inept. His overall contribution clearly overshadowed his few human frailties and he demonstrated the best use of the limited time he had available for all his activities.

- It should be observed that during 28 years of public service and being at the top of the ladder of the public service, dealing in 'treasury' matters for most of that time and even dealing in numerous politically sensitive enquiries (banking, land, schools, Legislative Council) there was never a hint of scandal or ill-feeling. There was not one newspaper article out of the many hundreds printed about Lithgow, or one Governor's despatch that was not complementary and supportive. Lithgow performed well, was well liked and selfless in his approach to people–important or ordinary–he had time for everyone. He brought his Christianity and Church training into the practical arena and brought no ill will to his life. Lithgow was never in trouble with his Governors but they took the chance to speak their mind to this mild-mannered man on more than one occasion.

Lithgow reformed the Commissariat Accounts and the way they were prepared in the Colony. Even though the procedures were laid down and to be followed, his amending procedures were well received by the Commissary-General in Sydney and the Lords of the Commissary in London. He made the Commissariat responsible for all of its revenue and expenditures, in a way totally different to the methods of the first commissary-general, John Palmer. Palmer would be the last Commissary to make great personal gains from his position and influence. Lithgow received no direct benefits from his role as Assistant Commissary for Accounts, and his processing of the records was apparently transparent and verifiable.

Lithgow, along with Major John Ovens, revised the way convict work practices were undertaken and by forming 'work gangs' with performance targets increased output greatly by increasing productivity. From our knowledge of Francis Greenway's building program, Ovens and Lithgow almost doubled the output by the land clearing, road making and Lumber Yard gangs, over that achieved during the Macquarie period less than a decade earlier. Lithgow and Ovens reformed the assignment system for convicts and used the prison labour for a more valuable contribution to government services. Suburbs in Sydney received drainage, water and better quality streets since convict labour was now being put to public use instead of being reserved for wealthy pastoralists and landowners. One reason for this change was that by the end of the 40th year after the first settlement, the colony was completely self-sufficient in food production and in fact was a net exporter of foodstuffs, grains and processed goods to Britain. The convict labour could now support itself from the remaining government farms and the growing number of government operated factories.

Upon Lithgow's appointment as Auditor-General, his first task had been to implement the British Treasury's financial system of 1826. This was a major change from earlier recording and reporting systems and confirmed the Governor's role as chief finance officer in the colony, responsible for allocating revenues to prioritised needs. The Macquarie era of privatised treasury functions was over and, even though locally raised revenue had grown faster and more reliably than anyone ever contemplated, the colony was still commercially backward in 1832 when a local currency and a local treasury were introduced. Also in 1832 the first Appropriation Bill was introduced into the Legislative Council, which had been expanded and reformed in 1824.

Lithgow introduced major changes in the way funds were collected and paid. He streamlined the mechanism of approvals for expenditures and lowered the cost of collecting revenues, which under previous governors was quite high. For instance, since Governor King's time, the appointed 'Naval Officer' for the colony collected import duties, harbour fees, wharfage and water charges on a commission basis. Lithgow changed this role to a salaried position and immediately reduced the administration costs by over £3,000 per annum.

Lithgow's main triumphs were reserved for his committee work:

The Female Work Factory in Parramatta, of which he was a trustee along with Samuel Marsden, John Macarthur jr and John Oxley

The Reorganisation of the Colonial Public Service and the Government Departments

Establishing parity on the Public Service pay scales and introducing the equivalent of meritocracy
Dealing with corruption (in the Public Service and in the workplace
The Colonial Land Board
The School and Clergy Corporation Board
The Coal Board
The Board of Directors for the Bank of New South Wales
The Trustees of the Savings Bank of New South Wales
The Board of the Bank of Australia
A magistrate and a Justice of the Peace (J.P.)
A member of the Executive Council
A member of the Legislative Council
Lithgow served on numerous Select Committees in the Council and prepared many reports for the consideration of Council members including those on the contentious issues of transportation and immigration.

The majority of these contributions by Lithgow will be outlined and discussed.

F. Lithgow and Convict Work Practices

On 2 October 1824, Brisbane conveyed to Bathurst his pleasure at the establishment of 'an Accompant department in this Colony', but then requested Bathurst to allow him to appoint Lithgow as 'Auditor of the whole Colonial Revenue' in lieu of just the Commissary operations. It can be assumed that Brisbane with this reference (made in an 1824 despatch to Bathurst) to 'Accompant' was implying that Lithgow would be his confident and trustee in his mission to regularise not only the Commissary accounting, but also the Colonial accounting. Brisbane was aware of the reputation of Balcombe, who had only just arrived in the Colony, but news of his circumstances and standing had arrived before him. In an attempt to dismiss his concerns about Balcombe, Brisbane wrote (to Bathurst–Governor's Despatches 1824) 'I am happy to bear testimony to the value I attach to Mr Lithgow's services since his arrival in the colony, and would like to offer him an extra £100 out of the colonial revenue annually for carrying out these extra duties.'

Early the following year (8 February 1825) Brisbane proposed a Board of Inquiry into the Rations of Convicts. The Board would include a Brisbane aide and confidante, Major John Ovens, and Lithgow. Brisbane was hoping that the outcome of the Board of Inquiry would result in significant savings in expenditure on convicts and in particular their food costs. This however was not to be, as the Lithgow-Ovens report recommended more convict grown food supplies, and there was an additional cost to the Treasury to implement these recommendations. Differential rations were eventually introduced but were the subject of much complaint and criticism and eventually abandoned.

Brisbane set down the terms of reference for the Board

The Commissary officers are to be responsible for issuing rations only in terms of government instructions

The overseers will ensure a daily muster of all convicts

Details of the mode of commissary accounting for rations to 'detached' and clearing parties, and prisoners in gaols and other work gangs

Convicts are to be classified into 7 categories for counting and rations. These included

Grose Farm
Longbottom Farm
Emu Plains Farm
Rooty Hill Farm
Female Factory
Lumber Yard and its subsidiaries (Male Factory)
Hobart Town operations

In setting such precise terms of reference it would seem that Brisbane was directing, if not anticipating, the recommendation of the Board. In fact Ovens and Lithgow concluded that differential rations were not practical, nor were they a means of being used to reduce expenditure and suggested an expansion of government farms and livestock facilities. The expected savings would come from having surplus production available for commercial sale through the commissary. These expectations could not be put into practical effect because of the growing numbers of convicts arriving in the colony, and the inefficient accounting and reporting practices that should have recognised this 'convict production' but which practice was disallowed by the Treasury. Obviously, suggested Lithgow, the value of goods produced by convicts should be measured and recorded in the accounts of the colony. At this time, convicts were extracting all the coal required for heating military and convict barracks, as well as government offices and other facilities, and in the process of using this coal was saving the British Treasury a great deal of expenses but its value was not recognised.

The first Ovens–Lithgow Report on Convict Work practices was released to Brisbane on 25th June 1825, and recommended the maintenance of the convicts by their own labour. The Report stated

'It will appear that the productive labour of the Prisoners, employed on the part of the Government, is not only sufficient to support the capital advanced for their lodging, Food, Religious Instruction and Medical Attendance, but likewise to afford an overplus (surplus) to the Crown. I have reason to believe that the labour, services and talents of the convicts are fully adequate to accomplish this desirable end in supporting their own maintenance and producing excess in favour of the government. To ensure this, however, an unremitting vigilance is absolutely indispensable to remove temptations as much as possible from the overseers and their men to do wrong, and to thwart the numerous means they may employ to evade their work. The propriety of this strict surveillance is not only obvious from ensuring the benefit of their services, but in producing a moral effect on their ideas and habits.'

Other recommendations included:

Replacing additional rations for overseers and supervisors with money payments, provided the target work was achieved

Substitute money payments in lieu of rations from the public stores in remote locations

Rescheduling the daily ration quantities to differentiate working convicts; gaol prisoners; female convicts and children

Substitution of articles in rations depending on availability of grain, meats, sugar etc
Diminished rations for unoccupied prisoners
Exemptions from established scale for certain classes eg lunatic asylum patients, hospital patients, colonial sailers
Rations for assigned servants

From the report, we are left wondering just where the overseers and supervisors would expend their money. Obviously some of them would bring their food and provisions for country work from home and this ex gratia payment would cover those costs (and probably to the overseers' advantage) but in the remote areas money was next to useless if there was nowhere to buy goods'.

Perhaps because of the extra workload imposed on Lithgow by Brisbane and the fact that it was without remuneration, Brisbane wrote to Earl Bathurst on 28 July 1828 again commending Lithgow's services. 'I express my high sense of zeal and talents of the commissary of accounts, Mr Lithgow, on this as on every other occasion for the furtherance of the public service.' Some 18 months later, Darling wrote to Earl Bathurst in similar language, advising Bathurst 'as to Zeal, I can assure you from long experience that no one has stronger claim to, nor is better qualified to serve in the post of Colonial Auditor'. One can only assume that Lithgow demonstrated great enthusiasm and commitment.

The first Inquiry on work practices was the precursor to the second Inquiry into how productivity from the convicts could be further improved. McLeay and Lithgow reported to Darling in November 1826 on the proposed expenditure 'devoted to the maintenance of convicts'.

Dispute relating to responsibility for convict expenditures

The main purpose of this Report was to itemise the areas of expenditure, which were to be a charge against the British Treasury and those expenditures, which were to be met from local colonial revenues. This running dispute (between the Colonial Treasury and the British Treasury) would last right up to the time of self-government in 1856. During the intervening period, the Legislative Council would spend many hours complaining about the Colony being charged for all police and gaol services which would grow and amount to over £800,000 over the years. In 1826, Lithgow confined his opinions to more mundane matters:

'We are of the opinion that, in addition to the expenses of colonial vessels and food and clothing for the convicts, which have previously paid by the commissary by Bills drawn on the British Treasury, the salaries of officers and other persons, employed in the convict establishments should be defrayed by the Home Government and disbursed by the Commissariat Department: eg.

The office of the Superintendent of Convicts
Prisoners Barracks at Sydney, Parramatta, Newcastle and Liverpool
Female Factory at Parramatta
Penal settlements in numerous locations
Agricultural Establishments at Grose Farm, Long Bottom, Rooty Hill, Emu Plains, Bathurst and Wellington Valley
Convict Hospitals
Civil Establishments (as to 2/3rds of the total expense) such as Police and Gaols
Justice establishment'

The continuing dispute between Britain and the colonists concerning which entity was responsible for paying for the care and maintenance of the convicts was apparently based on a misunderstanding between the two groups. W.C. Wentworth, who was leading the opposition to the Colony bearing the policing and gaoling expenses of convicts, claimed that the British Government had committed to meeting these costs, whilst allowing the Colony to collect local revenues, and expend these local taxes on improvements to the colony that the British Government did not think essential. Instead, having paid for the shipping and provisioning of the convicts from Britain to the Colony, the British Treasury claimed that it was the Colony's responsibility to supervise them (provide the policing services and gaol facilities) whilst they were under sentence. Their argument also included the fact that Governor Hunter had accepted this practice by having the settlers contribute in kind and with labour to the building of a new gaol when the original one was burnt down as an apparent act of vandalism in 1802. It was when that private effort failed to complete the gaol that Hunter imposed local taxes. This argument neglected to reveal that the settlers requested a gaol of the Governor in order to protect themselves from bad behaviour by the convicts against the few free settlers in Sydney Town. The settlers offered to pay for the gaol as an act of self-preservation, since it was unlikely that the Treasury would have funded a new gaol in the circumstances. From this juncture, Wentworth claims that the failure by the British Treasury to support this policing requirement had cost the colony treasury over £700,000. Wentworth never produced the numbers to support this claim, but as both a Legislative Councillor and an Executive Councillor, he exercised his antipathy to this situation, by voting against the estimates and the appropriation bills every year. This supposed miscarriage was still smouldering in 1856 when the Colony achieved self-government and Wentworth negotiated the remittance of crown lands revenue in exchange for the Colony meeting all civil list salaries.

Lithgow, as part of the report, valued the 'probable annual expenses of these establishments at £215,500, made up of salaries from each of the establishments contributing to the convict operations, eg housing, food, clothing, work, and transportation. This worked out at approx 3 pence per day per head for upkeep This sum also included the area in dispute between the British Treasury and the colony, which portion was approximately £72,000 per annum.

Lithgow wrote a supplementary report to Darling dated 29 February 1827 recommending further changes in the sharing of expenses and using production by convicts to offset their support costs:

The Lumber Yard section which was making shoes and clothing should be selling (as opposed to having it recorded in the Blue Books at no value) their output to the Commissary;

Conveyance of coals from Newcastle should be a Commissary expense instead of Colonial revenue offset. Lithgow's concern here was that the production of coal was undertaken by convict labour; the cost of transporting the coal to Sydney was paid for by the Colonial government, and the Commissary received all the revenue; he was proposing that the Commissary pay for the transportation costs. Production of coal was by convicts but the Commissary sold the coal to local settlers or exported it overseas;

Conveyance of tools and stores to new settlements, eg Western Australia and Melville Island, should be at the expense of the British Treasury rather at the expense of colonial revenues;

Cost of transporting fuel to convict establishments, hospitals and gaols outside Sydney should be met by the commissariat department and not colonial revenue.

The effect of these Lithgow recommendations would be a significant increase in the cost burden of the British Treasury, but one which would have been fair and reasonable. By the British Treasury accepting responsibility for these costs, the Colonial revenue would have been much higher and the result would have been to improve the Colony at a much faster rate than was possible under the limited revenues available to the governors. The reason Governor King had commenced raising local revenues in 1802 was so that the governor would have some discretionary funds to use in improving the lives of the settlers. King, Hunter and Bligh were all very restricted in using any discretionary spending but Macquarie expanded the revenue base, using locally raised funds to improve the Colony visually as well as commercially. The people's markets were relocated from the Circular Quay to the site of the present Queen Victoria Building and this served to promote private sales of grain, vegetables, meat, poultry and hand-made clothes.

In response to a request by the Secretary of State to limit the cost of local buildings to £200 before specific authorisation was to be made to London, on 12 March 1827 Lithgow advised the Governor that the weakness in that plan was that the 'great proportion of value added in any new building was carried out without recorded cost, eg the making of bricks and tiles, the supplying of timber, the use of convict labour'. Lithgow recommended just going along with the request and not valuing any of these items, even though he knew they each had a true value. In a separate letter to the Colonial Secretary of the same date, Lithgow suggested that if a 'value' was to be assigned to convict labour it be done at the rate of 1s 3d per day for each man. 'This charge for labour, however, ought only to apply to establishments not considered penal', i.e. work gangs etc. This was Lithgow's estimate of the production value of a convict compared to a free settler. Free settler labour, if it could be found, was being charged out between 5/–and 6/–per day, depending on the task being undertaken. Lithgow's figure placed the productivity level of a convict at about 30% of a free worker, which is the accepted by Timothy Coghlan some 70 years later in his four volume work *Labour and Industry in Australia.*

Lithgow analyses the general Commissary operations

Lithgow, in conjunction with Major Ovens, undertook an interesting analysis of the operations of the Lumber Yard, Dockyard, Government Farms and Female Factory. The findings make for an understanding of Commissary-sponsored work practices in the Colony during the its transition from penal settlement to a free enterprise economy. Since the Commissary had been Lithgow's specialty work area for almost 20 years of his working life, his interest in Commissary-operations and their improvement was genuine and his opinions persuasive. His conundrum was how far should he should push for change and improvement with British financial support (always with strings attached) as opposed to change supported by local self-sufficiency.

The Commissary controlled the operations of the Government Farms, the Female Factory, the Dockyard, the Timber Yard and the Lumber Yard. We learn from the Ovens-Lithgow Reports on convict work practices where these various facilities were located, and the number of men and women convicts they employed.

To increase our understanding of Lithgow's recommendations and work experience, there is some further information about the Lumber Yard that we need to know. By his work association, he had been involved with commissary operations for the first 20 years of his working life, first in Heligoland, then in Mauritius and finally in the Colony of NSW. To his enquiry into convict work practices and commissary operations, he would have brought a full understanding of the needs of the settlers and the colony generally and the need for supporting convicts in the colony and receiving the optimum possible work output from them. His contribution would have included a detailed working knowledge of all aspects of the commissary operations, their location, and potential to be improved. With respect to the Sydney operations, the largest workplace was the Lumber Yard and Lithgow would have enquired into numerous questions, including:

Its size and building configuration
How its harvesting operations (through the Timber Yard) were carried out
The locations of its main forests located and where and how harvesting and movement of logs took place
Where and how the Lumber Yard cured the timber
How the timber was transported from the forests to the Yard
The type of timber they produced and the most common dimensions
How much finished timber was kept in the Yard
Who used the timber and how much did it cost to buy
The security and fire prevention methods in use
Where the nails and screws and specialty fasteners came from
The most common method of joining the timbers

Before the importance of foundry work was recognised, timber cutting, drying and trimming was the largest part of the early Lumber Yard, and Lithgow's activities would have involved understanding the nature of colonial timbers and their potential, both for local use and as an export commodity. So it is that, in understanding Lithgow, we need to understand his working knowledge of the largest government commercial operation in Sydney Town and the type of work it undertook.

There are only a few sources that can assist in answering these questions.

Susanna de Vries-Evans in *Historic Sydney*
Joseph Fowles in *Sydney in 1848*
Peter Bridges in Foundations of Identity
David Collins in An Account of the English Colony in New South Wales
Geoffrey Scott in Sydney's Highways of History
The Ovens-Lithgow Report to Governor Darling

Before researching the original sources such as Historic Records of NSW and Historic Records of Australia, we should see what we could learn from the above named secondary sources.

Historic Sydney tells us that the Lumber Yard was located on the corner of George Street and Bridge Street. Bridge Street earned its name from having the first wooden bridge constructed over the Tank Stream and:

'The bridge was a rough affair of large logs, hastily rolled into place by convicts in 1788, but it soon collapsed and left the developing town once more divided into two by the stream. In June 1803, the Sydney Gazette reported that stonemasons and labourers were working on the foundations of a new bridge which would, upon completion, greatly add to the appearance of Sydney.'

Governor King had made it compulsory for all residents of the town to work on construction, either by supplying goods or labour. De Vries continues:

'These lumber or storage yards were a standard feature of British colonial penal settlements. They were in fact convict work camps and the Bridge Street Lumber Yard contained workshops for blacksmiths, carpenters, wheelwrights, tailors and shoemakers. There was also a tannery where the convicts made their own leather hats and shoes. Nails, bolts, bellows, barrels and simple items of furniture for the officer's quarters and the barracks were also made in the Lumber Yard. Convicts wore identification on their uniforms–P.B. for Prisoner's or Hyde Park Barracks or C.B. for Carter's Barracks. They worked from sunrise to sunset. If they failed to fulfil their allotted tasks they were flogged at the pillory, conveniently situated nearby, also on Bridge Street.'

Sydney's Highways of History reminds us that Captain Dumaresq was the superintendent of the Lumber Yard and that Bridge Street was possibly the second oldest street, and for some years, the most important, street in the country. It connected High Street (George Street) and Government House and the residences of the senior administration officers (the Commissary, Judge-Advocate, Chaplain and Surveyor-General). Between Bridge Street and the Tank Stream, Simeon Lord and other merchants built their homes and warehouses. Across the stream to the west was the Lumber Yard, the great Government storehouse and factory where the convict mechanics laboured. The Lumber Yard adjoined the lease of Garnham Blaxcell, one of the builders of the Rum Hospital, and was opposite the elaborate garden of Lieutenant Kent, whose big brick house was purchased by Governor King in 1800 for an orphanage. The Lumber Yard continued in use as a convict workshop until 1834, when it was cut up and sold for up to £25 front foot (for the best lots).

Foundations of Identity reveals that:

'. . . contracting for government work was a common path to independence for building craftsmen. Convicts or emancipists employed as supervisors of the government building gangs seldom wished to remain in service longer than they had to and there was always a shortage of reliable men to take their place. Macquarie, in his efforts to retain his supervisors in government employment, permitted them to combine their official duties with the business of private contracting. The supervisor would undertake the management of a building project to which the government contributed labour and materials from the Lumber Yard. The Superintendent of the Yard at that time, Major Druitt was unable to suppress the open practices of government men and tools being 'borrowed' and government materials from the Yard being diverted elsewhere.'

Already by 1791 the Government (Lumber) Yard had been established on the western side of the Stream to collect and prepare timber for building and was the recognised meeting place where the gangs picked up their tools and materials and were assigned to work. Here building materials were collected, prepared for use and distributed to the various work sites, tools were issued and gangs allocated and checked. It became the core of the government labour system after the devastating Hawkesbury floods in the winter of 1809. Lt-Gov Patterson had the Sydney working parties gather there for victualling before going to the relief of the settlers. Under Macquarie's expanding work program the Lumber Yard became the centre of the largest single industrial enterprise in the colony. Captain Gill, as Inspector of Public Works, exercised the general direction of the working gangs and controlled the issue of tools and materials, while William

Hutchinson, the Superintendent of Convicts distributed convicts to the work gangs.

With so much activity the Lumber Yard was an easy target for thieves and, by September 1811, the loss of tools, timber, bricks, lime, coal, shingles and nails from the government stocks had become so great that a General Order was issued directing that offenders, including conniving supervisors, would be punished as felons. The same order directed that all tools had to be handed in and counted at the end of each day and banned men from borrowing tools or doing private jobs in the yard after normal working hours. (*Sydney Gazette* Sept 1811).

Gill's successor, Major Druitt, expanded the Lumber Yard to cope with Macquarie's work program. He took over the adjoining land in Bridge Street now abandoned by the debt-ridden merchant Garnham Blaxcell, who had fled the colony; and built new covered saw pits, furnaces for an iron and brass foundry and workshops for blacksmiths, nailers, painters and glaziers, and harness makers. He raised the walls surrounding the Lumber Yard and built a solid gate to discourage truancy and pilfering; he built moveable rain-sheds for jobs around the town and provided two drags drawn by draft animals to replace the 90 to 100 men previously employed on the laborious task of rolling logs from the dock to the Lumber Yard. (HRA I/9 832; ADB I-324-5)

Men were selected off the convict transports based on their skills and background. They were told to find lodgings in the Rocks area. As described by Bridges in *Foundations of Identity*, each morning a bell:

'. . . would call them to the Lumber Yard where they were set to work according to their trades or capabilities. Some went to the workshops, others to building sites or the Brickfields where they dug and puddled clay and pressed it into moulds for firing in the kilns. Unskilled labourers were allocated according to their physical condition; the fittest went to the gangs felling trees and cutting logs to length, others to barrowing heavy stones or dragging the brick carts to the building sites, with assignments often used as punishment for the recalcitrant. The unfit were not spared; weak and ailing men went to gangs tidying up the streets or weeding government land, a man without an arm could tend to the stock and a legless man could be useful as a watchman. The days work started at 5 am, and there was a one hour break for breakfast at 9 am and again at 1 PM for lunch, and at 3 pm the men were free to go and earn the cost of their lodgings. When in 1819, Macquarie tightened the convict system, he housed them all in Hyde Park Barracks, and the working day was extended to sunset, and only married or trusted convicts were allowed to live in the town). The men from the Barracks were marched down to the Yards but 'control was lax and as they went through the streets, some would slip away to follow their own devices. As a result of Macquarie's building activities, and partly as a means of employing more and more convicts, the range of activities expanded in the Lumber Yard.

Every kind of tradesman was gathered: carpenters, joiners, cabinet makers, wood turners, sawyers, wheelwrights, cart-makers, barrow-makers, blacksmiths, whitesmiths, shoeing smiths, agricultural implement makers, tool makers, nailers, bell founders, iron and brass founders, brass finishers, turners and platers, brass wire drawers, tool sharpeners, steelers, tinmen, painters, glaziers, farriers, horse-shoers, saddle and harness makers, bellow makers, pump borers, tailors, coopers and many more. The organisation was simple: the big work-sheds faced the central log yard where logs and sawn timbers from Pennant Hills and Newcastle were stacked. The Lumber Yard was the source of many of the colonial-made goods and the centre of the Government's engineering and building activities. It was the first step in the creation of the Public Works Department. Although the Lumber Yard serviced most of Macquarie's building needs, he badly required the services of a skilled architect and he found those skills in a convict, Francis Greenway. Greenway had a solid background of practical experience as well as theoretical training and he became influential in translating Macquarie's aims and ideas into reality.

Bridges records that 'Nathaniel Lucas was one of Sydney's earliest building contractors; Lucas was one of the few skilled craftsmen to come with the first fleet. Colonel Johnston appointed Lucas superintendent of carpenters at the Lumber Yard but in 1814, he returned to private contracting'. It was this confused state that confronted Ovens and Lithgow in their endeavours to evaluate and reform the convict work organising.

Major Ovens and Lithgow Reorganises the Clearing Gangs

On 27 January 1824, Sir Thomas Brisbane forwarded a from memorial from timber merchants in the Colony to Earl Bathurst quoting that in the previous year 1823-24 a large quantity of timber (15,994 tons) was imported from Britain and only 7,235 tons was exported from the colony back to Britain, but those exports were attracting a duty on entry into Britain. The local timber merchants (in Sydney) wanted the duty removed under the Act 3 Geo II, C 96 that allowed duty free timber into England, especially on cedar. Lithgow supported this claim and,\ in a memorandum urged Brisbane to recommend a waiver of duty on all timbers from the Colony.

Major Ovens had arrived in the Colony with Brisbane and was set the task of organising convict work gangs leading to more control and better productivity in conjunction with Lithgow who had performing this task since his arrival in the Colony. Ovens is relevant to an understanding of Lithgow as they both sat on a number of committees, including the Female Factory and the Convict Work Practices Committees, which were responsible for evaluating and analysing, before reporting to Brisbane and then Darling with a series of recommendations for improvement in practices. They reported to Brisbane late in 1824 recommending that 'clearing' gangs (land clearing before grant and or settlement) be split into two divisions, each under a Superintendent, who in turn would be responsible to the Chief Inspector and Chief Engineer. The 'Southward' would be headquartered in Liverpool, whilst the Northward gang would headquarter in Rooty Hill.

Ovens reported that the food rations, (including clothing, sugar, tea and tobacco) made available to the 1,150 convicts working on the gangs amounted to approx £21,000 per annum (HRA) whilst the value of the wheat being able to be grown on the 9,000 acres cleared would be 7 bu / acre x 9,000acres x 8/6 /bu = £27,000. With these numbers, Ovens was justifying the value of the clearing work, not as an addition to the selling price of the land per acre, but based on the yield of grain recovered which was so badly needed by the Commissary. Ovens recommended that 23 men be included in each gang under one supervisor, with 50 gangs in total (50 x 23 = 1,150 convicts). The amount of clearing by each gang was to be 15 acres monthly or 180 acres per annum, or 9,000 acres in total each year (50 x 180 = 9,000). The incentive payment to each supervisor was 3/6 per acre, and to each convict was ½ lb tea, 6lb of sugar, 10 2/3 oz of tobacco. Land clearing and timber harvesting were not the same operations as few semi-open areas that required clearing contained standing timbers worthy of logging and hauling back to the Timber Yard. The best standing timber for harvesting was being found in the Pennant Hills and Castle Hills areas with the capability of floating the cut logs down the adjacent River (past Hunters Hill) to the Dockyard in Sydney, thus saving a great deal of handling and convict labour. Ovens noted that only certain of the timber being cleared was suitable for milling and he would arrange for transportation of these logs to the Lumber Yard. The most cost effective timber harvesting was completed in the land set aside with suitable and quality standing timbers.

Timber was so important to the new colony, especially for its construction (housing and barracks) program, that special attention was given to the various timber varieties and applications. This preoccupation with timber goes back to a justification for the original investment in the colony itself.

One original purpose of the Colony was to find strategic timber reserves

It is worth noting that the final paragraphs of the *Heads of a Plan*, prepared by James Matra included three non-convict motives for the colony of New South Wales

The obtaining of a supply of flax to make canvass, cables and cordage for British ships in Indian waters

The obtaining of standing timber for the supply of masts and spars for Royal Navy ships

The cultivation of 'Asiatic productions'

Of these three, the sourcing of masts and spars was by far the most important, as there was a crisis in Britain's supply of these naval materials. At this time, British ships were exclusively composed of timber, flax and hemp; their frames and hulls were of English or continental oak, their masts and spars were mostly made from Baltic and British flax and hemp. As Blayney writes in *The Tyranny of Distance*, 'to a maritime nation such as Britain, timber, flax and hemp were then as important as steel and oil became in the 20th century.' The argument here is that, if their need was so great to Britain and without any knowledge that the Pacific area could supply these naval materials, why had no experts been included in the First Fleet to investigate what was available. The recommendation to establish Norfolk Island as a timber source was an afterthought, to be pursued only after Botany Bay was settled

Frost conjectures in *Botany Bay Mirages:*

'conventional wisdom is that it was only during the last decades of the 18th century that there was a crisis in Royal Naval timber supplies. However, Britain's naval failures after 1763 are directly attributable to a lack of suitable materials'. Another view submitted was that 'there was no real shortage of large masts in the period 1775-83, but it was the lack of skilled artificers that the Royal Navy then lacked' (R.J.B. Knight Forests & Sea Power) He goes on to record that "When the North American supply was cut off in 1775, the Baltic filled the gap effortlessly'.

Why then the inclusion of sourcing masts and spars as a role for the Botany Bay settlement? Frost claims it is a matter of perception. In the '1770s influential people thought there was a problem. For instance, Sir John Jervis in explaining the peace settlement by the Shelburne Administration, refers to the want of sticks of a proper size for masts, and the shameful neglect in working them up, particularly the cordage, which is the worst in Europe.' He concludes:

'Given the centrality of timber and fibre to Britain's national life in the late 18th century, it was inevitable that people then should think of exploiting the perceived resources of the Pacific area. When in August 1783 James Matra justified his colonial proposal on the grounds it would give rise to sources of timber and flax, he was only reiterating an idea that had been in the air for fifteen years.'

Suitable timber supplies and other naval materials were obviously of great importance to Britain. In a document dated December 1807 written following his retirement and return to England, and addressed to the Board of Commissioners in London, ex-Governor King outlined the nature of some native Australian timbers:

'The iron & stringy barks are straight and from 40 to 80 feet high, and 18 to 20 inches in diameter, generally sound throughout, without much crooked or compass timber. It is heavy, but the latter not more so than oak. Both are well adapted to the different purposes of keels, beams, uprights and floor timbers of large scantling, and many other purposes where straight and durable timber is required. Of the stringybarks several ships have had lower masts. The Buffalo now has a fore and mizzenmast and boltsprit of that wood, and two cheeks of the mainmast, all of which she had in 1799, and have had them ever since. Their excellence, as well as that of studding sails and other booms, was sufficiently tried in the blowing weather and high seas she experienced in two voyages round Cape Horn. Fifty-gun ships' foremasts and mizenmasts might be selected, and it may be presumed that spindles for larger ships' masts maybe made from those trees, which abound in all parts.

The box is a very fine timber and grows in great abundance about Parramatta from 60 to 100 feet high, and from 18 to 26 inches in diameter, tapering but little. The crooked wood, being the branches are of small size; but this timber answers every purpose of the foregoing species, except that growing so very straight it might not answer so well for floor timbers; but for every kind of straight work, gun-carriages etc is equal to any wood in the world. Much of it has been used at Portsmouth Yard for tillers of all rates.

The blue and black-butted blue gums are esteemed good woods and ideal in vessels.' (HRNSW 6: P397)

Gov. Hunter built a 150-ton vessel frame to demonstrate the variety of timbers and 'after 7 years it was still perfectly sound'. In June 1803, Gov. King issued a Government Order relating to the general consumption of timber in the Colony

'The great consumption of timber, and the requisition made by the Government for as much as possible being preserved for the use of the Navy, the following regulations are to be observed.

Timber in this colony includes she and swamp oaks, red, blue and black-butted gums, stringy and iron barks, mahogany, box, honeysuckle, cedar, lightwood, turpentine etc, the property of all which lies in the proprietor of the land, either by grant or lease, excepting timber for naval or other public purposes, which may be marked, cut and removed from any situation, public or private. None may cut timber suitable for ship-building, buildings, masts or mechanical purposes, without being answerable to the Governor.'

A further letter from King to Earl Camden of 20 July 1805 intended to reserve all timbers or the use of the Crown.

In 1793, Lieutenant David Collins remarked early in his diary about the Norfolk Island pines:

'They have been found not to meet the purpose intended of them. Strikingly straight and tall, they are often hollow and unsuitable for large masts. They are shaky or rotten at thirty or forty feet from the butt; the wood is so brittle that it would not make a good oar, and is so porous that the water soaked through the planks of a boat which had been built of it. (Collins: An Account of the English Colony in New South Wales P63).

Even Watkins Tench recorded in his diary of 1792 his observations about the future usefulness of Norfolk Island:

'The New Zealand hemp, of which so many sanguine expectations were formed, is not a native of the soil of New Holland; and Norfolk Island, where we made sure to find this item, is also without it. So that the scheme of being able to assist the East Indies with naval stores, in case of a war, must fall to the ground.' (Tench P74)

As if expecting to be censured for not performing in his duty of finding suitable naval materials, Governor Phillip wrote to London:

'The pine trees, in the opinion of the carpenter of the Supply, who is a good judge, are superior to any he has ever seen; and the island (Norfolk Island) affords excellent timbers for ship-building, as well as for masts and yards, with which I make no doubt but his Majesty's ships in the East Indies may be supplied'. (Phillip to Lord Sydney 28 September 1788 HRNSW)

Is the mistaken impression that the Colony could supply naval materials, evidence that the British Government might also have erred in its other preconceptions of conditions at Botany Bay? These included the facts that of Phillip had arrived ill prepared; his convicts were not an effective work force and he had no one to direct them? The British Government had mistakenly assumed that convicts with few useful skills, used to manual labour and hostile to authority, could turn themselves into pioneers 'capable of taming a wilderness' (Bridges: *Foundations of Identity*)

Lithgow would have been aware of the need for naval timber stores as well as the great export potential of timber from the Colony back to England. As with many other raw materials reaching England, the Government was cognisant of deriving strategic supplies from a friendly source rather than becoming captive to European suppliers. Lithgow welcomed the announcement by his merchant friends that they were assembling exports of timber to England. He advised the governor of the discriminate tariff being levelled at imports from the Colony, and recommended that Darling make suitable representations to the Secretary for the Colonies to have the duty withdrawn. When that failed he recommended that timber merchants themselves make direct representations to London.

Timber of useable quality was not to be found around Sydney Cove so Phillip required pine from Norfolk Island until he found good stands of eucalypts, blue gum, Blackbutt, flooded gum and box around the upper reaches of Lane Cove River and Middle Harbour. These logs were so heavy and did not float, so they had to be cut to length for moving by boat. There was plenty of good stone and clay for bricks, but a shortage of skilled labour made these materials unusable in the early days of the Colony. Bricks began to be more usable in 1789 when the early timber constructions were decaying and in need of replacement. Roofing tiles became necessary as well, to replace the grass or reed thatching previously used for storehouses which was too fire-prone for the storage of valuable foodstuffs and other stores. Collins records that the living huts were constructed from pine frames with sides filled with lengths of cabbage palm plastered over with clay to form 'a very good hovel'.

In the Colony, close confinement was neither necessary nor practical and, except for hospitalisation, most convicts before 1800 had to find their own shelter. Building huts for convicts had not been part of official building policy, although some huts were built especially for them. In Rose Hill for instance, Phillip designed and built huts as part of his town layout. Since the sawn timbers were used for officer housing or public buildings, convicts building their own huts would use saplings covered with a mesh of twigs and walls plastered with clay. Convicts were given no access to the limited quantity of building supplies, such as ironmongery and glass, which had been brought from England so that windows were covered by lattices of twigs. The best buildings in the town were those for Government use such as the stores, the barracks, the hospital and housing for officials. Only when convicts became free or went on ticket-of-leave status was there any call or need for private building, and then a building industry began to emerge.

When Phillip returned home in 1792, Major Grose reallocated convicts to officers and small farmers, succeeding in depleting the government work gangs, which could only complete public works by paying soldiers to supervise the convicts at a rate of one shilling a day in addition to their military pay. 'With the depleted government gangs and with no firm direction', Bridges writes that roads and buildings were neglected and fell into disrepair. For lack of barracks, soldiers built their own homes along the road to the brickfield. David Collins reflected on the difficulties of the time:

To provide bricks for the barracks, three gangs, each of 30 convicts with an overseer was constantly at work. To convey materials from the brickfields to the barracks site, a distance of about ¾ ths of a mile, three brick-carts were employed, each drawn by 12 men and an overseer. Each cart held 700 tiles or 350 bricks and each day, the cart made 5 loads with bricks or 4 loads with tiles. To bring the timber to the site, 4 timber carriages were used, each drawn by 24 men. So 228 men were constantly used in heavy labour in the building of a barracks or storehouse, in addition to the sawyers, carpenters, smiths, painters, glaziers and stonemasons.'

Bricks were used mainly for government buildings or official houses because of the cost, and private housing continued to use timber framing. Private building activities increased and slowly improved, and in the year following Phillip's departure 160 houses were built in Sydney, with an allowance of 1,400 bricks to each dwelling for building the chimney and floor. When Hunter finally arrived, public works had languished and his first action was to plaster soft brick buildings as some protection against wind and rain. He ordered the collection of foreshore shells for lime-making and plaster. In a map prepared by the Frenchman Leseur in 1802 some 260 houses are identified, but in 1804 an official count listed 673 houses in Sydney, indicating a rapid building program between 1802 and 1804.

There was constant pressure on scarce funds within the Colony, as the authorities had not planned on any urban development. Hunter promoted the common cause and encouraged private contributions of material and labour to build bridges and public gaols. In building the Sydney gaol, Hunter directed each settler to bring in ten straight logs of nine feet in length and seven inches in diameter, weekly. When this scheme did not succeed, Hunter 'loaned' the Gaol Fund £1,000. To repay this sum, he imposed a levy of sixpence on each bushel of wheat delivered to the Commissariat store and, when that did not produce sufficient, he imposed a 'landing fee on spirits, wines and other strong drinks'. This was the very first tax imposed on the colonists for local discretionary use by the Governor.

Major Ovens reported on the convict work operations in the Colony

In their report to Governor Brisbane of June 1825, Major Ovens, who had arrived in the colony as part of the Governor's staff, and Lithgow recommended a 'government contract' system. Lithgow's association with the report was invaluable as it was Lithgow's numbers and analysis that made the report practical, complete and so useful.

Oven's introduced the report by stating that:

'. . . this colony was formed with a view prospectively of becoming in the course of years a useful appendage to Great Britain, and in the prospect of serving as a place for exercising that degree of discipline over the larger portion of its population who, forfeiting all claims to the more lenient laws of their own country, had rendered themselves fit subjects for a more coercive system of restraint. In the first case, therefore, it was only reasonable that the Colony should be indebted to the Mother country for a large outlay of capital in its principal institutions; and in the second, that the labours of the convicts should be rendered available for that purpose. Hence the numerous works and Establishments, that became necessary in the march of the colony's progress, were furnished from the industry and labour of that class of its inhabitants.'.

Having tried to justify both the development of the colony and the use of convicts for that purpose, Ovens went on to suggest that the assignment system should be temporary and 'used only when a benefit to the colony of enhancing it natural productions, or improving the value of its material by the skill and industry of the convict labour'. In other words, convicts should be placed into service, where they can do the most good, and reap the largest reward. He pointed out that, up to that time, priority has been given to town development but the priorities should now change and attention given to developing 'agricultural and pastoral industries'. Although the previous priority

'. . . was not the most consonant to the principles of political economy, it was the most natural at the then existing state of society; when the extent of the Agricultural resources of the country became better known, clearer and more enlightened views on the subject were entertained, and the labour of the prisoners could be applied to such pursuits as were eventually most likely to add to the wealth, comfort and independence of the community. A practical example of the happy result of such measures may be instanced in the system adopted in clearing the country by means of convict labour, and bringing into cultivation large tracts of land which otherwise would be dormant and useless to the colonist; this work has also improved the moral condition of the convicts as well as their habits assimilated to those of farming men.'

Ovens then noted a new incentive system for the land clearing gangs in the country areas. He suggested that convict labour should be used not only for land clearing, road making, and public works in the towns (government buildings etc), but for repair work as well (rather than free contractors imposing costs on the colony). The Ovens/Lithgow Report was full of minor cost-benefit analyses. These comparisons would set down the economic value of the land, after clearing and cultivation, and compare these benefits with the costs of clearing the land by these convict gangs. The numbers used related mostly to grain production, indicating either that wool production had not yet reached its full potential or that the emphasis in the colony was still on food production rather than the export market.

Ovens noted four commonly held objections to the privatisation of contract work. To coordinate the government contract system, he recommended establishing an engineer's department, in order 'to give a systematic effect to the labour and exertions, as well as to the skill and mechanical arts of the prisoners'. This recommendation was accepted and implemented as part of the Darling revised Public Service structure, and departmental reorganisation.

Operating the Dockyard

After the Lumber Yard, which utilised over 2,000 men per day, the most active area for employing convicts was the King's Dockyard. Of the two operating 'subsidiaries' of the Commissary, the 'heaving down place' located on the east bank of Sydney Cove, was originally not intended to exist. The East India Company enjoyed a monopoly of trade, and to protect this monopoly, the Crown directed:

'That you do not on any account allow craft of any sort to be built for the use of private individuals which might enable them to effect such intercourse, and that you do prevent any vessels which may at any time hereafter arrive at the said settlement from any ports from having communication with any of the inhabitants.' (Instructions to Arthur Phillip 25 April 1878 by George III)

The same instructions were issued to King, Hunter and Bligh over successive years. But the circumstances of the settlement soon conflicted with the original instructions, and limited facilities for building and repairing boats were set up in Sydney Cove. David Collins in *An Account of the Early Colony* writes 'Mr Reid, the carpenter of the *Supply* undertook the construction of a boat-house, on the east side (of the Cove) for the purpose of building, with the timber of this country, a hoy capable of conveying provisions to Rose Hill, and other useful and necessary purposes'. What was to become the *Rose Hill Packet* carried ten ton of cargo and was not launched until 1789.

Construction of the Dock Yard began in 1797 when, according to Collins, 'a spot of ground' was marked out on the west side for a 'ship yard'. The next *Return of Labour* in 1800 gave some idea of the trades carried on there: 'Shipwrights, caulkers, boat-builders, labourers and watchmen, brick and stone layers, plaisterers . . . 'Collins, in his account of public work carried out during Governor Hunter's term said, 'boat repairing was paled in a naval yard on the west side of the cove and erected within it was a joiner's and a blacksmith's shop, with sheds for the vessels while repairing, and for the workmen: with a steamer, a storehouse, a warder's lodge and an apartment for the clerk'

From these humble beginnings, the Commissariat Store, Boat Repair Yard and the Dockyard developed into a three-story warehouse with attached wharf for the loading and unloading of ships. The Commissary wrote (Governors' despatches–Phillip) that "shipping was the life-blood of the town: ships brought in food and supplies, new faces and news of the outside world; ships meant that the isolated settlement had not been forgotten by the British Government; and the seaways and rivers were the means of communication with Rose Hill, Hawkesbury and Norfolk Island". The Dock Yard became as important to the colony, employing nearly 1,000 convicts at the height of its activities, as the Lumber Yard itself.

Operating the Lumber Yard

Ovens and Lithgow had reported on the state of the Lumber Yard. Here are selected extracts from that report taken from the HRA XI P653.

Relatively little is known about the operations of the Yard, except that it was the focal point of colonial 'industry', and employed the majority of the convicts. It was part of the Commissary operations and was originally located on the corner off Bridge and George (High) Street. When Blaxcell went bankrupt and was forced to leave the colony, his property was purchased by the Commissary for use as an enlarged Lumber Yard. There were well over 1,000 convicts on site prior to the Macquarie years and many more afterwards.

In his report to Governor Brisbane, Major Ovens unveils a little about the operations of the yard:

'In the Lumber Yard are assembled all the indoor tradesmen who work in the shops such as Blacksmiths, carpenters, sawyers, shoemakers, tailors etc. The workmen, carrying on their occupations under the immediate eye of the Chief Engineer are probably kept in a better state of discipline than those, who working more remote, are dependent on the good behaviour of an overseer for any work they may perform.

Whatever is produced from the labour of these persons, which is not applied to any public work or for the supply of authorised requisitions, is placed in a large store and kept to furnish the exigencies of future occasions; the nature of these employments, also renders it much easier to assign a task to each, for the due performance of which they are held responsible.

In the Timber Yard adjoining the Lumber Yard is kept assorted all the timber, scaffoldings etc required for the execution of public buildings: and whatever materials are carried away from hence for these purposes to the different works, the same have to be returned, or the deficiency accounted for. The storekeeper of this Yard has charge of such timber as is brought from the out stations, or sawn and cut up in the Yard, such as flooring boards, scantlings, beams etc; and when these supplies exceed the demand for government purposes, the excess is sold by public auction, and the amount of the proceeds credited to government.'

We can assume that there was some form of 'inventory' control of tools; otherwise the Governor could not have been advised that tools were missing (assumed) stolen. In the centre of the half-acre site, there was a large open, but roofed building, under which the logs were stored, debarked and sawn

Ovens lists the workforce by category as well as their expected output (HRA Vol X1 P655-7):

Carpenters' Gang	50 convicts + free apprentices
Blacksmiths' Gang	45 convicts
Bricklayers' Gang	10 convicts
Sawyers' Gang	25 convicts
Brick-makers' Gang	15 convicts + boy apprentices from Carters barracks
Plasters' Gang	8 convicts these men carry out lathing, plastering and whitewashing)
Quarrymen	15 convicts
Loading, carrying, clearing the Quarries	3 bullock teams + 5 horse trucks–19 convicts
Wheelwrights' Gang	23 convicts (wheel, body and spoke makers)
Coopers Gang	6 convicts
Shoemakers' Gang	8 convicts
Tailors' Gang	8 convicts (the cloth is made at the Female factory in Parramatta)
Dockyard	70 convicts working as mechanics and labourers
Dockyard Town gang	22 convicts used for loading or discharging vessels
Stone-cutters and setters	13 convicts
Brass Founders' Gang	9 convicts (casting iron for all wheels and millwork)

Other occupations of convicts employed, included: foundation diggers', rubbish clearers; Commissariat Store gangs, grass cutters, boats' crews; boat conveyance crews, gardeners

An overview plan shows the presentation of the Yard operations. Convicts were marched, as arranged by Macquarie, from the Hyde Park Barracks along Macquarie, Bent and Bridge Streets to the entrance to the Yard, which faced High Street. Inside the entrance, which was two large solid wood gates set into a high brick wall. We can picture a supervisor's office, with room for clerical staff. A tool shed would have been located near the front gate so that convicts could be issued with tools and have them collected at the end of the working day. Along one side of the site, probably the back boundary adjacent to and running parallel to the Tank Stream, the five operating divisions would have been housed, probably also under an open sided roofed building. These five independent areas included workshops for:

Blacksmiths
Carpenters
Wheelwrights
Tailors
Shoemakers

Sawpits were located in the central area, (2 sawpits of about 70 feet in length, + 1 in the Timber Yard + 1 in the Dockyard–Ovens) whilst furnaces, for safety reasons would have been located on a third boundary wall. The fourth boundary wall would have contained materials storage, since bricks, tiles; sawn lumber would have been stored in the Yard. Quarries were located at Cockle Bay, the Domain, the Gaol quarry, and the High Street quarry. Stored items included:

Bricks
Lime
Coal
Shingles
Nails
Tools
Timber in process of drying
Logs awaiting cutting
The products despatched from the Lumber Yard, included:
Sawn timber for framing, roofing battens, flooring supports (if used instead of bricks), window frames, doors and frames
Nails
Bolts
Bellows

Barrels
Furniture for the various barracks

Convict Employment Categories

Employment was considerable, and was categorised into at least these groupings for control purposes:

Construction gangs for building, houses, public buildings, wharves, bridges
Gangs for moving logs from the wharf behind the commissary, further up High Street, to the Lumber Yard
Gangs for dragging 'materials' carts from the Yard to building and construction sites
Gangs for dragging the portable 'rain-sheds' to the various construction sites.
Gangs for dragging brick-carts to and from the Brickfields
Gangs for dragging the 'roofing tile' carts from the Brickfields
Gangs working in the Stone-yard on the west side of High Street
Gangs for dragging carts with large stones from the Stone-yard to building sites
Gangs for land 'clearing'
Gangs for felling trees in the selected timber harvesting areas (Pennant Hills and Castle Hill)
Gangs for Road making

In all, over 20,000 convicts were organised from the centre of manufacturing, with about 2,000 employed within the yard itself.

Commissioner John Thomas Bigge gives us a preliminary opinion of the convicts at work in his First Report on the Colony published in 1821. We also have the written report by Major Ovens and Auditor Lithgow to Secretary Goulburn in June 1824 to show how the clearing gangs and road gangs were re-organised under Governor Darling. Commissioner Bigge's report provides an interesting insight into convict operations as will see later, but he makes a couple of observations about the Lumber Yard.

'The able bodied men who are lodged in the Hyde Park barracks and the Carter Barracks are divided into gangs, and are employed in the Lumber Yard'

The principal place of convict labour, Bigge reported, 'is in the Lumber Yard, a large space of ground now walled in, and extending from George Street to the edge of the small stream that discharges itself into Sydney Cove.

The trades carried on in this place are those of: carpenters, joiners, cabinet makers, wood turners, sawyers, wheelwrights, cart-makers, barrow-makers, blacksmiths, whitesmiths, shoeing smiths, agricultural implement makers, tool makers, nailers, bell founders, iron and brass founders, brass finishers, turners and platers, brass wire drawers, tool sharpeners, steelers, tinmen, painters, glaziers, farriers, horse-shoers, saddle and harness makers, bellow makers, pump borers, tailors, coopers and many more.'

Based on the Bigge assessment, other observations of the convict work in the Colony can be made as follows:

In the seven years between January 1, 1814 and December 20, 1820, Bigge tells us that 11,767 convicts arrived in the colony.

Of the 11,767 only 4,587 were placed into government service, whilst the remainder of 7,180 were assigned to the military officers and other land grant beneficiaries

The government assignees (the 4,587) were placed into various enterprises as mechanics and labourers–they all (except for 594) were required to live in government barracks in Sydney (Hyde Park or Carters) Parramatta, Windsor, Bathurst. They were employed on Government farms, growing or looking after:

Vegetables	150
Cattle	11
Hay/charcoal	110
Wheat/maize	269
Timber cutting	73

Lime preparation	27
Road making	362
Land clearing	386
Stone quarries	69
Cart operators	268
Brick/tile makers	124
Boat navigators	12
Official boat crews	120
Dockyard operations	47
Lumber Yard	1,000
Construction work	1,450

There were over 1,500 convicts employed as supervisors, foremen, leading hands and clerical assistants, as well as in the Governor's and official government offices. The hierarchy was equally as simple in structure. The Governor was obviously the final arbiter, whilst the Chief Engineer, Major Druitt, had overall responsibility for the works program–planning and completion. The principal superintendent of convicts was William Hutchinson, and the other two important figures were the chief architect for public buildings and quality control as well as convict productivity (Francis Greenway), and the design chief for military and civil barracks and police posts, Lieutenant Watts of Macquarie's 46th regiment.

Lithgow's understanding of the real costs of operating the Lumber Yard (which was an important and significant part of the Commissary operations) was invaluable in the analysis of what improvements could be made and what financial benefits would flow from changes. In turn the Ovens analysis gave Lithgow a much clearer understanding of the value of convict work. The Second Lithgow/Ovens Report is entitled *Public Labour of Convicts maintained by the Crown at Sydney, Parramatta, Hawkesbury, Toongabbie and Castle Hill* and includes the following:

'The work undertaken by the convicts includes:

Cultivation–Gathering, husking and shelling maize from 2000 acres sowed last year–Breaking up ground and planting 1230 acres of wheat, 100 acre of Barley, 250 acres of Maize, 14 acres of Flax, and 13 acres of potatoes–Hoeing the above maize and threshing wheat.

Stock–Taking care of Government stock as herdsmen, watchmen etc

Buildings–Convict labour is being provided at the following building sites:

At Sydney: Building and constructing of stone, a citadel, a stone house, a brick dwelling for the Judge Advocate, a commodious brick house for the main guard, a brick printing office
At Parramatta: Alterations at the Brewery, a brick house as clergyman's residence
At Hawkesbury: completing a public school

A Gaol House with offices, at the expense of the Colony

Boat and Ship Builders: refitting vessels and building row boats
Wheel and Millwrights: making and repairing carts

Manufacturing: sawing, preparing and manufacturing hemp, flax and wool, bricks and tiles

Road Gangs: repairing roads, and building new roads

Other Gangs: loading and unloading boats'

(Historical Records of NSW–Vol 6 P43)

Lithgow's accounting knowledge and inclinations told him that the Blue Books were missing an important concept. The British Treasury had refused to allow the output of convict labour to be valued and included in the accounting reports being sent back to London. If they had been, the 'returns of the colony' would have offered a very different picture. Some instances serve to illustrate Lithgow's concerns:

Only at the end of Darling's period as governor was an attempt made to include the 'cost' of land clearing (by convicts) into the selling price of crown land. Buyers were offered cleared or uncleared land, at differential prices. This scheme was not successful and was abandoned as a marketing practice, at the same time; land clearing operations were also ceased.

Lithgow had previously itemised and reported on convict production that was being sold to the settlers but not accounted for. These items included coal, food and meat from the Government farms which the Commissary sold to settlers which had 'no value' as far as commissary records were concerned. The Female factory produced a wide range of garments for male and female convicts with a limited range of goods being sold through the Commissariat. Again, no recognition was made as to the cost of these items as an offset against their revenues. Convicts operated the ferryboat operating between Sydney and Parramatta and revenues were recorded in the Colonial accounts as 'sundry' income, and was not attributed to convict labour.

These were the circumstances that Lithgow was most concerned about in his accounting records. However another element of convict labour, apart from production of consumables had been discussed by Bigge. This was in the context of waste and unnecessary expense in constructing a wide-range of public buildings under Macquarie, which Bigge considered extravagance. Bigge received submissions on the valuation of these buildings and the costs of construction. (Refer Appendix D for a full list of Macquarie Buildings and their cost estimates.)

Henry Kitchen, a free settler architect, and Francis Greenway, a convict architect, offer us a brief sample of the value of work performed by the convicts. Kitchen estimates £922,857.13.11 as being the cost of the Macquarie era building program. Since the actual material cost total for the estimated construction work completed in the Macquarie era was less than £500,000 (refer this author's valuation of each building–Material Content only–Appendix B), it is most unlikely that the total could have reached £922,000. Therefore, it is safe to assume that Henry Kitchen, in producing this misleading estimate to Commissioner Bigge, did so with the intention of further blackening the names of Greenway and Macquarie, both of whom disliked Kitchen and were, in turn, disliked by Kitchen. This estimate by Kitchen, offered to Commissioner Bigge in evidence, was a deliberately malicious and deceptive piece of disinformation.

There is another possible explanation that stretches credulity somewhat but could be justified as a possibility. It was always assumed that convict labour was essentially 'free', and should therefore not count or contribute to the total cost of the finished construction. This is not necessarily the case. Some of Lithgow's peers (eg Ridden and Riddell, both Colonial Treasurers) have indicated that 1/3 per day was an appropriate rate of compensation for the non-skilled convict labour. If we make a number of assumptions concerning day rates of equivalent pay, and about the productivity level of the convicts in a major construction job, keeping in mind they were supervised by other convicts, then we may be able to say that the £400,000 of cost assembled is for materials and that the equivalent value of the convict labour makes the difference of the £22,000 to bring the total estimate up to Kitchen's estimates. In other words, convict labour, if valued, would result in approx £900,000 of value for the completed buildings

The relevant assumptions are (based on Greenways cost estimates reproduced in this author's study of building costs during the Macquarie period)

The number of days of mechanics labour to complete the Government House Stables was 16,686.5

The average cost per man day was 1 shilling

Labour reflected a 33% content of the total finished cost.

So applying these assumptions to the construction work, we find that all the Macquarie projects would have taken 2,683,108 days of mechanics labour or approx 8,450 man years. The convict population increased between 1812 and 1820 by 10,800 men and totalled 19,000 men by 1820, and to suppose that 44% of the male convicts were employed in construction work is not unreasonable. At the minimum rate of 1s per day, our labour cost total becomes £134,155; thus, at an average of 3 shillings (compared with Coghlan's cost for 'free' mechanics at 5s per day, we would achieve the difference of £480,000. Coghlan estimates that a convict would only produce about 60% of a 'free' labourer's output' so that 3/–on average is not unreasonable. Our conclusion, if we stretch the point, is that Kitchen's estimate of a construction cost for the period of £900,000 is valid if our materials are valued at£402,000 and our labour accounts (at the average rate of 3 shillings per day) to a further £470,000. In the end result,

Kitchen was almost correct but only if certain assumptions are made, but it would be unreasonable to attribute both good or reasonable motive and mathematical abilities to Kitchen in 1822.

It is these details that Lithgow would have studied, together with his friend and colleague Major Ovens, in formulating a 'valuation' of the overall efforts by the convicts in the colony and in revamping the work processes in order to improve the output by the convicts. This means that the Lumber Yard was the focal point of industry within the Colony. The Commissariat was the operational means to an end and the role of the Deputy-Commissary of Accounts (Lithgow) was very important, especially with the difficulty in planning, analysis and interpreting the actual results.

Lithgow was constantly undertaking cost-benefit analyses, by the very nature of his work, and the type of questions that would have been asked of him, by the governor. Surely the most important one he could have undertaken, and a valuable one we should undertake is a cost-benefit analysis of the British contribution to, and the benefit received from, the Colony. It is not an exercise in futility. but rather a mathematically reasonable attempt to quantify a series of expenditures by Britain in the Colony, and a listing and valuation of benefits Britain received in return. One of our original assumptions is that Britain saw the Colony as having a successful commercial, military and trade outcome, so it is not unreasonable to try and assess if the actual outcome was worthwhile.

The colonial investment returns great benefits to Britain

The estimate of direct gains by the British authorities from the original and continuing investment in the Colony of New South Wales can be based on five identifiable and quantifiable events:

The opportunity cost of housing, feeding and guarding the convicts in the Colony compared with the cost of doing the same thing in Britain. The original estimates, in this category, were based on an estimated differential of ten pound per head–an arbitrary assessment of the differential cost. However recent and more reliable information has come to hand which gives further validity to a number of £20 per head per annum, compared with the original £10 per head per annum. Adopting this cost as a base for comparison purposes, it means that the benefit to Britain of the Colony increased from £140,000,000 to £180,000,000. This benefit assesses the Ground 1 benefit at £84,000,000. A letter to Under Secretary Nepean, dated 23 August 1783, from James Maria Matra of Shropshire and London assists us in this regard. It was Matra who first analysed the opportunity of using the new Colony as a Penal Colony; only his estimates were incorrect and ill founded. He had advised the Government that it would cost less than £3,000 to establish the Colony initially, plus transportation cost at 15 pound per head and annual maintenance of £20 per head. In fact the transportation was contracted for the Second fleet at £13/5s per head and Colonial revenues from 1802 offset annual maintenance. However, Matra made a significant statement in his letter to Nepean, when he pointed out that the prisoners housed, fed and guarded on the rotting hulks on the Thames River were being contracted for in the annual amount of £26.15.10 per head per annum. He also writes that 'the charge to the public for these convicts has been increasing for the last 7 or 8 years' (Historical Records of NSW–Vol 1 Part 2 Page 7)

Benefit to Britain on Ground two is put at £70, 000,000 pound which places the value of a convicts labour at £35 per annum. Matra had assessed the value of labour of the Hulk prisoners at £35/17s.

The valuation of convict labour in the new Colony should reflect the convicts not only used on building sites, but also on road, bridge and wharf construction. This would add (based on £35 per annum) a further £21,000,000.

The Molesworth Committee (a House of Commons Committee investigating transportation) concluded that the surplus food production by the convicts would feed the military people and this, over a period of 10 years, would save £7,000,000 for the British Treasury. The benefits of fringe benefit grants of land to the Military etc can be estimated (based on One pound per acre) at over £5,000,000 before 1810.

We learn from Governor King's Report to Earl Camden (which due to a change of office holder, should have been addressed to Viscount

Castlereagh as Colonial Secretary) dated 15 March 1806 that the convicts engaged in widely diverse work.

Thus the total benefits from those five items of direct gain to the British (set out above) comes to well over £174 million, and this is compared to Professor N. G. Butlin's proposal that the British 'invested' 5.6 million, at great inconvenience and cost. The real point is that the 'investment' was carefully and calculatingly designed to show a 'return' and this return came in the form of increased trade to British shipping fleets; increased use of British seamen, increased use of British insurance and trade finance, increased utilisation of public docks and warehouses, and greater access by British manufacturers to raw materials and removing the reliance on European suppliers. Lithgow reported to the Colonial Secretary that the transportation program was valuable to Britain and, even if it was 'costly' to the British Treasury, there was real value in the whole program.

It was these circumstances that had to be considered and brought to account by Lithgow in his second report to Governor Darling which outlined how the colonial accounting system would account for the diverse work practices, tools and materials used and valuing the output of convict work gangs.

Lithgow and the Land Board

The Land Board had been created in response to the decision to slow the staggering rate of land grants and commence the sale of Crown lands. It was designed to be a regulating body, with the authority to enforce the collection of fees and quit-rents associated with grants of crown land.

In 1826 Lithgow was appointed a member of the Board by Governor Darling with expectations that the very large job of surveying Crown lands, both granted and sold, would become current and continue to meet demands for surveys of new townships, and the large pastoral lands that needed to have boundaries surveyed, for identification purposes. Lithgow as a member of the Land Board officially wrote to Governor Darling on 11 March 1826 concerning the delay in surveying land granted during the past 5 years. The letter recites:

'The surveyor-General (John Oxley) states in his report 'that the principal portion of 400,000 acres, granted by the late Governor Macquarie remained unsurveyed at the time of his departure, and that out of 1,068,000 acres appropriated by Governor Sir Thomas Brisbane by grant or sale, or as Crown reserves, the boundary lines of at least half remain unascertained.'

The letter urged Darling into action to recruit more qualified surveyors from Britain. The letter also responded to Darling's instructions ordering the division of the country into counties, hundreds and parishes. The Land Board explained that the policy could be implemented only if further manpower was provided. We can see Lithgow's concerns in a further letter from the Land Board to Darling dated 29 March 1826. The submission states that the Surveyor-General's Office was far too busy with boundary surveys to be collecting quit rents. Instead Lithgow and other members of the Board (including J.T. Campbell and William Stewart) recommended that the position of Collector of Land Revenue be located within the office of the Colonial Treasurer.

The Land Board was required to handle many disputes, and the report of one such dispute was handed to the Governor on 25th December 1826 along with a stinging rebuke on a flawed policy:

"The board recommends that the governor does not grant further lands to applicants who do not even intimate any intention ever to become resident in the colony, which will reduce the great abuse in the future distribution of crown land in the colony" (Government Despatches–*Land Board*) Lithgow also recommended that locals residents not be allowed to act as 'agents' for absentee landlords, especially those who used their influence in England to gain an unfair advantage.

The Land Board remained in existence until the Robertson Acts installed a Board with broader powers in 1858.

The Sale of Waste Land Act of 1828 raised the minimum reserve price of crown land to one pound per acre, except that large remote areas might be sold at a lower price, and established a formula for the use of the land revenue; fifty percent was to be spent on immigration, the rest was to be expended by the Governor in accordance with British Government directives from time to time. The Governor was to continue to have power to issue depasturing licences and to make regulations for the use and occupancy of unsold lands, but the existence of the Sale of Waste Lands Act placed an important restriction on the colony by implying a prohibition against the Legislative Council legislating on these matters. The first directive on how the Governor was to spend a portion of the fund, enjoined the Governor to spend a proportion on Aboriginal protection and another on the roads; he was left free to hand any surplus over to the Council for appropriation; but it was made clear that the whole of the fifty percent was to be considered as an emergency reserve if the Council proved difficult". McMinn sheds some further light on the Crown Lands mystery but there still remains the question of whether, year after year, these funds were fully used or just included as a contribution to general revenue. It would appear that somewhere there is a firm directive from the British Treasury that the revenues from Crown Lands sale was to be used to 'offset' British costs of maintaining the Colony. The 'Blue Book' is evidence that as general revenues, these funds were already being used to pay for the costs of feeding, clothing, housing convicts, and we know they were specifically used to pay for 'sponsored immigrants', aboriginal 'protection', and now roads. The costs of the military establishment were charged against general revenues so in the quite large 'pot', nearly all Colonial expenditures were subsidised or offset by revenues from the Sale of Crown Land. Britain it seems, offered to pay only for the shipping and supplies costs of getting their prisoners to the Colony. After 1828, we know that convict production–both agricultural and mineral–went a long way to paying their expenses, so perhaps the British Treasury did in fact get off very lightly indeed, especially for the benefits it derived.

The question of Crown Land's revenues still remains. It is apparent from the 'Blue Book' notations that this revenue was initially 'reserved' for specific allocation by the Crown and remained in the Colony as an offset against British Government fiscal obligations (eg Civil List salaries) until self-government in 1855. A relevant quotation from the 1887 Financial Statements of the Colonial Treasurer of New South Wales follows:

'Prior to the passing of the Constitution Act, the Territorial Revenues of the Colony belonged to the Crown, but upon that coming into operation in 1855, they were placed at the disposal of the local Parliament, and together with the taxes, imposts, rates and duties were formed into one fund, under the title of the Consolidated Revenue Fund. In lieu of the Crown Revenues thus given up to the Colony, an annual Civil List of 64,300 pound was made payable to Her Majesty out of the Consolidated Revenues of the Colony."

What this means is that the British Treasury allowed the offset of all direct British payments made on account of the Colony against revenues raised by the sale, rent or lease of Crown lands until 1838, when the decision was made to allocate a 50% portion of Crown Land Revenues towards subsidising immigration to the colony, and a further 15% towards the support of 'natives' in the colony, and the balance was to be made discretionary, although Britain chose to use most of the excess for administrative (eg civil salaries) purposes.

Lithgow provides the Blue Books later than required to Treasury in London

A number of reasons, bordering on excuses were made for and on behalf of Lithgow to explain the lateness (in excess of five years) of the Blue Books being transmitted to London. Lithgow himself was instrumental in extending this situation by:

Taking extended leave when he was sick
Failing to budget for sufficient qualified staff
Having to wait for vouchers from revenue officers that never arrived
Being overworked by sitting on too many government boards and committees
Commencing the audit of the Port Phillip accounts which grew (in volume) very rapidly and took much more time than planned
Being unprepared to cope with a growing economy and the measure of a busy economy is the number of transactions taking place in government circles.

These excuses were made by the Governor, the Colonial-Secretary and Lithgow himself to the Lords of the Treasury, Whitehall, the Secretary of the Colonies and even the London–based Commissary-General himself. All the explanations are plausible but could have been solved very simply.

Lithgow was a meticulous auditor and, wanting to keep the overview of the colonial accounts for himself, he infrequently passed on work for completion by others.

Once threatened with dismissal, Lithgow was able to so complete the five years of overdue Blue Books quickly, even if with less than in his usual meticulous accuracy. This does not suggest prior laziness on his part; he lost control of the situation for a variety of reasons:

He was pre-occupied with his committee work, and being acting chief executive in the Colonial Administration

He was under enormous pressure by being understaffed in his office

The system was cumbersome, unwieldy and over bureaucratic

The British Treasury in 1829 did request that, in order to assist the work of a House of Commons Committee, they need 20 copies of the Blue Books for the previous year and these should be handled and, indeed, printed in the Colony. The colony did not have the capacity or the capability to print such a large volume of work, not did it have the paper supplies. Lithgow decided to await the next shipment of paper from England and try to upgrade the Colonial printing press. He became preoccupied with this request and this caused further delays in current work

The growing volume of work did not assist his planning for 'auditing' the Blue Books.

It is not surprising that, when Gipps threatened him with dismissal if the long overdue accounts were not completed in a hurry, in the auditing of the previous five years of Blue Books was completed less than one year. Of course, the system was cumbersome and difficult, as were the regulations passed down by the Lords of the Treasury in London. The accounting system had to be changed if a speeding up of auditing checks was to be accomplished. Ledgers were kept open until the full and original allocation of funds for any project was spent and/or the project was completed and some projects continued for three or more years. It was surprising that, when Lithgow was confronted with the most severe of penalties the system could be made so flexible and he could achieve results previously considered impossible.

Of all these challenges presented to Lithgow by the British Government, albeit filtered through five different governors, the most difficult and harmful was this criticism arising from his failure to deliver the annual returns (the Blue Books) of the Colony on a timely basis and in the timeframe required by the Lord Treasurers in London. He was chastised by the Secretary of States, the Lord Treasurers themselves, the Lords of the Audit Board, the British Parliament the Colonial Secretary and the governors. On each occasion he had an explanation, if not an excuse, for his omissions but when his returns became over 5 years late, the threatened dismissal, even if unfair, brought about a most remarkable response. The question may be asked–was this laziness on Lithgow's part that had got out of control, or was it the system of recording, inspection and validation of the accounts or perhaps the assembly process of the Blue Books, the pressure of other work, or the shortage of clerks? The governors of the time, Bourke and then Gipps had obviously knowingly contributed to the Lithgow dilemma but they never publicly accepted any responsibility. Their actions, in reducing the clerical manning numbers by nine, if not contributing directly and fully to the problem faced by Lithgow, certainly topped of the list of plausible explanations for the delay. Another explanation on the list was the constant placing of Lithgow onto so many Boards and Committees. A list of his 'extracurricular' work shows that he was at one time involved in 27 committees and boards over a three-year period as well as in the writing or co-authoring of many of the reports coming from these bodies.

In retrospect Lithgow was probably vulnerable by accepting an overload situation, and then wanting to please his masters. Certainly preparation of the Blue Books was cumbersome and protracted. The data would be assembled in normal record-keeping but then it would have to be rearranged and copied onto pre-printed forms, which had been determined in England as being information that in some way and on some day, may possibly be useful or needed. Little, if any, thought had been given as to the clerical labour required to complete all this information. Lithgow submitted a number of changes for consideration by the Lords of the Treasury, but their response was (Governors despatches–1833) the Blue

Books are common to all colonies and we cannot change for one colony without disturbing all of the other returns.

Although Lithgow played catch up with the backlog of unaudited and uncompiled accounts, and completed five years of Blue Books ready for dispatch in as many months, his reputation had been bruised by the criticism from both home and abroad, and it took a minor scandal for Lithgow to reclaim his earlier quest for zeal. As the means of recovering his reputation, he presented the Governor with an event that demonstrated the Lithgow diligence. He had located a misappropriated sum of money and those funds had now been returned to the Colonial coffers.

What had happened was that the Agent-General in London, a Mr Barnard, had been accumulating funds in London and not accounting for them to his Colonial Treasurer. As Governor, Charles A. Fitz Roy advised Early Grey on 21 December 1848, 'certain sums have been remitted to the Colonial Agent-General by the British Treasury, but which had not been carried to the credit of the colony'. Lithgow had located and tracked these sums over an extended period and had first advised Fitz Roy that the amount was £3410.2.9. However on 16 December 1848 he amended his advice to the Governor and increased the amount he was tracking to £5928.3.2. The extent of the missing funds and its discovery made Lithgow something of a hero, and corrected all those negative thoughts that had travelled through government circles over the last few years.

The actual Dates of Transmission of Blue Books from Sydney to London for the years 1832-1842 are listed below. The fact that they were officially due within 12 months of the end of the calendar year should be kept in mind.

1832	24.7.1834
1833	5.10.1836
1834	8.6.1839
1835	31.12.1840
1836	26.6.1841
1837	31.1.1842
1838	6.2.1843
1839	12.4.1842

1840	12.4.1842
1841	16.5.1842
1842	2.10.1842

CHAPTER 6

LITHGOW AND HIS GOVERNORS

Lithgow served five Governors between 1824 and 1852, and lived under a sixth, Sir William Denison, between his retirement in 1852 and his death in 1864. The Governors he served between 1824 and 1852 were:

Sir Thomas Brisbane	1821-1825
Ralph Darling	1825-1831
Sir Richard Bourke	1831-1837
Sir George Gipps	1838-1846
Sir Charles Fitzroy	1846-1854
Sir William Denison	1855-1861

Most of the 'notable' historical biographers such as Yarwood, Butlin, Ellis and even the recognised historians have overlooked William Lithgow and his contribution to the growth of the colony, in which his character and role in the economy made him a prominent and important figure in Colonial affairs. For example Ellis, the biographer of Caroline Chisholm, John Macarthur and Lachlan Macquarie, each of whose lives and activities crossed over into the Lithgow period within the colony, does not once mention William Lithgow.

The main, but not the sole, purpose of recalling the days of the governors who Lithgow served, is to put into a political and economic context the most significant events of the day and how Lithgow may have been involved, or even affected by them, in his dual role of Commissary of Accounts and Colonial Auditor.

Governor Sir Thomas Brisbane–1821-1825

Lithgow arrived in the Colony at the end of 1824, shortly before Brisbane's departure. Brisbane had faced a number of contentious issues during his administration, the most important being:

In 1824 Brisbane received instructions to install an appointed Legislative Council in the Colony, made up of 'official' nominees ('five principal officers') and two other independent nominees, including John Macarthur and Charles Cowper

In that same year of 1824, trial by jury was 'conceded' with the Act cited 4 Geo IV cap.96 (later repealed by 9 Geo IV cap 83) and implemented, empowering the Crown to establish Courts of Judicature in NSW, to be styled the Supreme Court of New South Wales. A Chief Justice was to be appointed, and a Charter of Justice implemented.

He removed the censorship exercised over the Press, which had the salutary effect of having two competitive journals to the *Sydney Gazette* to be opened viz Dr. Wardell and W.C. Wentworth's *The Australian* and the E.S. Hall *Monitor*

He established a local 'colonial' currency in 1824, which raised the pound sterling by 25%. The discontent caused by the commercial embarrassment which followed this action led largely to his recall. It is not known whether Lithgow participated in this decision or even supported it but it is most likely that he was forewarned about it and knew of its introduction. He must have visualised the impact it would have on the colonial economy in general, and the Commissary in particular. As Deputy-Commissary of Accounts, Lithgow would have been aware of the impact on the Commissariat costs and accounts from this move, and the resulting effect on all families relying on the Commissariat for food handouts or buying from the commissary store.

A brief understanding of the important role of the Lithgow friend and colleague, Major John Ovens, will be useful. The *Australian Dictionary of Biography* records with reference to Ovens:

'When Brisbane was appointed Governor of New South Wales in 1821, he brought Ovens with him as aide-de-camp and made him acting chief engineer. In that capacity Ovens had general supervision of convict gangs. He generally improved the efficiency of the convicts employed on public works; supervised 'clearing' gangs with much success and ultimately had 50 gangs preparing 'extensive tracts of land into a state for cultivation by the settler'.

He also accompanied Captain Currie on an expedition to the Upper Murrumbidgee and Monaro Districts in 1823, and helped John Oxley to survey Twofold Bay in 1825. Brisbane wrote 'no public officer here has rendered me the same essential service, the colony such general benefit, or imposed upon the Mother Country such a heavy debt of gratitude'.

'The Governor appointed Ovens as his private secretary when he found Frederick Goulburn (a Lord Bathurst appointee) unco-operative. In 1824, in recognition of his services, Ovens was promoted to Major and received a grant of land (200 acres) at Concord, now a suburb of Sydney. Planning to retire to this property Ovens, died just six days after Brisbane left the Colony in December 1825'. (ADB)

Lithgow and Ovens had worked together under the watchful eye of Brisbane and produced two well-received reports for Brisbane on how to improve convict work practices and organisation. Ovens was a trusted and long time army friend to Brisbane and carried out the dual roles of private secretary to the Governor as well as Chief Civil Engineer, responsible for the Lumber Yard operations, the work gangs of convicts and the planning of output by convicts in order to make the colony self-sufficient. Brisbane had responsibility for only slightly more convicts than had been in the colony during Macquarie's period, but could sense that reform, in the area of convict work organisation was necessary, if the additional convicts, as planned by the British Government were to be shipped to the colony. The Ovens/Lithgow Reports were well planned and methodically analysed the output projected from the arrangement of convicts into work gangs, and also set down the best method of supervising their work, and the optimum size of the respective work gangs, be it road-making, road-repair, land clearing, dockyard or lumberyard assignments.

Sir Ralph Darling–1825-1831

Lt-General Ralph Darling was the seventh governor of the Colony of NSW and accepted the office after a lengthy stay in Mauritius as the Britain's senior military representative, on 19 December 1825. Although he had been appointed in late 1823 whilst still in Mauritius, he chose to return to England and tidy up his personal affairs, prior to taking up his appointment. During his brief stay in England, he discussed with the Secretary of State changes desired to be made in the colony. When he arrived in Sydney he was armed with a variety of written instructions, covering a wide range of matters, from operating the Commissariat store, to instructions for restructuring the financial system, creating trial by jury and improving the colony's criminal and civil code.

Darling placed great emphasis on his small group of close advisers, including Lithgow, and this contributed to a significantly Lithgow's extra workload. This group of close confidents, given the name of 'The Board of General Purposes', made recommendations to Darling on a variety of matters from public administration to internal communications between departments and the Governor.

To put the Darling era into further context and outline some of the matters laid before Lithgow, here are some highlights of the Darling administration:

After his arrival in the Colony, one of Darling's first official acts was to appoint new Executive and Legislative Councils. The Executive Council selected by Darling consisted only of the 'official members' of Legislative Council, the Lieutenant Governor, Chief Justice, the Archdeacon, the Military Commandant and the Colonial-Secretary. Lithgow, as Auditor, was to be first appointed as Secretary to the Council, until eventually being appointed to this Executive Council in his own right. He would assume even more responsibility in the Darling administration when he became the Governor's financial representative in the Legislative Council and he remained active for 25 years in this capacity.

In February 1826, Darling tabled before the Legislative Council meeting an extract from the Crown's Instructions, which laid down rules for observance in the enactment of laws being prepared for Royal Assent:

No perpetual law was to be part of any temporary law
No law was to be re-enacted once Royal Assent was refused
No law was to be made to continue for less than two years
No law could be made to lessen or impair revenue without special leave
No law could be made to naturalise aliens
No divorce laws could be made nor laws giving good title to lands owned by aliens

An Act for vesting the Orphan School Estates in the Trustees of the Colony's Clergy and School Lands was passed in August 1826. Lithgow was appointed to the Church and Schools Land Corporation, and to the Land Board. In many respects, these two appointments led to a conflict of interest for Lithgow but, since he was entitled to an official emolument from each position, he had little public complaint about any conflict. The potential conflict came about because the Land Corporation (as trustee for Church and School lands) was in policy conflict with the Government Lands Board which had different goals and responsibilities. The Land Board was created by Darling, and had as its core responsibilities:

The survey of all lands, as grants were made, towns designated for settlement, and pastoralists moved westward

The formal creation and mapping of the nineteen counties designated by Darling

Reservation of public land in each county including land set aside for the Clergy and School Estate, in each of the proposed parishes

On the other hand, the Church and Schools Land Corporation was caught in the web of needs without means as they were limited in funding but unable legally or politically to sell the prime land granted to them. They also complained about it being in unacceptable locations, the results of insufficient consultation between donor and receiver. The facts relating to the Church and School Corporation are:

By Charter of 1826, the lands now referred to as belonging to the Church and School Land Corporation had been dedicated to particular public uses, subject to a power reserved to the Crown, 'to be held, applied and disposed of in such a manner as should appear most conducive to the maintenance and promotion of religion and the education of youth in the colony'.

The *Imperial Land Sales Act* 5 & 6 Vic. Cap 36, provided that the lands should not be dealt with as waste lands, but in the event of sale, reserving to the Crown the power of disposing of such lands for any purpose of 'public safety, convenience, health or enjoyment', and 'saving existing promises, engagements and contracts'. (Land Sales Act)

These lands, with their chequered history and ownership disputes, were not to be considered as or treated as 'waste lands' and were therefore out of the bailiwick of the Lands Board, and any sale proceeds reverted as a restricted attachment of the Crown. This argument became part of the annual debate in the Legislative Council, but was resolved and legitimised in 1856–constituted in the Imperial Act (Constitution Act of 1856) 18 & 19 Vic. Cap 54

The Lands Board annual report of 1834 opined 'we think that it is competent for the Governor, without any risk to impound the annual receipts of these lands, and to stay the issue of further leases or grants until the question may be settled by an Act of Parliament, or by a legal decision.' (SRO)

The Australian Agricultural Company had commenced operations in 1826 on a large scale, causing an inflationary price spiral for livestock. A severe three-year drought had burst the bubble of the livestock market and, in turn, hurt many 'investors' and pastoralists, forcing them into bankruptcy. The result of the AAC speculative cycle was a remarkable rise in the price of livestock followed by a rapid accumulation of wealth by the larger pastoralists who had supplied the markets; 'A mania for possession of flocks and herds possessed all classes of the community in consequence' (*Official History of NSW*–Richards 1883). This 1827 recession was a precursor to the major depression of 1841-1843. Lithgow's interest in the AAC was part of his general interest in agriculture and especially pastoral investment. He had a large pastoral run in the Southern Highlands region (the Monaro), and had become active in two of the Grazing Societies. The AAC had greatly influenced greatly the market price of livestock, and Lithgow was a supporter of optimising the wool returns to growers.

Two of the first Acts passed in 1828 were specified as the *Census Act*, and an *Act for enabling the Governor to Grant Letters of Denization (*citizenship*) to Foreigners*. The census planned for the latter part of 1828 the first during t Governor Darling's term and it was important for him to be seen to be expanding the Colony. The results were that early in 1826 the population was estimated at 34,649, whilst the late in 1828 the census confirmed the population at 36,598.

Darling introduced further land reforms in September 1929, when he signed a bill *For the more effectual Resumption of Crown and Church and Schools Lands* authorising the exchange of Corporation lands to more convenient locations, the sale of some limited areas and the placement of these revenues into a government appropriation account rather than consolidated revenues.

When the Council resumed after a sixteen month lapse, Darling presented the it with a *Statement of the Revenue and Expenditure* of the previous year, together with a Comparative Statement of the same for 1829 and 1830. This was the first stage before the first Appropriation Bill was presented to the Council in 1834 by Darling's successor, Governor Bourke, and was the first time the Legislative Council had been privy to current 'official' treasury figures.

Darling was also committed to exploration. The outcome of the drought of 1812 had been the discovery of the fertile plains beyond the Blue Mountains. A legacy of the big drought of 1826 was to be the discovery of the Darling River by Captain Sturt, leading to the creation of the new province of South Australia. Lithgow's interest in pastoral activities ensured his support of the opening up more and more grazing lands, especially in the Riverina Regions where he had his own 'sheep run'.

On 2 August 1831, it was officially advertised in the *Sydney Gazette* that future Crown Lands would be disposed of by auction sale only, and at a minimum price of 5s. per acre. This announcement was received with surprise and grave concern. Lithgow's Land Board had made the recommendations as a means of raising more local revenues but the British Treasury initially wanted such revenues reserved to repay the early official expenditures of establishing the Colony.

We learn from the Darling diaries that Lithgow was in regular officer contact with Major-General Darling, whilst they were both located in Mauritius, and that Darling, as the nominated Governor of NSW, was instrumental in transferring Lithgow from Mauritius to Sydney. However, Brian Fletcher, as the biographer of Governor Darling (*Darling–A Governor Maligned*) makes only two passing references to Lithgow's existence. In one Fletcher quotes from the ADB when he states, 'In April 1823, William Lithgow was brought from Mauritius, where he had served with Darling, and given charge of the commissariat accounts'. Fletcher points out that only two years later, Darling invited another Mauritian resident to come to the Colony and head up the new Police Force–his name was Francis Rossi. In fact Fletcher is mistaken and it can be verified that Lord Bathurst personally issued that invitation but it can be confirmed also that Darling requested Lithgow's transfer to the Colony of NSW in anticipation of his own arrival as Governor but that Lord Bathurst, wanting to influence the constitution of the colonial civil service, issued the instructions to appoint Lithgow, Rossi and a number of others as set out below (refer also the section on the civil service and new administration in Chapter 2).

The Governor was surrounding himself with carefully hand-chosen departmental supervisors, most of whom had been initially handpicked by Bathurst, for example:

Frederick Goulburn, as Colonial Secretary
William Balcombe who became the first Colonial Treasurer in 1823
Frederick Healy, a tried and tested Superintendent of Convicts
William Lithgow in charge of Commissariat accounts
Francis Rossi became the Superintendent of Police
John Piper was the Naval Officer responsible for collecting Harbour charges and import duties
John Oxley was the Surveyor-General

Each of these supervisors had a defined role with the colonial secretary filling the top spot. The colonial secretary was responsible for intervening between the public service and the governor, and was central to the colonial administration. The Colonial-Secretary was directly responsible for 'Making out all grants, leases and other public colonial instruments . . . along with the care of indents or lists sent with convicts and every other official transaction relating to the colony and government'. He transcribed public dispatches and was custodian of official records, except those of the courts. Originally he performed the duties of private secretary to the governor, but this practice ceased after the clash between Governor Brisbane and Goulburn. In 1824, Lord Bathurst decided to end the friction between Governor Brisbane and Major Frederick Goulburn in the administration of the Colony of NSW by recalling both officers and replacing them with General Darling and an experienced civilian assistant.

Goulburn's departure was followed by the appointment of Major Ovens (the Governor's brother-in-law) who effectively created a separate secretarial division. Following this precedent, Darling brought Henry Dumaresq into his administration as private secretary and offered to appoint Alexander McLeay as Colonial Secretary. It took some persuasion by Bathurst before McLeay was induced to accept this appointment as Colonial Secretary at a salary of £2,000 per annum. The British Treasury insisted that he be paid from Colonial Funds. (Refer also the history and establishment of the colonial secretary's office in the colony in Chapter 2).

Lithgow replaced Dumaresq (who was travelling overseas) between mid-1827 and 1829. The ADB informs us that:

'Darling's concept of government was one of military simplicity: strict adherence to regulations, and the unquestioning personal allegiance of his subordinates. He found these qualities in his private secretary Henry Dumaresq, who he had brought with him from Mauritius and whose sister Eliza he had married, in his Colonial Secretary Alexander McLeay whose daughter Dumaresq had married, and in his own nephew Charles Darling, who arrived in 1827 and was appointed assistant private secretary but in few other among his senior officials. With this family circle behind him, Darling saw himself as the chosen defender of the King's authority in an immense territory, where he suspected even the loyalty of even the small garrison outnumbered though it was more than fifteen to one by a largely convict population. In his zeal for efficiency, Darling introduced many long-overdue improvements in the machinery of the local government, not the least of them being an expertly integrated and supervised civil service. He wanted his officials to be respectable as well as efficient and in 1826 he told the Colonial Office in London Surely there is no colony under His Majesty's Government where attention to the selection of individuals is so important . . . not only the character of Government, but the moral improvement of the people mainly depend on it.'

Darling can be assessed as a reformer who achieved significant changes in the public service of the colony, without ever really getting the colonial economy in top shape. This progress was to await the arrival of Sir Richard Bourke and Sir Charles Gipps. Lithgow's acceptance into the Darling bailiwick was through his active participation in the Board of General Purposes (refer Chapter 2).

Darling found that 'every department appeared to act for itself, without check or control and indeed without apparent responsibility' decided to reorganise the government departments and transferred both the Civil Engineer's Department and the Lumber Yard to other superintendence. In February 1826, *The Australian* described the Chief Engineer's Department as 'establishing a superintendence over almost everything–public works and prisoners; road-making and clearing gangs, the Dockyard and Telegraph'. The reorganisation of the public service, with Lithgow being an influential part of this revised structure (refer Chapter 2) affected those close to Darling, especially Alexander McLeay, who pushed the overall process. Lithgow was appointed to the newly created Land Board, and was also to advise on rearranging 'public departments according to their nature and operations' whilst Lithgow and Ovens associated to assist Darling by planning a major improvement in convict work practices. Part of Darling's philosophy was to rely heavily on his close confidants. Macleay, Lithgow and Dumaresq all fell into this category, and on these three fell the review and analysis of many matters requiring attention. Between 1826 and 1831 at least 27 matters were 'investigated', of which Lithgow directly participated in the following,

Board of General Purposes
Board of Trustees of the School and Clergy Council
Board of The Church and School Land Corporation
Director–Bank of New South Wales
Committee drafting responses to the attack by William Hume MP in House of Commons
Board of the Female Work Factory in Parramatta
Director–Bank of New South Wales
Committee drafting responses to the attack by Hume MP
The Land Board
Committee responding to allegations by Dr John D. Lang
Settling estate of Darling Brother-in-Law Major Ovens
Pay disputes for public servants
Work practices and employment numbers in the public service
Committee on operating an independent government printing office
Committee to improve work practices in the commissary
Committee on assignment practices for convicts
Committee reviewing operations of the post office and the naval officer–both were made salaried positions in lieu of commissioned or fee positions.

From this listing of his committees and boards, Lithgow obviously had a very heavy work schedule on top of his duties as head of Commissary accounts and as the acting private secretary to Governor Darling. He sat on, and wrote reports for, committees dealing with 15 of the 27 matters referred to the 'Board of General Purposes' by Darling. Most of the important roles exercised by Lithgow (as listed above) are discussed in detail elsewhere. Not all of this work occurred at any one time, but even a few extra-curricular meetings each week would be sufficient to interrupt his regular six-day week, nine hours day, work schedule.

On 13 September 1826 the British Treasury 'issued minutely detailed instructions' concerning the 'Revenue and Expenditures . . . and the mode of accounting for the same'. The instructions required a distinction to be drawn between fixed and contingent expenditures, whilst fixed were broken into long term and short term, and contingent expenditures were broken into recurrent and non-recurrent. These were relatively meaningless distinctions and the clerical costs of execution were greater than any possible benefit. Darling, based on his experience in Mauritius, had recommended even before his arrival in the new colony that the public accounts be examined by the Commissary of Military Accounts, as was the practice elsewhere. He eventually placed Lithgow (in early 1827) in charge of the reorganisation and implementation required by these Treasury instructions and relieved him of his Commissariat duties. Darling had changed his mind about third-party examination of public accounts, at least for the time being.

Darling wrote of Lithgow as 'a man of outstanding merit, who possessed a perfect knowledge of business and information on all points connected with official details'. In 1826, Lithgow's problem, as in every year thereafter, was that of having too many commitments on his time and not enough hours or assistance to complete his regular tasks of office. In part this became the Governor's responsibility. Even whilst being informed that the audit work was slipping behind (it was eventually five years in arrears) Darling kept deploying Lithgow on to more and more committees and situation analysis for his own purposes, not showing any fairness, even-handedness or concern about the Lithgow overload.

Evidence of this overload is recorded in various Governors' despatches where observations were made of the extra work being handled by Lithgow as well as the application for a salary increase by Governor Darling. It is also evidenced in the granting of this increase of £200 per annum by Lord Bathurst who further commended Lithgow for his hard work and diligence. This overload, however onerous on Lithgow, was probably in keeping with Darling's regular policy towards public servants. Having hounded convicts from the ranks of the public service, Darling endeavoured to ensure that only men of ability, hard work and integrity filled clerical positions. He offered salaries commensurate with those paid by private employers and established the principle of promotion by ability, not seniority.

Another contributing factor to the Lithgow overload was that there was unprecedented economic development in the colonial economy under Darling, and the bounds of settlement were pushed further afield, giving rise to the need for more Crown land to be surveyed, more small settlements to be surveyed, more land board adjudication and the need to build more roads, undertake still more land clearing, and promote greater productivity from the convicts. This development did not always equate to growth or boom times–in fact Darling faced a mini-recession in 1827. Lithgow was in the centre of all this activity and as number two in the public service had many responsibilities. The arrival of 16,500 convicts in the 1825-1828 period added to the burden of administration and of public administration costs. Darling understood the additional burden on the economy and on Lithgow but he paid lip service only to the problem, whilst still pouring more and more duties on Lithgow. Darling observed rather callously:

It would be impossible to point out the extent of the arrears in business generally" and he instanced the Auditor-General's office where the 'indefatigable Lithgow has been unable to do more than commence the examination of the "Store Accounts" of the government which were years in arrears'. (Governors' Despatches1828)

Darling was referring to the growth in employment but the continuing delay in being able to replenish reserves for the Commissariat from within the Colony. Demand outstripped the supply colony wide and this pressure translated into the demand for more free settlers and immigrants to replace the convicts who, although many in number, contributed less than 40% of a free worker's output in any period. (Ovens' Report)

On the larger question of convict work practices productivity and punishment, it appears that Darling and Lithgow had different opinions. On one hand the Lithgow-Ovens Report on work practices supported the cost effectiveness of convict work gangs (under proper supervision) and recommended its continuance. On the other hand Darling, having read the report, decided on a number of steps, quite contrary to Lithgow's expert opinion:

The work gangs initially included a number of unskilled convicts drawn from Brisbane's clearing parties, which had been disbanded by Darling. Darling had earlier drawn his magistrate's attention to the fact (or rather, Darling's opinion) that many convicts transported for relatively minor offences were sometimes left 'in a state of absolute idleness, at least without rendering any material service', which caused the inhabitants to 'suffer for the lack of labourers on their farms'.

The difference of opinion between Darling and Lithgow on reform of convict work practices was one of casual observation: Darling considered some of the convicts to be underemployed whilst Lithgow took the cost-benefit approach and wanted to see productive work gangs reaching their goals and targets even if some of the members were underemployed. Contrary to Brisbane's view, Darling did not believe that 'the gangs also served as a means of punishing offenders, particularly those whom settlers had returned to government as unsuitable or troublesome'. This type of offender, decided Darling, was to be transferred away from Sydney and to work in groups of 32 under the supervision of a trusted convict. They were under the overall supervision of, firstly the Civil Engineer, then the Inspector of Roads and Bridges and finally, under the Surveyor-General. For Darling it was a matter of 'out of sight, out of mind'.

Darling had supported the use of a 'hulk' in Sydney Harbour as a penal gaol for the malcontents until a larger public gaol could be built and the *Phoenix* became the vessel used for convicts sentenced in NSW. The number of inmates ranged from 84 (early 1826) to 135 (in 1828). Darling encouraged magistrates to separate repeat criminals from boys younger than 16 (who were to be sent to Carter's barracks) and newly arrived convicts who were thought to be itinerants under government care (these men were housed in Hyde Park Barracks). Although Commissioner Bigge had recorded in his report to Lord Bathurst that the Carter barracks was 'the best conducted of all the convict establishments in NSW', Darling found it necessary to make further changes and directed his aide Captain Thomas De la Condamine, together with Lithgow to conduct an enquiry into 'how to trim further the operating cost, per head, of convicts'.

On his arrival in the Colony, Condamine had been appointed military secretary without pay, and in 1827 was recommended by Darling for appointment as Collector of Internal Revenue in lieu of Captain John Piper. At that point he resigned his military commission, but the Secretary of State (Lord Bathurst) declined to confirm the appointment so, for the next two years, Condamine acted as private secretary at a salary of £300 per annum and then as Clerk of the Legislative and Executive Councils with a further £800 per annum. Condamine's were in the traditions of the military–loyalty, compromise and future reward. He joined Lithgow in other roles, and became number two in ranking to Lithgow when the office of Colonial Treasury was diminished by the appointment of Charles Riddell, who fell into open conflict with the Governor, the Legislative council and most of the Government Department heads.

The Lithgow/Condamine Report recommended closer supervision over all convict barracks in order to trim rations, establish better work practices and operate the barracks at a cheaper cost per head. Darling also decided to treat the 'boys' aged 17-20 in a different way. They were to be kept separate from the older men; they were to be trained in a skill such as carpentry, stonecutting, shoemaking, blacksmithing or rope-making. They were to be instructed in writing, reading, and ciphering by a schoolmaster, John Kingsmill, who was appointed in March 1826. Kingsmill wrote a lengthy report, including a syllabus and lessons and it became part of the history of early education in NSW.

Darling's biggest concern was for the inmates of the Female Factory at Parramatta, founded in 1804 by Governor King and, due to overcrowding, redesigned by Greenway and re-built during the Macquarie era. The Factory served as a place of confinement for women convicts who were not in private employment. The inmates were employed in the factory knitting socks and manufacturing convicts clothing ('slops'), sheets, nightcaps, hats and shirts. Although the building was relatively new, conditions in the factory left much to be desired and a Grand Jury, which made an inspection in August 1825, drew attention to the poor food, shortage of beds, shoes, and clothing which existed. Darling appointed a Board of Enquiry in March 1826, to which Lithgow was seconded as the Governor's representative. After its initial report, the Board continued in existence as the Board of Management to oversee operations. The next disagreement between Darling and the managers of the Factory was about its size and usage. Darling wanted female convicts to be assigned as quickly as possible, in other words to be put to productive work and off the expense of the government. The managers disagreed with this approach to welfare: they felt the system concentrated more of profit that rehabilitation or training.

On 14 October 1831, Governor Darling received his recall and embarked shortly thereafter for England. Lithgow was associated with most, if not all, of these matters due to his main Board positions:

The Board of the Female Factory
The Land Board
The Board of the Clergy and Schools Lands

However, Lithgow was to equally serve the needs of Darling's successors, during the full terms of Governors Bourke and Gipps. It is of value to repeat the highlights of these next two administrations and determine the extent of Lithgow's influence.

However, first, why did Darling have such a profound effect on Lithgow, and why did Lithgow demonstrate such talents, interest and commitment to the Public Service during Darling's governorship? Lithgow planned on making the public service a career for life and resolved to be both likeable and charismatic. He got on well with his colleagues as well as the governors and colonial secretary and became a favourite of Darling. Although Darling's high opinion of Lithgow was grounded in his experience in Mauritius and led to his recommendations of Lithgow to join him in the Colony of NSW, Lithgow obviously had a different view of Darling to that held by the general population. Lithgow saw in Darling, a man of vision and compassion.

Lithgow supported Darling's vision for a master road system, especially the second of the 'great roads' which ran from Parramatta to the Goulburn Plains, and by late 1826 the 'track' had already reached Goulburn. Under Darling the track was re-routed and converted into a properly constructed road, thus reducing the journey. Lithgow had more than a little self-interest in this 'vision' as his sheep run at Gundagai used this Goulburn road for most of its access and delivery of livestock. Darling's compassion can be seen in his adoption of the 'trial by jury' legislation, also supported by Lithgow, and the attitude of the Governor to the concern Major Mitchell had of his own well being in the colony.

An explanation of this special Lithgow/Darling relationship is possible. Lithgow was young; he had risen quickly to the number one financial posting in the colonial Commissariat, and had became adept at understanding the governor's intentions in policy matters that required the transparency of a committee or Board. He was the governor's main man in the financial affairs of the Colony. The official role of Colonial Secretary was in transition, from private secretary (under Macquarie) to number one public servant. As senior non-political officer, the Colonial Secretary during the Darling Administration was Alexander Macleay, and his understudy was Edward Deas Thomson. Darling was influenced greatly in his judgement by figures and statements of accounts, rather than being confronted by a wide range of people each with demands and requests. Not all governors were interested in or influenced by the Statements of Financial Affairs of the Colony as expressed in the Blue Books. That Lithgow had known and worked with Darling in Mauritius was a great advantage generally, and especially in the colony of NSW, as patronage was the source of nearly all promotions and progress up the ladder. Darling became Lithgow's effective patron after he had specifically requested Lithgow's services in the Colony and continued to promote him. Lithgow never again had the strong personal support of a governor although he grew to respect most of the governors he served. When Darling was recalled and returned to England, the community was jubilant with signs all across the town, and banner headlines in T*he Australian* of 'He's Going!' A large crowd jeered Darling on the Dock, as he embarked. Lithgow, on the other hand, was unhappy (expressed in a letter to Commissary Boyes in Hobart–ML) at having to undergo another change, even though by word of mouth, Bourke's reputation as a successful leader had preceded him. Lithgow was appreciative of the kind words Darling had written about him to London and the knowledge that his position in the colony was secure.

Governor Sir Richard Bourke–1831-1837

Bourke may only have overseen the Colony for six years, but they were most successful and filled with many highlights. 12 of these high events are set down to demonstrate Bourke's inclination towards economic and financial planning, and his apparent pre-occupation with appropriations, budgets and financial statements. Lithgow was an active participant in the fiscal matters and grew to respect Bourke, to the extent he contributed a significant sum to the Monument fund to erect a statue when Bourke retired.

Major-General Sir Richard Bourke KCB arrived in the colony on 2 December 1831. He called the Legislative Council into session and immediately re-presented the Jury Act of 1829, which had expired at the close of 1831. Lithgow, as a magistrate (appointed in January 1827 on Darling's recommendation), supported this Act through the Legislative Council.

Bourke advised his Council, in June 1832, that 'an abstract of the Revenue and Expenditure' for the colony would be submitted, as also would 'Estimates of the Probable Expenditure of the current year and of the Supplies by which the Expenditure would be defrayed'. This abstract of Revenue and Expenditure was a giant leap forward in Colonial financial reform, and was encouraged and supported by Lithgow. It was the first time than that an appropriation Bill was presented in the Legislative Council. The situation had become disturbing. With Lithgow's delay in auditing government records before they could be recorded in the Blue Books, the Council relied on Lithgow's verbal assurances that the Colony was financially secure, but now the legislative system could be vastly improved and the presentation of the Appropriation Bill offered the Councillors a picture of the departmental and Governor's plans for the colony. They became the predecessor of the annual budget. In presenting an address to the Council on Thursday 19 January 1832, Bourke is recorded in *Votes and Proceedings* as saying

"the abstract will be accompanied by Estimates of the Probable expenditure of last year, and of the supplies by which the expenditure is to be defrayed. To these estimates I request you give your particular attention, and that you will give your opinion upon them in detail: and, I assure you, I shall feel great satisfaction in diminishing any expenditure that may be shown to be necessary. You will perceive in these estimates several items made chargeable to the colony, which have not previously been brought forward, but have been left as a matter of account between the Colonial Government and the Commissary. A claim has been made by the Commissary against the Colonial Government, and it will be for you to adjust this claim to its speedy liquidation. No arrear of this kind is likely to occur again." (V & P 1832)

Bourke also advised the Council that 'the revenues of the last year (1831) had been unusually productive, and a considerable balance remained in the Treasury after discharging all demands against it'. (Official *History of NSW* and V & P 1832)

Bourke advised his Council during this first session that he would be recommending in the appropriations additional provision for extra support of public schools and places of religious worship. The formation of roads and the repairs and erection of public buildings required particular attention as they had fallen into disrepair under Darling. The Board of General Purposes, on which Lithgow sat, had prioritised expenditures within the Colony.

'No progress had yet been made in the disposal of Crown Lands suggested under the latest Royal Instructions (of 1831 to Darling). The new system (confirmed Bourke) would be strictly adhered to, and it would tend to the improvement of the colony in the most essential respects.' Bourke, encouraged by Lithgow, thought that if the land plans was implemented revenues from Crown land sales would remain in the colony and be available to the Colonial treasury and government. Both Bourke and Lithgow were very surprised when word was received that the revenue was to remain the sole entitlement of the British Treasury and it would be used it to offset past contributions to the cost of establishing the Colony. However, we learn from the V & P, that the authorities had not planned on the strenuous exceptions and opposition from leading colonists including non-official members of the Legislative Council. This unexpected opposition caught government officials by surprise and without any cogent explanations or rational policy. W.C. Wentworth led the opposition, whilst the Council formed a general committee to advise the governor, Lithgow participating in this committee's deliberations. Wentworth was not easily convinced of the bona fides of the British argument of 'terra nullius' and did not accept that the land was theirs by right and legal claim. Wentworth was also aware of the broken promises by Britain that had cost the colony dearly. Lithgow had submitted the report that supported the numbers stated by Wentworth as to the cost to the Colony. Lithgow, and Wentworth, had rightfully claimed that the British had committed to support the Colony's convict costs, whilst other 'operating' costs by the Colony through local revenue.

Governor King had commenced raising local revenues in 1800 by applying duties to all imports. By 1831, when Bourke arrived as Governor, the Colony was doing quite well with its revenue raising, and for the year 1832 raised £135,847 in revenue over which the Council had authority to disburse that sum in aid and support of the colonists. Wentworth's valid complaint was that the British Treasury had promised to meet the costs of the operating the Colony's police and gaols, but had then reneged on this promise. Darling had supported the Council in this cause, but Bourke was yet to be convinced to oppose the British position. By compromise on the question of disbursing land sales revenue, Wentworth led the Council (supported by Lithgow) into an arrangement whereby the revenue would be used to financially support a migrant sponsorship scheme, allocating up to 50% of the total revenues. In British eyes this would assist in relocating the poor and lower class people of Britain to the NSW. As a concession to the Anglican Church and its local missionary endeavours, the agreement also extended 15% of the revenues to aid and assist the colony's 'natives and aboriginal peoples', this move being strongly supported by the Rev'd Samuel Marsden. Lithgow had been an initial supporter of retaining Crown land sales revenue within the Colony to reduce the high imposition of import duties on all foodstuffs, clothing, furniture and consumer goods. He disputed (V & P 1833) the idea that Britain had sovereignty over all land, and remarked that the Canadian system was more appropriate. However, realising that his argument would be overturned by Westminster, he espoused the Bourke compromise position of keeping 50% of the revenues, not as consolidated revenues but as the means of paying for immigrants to be brought to the Colony as better than no position. Lithgow was closely involved in the preparation of the estimates and, as a member of the Board of General Purposes, he was partially responsible for the Colony's planning expenditure priorities; he became responsible for submitting the unaudited and incomplete expense records to the Council for the past year.

Formation of the new Land board

During the Council Session of 1833, Bourke submitted a Bill for Appointing and Empowering Commissioners to hear and determine upon claims to grants of land under the great seal of the Colony of New South

Wales. This was passed on 28 August 1833 and, as a result, Lithgow was appointed a Commissioner of the Land Board.

On that same day, the Clerk of the Legislative Council tabled a report by the Sydney Cove Redevelopment Committee, which had been appointed on 12 July 1833 'to examine certain plans and report, relating to the construction of a Quay at the head of Sydney Cove'. Lithgow had been a member of that Committee, chaired by Charles Cowper, which was established to review the development options for the Cove, as well as cost the proposed engineering and construction work. The committee heard competing interests from the Commissariat operators and the Campbell stores over allocation of wharfage space, and from merchants and ferrymen over the exact purposes of the Cove. Engineering plans were sketched showing conversion plans for the low tide mud flats to an area of filled-base able to support new wharves adjacent to the point of deep water sufficient for ferries, barges and even ocean going sailing vessels.

The Land Board was initially established to reconcile policies differences of the grant system and the new system for the sale of land. Considerations demanded of the Land Board included:

Who would be entitled to purchase land, and on what terms and conditions
Would speculation in land be tolerated
Would squatting be accepted on Crown land
What would the capital needs be for purchasers of crown lands
Should development and improvement of purchased land be demanded within a certain time

On a more mundane administrative question, the collection of payments from sales, as well as quit-rents and fees was to be determined. Was this a treasury function or a Land board function? By default, Lithgow was made responsible for these and other fiscal matters.

The Council took heart about the decision to use half of the land sales revenue for immigration purposes when Bourke tabled a report showing that between 1829 and 1831 over 1,430 unassisted immigrants had arrived whilst sponsored immigrants numbered 1,253. The overall level of assisted immigration was high, with 47% of those immigrating between 1829 and 1831 being directly assisted and 34% between 1833 and 1840. The cost to the Government was high, especially as the shipping companies increased their prices for travel to the colony, when they learnt that the government was paying the passage. The general opinion was that the migrant intake would swell the colonial population if greater sponsorship and attractive work prospects were to be offered. In 1833 these numbers grew to 6,021 of which 2,045 were assisted. Lithgow also sat on the Immigration (Advisory) committee.

In July 1834, Bourke laid on the table of the Council a *Bill for regulating the affairs of the late Church and School Lands Corporation*. By this Bill all lands and other property belonging to the old corporation were declared to be vested in the Crown, and a new commission was to be established. Lithgow had sat on the board of the Church and School Land Corporation and Bourke now him to sit as a Trustee on this new Commission.

On 18 September 1835, the Commission on Immigration brought up their final Report. Lithgow, still an ordinary member of the committee, had been charged with recommending the means by which a variety of immigrants could be attracted to the settlement, the cost and the source of funds from which to pay for the cost of subsidising them. The report opined that:

'. . . the funds arising from the sale of lands should be appropriated exclusively for the purpose of introducing a moral and industrious population; that they considered this appropriation alike indispensable to the present interests, and the future prosperity and character of the colony; and that they regarded the opinion expressed by the Secretary of State, and approved by the Lords of the Treasury, in the light of a pledge by His Majesty's Government that the Crown lands of the colony should be held sacred to the promotion of immigration.'

This debate is further discussed when the *Sydney Gazette* editorial comments are outlined a little later in this work. The 1836 session of the Legislative Council commenced with a speech by Bourke in which he announced that:

'. . . in no former year had the Revenue equalled the amount of the last year, nor had the exports and imports been so large. The influx of foreign capital had been considerable. Collegiate and Educational Institutions had been established, and a taste for fine arts was beginning to show itself. To extend the blessings of wholesome education to the poorer classes, it was necessary to introduce a system of general instruction. Considerable progress had been made in the general improvement and completion of the great lines of road throughout the colony.'

Lithgow and Major Evans had also sat on the committee overseeing future planning for roads and inland settlements and had guided the Colony in recording and reporting on the overall state of the financial accounts. To the question of whether Lithgow influenced colonial revenues, the answer must be that with his interest in and commitment to economic development, decentralisation, new settlements and communications, Lithgow's influence was considerable and he made a significant contribution to improving economic conditions in the Colony and of raising levels of colonial revenue.

Lithgow's close association with Ovens may well have been influenced by the fact that both were educated for the Church, Lithgow in Scotland and Ovens in Ireland. This committee role was the start of a lifelong interest in immigration to the Colony that Lithgow pursued vigorously in the Legislative Council. During 1836, Lithgow's Land Board reported that for the previous year (1835), land sales revenue was a gross £131,998.10.3 of which only £11,139.15.3 was spent on assisted migration. These figures meant that the Immigration Committee's hope of having sufficient funds to continue to attract a high level of suitable immigrants could be achieved.

Lithgow sponsored a bill presented to the Council on 28 June 1836, restraining the unauthorised occupation of Crown lands. He remarked (*Sydney Herald* 29.6.1836) that the 'interference of the government had lately been sought by a number of respectable colonists, who represented that the commission of various offences was occasioned and promoted by the indiscriminate occupation of these lands'. He may well have been speaking and acting on behalf of the Governor, whose intentions were to assist the pastoralists and spurn the growth of the squattocracy.

Lithgow assisted on the fringe of inland exploration in an unusual way. His interest had been in the pastoral area for some time, suggesting that his parents may have been property owners in Scotland and Lithgow himself may have grown up on a small holding. However, Lithgow encouraged the exploration of the Riverina district, after Hume had made his first southern trek. He also befriended Mitchell, the colonial Surveyor-General whom he knew well from mutual membership on the Land Board, and encouraged him to survey the Riverina area as a priority. Mitchell was also helpful in selecting for Lithgow a riverfront sheep run in the Gundagai-Monaro region. Lithgow was thus allowed to operate this earliest of sheep runs, through a Manager, at present day Gundagai but never once did he visit the site. Bourke had sponsored Major Mitchell by fitting out, at public expense, an expedition to follow the Darling River from its source in the Dividing Ranges to the Murray. Mitchell had also come to Lithgow seeking advice on the question of personal liability as a member of the expedition. Lithgow arranged a letter indemnity (of questionable worth) to soothe Mitchell's concerns, and the expedition moved off and achieved its goal.

When Bourke decided to retire and return home to England, Lithgow joined numerous other colonists in subscribing money for a statue of Sir Richard Bourke which now stands in the Macquarie Street entrance to the Governor's Domain bearing an appropriate inscription. This shows another side of the Lithgow character, suggesting he had strong bonds of loyalty and great respect for those whom he served.

Bourke left the colony on 5 December 1837 and the settlement, after 50 years of existence, was a much better place for the five years of his administration. Bourke had guided a very active and successful economy, with low levels of unemployment, solid growth, and well-deserved material gains for its citizens. In his first year revenue amounted to £135,847; it had risen to over £354,800 in his last year. In the same five years (1832-1837), population, grew from 53,524 to 85,267.

Although Bourke may have taken over the economy in an upward cycle, it is not always the case that a successor can maintain the momentum of growth. In Bourke's case, he not only maintained an upward trend but also improved on it. His successor was not as lucky; having inherited a strong economy, he led it into decline and then watched it enter the worst recession in the Colony's short history–the recession of 1842-43. Sir George Gipps did not enjoy the people's respect for very long. If Bourke had served at an opportune time, then Gipps served at an inopportune time, at least economically. Every governor had strengths and weaknesses but each left his mark on the Colony and the public service. Gipps left an indelible impression on the whole colonial economy

Governor Sir George Gipps–1838-1846

Gipps was the Colony's ninth governor, taking over a strong economy from Richard Bourke. However, the Colony's economic growth could not be sustained for, l even in Gipp's first year, total revenue fell far short of that of Bourke during his last year. Before long Gipps would find that the speculative bubble would burst and the Colony would be plunged into its biggest depression to date. The Colony had faced a series of peaks and troughs in its short economic history but the Depression of 1842-44 was man-made and largely underpinned by events in Britain. It was a real setback to the Colony and, although it was short-lived, it affected many settlers and took its toll on major financial institutions.

Through all these years, Lithgow was the Auditor-General but he did not admire or support Gipps in the same way he admired and supported Bourke and his predecessors. Lithgow's approach is evident in the tenor of his reports and writings, and his overall attitude towards the Colony during this period. Gipps did not accept Lithgow's explanations as to why the Blue Books were late in being despatched to London, especially since Gipps was on the receiving end of growing correspondence from the Lords of the Treasury as well as the Audit Board within the British Treasury. In one response to an enquiry from the money 'Lords' Gipps, not known for his loyalty or support of senior public servants (this observation comes from a private letter from his Colonial Secretary to a friend), wrote to the Treasury in London that he would dismiss Lithgow if the delays were not corrected and all the late reports were not brought up to date quickly. As we have already observed, the delays were not justified but could be explained and in fact, the fault lay mostly in the accounting system, which had been imposed unilaterally on the Colonial treasury, rather than on

Lithgow or his office management. That the delay was in the understaffed and poorly managed local Treasury rather than in the audit office did not concern Gipps, but does show that Lithgow was considered to be the senior Public Servant of his day, on whose shoulders the blame for Gipps' problem could be laid. Having been threatened with dismissal, Lithgow hastily caught up the arrears in the Blue Books and delivered five years of arrears in less than 12 months. This does not suggest prior laziness on Lithgow's part, but rather correction of an underlying problem (changing the audit processes) and a lot of extra hard work by Lithgow and his staff.

One can review each year of the Blue Books and determine where Lithgow cut corners in order to deliver current information. During this period, there is a growing number of arithmetic errors which would not have been normally been made and, if they did occur, they would have been detected and corrected before going into print. Many may have been simple transposition errors, when figures were being transferred from operating reports to the Blue Books, which were a compilation. Many 'project' costs were not complete in the year during which the funds were allocated, and Lithgow effectively anticipated the necessary changes to the system and made them in advance of their promulgation. The intent was not compromised and the overall system provides the required information; however, it is the numeric accuracy that is in question and left wanting.

In June 1838, an interim report from the Committee for Immigration (of which Lithgow was a member) was presented showing that the total number of immigrants in 1838 was 7,580 of which 4,480 were assisted immigrants. These numbers continued to grow, and the Colony benefited from their influx. However, with the coming financial crisis in 1842, this increase in assisted migration was not helpful. The number of unemployed men also grew and the Colonial administration eventually had to step in and create paid work for this rising tide of out-of-work settlers.

Gipps faced growing problems within his Legislative council, whose members wanted more authority and independence from the Crown and British Parliament. There are 12 major events, most of which involved Lithgow, that marked Gipp's administration:

By 1838, the Port Phillip district had attracted a large number of immigrants, as agriculturalists, merchants and general settlers. With regard to disposal of land to the people, the Historical Records of Victoria and of Australia inform us:

'Sir George Gipps, anxious to fill the public treasury, adopted the policy of throwing into the market only a small quantity of land in proportion to the demand. Consequently, the price of land in the Port Phillip district became enormously high, and the settlers were therefore handicapped by having to part with so much of their capital in purchasing the land. Lithgow as a member of the overseeing Board (the Land Board) did not agree with this Gipps policy, but remained supportive of building up overall revenue from Port Phillip in order to balance revenue and expense in the latest southern settlement.' (HRV 7: 228)

'The extensive immigration which was taking place was attended by a large influx of British capital. There were only three banks then in existence–the Bank of New South Wales (on which Lithgow sat as a director and as the government representative), the Bank of Australia (in which Lithgow was a charter stockholder) and the Commercial Banking Company.' (HRA I: 6 p742)

With only these three banks, the amount of new deposits was almost overwhelming and created two problems. An overload situation existed for the three banks creating difficulties in finding sufficient qualified or experienced staff to handle the situation. Most new staff was brought in from the City of London. The second problem was the opportunity for new banks to arrived and set up operations. With virtually no prudential supervision, the new banks were not well regulated or managed and, as branch banks from England, were remitting their bills and notes back to their head offices for discounting and negotiation.

The government, through the Colonial treasury, was a depositor of large amounts into local banks, being the proceeds of land sales. The average interest rate was of 4 % but Gipps insisted on a rate of 7-7.5%. This he obtained but, in order to pay this rate, the banks had to enlarge their discount rate (from an average 10% to over 12%) in order to support the higher borrowing rate. Lithgow, as a director of the Bank of New South

Wales, was placed in the invidious position of co-signing the letter from the Bank to Gipps in which the dire consequences of this new policy was spelled out. By increasing the discount rate, the banks believed they had crossed the margin of safety as the

'. . . rage for speculation now seized the colonial public with even greater vehemence than during the sheep and cattle mania of Darling's time; the most unbounded extravagances of living were now indulged in; everyone bought land and livestock at enormous prices, till at last, the obligations to the banks came due and the inevitable crash came.' (Official History of NSW)

The Bank of Australia was involved in the ruin, and fell in June 1842. Lithgow's investment of approx £500 was now worthless; he, too, had gambled and lost.

A great outcry also followed Gipps' interference in the squatters' rights as to Crown land; meetings were held; inflammatory speeches were delivered; petitions were signed, and new organisations came into being. A society called 'The Pastoral Association of NSW' was formed, as was the Stockowners Society of which Lithgow was a sponsor and a committeeman. Although this was not a direct conflict of interest for Lithgow, he stood to gain personally from having stronger banks, an organised pastoral sector, stronger land laws and government control of squatters.

With the separation of Port Phillip. the next particularly difficult issue was the legislation introduced concerning New Zealand. Lithgow was a member of the standing committee of the Legislative Council that determined the course of the bill in the Council. Lithgow argued in the Council that, if the New Zealand Land policy had been introduced in the Colony of NSW, most of the problems faced by the Land Board would not have existed. The *Sydney Morning Herald* reported the matter in this way:

'Up to the time that New Zealand was taken under the protection of the British Crown, the sovereignty of the chiefs as ruling over an independent people had been admitted, and their flag was acknowledged in such ports as their vessels had visited; the declaration of independence by the confederated chiefs had been approved, and ordered to be printed as a State paper by the Home government. In a recent treaty between Captain Hobson and the NZ chiefs the latter agreed to forgo their right of selling land to any but the British government, thus giving the Crown the right of pre-emption: but if the chiefs had never had that right, why were they called upon by that treaty to relinquish that which they never possessed?

Wentworth argued, in the course of a long address to the Council, that for a proclamation to be binding, it must be founded upon some law previously existent; and if the proclamations in question were founded upon law it was for those who had issued them to show what the law was. The principle contained in the preamble of the New Zealand Bill–that no chiefs, or other individuals of tribes of uncivilised savages, had any right to dispose of the lands–occupied by them–was at variance with British law and the Law of Nations, claimed Wentworth. The 'Law of Nations' assumed that the Queen Victoria had a right to the island by virtue of discovery, but that assumption was denied by Governor Gipps, who in response, stated that discovery gave no right to the occupation of an inhabited country; nor would the Law of Nations acknowledge the property and sovereignty of any nation, unless it had really taken actual possession, and had formed actual settlements, or made actual use of the country' (SMH 25.6.1838)

In his formal reply to the debate over the Bill on colonising New Zealand, Gipps addressed the Council at great length in refutation of the positions maintained by the members in opposition to the Bill. Gipps stated inter alia

'Firstly, the uncivilised aboriginal inhabitants of any country had always been held to have but a qualified dominion over it, or a right of occupancy only; and that until they established among themselves a settled form of government, and subjugated the ground to their own uses, which, by the cultivation of it, they could not grant to individuals, not of their own tribe, any portion of it, for the simple reason that they had not themselves any individual property in it.

Secondly, if a settlement were to be made in any such country by a civilised power, the right of pre-emption of the soil, or in other words, the right of extinguishing the native title, was exclusively in the government of that power, and could not be enjoyed by individuals without the consent of that Government.

Thirdly, neither individuals, nor bodies of men belonging to any nation, could form colonies except with the consent and under the direction and control of their own government; and that from any settlement which they might form without the consent of their government they might be ousted; so as far as Englishmen were concerned, colonies could not be formed without the consent of the Crown.'

This statement, as reported in the *Sydney Morning Herald* of 25 June 1838, was really not to Lithgow's liking (he had opposed the bill when first introduced into the Legislative Council). As a licentiate of the Church of Scotland and a long-term civil servant, with previous postings to two other colonies, Lithgow was not so much concerned about the legality of occupancy of the land but, as a Land Board member, he was interested in the right of the Crown to sell that occupied land. Lithgow stood damned if any threatened legal challenge was made to the legality of the Land Board's operations. Public servants held no indemnification against wrong doing as was evidenced when, after ten years of revenue-raising in the colony, the Governors' actions in imposing such duty had to be validated by a back-dated Act of the House of Commons, this move offering indemnity of a limited variety to the Governors and senior government officials.

The gain in land sales revenue was almost frightening in the rapidity of its growth. It had been proposed:

'. . . under the permission which had been given by the Lords of the Treasury, to apply to the ordinary expenses of the colony those portions of Crown Revenue which were derived from Quit rents, leases, licenses to use crown lands, and which formed no portion of the funds application to immigration.' (HRA I: 7 P334)

Lithgow proposed charging the Land Fund with the expense of each survey, as well as the cost of land clearing by convict work gangs, and enforcing payment of a portion of the arrears of quit rents in order to cover a portion of the expense incurred in the erection of churches and schoolhouses. The balance of the cost of building would come from the sale, from time to time, of portion of the extensive estates of the late Church and School Corporation, under the general instructions received from the British Government. This later recommendation is also attributed to Lithgow. Lithgow wrote to his friend Boyes 'Crown lands had been wonderfully productive and had contributed very largely to the means of keeping up immigration.' (Crowley: Select documents)

The protest successfully raised by Wentworth about the Colony being charged with the whole expense of the Police and Gaol establishment was also signed by Sir John Jamison and John Blaxland and transmitted to the Secretary of State in London for further review. Lithgow had also voted in favour of this action as a means of determining the validity of a potential debt by the British Treasury to the Colony of an amount in excess of £700,000. Hannibal Macarthur, nephew of John Macarthur, presented further resolutions to the Council, to the effect that Britain should at least share half of the costs of police and gaol operations. This protest commenced a 'running sore' in the colony, and pitted the British Government against just about every free settler who was outraged against the actions of the home government.

Returns by the Immigration Committee show that at the peak of the speculative period in land purchases, there was still a high level of immigration to the Colony, at a time when immigration to the United States was both closer and cheaper. The returns showed that for 1840 the immigrant numbers rose to 8,536, only 513 of whom were unassisted, the assistance costing £156,760.1.10, or £19.10.0 per head. This successful assisted-immigration program met the targets set by the Lithgow led Board of Immigration Advisers, and established a pool of labour upon which the growing industrial base of the colonial economy could draw upon. Had it not been for the Gipps-sponsored financial crisis, this would have brought about a competing source of manufacturing in the Colony, sufficient to replace most of the imported manufactured goods which had dominated the colonial market since the first settlement.

The Governor addressed the Council on 6 July 1840 and congratulated its members on the marked increase in revenues for the past year. Ordinary revenue showed a full 31% increase over the previous year whilst Crown revenue increased more than 100%. The Governor credited (or blamed) speculation in land as being the main reason for the increase. Lithgow, being responsible for land sales, was torn (policy wise) between wanting to sell more land, thus raising much needed revenues but creating speculation in the market through growing numbers of absentee landlords, or continuing with the steady 'status quo'. He supported the non-inflationary aspect of land sales and thus 'maintenance of the status quo', so that local buyers could afford to purchase larger holdings and create a network of family farms. However, the speculators won and their efforts led to the big financial crisis of 1842. The nature of the land market in the Colony was speculative with reducing interest in broad acre purchases. The rising cost of livestock and the shortage of experienced herdsmen had contributed to this lack of interest but, if more land had been released for sale, this could have helped control speculation. The price of land was high because it was being kept in short supply artificially and the only purchasers were wealthy absentee landlords who wanted a speculative outlet in the colonies. The Land Board had considerable power over the market in terms of supply but interest rates in England were much lower than those in the Colony (again a matter of supply and demand) and this further added to the speculative market from overseas.

Under Gipps, the population almost doubled from 97,912 to 181,556; general revenue and imports fell per head of population whilst exports and land under cultivation rose proportionately. Gipps' contribution was an important one, although he did not appear to handle the depression very appropriately, and the economy was driven by speculation rather than solid economic growth.

At the time of Gipps' retirement in July 1846, Lithgow had been in government service in the Colony for 22 years. He was still upset by the threat of dismissal by Gipps and his disappointment and at being treated so harshly led to thoughts of retirement. He disposed of his Hunter's Hill property and of his Gundagai pastoral run and commenced development of the Hunter River property he had acquired not long before. He was obviously taking his retirement planning very seriously. Because of the nature of his work and the associated forward commitments, the training of junior staff and the long period required for transfer of a senior job to more junior people, it took Lithgow a further six years to put his house in order. During this time he saw the needs of the new governor met and hoped he could be the beneficiary of one final promotion to the pinnacle post of the Colonial public service, the position of Colonial-Secretary. He had briefly tasted the position but it had eluded him for so long and it by-passed him again in his last years before retirement. From the seclusion of the Legislative Council, he watched while the railway movement began, gold was discovered near his namesake town and the Colony experienced its first taste of real independence with the Self-Government bill of 1850. However, he was tired and unwell and his final decision to retire was communicated to Fitz Roy in 185. He departed the role of Auditor-General in mid-1852, Gipps reluctantly giving him a pension of not quite 'half-pay' which, although generous (in policy terms), was miserly in terms of over 40 years of Government service.

Governor Sir Charles A. Fitz Roy–1846-1854

Fitz Roy was the fifth and last Governor that Lithgow served. When Lithgow retired in 1852 at the age of 68, he had been in the service of the public for nearly 50 years, serving four monarchs, eight Secretaries of State and five Governors. As we review some of the highlights of the Fitz Roy period, a few things should be kept in mind:

Lithgow was still a member of the Land Board as well as a Legislative Councillor. Fitz Roy's administration was almost scuttled by disputes about land prices, failing land sales and squatters.

A second matter to which Lithgow had a great deal to contribute and which occupied a lot of the Council's time was that of abandoning or retaining the transportation program.

With Lithgow's extensive practical knowledge of the affairs of the Colony, he was frequently selected to sit on Council committees established to consider a new constitution for the post-self-governing colony

The question of steam communication, by boat from London and of railways, also occupied a lot of Council time.

Much of Fitz Roy's time was spent working with the Legislative Council and its members. Unlike his predecessors, Fitz Roy delegated work to and through his departmental heads and liaised with senior members of the colony in order to reach consensus. His actions formulated a people's consensus, as well as holding the Legislative Council to the highest standards of a House of Review. This methodology eased the way for implementing the proposed self-governing principle of a bicameral system, using dual Houses of Parliament.

Although Lithgow's re-appointment to the Legislative Council had been ratified as one of the 12 non-elected members on 4 June 1850 for a six year period, his health had deteriorated. At the same time his commitment to retire from active public life had grown, and he retired on the 8 June 1852.

Fitz Roy assumed office from Gipps on 2 August 1846 and immediately called the Legislative Council into session. Some of the more significant highlights of the Charles A. Fitz Roy years, include:

Fitz Roy pleaded for the Council to support his agenda, in particular allowing him to promote the plans and instructions of the British Colonial Office. In his Opening Speech, he stated that: 'The estimates would be submitted with full reliance on the liberality of the Council to make such provision as the exigencies of the public service might require, and the prosperity of the public revenue might warrant.' (V & P 1846)

Land sales became and remained a contentious and difficult issue right through the Fitz Roy administration. Lithgow found himself caught in the middle but did agree with the earliest thoughts of the Council. Mr Robert Lowe moved a series of resolutions on the price at which land should be sold and the Council carried the resolution "that the raising of the minimum upset price of land, first to 12s and afterwards to One pound, has rendered wasteland unsaleable", by 12 votes to 7. Lowe had been made a magistrate for the County of Cumberland by Governor Macquarie in 1820. He took an active part in the affairs of Campbelltown district and was a member of the Agricultural Stock Club, vice-president of the Benevolent Society (together with Lithgow), and supported the Native Institution and the Society for Promoting Christian Knowledge amongst the Aborigines of NSW. His submission to Commissioner Bigge was that 'the prisoners would be better reformed if employed in agriculture than if kept in town, that if unskilled convicts could not obtain such work they should be placed in roads gangs and that tickets-of-leave were too readily granted'. (ADB)

The Governor tabled a despatch from the Secretary of State for the Colonies (Rt. Hon William. Gladstone) on 7 October 1846 announcing the intention of Her Majesty's Government not to alter the practice of transportation as far as NSW was concerned, without the general approval of the Colony, or of the portion of the Colony affected by such alteration. Lithgow was of two minds on this matter. On one hand he recognised that the growth in the Colony, especially manufacturing and exports, would be slowed unless additional labour became available. On the other hand, there was an enormous potential to attract free immigration, especially if there was a continuation of sponsored settlers bringing capital with them. The Colony had the perfect opportunity to move ahead as a free community, without convicts driving the growth. A Select Committee was formed with W.C. Wentworth as Chairman to analyse the consequences of abolishing transportation and he presented a petition to the Council, supported by the vast majority of settlers from all areas, opposing the 'revival of transportation.' The Committee's Report was, in effect, a tacit agreement with the Secretary of State's despatch, with recommendations for the 'importation of equal numbers of females and males, simultaneous immigration and the non-aggregation of convicts in masses'. The response was that the last boatload of convicts was rejected by both Victoria and NSW but reluctantly accepted into Moreton Bay. Only Western Australia wanted to accept more convicts but even that policy was short-lived when the British government placed a high cost for transportation housing, protection and supporting the convicts on the receiving colony.

Another Select Committee was appointed on 16 September 1846, 'to take into consideration the best means of establishing steam communication between the colony and England'. Lithgow chaired this committee, which reported on 27 October recommending the adoption of a route via Singapore and Torres Straits. As a means of providing for the expense, 'it is proposed to charge 1shilling on all letters transmitted by ship, payable at the place of despatch; and also that there should be a small charge on newspapers'.

The anti-transportation movement held further rallies in Sydney early in 1847 and then spread to Port Phillip. There was still concern that the rump of the pro-transportation movement could cause Britain to reconsider its policy, especially in Victoria which had never directly benefited from this 'free' source of labour.

Fitz Roy declared that the colony was in good shape economically and could afford to support by local financial means the subsidised immigration movement, which had been left without funds when land sales revenue declined. On 4 May 1847, the Council was informed that:

'. . . the amount already at the credit of the Crown revenue would enable the Government to pay off, in the course of the current year, the whole of the outstanding debentures, amounting to nearly 100,000 pound, which were issued to meet the expenses of immigration in former years. This would leave territorial revenue wholly unencumbered, and Governor Fitz Roy had strongly recommended to the British government resumption of immigration sufficient to recruit 5,000 statute adults.' (Official History of NSW)

Fitz Roy recognised that there was still a pressing demand for a further supply of labour: and he had been impressed with the 'persuasion that a regular and copious supply of labour was necessary to promote and maintain the chief objects of colonial industry'. (*Official History of NSW*)

In submitting the estimates for 1848, the Governor regretted having to state that certain areas of expenditure was being curtailed due to revenue shortfall, due to tonnage duties being reduced to one half; the reduction on duties for spirits; reduction of wharfage duties; and reduction on the assessment of livestock. Over the last four years this loss of revenue had amounted to nearly £30,000 per annum and he trimmed the public works budget by the same amount. This was not a bad move, as labour shortages would have increased government employment at the expense of the private sector with a further push on labour rates.

In 1846 Land sales revenue had fallen to one quarter of that of 1837, because of the commercial depression of 1842-43. In fact with the price now set at £1 per acre, between 1842 and 1846 the sum realised by land sales was two-thirds that of the year 1837. Whilst every other activity in the colonial economy was moving ahead with great activity and success, the settlement of the country stood still and 'the mind (said Fitz Roy) was astonished by the anomalous spectacle of an active colony, enterprising and energetic in all things, save in the one for which it was founded–colonization'. (*Official History of NSW*)

Lithgow wrote in the Land Board report for 1847 that:

'Out of a territory of 300,000,000 acres, not 25,000 had been sold in the last four years and if the 300 million acres was to remain desolate till bought at the rate of one pound, it would require 48,000 years for the completion of such an operation. The revised sales price per acre was still very small, only being the equivalent of three-fifths of a penny for each sheep (this was a new way of quantifying the production price equivalent of land prices (i.e. to quote the sales price in terms of cost per grazing animal or cost per unit of carrying capacity). It appeared that each run was to be capable of supporting at least 4,000 sheep. Nothing in the Act (stated Fitz Roy), authorizing disposal of Crown land, was preventing the Governor from disposing of the lands in other ways, provided it was for the improvement of the colony.'

In this way squatting became officially supported, merely by the inaction of the Governor to recover land from casual 'trespassers', and leases were granted for pastoral purposes to those unable to pay £1 per acre to purchase, but could pay to improve their selected land to the great advantage of surrounding settlers.

Lithgow sat on the Committee to review coal facilities in the Colony and, upon its presentation to the Council on 28 May 1847, another member a Mr Grant moved 'certain resolutions in regard to the monopoly of coal by the Australian Agricultural Company, which had been granted in 1826, by a mere letter from Earl Bathurst–the said monopoly being in direct violation of a statute by which the power of the Crown itself to grant any monopoly was expressly debarred for all time coming'. The matter was referred to another Select Committee for consideration. Coal had become an important 'export' item from the Colony, both to overseas destinations and to other colonies especially Victoria, who accepted almost sixty percent of the coal production in NSW. In the eyes of the NSW Government, coal had become an important economic weapon, one that could be used to persuade Victoria to co-operate on inter-colonial tariffs and taxes. The Victorian Government had imposed tariffs and taxes on goods transported along the Murray River, specifically on goods from Melbourne to the Riverina region. Because of its closer proximity to the southern town of Melbourne, this was the destination of choice for wool and livestock, and the origin of choice for goods coming into the southern NSW region. Coal also brought much needed earnings into the Colony, and utilised local loading facilities and locally owned shipping. The result of the committee deliberations was that coal production was to be de-monopolised, and made available to many more operators.

The Select Committee on Immigration reported on 14 September 1847 that 'at no period since the foundation of the colony had there been so great, so pressing a demand for labour as at that moment. The Council adopted a series of resolutions for the immediate introduction from Britain of suitable migrants in order to avoid the dangers of coolies from India and savage natives from Polynesia; to be followed by the expenditure of territorial revenue for the purposes of immigration.' The recommendation from the Committee was for more government funds to be made available for subsidising the passage of an increasing number of immigrants.

At the opening of the first Council session for 1848 Fitz Roy, who was looking to bring good news to the members and revive their flagging spirits after the continuing effect during the recession of 1842-43, stated that:

'. . . notwithstanding the commercial depression still prevailing in the mother country and the consequent low prices of colonial produce going into that market, the chief resources of the colony continued to increase in a manner alike rapid and surprising. The export of wool–its main staple–reached, in the year 1847, the large quantity of upwards of 22 million lbs, with an official value of £1,260,000, or a little less than 6 pence per pound, and an increase over the previous year of 5.7 million lb."

Fitz Roy announced further efforts to seek fresh supplies of labour from Britain as a means to restore that equilibrium between the two classes so essential to the general welfare and 'as no community in the aggregate could long continue to be prosperous where the fair profits of the capitalist were liable to be absorbed in the payment of excessive rates of wages'. Fitz Roy clearly understood the popular philosophy that suggested the economy could grow on the back of investment capital rather than allow the limiting factor in the colonial economic growth to be a shortage of labour.

It did not appear that the 'commercial depression in the mother country' was holding back the Colonial economy as anticipated. Using Lithgow's latest audited figures, Fitz Roy announced that 'the whole of the Land and Immigration Debentures had been paid off, and the territorial revenue had exhibited so prosperous a state as to have enabled the Governor to request the Home Government to send a further 5,000 immigrants, in addition to the 5,000 already pledged'. The Governor was riding high on a wave of popularity due to the rejuvenated economy, increased immigration, and the ability of the Colonial economy to absorb the increasing number of immigrants.

Earl Grey announced the basis of sending out exiles and ticket-of-leave holders from Britain, to be subsequently followed by their wives and families and by an equal number of free emigrants, all at the expense of the British Treasury. No colony could knock back or dismiss an offer like that, even if there was popular opposition to 'transportation of prisoners'. Earl Grey's announcement was published in full in the Colonial press 'for general information'. The announcement that growing numbers of misfits from the British lower classes were to be offered assisted passage to the Colony was not welcomed with much relish in Sydney. It was not expected that this group, consisting of the poor, the frail and the discontent, would 'pay their way' once they arrived in the Colony, and there were negative reactions to immigration monies being spent in such a potentially wasteful way.

Following the announcement by Earl Grey, Fitz Roy stated his intention to introduce a Bill dividing NSW into two colonies, the northern division to retain the existing name, the southern to be called Victoria.

Lithgow, the official auditor for the Port Phillip area, strongly supported this intention, as he was found this duty difficult due to the settlement's remoteness, slowness of the mails and their unwillingness to use standard NSW accounting formats and procedures. He thought it would relieve him rather difficult responsibility. The Fitz Roy Bill would provide for two Houses 'which is the ancient system of colonial government'.

Again guided by Lithgow, Fitz Roy advised the Council 'the Estimates for 1849 had been prepared with every regard to economy, but nevertheless showed a considerable increase to those voted for 1848'. The causes of the increase were:

The breaking up of the convict system, previously maintained solely at the expense of the British Treasury
Charges for schools and local purposes in new settlements beyond existing settled districts
Additions to police estimates
Additional public works

In spite of additional expenditures (relating to immigration subsidies)) it was still expected that there would be a surplus for the year 1849, with expected revenues at £324,340 and expenditures of £3313,179. The surplus would only be £311,160. The relevance here is that Lithgow had continually encouraged a balanced budget, and for most years, the governor produced a small surplus. Only during the dark days of the recessions in 1827-28 and 1842-43 did the economy produce a deficit. There was no public borrowing available and although in the last resort the governor could have called on the British Treasury, for the most part, cash shortages were met by borrowing from the Military Chest or the Commissariat funds.

Fitz Roy opened the 1849 NSW Legislative Council with talk of a:

'considerable depression partially contributed to by the separation of Victoria which had cost the mother colony because it took a net surplus of revenue over expenditure from the NSW Colonial budget, as well as directing most Riverina region economic activity south of the border. The commercial distress consequent on the political convulsions, which had for some time agitated some of the chief States of Europe, had extended its baneful influence even to this Colony. Wool–that great staple of the colony–had not escaped depreciation in value, which had now affected all property. There was reason to hope that with the restoration of tranquillity the price of colonial produce would again rise.'

Fitz Roy had an obviously pompous way with words but he was trying the tell the Councillors that the Colonial economy was on the mend, unlike the economies of Europe which were still weak, and that the local turnaround was largely due to the attractiveness of Colonial wool, and their record sales in the overseas market. He also had some good news:

'Since the renewal of immigration in 1848, not less than 54 ships had arrived in the colony, bringing 13,161 souls at the public expense. It had been necessary to raise the sum of £50,000 in debentures, secured by territorial revenue, to meet the obligation for immigration funding. However, if the immigration program is to continue some comprehensive arrangements would need to be made for raising further funding.'

In 1849 an important legislative measure was submitted to the Council for a uniform rate of postage. Postal services had been expanding in the Colony, especially since Lithgow had made the position of Postmaster a salaried one instead of a fee-based position. New services were being offered throughout the country areas but the postage rate was based on distance and accessibility. Now there was a move to introduce flat domestic postal charge. 'It is not practical to adopt as low a rate as existing in the United Kingdom, but there was no desire on the part of the colonial government to maintain a higher rate than might be found absolutely necessary to the actual costs incurred". The rates were fixed as follows: 2d for letters within the colony not exceeding ½ ounce; 1d each was imposed on newspapers and a separate rate was agreed for mail carried to England by steamship as opposed to sailing ship.

Because transportation of convicts had not been an issue in Port Phillip up to that time, the immigration question was of particular importance to that region and the Port Phillip representatives in the NSW Legislative Council were strong advocates of a fixed portion of subsidised migrants being assigned to that district. Victoria, as a separate state, became much more attractive and, following separation, the new government was persuaded to allocate funds to a locally sponsored migrant intake. This task was made much easier after the discovery of gold was announced.

The transportation debate heated up again, and the move to transport convicts only to Moreton Bay was abandoned. Earl Grey said this was because of the cost and the fact that an equal number of free settlers had been pledged. He proposed to advise Her Majesty to revoke the Order in Council by which NSW would no longer be a place for receiving convicts under sentence of transportation. Public meetings on the subject were held in almost every town and district in the Colony, resulting in a combined resolution to oppose the revival of transportation in any shape or form.

Lithgow again reported from the Land Board:

'In British North America, it was the subject of daily lamentation that by the course of progressive alienation large tracts had fallen into the hands of single individuals, to the great injury of the colony (Lithgow was making the point that he did not want the same degree of large landholdings in a few hands in the local colony, and unless changes to land policy were made, a monopoly caused by price as well as regulation would occur). The same policy had ruined settlement in Western Australia. The experience in NSW went to show that in all its early years an only nominal check was presented to the appropriation of Crown Lands, and there was nothing remarkable in its progress: but since a price had been demanded, upwards of a million pound sterling had been realised from Crown Lands, and applied in obtaining a supply of labour, which was still deficient; although the population had been increased by an immigration of nearly 63,000 persons, the means for whose conveyance had been obtained from the Land Fund, besides 18,000 persons who emigrated by their own resources after assisted immigration was established. It was by no means of the increase of population thus obtained that the colony had continued to advance in wealth and prosperity, and its character had been changed from a convict to a free Colony.'

Before the death of Sir George Gipps, it was well known that he thought that 'even the smallest coin in the colony was too large a price for an acre'.

Gipps had remained an advocate for free gifting of land to capital-rich settlers and immigrants.

One bill opposed by Lithgow but approved by the Council was the City of Sydney Corporation Bill recommending the repeal of the present acts incorporating the City of Sydney, that three commissioners be appointed instead of the corporation, that local revenues and powers should vest in the individual Commissioners and that a uniform rate should be imposed on all property.

The commencement of the railways movement

The railway debate was becoming very active in the Colony, and a positive reaction to rail communication between Sydney and Parramatta was greeted with as much goodwill as was the announcement of the line from Sydney (via Campbelltown) to Goulburn. A despatch from the Colonial Agent in London, transmitting various Railway Reports, was to be submitted for guidance of the Council and the great importance of establishing such a means of communication at the earliest possible time was pointed out. A similar despatch was also tabled stating that the use of steam ships between England and the Colony by way of the Cape of Good Hope had been approved. Lithgow, because of his remote pastoral holdings and, his interest in further economic development and decentralisation in all regions of the Colony, was a strong supporter of rail communication but he expressed the hope that much of the 'manufacturing' of the steel lines and steam engines (instead of just the carriages) would be carried out in the Colony (Lithgow to Boyes, August 1848)

The British Government had strongly supported colonial railways being developed along British lines by being privatised (privately owned) and privately constructed and financed. On 6 June 1848, the Legislative Council committee reported, recommending:

'The speedy formation of a company for carrying out such a means of transit, especially in districts where the population and internal traffic afforded reasonable prospect of success.'

'Crown Land in fee simple ought to be made to any company not only for the line itself but for adjacent development.'

'The Legislature ought to guarantee a dividend of 6% to investors, for a limited period of years.'

'The Government should encourage the State Savings Bank to invest 30,000 pound in such a company.'

The Sydney Railway Company appealed by petition to the NSW Legislative Council asking that it incorporate the company. On 28 August a resolution was carried by 13: to 4, and the incorporation, including a dividend guaranty, became part of the Sydney Railway Bill.

Gold is discovered in the Colony

At the beginning of 1849, a newspaper announcement(in the *Sydney Gazette)* that gold had been discovered in California caused a great exodus from the Colony. 'Amongst those who emigrated were a number of bounty immigrants. The NSW Legislative Council moved resolutions to the effect that sponsored immigrants could not leave the Colony until they had repaid the benefits received'.

William Lithgow was reappointed as a non-elected Member of the Legislative Council on 4 June 1850. Early in 1851, Edward Hargraves discovered gold in the Bathurst district and, in one of his last Legislative successes before his retirement, Lithgow was proactive in preparing a package of measures that would have far reaching ramifications. A new schedule of duties on imports was set to raise sufficient revenue to provide for public requirements; removal of discriminatory tariffs on articles from different countries; additional expenditure to 'ensure efficiency in the Public Service' would be made; Crown land policy would be re-thought; transportation would be finally brought to an end;

The extensive gold discoveries in the Colonies in 1852 raised the level of economic activity and government activity. A surge in population was expected; additional levels of licensing and law enforcement were anticipated, and a dramatic increase in official revenues was predicted. Fitz Roy responded well to the new problems suddenly facing his administration.

The Growth of the Pastoral Industry in the Colony

Macarthur's contribution to the Colony was impressive and important and, even if his principal intent was only to increase his personal wealth, the part he played can be considered in hindsight to have revolutionised the agricultural performance of the early Colony.

The term 'squatter' was applied to all persons who placed themselves without title on public lands, and it was applied to those agriculturalists occupying Crown lands for sheep-raising, with or without a lease or license. Until 1831, free land grants were made to encourage settlement and much land was taken up by a 'ticket of occupation' issued by the Government. This practice stopped under Governor Darling but, later in the 1830s, it became official policy that squatting was acceptable economic policy and appropriate laws were amended to provide for 'legal' squatting by payment of an annual license fee. However, in 1842 the British House of Commons passed the Sale of Waste Land Act, setting a minimum auction price for Crown Land sales and raising the amount per acre up to £1.

Governor Gipps (1837-1846) had made many enemies in his attempts to stop squatters in NSW from acting as if all grazing land belonged to them. The squatters' problems developed mainly because of officialdom's inability to define boundaries of freehold land (sold by the Government to settlers) and to define 'occupation' rights of Crown land (land occupied under a licence agreement by settlers). The problems of landowners and squatters converged in many instances because landowners could at the same time be squatters, own estates and occupy (livestock) runs on Crown land. By 1839 about two-thirds of the Colony's livestock was running on the 22 million acres of 'Crown land' held by both small farmers and big graziers. In 1831, Crown land had a reserve price of 5 shillings per acre, having been first made available to settlers in 1830 but, for a period, only the established settlers could afford to buy this land. \

In 1839 the reserve price was raised first to 12 shillings per acre and then in 1842 to £1. There was little reaction to these price rises because of the existing land boom but, in the depression that followed, graziers argued that only those with imported capital could afford to buy land at these high prices or else they could 'go beyond the current boundaries of

Government land and squat'. Governor Gipps operated under a policy of securing the highest price he could for land and this brought him into disfavour with landowners, although property owners of today would welcome such a declared policy. Squatters paid a flat fee of £10 per annum and they were generally considered to be landed gentry, since they usually required a minimum of £1,000 capital to buy supplies and livestock and pay employees. These 'runs' were starting to be sold on the open market, as if squatters had proprietary rights to the land, and Gipps became increasingly concerned that the land ownership Government's rights were being eroded by the proscribed rights of squatters. Then, in 1839, the Supreme Court ruled that a squatter's occupancy could be upheld against all intruders except the Crown.

Another non-farmer who rose to power and wealth was the first Minister of the Presbyterian Church, Reverent Samuel Marsden. Within 10 years of his arrival in NSW with the First Fleet, he was on his way to becoming one of the richest men in the Colony with 1,720 acres and 1,200 sheep. Like other farmers of the time, he was intent on improving his stock and consistently bred Suffolk sheep strain into his flock. A result of this better breeding can be seen in the improvement in total wool production over the following 30 years.

Livestock belonging to the government in October 1796

	Male	Female
Cattle	3	3
Horses	1	2
Young horses	2	2
Asses	2	4
Sheep		170
Goats		383
Swine		4,835

As can be seen in the above table, there were few horses for use in farm work or for transportation. Ken Austin in *The Lights of Cobb & Co.* writes 'The first draught animals in Australia were convicts: the first travellers traversed her forests on foot. For several years after Governor Phillip landed at Sydney Cove in January 1788, horses and cattle were few and very precious'. Nearly four years later, Judge Advocate Collins recorded in 1791 in his *Account of the English Colony in New South Wales* that the public livestock included one stallion, aged, one mare, two young stallions, two colts, and sixteen cows. These horses were still too valuable to be used for transportation purposes, so most of the officials continued to walk when carrying out their duties, and convicts kept hauling the wagons used in government service. Not until 1796 was Collins able to report: 'The timber carriages were now, instead of men, drawn by 6 or 8 stout oxen: and all the timber, which was used for building or other purposes, were brought to the pits by them. This was some saving of men, but 8 people were still employed with each carriage'.

Trends in pastoral and land holdings by size–1878-1886

	1878	1886
Under 200 acres	25,036	27,800
Between 200 & 1000 acres	10,501	13,174
Over 1,000 acres	2,340	3,980

Coghlan statistics show that in 1886, there were 10,750 holdings of more than 400 acres, an increase of 55% from 1878. The smaller holdings were close to towns and used mainly as gardens and orchards. Although many freeholders and squatter settlers did well, they all faced a harsh and unforgiving climate, disease and extremes of drought and debilitating floods.

When Commissioner J. T. Bigge reported to the British Colonial Office (Bigge: *Agriculture and Trade–1822*) he opined on the reasons for the major crop failure in the Colony in 1820. Among the many reasons he listed were:

'The uncertain climate that is not generally favourable to the growth of European grain varieties

A degree of heat that either too suddenly or too quickly follows long series of heavy rains, and scorches rather than matures the grain the smaller grains of New South Wales, although equal in quality to those grown in southern Europe, have to contend with frequent blights at Bathurst, and a regular outbreak of smut, as well as (in the dry years), an insect infestation like fly-moth, which eats a great quantity of grain.

A greater and more constant loss of grain is sustained from the devastation of the weevil, after the wheat is stacked, and as very few of the farmers in the Colony posses granaries, or even barns, the effect of the weather on open storage, and of insect infestations is dramatic.'

Bigge: Agriculture and Trade–1822

The Big Depression of 1843

A great commercial crisis followed soon after the introduction of the new Colonial Constitution in 1843. This constitution established the NSW Legislative Assembly with 21 members. The new leaders of the Assembly strongly advocated cessation of transportation, against British wishes, most members having won their seats on this policy. However, with the cessation of transportation came the withdrawal of large sums of British money from the Colony, this money having been used to support prison establishments, convicts and many public works. An unwise interference by British Authorities in the land laws caused much distress by discontinuing land grants and setting an auction support price for the first time on Crown land. Interest rates on land mortgages were raised and squatter's licenses were established. The depression saw the price of land and stock drop to zero, followed by a great many business failures. The most important was the Bank of Australia, whose shareholder liability was unlimited, and this resulted in many influential people seeking bankruptcy protection.

The Governor of the day, Sir Charles Fitz Roy, also oversaw other dramatic events. In addition to the final abolition of transportation, there were the separation of Victoria as an independent Colony in 1851, the discovery of gold in 1851 and the establishment of Responsible Government in 1855-56. However two powerful and influential groups together tried to bring transportation back. On this subject, pastoralists and squatters saw eye-to-eye since convicts largely supplied their indentured labour at low rates of payment (food and lodging). The British Government supported this move and sent two ships with prisoners to the Colony, but Port Phillip

(Melbourne) and Sydney both refused landing and the ships went on to Moreton Bay (Brisbane). Local support was low and, at various meetings set up by the Anti-Transportation League to seek public opinion, only overwhelming rejection was expressed.

Exploration

From 1810 there were new incentives to know what lay beyond the Blue Mountains to the west of the Sydney to Parramatta development. The Colony's flocks of sheep and herds of cattle were increasing in numbers and good pasture was becoming scarce, not for want of land, but because of overgrazing of the most suitable pastures and the effects of periodic droughts and floods. In the spring of 1810, a plague of 'army worm' caterpillars appeared and destroyed crops, gardens and pastures. Many crops were completely lost and, for the first time, fresh water in Sydney became scarce. 1811 was another drought year, but 1812 saw a return of the caterpillars to such an extent that stock on most farms was in very poor condition.

In the face of deteriorating crops and livestock, the pressure was on to cross the Blue Mountains and search for protected grazing land to the north, south and the west. A stream of 'explorers' followed–Blaxland, Lawson, Wentworth, Oxley, Evans, Phillip Parker King (the son of former Governor King), Hume and Hovell and many more. The land was harsh and hostile but recognition was given to the great strides needed to open up future settlement areas.

In early 1802, Governor King issued an official warning regarding convict escapes to cross the mountains to the west: 'The Governor has for some time been informed of a Report, as wicked as it is false, . . . that a settlement of white people exists on the other side of the mountain. Several prisoners have lately absconded from their labour in order to reach that settlement.' In late 1802, King gave a further warning in relation to those mountains: 'Even if present adventurers could reach the foot of the mountains, they must have languished and died for want of food before they could have got a mile into the mountains'.

Although there were several attempts by resolute and experienced explorers, including George Bass and Ensign Francis Barrallier, it was not until 1813 that Blaxland moved to make his successful assault encouraged by the changes that had taken place in the Colony during the previous decade. These changes included the fact that when King issued his warning in 1802, the population was just under 6,000. By 1813 it had doubled. In 1802 there were only 8,632 sheep and 1742 cattle. By the arrival of Macquarie in 1809, the sheep had increased to 35,338 and cattle to 12,442. By 1817 little of NSW remained unexplored and Governors were beginning to offer encouragement and incentives for settlers to utilise the newly opened land.

Ken Austin (*The Lights of Cobb & Co.*) concludes:

'It was by then clear that the limited amount of good grazing and agricultural land to be found in the area between the mountains and the sea was no longer sufficient for the Colony's needs. Blaxland himself admitted that the need for more and better land to accommodate the expansion of his own flocks and herds was his principal motive in organising the expedition.' in June 1813, after Blaxland, Lawson and Wentworth returned with their news of the extensive, well-grassed country beyond the mountains, Macquarie acted speedily. He sent assistant Surveyor Evans over Blaxland's route to confirm and extend his discoveries and, pushing on past the furthest point that Blaxland had reached, Evans found and named the Bathurst Plains on 10 December 1813. Much of the remote inland was about to be explored and perhaps new fertile regions suitable for the ever-expanding sheep population would be found. The general conjecture was that an inland sea might be discovered, surrounded by fertile soil and this led to Oxley, Cunningham, Sturt, Hume and Hovell, Eyre, Mitchell, Leichhardt, Gregory and many more striding across lands outside the NSW borders. These were areas which aborigines had settled thousands of years earlier, but they were not marked on any maps. Exploration brought new settlements and townships to these outlying areas, opening up vast areas of grazing and cropping land and finally placing the settlements on a basis of self-sufficiency.

Two types of exploration were actively under pursuit. The exploration for new land came because of pressure to expand the amount of pastoral land but exploration for minerals had been under-way since 1797, when Lieutenant Shortland discovered coal in Maitland, just out of Newcastle. Although coal was the black 'gold', much sought after to sustain the steam generation innovations shortly to become active with road, ship, farm engine and industrial engine motivation, there were other mineral discoveries prior to the official discovery of gold that assisted Colonial development and exports. They included silver discovered in Broken Hill and the associated development ofThe Broken Hill Proprietary Company; tin discovered between Tenterfield and Vegetable Creek in the far north of NSW and copper found in the central part NSW between the Macquarie and Darling Rivers. However the high cost of transport between mines and the nearest port, and a world price decline, slowed discovery and development activities for some time. Other minerals being pursued and mined were antimony, manganese and iron.

Marble, building stone, slate and fire clays were under development and the Colony became enriched by mineral discovery and extraction. However, iIt was Gold that attracted the most attention domestically and internationally.

The 'rum' rebellion

The NSW Corps, soon to be dubbed the 'Rum Corps', was destined to play an energetic but inglorious role in the Colony's development.

NSW had no monetary system since this was regarded as unnecessary in a community that was intended primarily as a jail. Accordingly, wages were generally paid in kind, and the articles used thus acquired a 'monetary' value but the high cost of living caused the value of such items rise, supported by the desire of workers to earn as much as possible. Other means of fiscal transactions in common use in the Colony became the 'government bill of exchange' issued on the British Treasury and paymaster's notes issued to the officers of the NSW Corps, which were consolidated as bills on the regimental treasury in England. Of the two, the paymaster's notes were much preferred, although the government could enforce the settlement of its debts using Treasury bills.

In 1797, after meeting with groups of settlers, Governor King fixed the rate of pay for a wide variety of tasks. By 1798, the retail sphere of the Colony was no longer exclusively controlled by the NSW Corp, and already a number of emancipist dealers had risen to the fore including Simeon Lord (cloth merchant), Isaac Nichols (the first 'postmaster') and James Larra, a Parramatta publican patronised by wealthy colonists and overseas visitors.

Some of these emancipist leaders began as middlemen fronting for officers of the Corps but others started by themselves in small ways, such as selling bottles of watered down spirits at high prices, thus accumulating sufficient capital to grow and expand. However, they had not completely supplanted the officers who also controlled the importation of all products and required retailers to enter into a bond, forfeited if goods were sold below preset prices. The wealth created by these officers enabled them to buy land in the Colony and, by 1800, 34 officers owned 15,000 acres of land, 3000 acres of which were cleared and running 4,250 sheep, 244 cattle, and 105 horses, besides goats and hogs. These figures represented the bulk of the privately owned livestock in the Colony. Around 1799-1800, a short-lived attempt by Governor Hunter to counter the officers' steel grip over commerce in the Colony resulted in the establishment of a Government store, from which all settlers could buy goods at reasonable prices. After taking this first step, Hunter made no effort to keep the store going and by late 1800 a serious crisis had arisen between the Governor and the colonists over the Governor's failure to reign in the power and influence of the officers in the NSW Corps. A group of settlers wrote directly to the Colonial Secretary, the result of which was the recall of Governor Hunter, and his replacement by Governor King.

In his reference book *The Rum Rebellion*, H.V. Evatt writes of the rise of the power and influence of the Rum Corps (p26-27):

'The explanation of many, if not most, of the difficulties which overwhelmed the three Naval Governors who succeeded Governor Phillip viz Hunter, King and Bligh, lies in the increasing ascendancy of the officers of the New South Wales Corps. They not only possessed the monopoly of violence, but they became an aristocracy. They were allowed to engage in trade and agriculture; gradually, they obtained control of the imports, particularly spirits; and the consequence was that, within twelve months of Phillip's departure, rum became the recognised medium of exchange. So much so that even labour could only be purchased with spirits. Under this system the officers reaped enormous harvest'. (Transcript of Bligh's testimony at Trial in London)

During Hunter's governorship, the officers repeatedly smuggled convicts away from government control to use them in private employment, including of course that of the officer's themselves. After Phillip's departure in 1792, the Colony was administered for three years by Grose, the commanding officer of the regiment, after which Paterson, the next in command, succeeded him. Under both Grose and Paterson, 'convict servants were lavishly bestowed, not only upon commissioned officers of the Corps but by most other Corp men'

The NSW Corps was eventually replaced in 1809 on the arrival of Governor Macquarie who had brought his own regiment, the 73rd Foot.

'Free' Immigration

Assisted 'free' emigration began in 1832, with the funds to finance the passage were raised through the sale of Crown lands in NSW and controlled by the authorities in London. However, insufficient care was taken in the selection process and a number of people were sent out who could not usefully be added to the Colony's workforce\, or whose moral reputation did not stand up to scrutiny. The mortality rate on the ships was high, especially amongst the children, due to poor food, poor accommodation and inadequate hygiene.

The immigration program was financed from 'local' funds over which the Colony had great control which caused great concern. The British Colonial Secretary of State Bourke modified the immigration scheme by allowing bounties for approved 'free' settlers upon arrival in NSW or for private employers who had arranged bounties by sponsoring new settlers. These two systems of 'free' emigration continued until transportation of convicts was suspended in 1840. Owing to immigration, both 'free' and penal, along with natural increase, the Colony's population grew from

51,115 in 1831 to 97,912 in 1838. In the same period, the proportion of free persons increased from 37.7 percent to 42.7 percent.

There was no doubt that immigration was the answer to the evils of both the old world and the new. In the old world it helped to cure pauperism and provided an invaluable market for British manufacturers, and a happy British alternative to radicalism, Chartism, socialism and all the other 'isms' that threatened the very foundations of Georgian society. In the new world, it helped to alleviate the chronic shortage of labour and provided a 'moral and industrious' working class as a substitute for the 'convict polluters'. In all the Australian Colonies (except Van Dieman's Land), labour was in intense demand, wages were high, and there was comfort, abundance and happiness for the workers.

Struggles in starting a 'free' colony

Although the first free settlement in Australia was on the Swan River (Western Australia) in 1829 and not very successful one, South Australia was the first British Colony founded on systematic principles as a home for free men with no convicts to be transported there. However, long before the South Australian Land Trust came into being as a means of raising capital from land sales, the Colonists in NSW were hard at work lobbying for fiscal equity between settlers and equal right and access to the Colony's assets.

An extract from Robert Hughes' "The Fatal Shore"(P288) is strong evidence of the struggles for economic independence in the early Colony

'In the "famine years", convicts were let off work at three in the afternoon so that they could raise their own produce. This dispensation became the custom and it survived for both private and government workers even after the shortages had passed. Convicts soon came to be paid wages for out-of-hours labour. They could sell this overtime elsewhere, if the master did not want to pay for it. Some items in the 1808 code of labour prices were: 10s for felling an acre of trees; 1 pound 4 shillings per acre for breaking up new ground; 66 pence a bushel for pulling and husking corn, and so forth. If a convict always worked the whole day for his master, not just the ten standard government hours, his surplus time entitled him to a shilling a day, or about 18 pound per year. He may even get a bonus of rum.

Not even Macquarie's creation of a holey dollar–a mutilated Spanish coin of Charles 111, whose center or 'dump' was punched out and given a value of one shilling and three pence could keep coinage in the Colony.

As a result, the first 25 years of economic life were a crazy quilt of barter, IOU's and sliding coinage, many of which were left in the Colony by visiting ships.'

The absence of currency was a deliberate policy as it was considered that a penal colony would not need such means of exchange. The convicts were the worst victims of these economic arrangements, since their paid labour was mercilessly exploited by this means of payment which was mainly in kind, at prices fixed by the free settlers. Sometimes they were forced to take goods they did not want. In the heyday of the Rum Corps, sugar was 7 shillings per pound, tea 6 shillings an ounce and spirits at 20 shillings a bottle. However, the most sought after commodity was rum. Nearly all settlers, both men and women, were addicted to alcohol and rum trading and consumption affected every level of the social framework. 'Families were wrecked by it, ambitions destroyed and an iron-chain of dependency forged. Bligh saw rum as an instrument of debilitation that helped an elite maintain its power'. (Hughes P290)

Governor Bligh's successor, Lachlan Macquarie, was ordered to arrest the leaders of the Rum Rebellion and take them back to England for trial. The leaders were John Macarthur and the Corp's second–in-command, Major George Johnson who had had arrested Bligh and taken charge of the Colony. However, they had slipped out of the Colony and left for England and to take their case directly to the Government. Johnson was later cashiered and Macarthur reprimanded, before he was allowed to return to the Colony.

In the early 1840s, a severe depression threatened livelihoods in all the colonies except South Australia, and many squatters resorted to slaughtering their sheep and boiling them down for tallow. But their faith in Australia as a sheep-walk remained unshaken. In NSW, squatters were enthusiastic about a scheme to introduce steam communication from Port Essington in the northwest corner of the continent to carry produce to London via India. Attempts to open up the inland route from NSW to the northwest coast continued, leading to continued speculation about what lay at the heart of the continent. Some said any exploring party in search of such a route would confirm John Oxley's prophecy that the interior was impassable. Others prophesied that they would find an inland river emptying into an inland sea, which would be used to 'convert that vast and mournful wilderness into a smiling sea of industry'. (Manning Clark–*History of Australia*–Vol 3)

From boom to bust–the economic ups and downs of the period 1827-1845

The Colony experienced numerous boom and bust cycles in its early years. Even after it had reached a point of quasi-economic stability following Macquarie, the 1827 depression arrived unannounced. The next depression, the commercial depression of 1842-43 was almost contrived by Governor Gipps, who made little effort to anticipate it, limit its severity or shorten its longevity.

The Big Depression of 1843

We briefly touched on the depression of 1843 previously, but there was one interesting side issue flowing from the economic downturn that affected so many merchants and pastoralists. This financial and commercial financial crisis led to the Insolvency legislation. In the years 1842-44, insolvencies numbered 600, 535 and 221 in each of the three years. In Melbourne the figures were 113, 124, and 45 making all together 1,638 sequestered estates with collective debts of £3.5 million. Some relief was to be found in new legislation in NSW, which provided for advances against wool sales, providing £680,000 of relief. (NSW Legislative Assembly–V & P–1845)

In 1843 a new insolvency law had made it easier for insolvents to settle their affairs with their creditors and exempted them from the immediate prospect of imprisonment except for fraud. By the end of December

1842, 600 people had been confirmed as bankrupts by the Supreme Court and few ever repaid much money to their creditors. Men who had begun wholesale and retail businesses with little or no capital became unemployed, they were often also unemployable. This table shows the occupation of those using the provisions of the insolvency legislation:

Principal occupations of the insolvents–1842

Settlers, farmers and graziers	78
Clerks and shopmen	44
Publicans, brewers	42
Gentlemen and yeomen	31
Merchants	29
General dealers	27
Mariners etc	17
Storekeepers	16
Butchers	16
Boat builders	16

To place this in the context of the times, N.G. Butlin in *The Economy Before 1850* writes:

'The official history is pre-occupied with pastoral expansion in New South Wales, the growth of grain production in Van Dieman's Land, and mining in South Australia. This conventional interpretation must be challenged. We can be reasonably certain that the notion of the Colonies being dependent simply on rural activity is equally unacceptable, and that a great variety of economic activity developed at a very early stage. Rapid expansion tends to be unstable. The Colonies were subjected to severe depression in the early 1840s but what is novel in the data available is the linkage of this depression with British Economic conditions. This linkage is evident in trade and pastoral production but also in public finance, with Britain drastically curbing its expenditure on Australia in the early 1800s through 1840.'

It is possible to conclude that the challenges heaped upon the British authority's local representative, the Colonial Governor, were satisfied. These challenges included:

Produce food sufficient to feed the growing population
Become economically self sufficient in other respects
Make the Colony attractive for 'free' settlers
Keep the military satisfied
Land grants

Extensive land grants were provided to many people before it was seen that this was a potential source of revenue. The British Parliament first legislated in 1823 (59 Geo III c.114) to designate revenue from Crown land sales, Crown land leases and the associated financing charges to the account of the British Treasury and this was confirmed in two successive and related pieces of Colonial legislation under George IV. Obviously, in the mind of the British Colonial Office, revenue from Crown Land (initially Waste Lands) was of great potential and was to be reserved for British Treasury use. Evidence of the movement to self-sufficiency is found in the number and size of land grants to new settlers, ex-convicts and military personnel:

NSW land grants 1789-1840

Year	No.	Acres
1789	1	30
1790	0	
1791	36	1,620
1792	46	2,225
1793	34	2,250
1794	248	9,050
1795	181	5,526
1796	37	2,114
1797	83	2,116
1798	40	2,417
1799	117	12,816

Year	No.	Acres
1801	2	348
1802	45	82,820
1803	87	27,587
1804	118	20,230
1805	18	9,630
1808	24	15,064
1809	344	66,641
1816	215	44,862
1823	568	199,294
1831	246	55,091
1839	418	310,250

CHAPTER 7

CONCLUSION AND SUMMARY

We know William Lithgow from his career, his friends, his colleagues and the historical setting of his days in the Colony. We know him even better from his public service activities and we can draw a number of conclusions from his lifestyle and career positions. The title of this work tells us a great deal: we know more about the times in which he lived and his colleagues than we do about his own career.

What can one conclude about the life and times of a person that we hardly knew? Does the fact that we know little diminish a very favourable and positive opinion about our subject? The answer must be, not in the least. We know enough for him to keep his place on the pedestal but what we do not know matters. He would have gone to school in only one of two kinds of schools–one a public school operated by the Church of Scotland in small regional towns, such as Lanark, or a government school in the town for children of the poorer folk. That Lithgow chose the University of Edinburgh would suggest either that his parents were wealthy enough to pay his way or he was scholarship material with some assistance from his parents. Did he choose the Church for religious or for hereditary reasons? Did he do well at school? He must have at a minimum reached the level which put him into the university entrance grade. Where was he born? We have sound reason to believe he was born in the family residence around Lanark, south central Scotland. What position did his father reach? It should have been a prominent position for the present head of a prominent family. If there were, indeed, two sons, we learn nothing of the other son, who gains no mention in Lithgow's life. It would seem that

Lithgow, carrying the family name of William, may have only had a sister, and his sister's early death may have contributed to his inclination towards a solitary life.

This however is mostly surmise. Our definitive knowledge about Lithgow comes from his colleagues, his committee work and his public service in the early Legislature, particularly as an appointee to the Executive Council and then as an appointee and finally as an elected member of the Legislative Council.

As a financial analyst, in the broadest sense, he was a good accountant and he was able to think laterally, not only in terms of productivity and outcomes but also in terms of recorded details being presented fairly, accurately and meaningfully. At the best of times, auditing is a slow and tedious task but in the early colony, where new systems were being implemented and the quality of clerical assistance left much to be desired, Lithgow's challenge was to find competency in any field. He showed himself to be a generous man, not inclined to hasty decisions, but using his religious training as a cloak of human kindness. He evidenced compassion (Explorer Mitchell), caring qualities (Female Factory) and understanding (convict work planning).

As a senior and important adviser to a succession of governors, Lithgow developed great expertise which interlinked from one task to another. For instance, as the Commissariat accountant, Lithgow was knowledgeable about rations for convicts and settlers and sources of supplies from overseas and within the colony. He was familiar with many of the ships coming into Sydney Harbour with supplies for sale, and all this added together made him familiar with, and knowledgeable of, the cost of the commissariat operations to the British Treasury, as opposed to him being a mere recorder of events. His knowledge of the Commissariat equipped Lithgow for assessing the role and work practices of the convicts; and led to successful management of Government business enterprises. The Female Factory and the Lumber Yard were responsible for producing so much of the vital supplies and productive work in the colony, and its outposts and were the most important part of the Commissariat operations.

Prior to their leaving Mauritius, Darling had advised Lithgow that the basics for a monetary crisis developing in the Colony. Such a crisis developed within months of both Darling and Lithgow arriving, but from a very different source. Darling had anticipated a crisis within the monetary system because the Colony had no treasury, no currency and only basic banking. In fact, the monetary crisis developed within the Bank of New South Wales initially because it was short of specie (coinage was very difficult to keep within the colony, even the 'holey' dollars, which could not have been used elsewhere in the empire), but a surprise inspection by Lithgow uncovered a fraud involving Colonial funds–Treasurer Balcombe had been treating public funds as his own property.

Thus Lithgow started life in the Colony in the 'hot' seat and, indeed, he finished life in the Colony in a 'hot' spot. He grew resentful at the work load imposed on his office by the discovery of gold and the unending bureaucratic demands of Governor Bourke including approving licences, claims, food supplies to the gold fields, gold escorts from the goldfields, welfare on the goldfields, and so on. These demands, together with his age, ill-health and once again being overlooked for the top post of Colonial Secretary, caused him to consider retirement, without waiting for the *coup d'grace* of self-government and a fully elected parliament.

Lithgow's other interests as a public servant in and of the colony included technical education and the land planning opportunities that came before the Land Board.

It would be very difficult to nominate one other person in the Colony between 1788 and 1855 who covered so much ground and was so knowledgeable as a public servant. The conclusion that Lithgow was the man of 'zeal' spoken of Darling and Brisbane can be drawn from *A Life and Times of William Lithgow.*

One reason for entitling this work *A life and times* is that we have so little definitive knowledge of Lithgow, and it would be presumptuous to entitle it *The life*. A life allows a lot of room for interpretation, and interpretation is what we need a lot of.

Allow me to list finally what I see as the main factors determining Lithgow's character and the events that would be influential in his lifestyle and career:

He trained for the priesthood, albeit the Church of Scotland, and this would have instilled in him a wide range of Christian characteristics as regards fairness, coveting, theft and misappropriation. Excellent training for an accountant

His closest friends were a mixture of professions and backgrounds but at least two others had also been 'men of the cloth' (Ovens and Boyes).

His was the second most senior position in the Colony, and was relied upon by the governors and the Colonial Secretary. He offered stability in an otherwise changing workplace. He offered a sense of continuity to those occupying the two senior roles, as well as department heads. He was a public servant for a total of 40 years, serving the Colony of NSW for 30 of those years. He represented stability, continuity and permanence.

The *Sydney Gazette* of 20 May 1826 offered Lithgow a boost in reputation when it wrote of Lithgow's appointment to the Board of the Bank of NSW. 'He is the first financier in the country, but also a gentleman of undoubted honour and integrity'.

He was an experienced committeeman, and to the extent he was asked to formulate recommendations for general action, he would have been a consensus man

He was mostly a numbers man–an accountant–not formally trained but trained by experience and variety. That he was consistently sought to sit on committees and Boards suggests he was a man of action, perception, broad-minded and well spoken. He could certainly write cogently, and his reports are models of simplified logic and persuasive argument. He would back his recommendations with a clear determination of mathematical conclusion. The report into convict work practices he co-sponsored with Ovens was full of cost-benefit analyses as to the work convicts could complete on land-clearing, road-making etc, the costs of completing that work and the quantified benefits that should flow.

There are no records of disagreements between Lithgow and those he worked with. The Governors wrote only glowingly of his support and contribution to the government service. Both Brisbane and Darling wrote that he was hard working and a 'man of zeal', although Darling also wrote the same words about at least another three other Lithgows's compatriots. Having written to Bathurst that Lithgow was a well-organised public servant, Darling certainly put this concept to the test, by appointing him, over a period, to 27 Boards, committees and other public bodies. Darling was not intending to let the grass grow under Lithgow's feet, and we can only wonder as to his motivation. Was Darling the ultimate direction finder and allocater of jobs for the boy, or did he merely want to off-load much of his own work so he could enjoy the limelight and vice-regal pompousness. Lithgow appeared to get along well with his colleagues.

Lithgow's off-duty interest was in the pastoral industry. It was not a passing interest and, like his other duties, he appeared to take his pastoral activities seriously, with logic and based on the optimising of a return. It could be that he came from a family of landowners in Scotland and possibly he was familiar with the Scottish longhaired sheep. It would be unusual for a new settler, already on a good salary and citified, to learn a new hobby of sheep-raising without there being an interest from an earlier time. Lithgow appointed a manager for his two runs and carefully selected locations based on the selection of 'experts'. It was Oxley and Mitchell who told him about the Gundagai area in the Riverina region, shortly after it had been opened up for settlement. His other runs at Kissing Point and the Hunter Valley gave him the opportunity for diversification. His interest in pastoral activities was very professional and he supported the Southern Pastoral Association, which covered his Riverina property. He also became an active office-holder in the two other active and powerful agricultural lobby groups.

The section on corruption in this work is a reminder of just how different those days were, and the different that standards existed then. However, in the almost 50 years that Lithgow was in public service, and with all the evidence of scandal and malfeasance going on around him (even in his adjacent office–that of Balcombe), there was not one hint of scandal, financial trouble or conflict of interest attributed to Lithgow, a remarkable record that shows great strength of character.

Although Darling issued regulations against speculation in land grants, it did not occur to Lithgow that 1,900 acres in St. Leonard's was speculating. He must have just wanted a Harbour front block with a site suitable for a large house and plenty of space away from his neighbours. His other land holdings in the Monaro and the Hunter Valley showed how broad were his interests in agriculture.

Lithgow could not be classified as a man of property but he certainly was a man with plenty of property. St. Leonard's, Kissing Point, Hunter Valley, Gundagai (Monaro), Macquarie Place and Elizabeth Street in Sydney town. He had been offered a grant of land for a home site in Hyde Park, but he decided not to take up that prestige property and purchased the Elizabeth Street property instead.

During his lifetime, he must have accumulated a reasonable amount of wealth and we need to determine how his will was written upon his death. Without any heirs or family, Lithgow was restricted as to whom he could leave his assets. In fact, he had planned as carefully for his death as he had done for his life. He left many bequests and legacies, to friends, charities and institutions; the largest being to the University of Sydney to endow the Lithgow Scholarship which still operates today.

Lithgow died, not at his retirement property in the Hunter Valley, but at St. Leonard's Lodge, his home in Sydney. In anticipation of retirement and death, he liquidated his various properties, holdings and livestock, and remained for most of his last 10 years (he had retired in 1852 and died in 1864) in the Hunter Valley, before returning to Sydney and dying 'at home' in June 1864

We can safely conclude that Lithgow was a proud, conservative, loyal, active and honourable man, completely committed to his work as a servant of the public and to the Crown. What better epitaph can we offer than *William Lithgow was a colonist that left behind much more than he brought and left the new land a better place.*

We commenced with a brief synopsis of the Lithgow life. We should conclude with a review of his life as we know it and can interpret it from the facts and circumstances. It is important and relevant that we remember that the First Fleet was despatched without Governor Phillip having money to buy or trade for goods en route. His instructions on the recording and reporting of expenditures were meagre and it was not planned that he should develop the Colony into other than a self-sufficient prison. He was directed to purchase goods and services only when and if necessary, by means of issuing bills drawn on the Treasury in London. It was not foreseen that he would run out of food and would be forced to either buy food from visiting ships or send a provisions ship to Batavia, again paying by Treasury bill.

The theory behind the transportation program was that there was absolutely no intention of creating the need for coinage or receiving payment for goods. In its simplest outlook, the Colony would initially rely on provisions from British merchants and manufacturers, and would export timber, flax or minerals on account of the government of the day, in which case no provision need be made for coinage, currency or conversion rates. Pay for military personnel, and those on the civil list, would be made by way of notes drawn on the Paymaster General in London. The Commissariat would be issuing rations rather than selling supplies to free settlers, and it was planned that it would also establish and operate government farms, utilising convict labour, in order to supply sufficient vegetables and foods for the settlements. It was also planned that convicts would be the manufacturers of implements and furniture from local timbers. Housing and barracks were to be also built from local materials and public buildings could be erected from locally-quarried stone and brick and erected by convict labour.

Therefore, it is not surprising that there were no written instructions for recording or reporting income and expenditures. This could all be done in and from London. The British Treasury would be in total control. The plan as given to Phillip was simple 'Our will and pleasure is that all public monies which shall be raised be issued by warrant from you and disposed of by you for the support of the Government or for such other purpose as shall be particularly directed and not otherwise.' (Phillip's second commission HRA 1.1.7)

S.J. Butlin reached the same conclusion as to the operations of the economy when he writes: 'The pay of the military and civil officers was looked upon as normal army and navy routine and no special arrangements were made. The colony was conceived as a large prison where only a slight but authoritarian economy would be necessary and where the convicts would soon become self-supporting (Butlin: *Foundations of the Australian Monetary System* p.12).

Later Governors took over an established financial administration, albeit under sufferance and with complaint, even though they had received the same written instructions. Hunter expressed his concerns on behalf of all the early Governors when he wrote to the Duke of Portland in May 1798 'Your Grace can scarcely suppose me responsible for the system of errors established for the management of this colony long before it fell to my care . . ." (HRA 1.2.149) The problem was the circumstances that local revenue purely for local disbursement was not available and that the actual cash for the Governors (Phillip, King & Hunter) was retained in England. In spite of the development of common practices, it was not until Lithgow arrived that an authoritative set of instructions was prepared and written for the local treasury.

The Commissariat's role was not only to operate the government farms, the Dockyard, the Lumber Yard, quarries and milling operations. It had a specified financial role as well. The first Commissary, Miller, managed the stores and supplies, arranged for their issue and replacement and drew bills in payment, subject in all details to the direct control of the Governor. Instructions regarding operations of the Commissariat were as vague as those for the treasury functions. In 1796, Commissary John Palmer complained to Governor Hunter about the lack of orders:

'. . . relative to the manner of my keeping the public accounts of the colony, as Commissary of Stores and Provisions. I was provisionally ordered (by Phillip) to keep the accounts as would a purser on a man-of-war . . . but my duty as Commissary is something more than a purser, from being obliged to keep a particular account of all kinds of stores received and expended in the colony, and to transmit accounts of all ordinance, naval and victualling and hospital stores that may be received and issued from the different Boards; all which must necessarily occasion a vast deal of time and require a great allowance of stationery' (HRA 1.1.650 August 1796).

It was not until 1802 that Governor King made a detailed statement of the function and importance of this office. Macquarie also took the opportunity to fine tune Commissariat operations in 1813 but by then it was extremely busy with many more responsibilities and a growing number of convicts to oversee. In 1813 the Commissariat was reorganised as a branch of the Army Commissariat in London, itself a sub-department of the British treasury. Thereafter the Commissariat was controlled by the Lords Commissioners of the Treasury whose instructions were superior to those which the governor might give in his capacity of Captain-General.

Although local revenues were raised as early as 1802, it was not until 1823 that Lord Bathurst directed Brisbane to appoint a special Colonial Treasurer to be responsible for the collection of Internal Revenue, the payment of salaries to the civil establishment, the issue of licences, the auctioning of tolls on bridges and ferries, etc. The first Colonial Treasurer was William Balcombe who took up his position on 28 October 1823. The second string to the Bathurst/Brisbane bow was the appointment of William Lithgow as the first Commissary of Accounts, to cope with the needs of a rapidly expanding colony. This accounts branch of the Commissariat was established in 1824 and was probably intended as a check on the activities of the Deputy Commissary-General, following a long period of maladministration, a possibility intimated in an instruction given to Commissary Lithgow when he was appointed to the new branch:

'You will take care that the officer in charge of the Commissariat conducts the duties of the Department in strict conformity to the instructions communicated to him by the Board, or to the directions which he may from time to time receive from the Governor.'

This was our initial introduction to Lithgow. We can track him from the University of Edinburgh through two years of a post graduate licentiate and then his recruitment by the Commissariat in Scotland for government service in Helgoland (Germany), then to Mauritius and an elevation in position to Assistant Commissary, before his transfer to the Colony of NSW at the request of Commissary David Allen and Governor Darling (both of whom he served with in Mauritius). By virtue of his acquaintance with these two, amongst numerous other officers who had previously worked in Mauritius, Lithgow's reputation preceded him and his appointment and arrival were warmly welcomed. It is incumbent on our search for the life and times of William Lithgow to extend our story to understand and analyse his achievements, his colleagues, his professional appointments and accomplishments.

Detailed instructions from the Imperial Treasury accompanied the formation of the accounts branch. Lithgow was to receive duplicate monthly accounts from both the NSW and VDL Commissariat departments, and he was instructed to examine these thoroughly before sending them to London. He was also to counter sign all bills drawn by the Commissariat. (HRA 1.11.379)

Writing to Bathurst in October 1824, Brisbane expressed gratification that the branch had been established and then continued:

I have the honour to solicit your Lordship in order to render that appointment complete and effectual in its operation, to entreat you to allow me to appoint Mr Lithgow Auditor of the whole colonial revenue in order that he may have the entire financial state of the colony under his eye.' (HRA 1.11.379)

For this duty, Lithgow was to receive £100 per annum over and above his salary as Commissary of Accounts. He was officially appointed as the first Auditor General in the colony on 8 November 1824 and Bathurst, in a letter to Brisbane in June 1825, approved the appointment.

Prior to Lithgow's appointment all accounts of receipts and expenditure had been recorded either in London or, since 1802 and the introduction of the first local revenues, the recording had been privatised. The Rev'd Samuel Marsden, acting as Treasurer and Board member of the Female Orphan Fund, had personally handled 1/8th of the revenues derived from customs duties, harbour dues, auction and hostelry licenses, and expended such receipts on operating the orphanage. Darcy Wentworth, as Treasurer of the Police Fund and Police Magistrate operated his fund with 7/8ths of the revenue, which he used to repair roads and bridges, catch runaway convicts, maintain gaols, cemeteries and official buildings. All accounts had supposedly been received and reviewed by the Lieutenant Governor and an audit committee and then published in the *Sydney Gazette* each quarter, before being transmitted to the Lord's Commissioners of the Treasury. Even though the two sets of accounts passed through numerous hands, there remain numeric errors in the published figures.

Lithgow's new duties were limited to auditing the local revenue and expenditure accounts. The accounts kept by the Commissariat connected with the expenditure for the maintenance and supervision of convicts were, as formerly, forwarded periodically to the Imperial Government, and the business of that Department continued under the sole and immediate control of the Governor. Even after the appointment of Lithgow as Auditor General and up to 1855 the accounts of the Crown Lands Revenue of the Colony were transmitted annually to the Imperial Audit Office.

In theory, Lithgow's role was an important one, especially since the Colony had no treasury until in 1817 when Macquarie provided an illegal charter to the Bank of NSW to commence operations in the Colony. From 1802 local revenues, and thus expenditures, grew rapidly due to the growing population of the settlements, the increasing convict population and the rising wealth of many free settlers. There was an increasing demand for imported goods, and in line with British economic policy, imports were kept in line with exports. There was no room for a balance of payments problem–trade was kept tightly in balance. The mills in England had accepted colonial wool and there was a clamour for all available quantities of Australian wool. There were other export items, such as sealskins, whale and seal oil and timber. All this trade increased the funds able to be matched with imports of consumer and capital goods.

The Commissariat was undertaking more and more work and responsibilities. The Lumber Yard, manufactured a wide range of 'forged' products, as well as a full sizing of timber to construct housing and public buildings; the Dockyard handled all imports and exports and the loading of ships; the government farms grew vegetables and raised cattle and sheep for meat; the Commissariat had its own killing works for slaughtering and preparing government livestock and traded in grains purchased from local farmers, as well as purchasing maize, wheat, corn for seed. The Commissariat controlled bread production in the settlement and ran 'farmers' markets on the site of the present Queen Victoria Building.

The Commissariat accounting branch was a busy place and Lithgow was kept well occupied, even before taking on these extra auditing duties. Brisbane recognised this load and decided to make Lithgow the full time auditor and also a general government adviser and representative on numerous boards and committees.

It is these duties and responsibilities that we can follow between 1824 and 1852–28 years of loyal and dedicated public service.

APPENDIX A

EXPLANATORY MEMORANDUM of the Financial System of the Colony of New South Wales, &c.

(Written in May, 1879, for the information of the Imperial Government.)

Chiefly the Constitution Act of 1855 and the Audit Act of 1870, and in matters relating to Trust Funds and Loans by Special Appropriation Acts of the Local Legislature regulate the Financial System of the Colony of New South Wales.

THE CONSTITUTION ACT

The Imperial Act conferring a Constitution on New South Wales and granting a Civil List to Her Majesty was assented to on the 16th July 1855, and came into operation in the Colony on the 24th November of that year. This Act provides for Legislative Council and a Legislative Assembly. The Governor with the advice of the Executive Council nominates the Members of the former, and the Members o9f the latter are elected by the inhabitants of the Colony. All taxation and Appropriation Bills must be originated in the Legislative Assembly, and these are generally introduced by the Treasurer and Secretary for Finance and Trade, who must be not only a Minister of the Crown but a Member of the Assembly. The Ministry consists at the present time of the following Officers of State:–

The Colonial Secretary (At present The Premier)
The Treasurer and Secretary for Finance and Trade
The Minister for Justice and Public Instruction (see note)

The Attorney General
The Secretary for Lands
The Secretary for Public Works
The Postmaster General
The Secretary for Mines.
The Vice-President of the Executive Council (without Portfolio).

These Officers form with the Governor as President, the Executive Council. All appointments, whether salaried or not, are vested in the Governor with the advice of the Executive Council.

Prior to the passing of the Constitution Act the Territorial Revenues of the Colony belonged to the Crown, but on that Act coming into operation in 1855, they were placed at the disposal of the Local Parliament, and together with the taxes, imposts, rates, and duties, were formed into one fund, under the title of the Consolidated Revenue Fund. In lieu of the Crown Revenues thus given up to the Colony, an annual Civil List of 64,300 pounds was made payable to Her Majesty out of the Consolidated Revenue of the Colony. This sum was to provide for,–

1st The salaries of the Governor, the Judges, and certain high Officers of the State.

2nd Pensions to Judges and to certain officials who were allowed to retire on political grounds, when the new Constitution came into operation, as well as pensions to other Government officials who could retire from office in accordance with certain regulations and rates fixed by the Superannuation Act of the Imperial Parliament, 4th and 5th Wm. IV, c. 24.

3rd For the maintenance of Public Worship.

The Constitution Act also provides that the Legislature of the Colony shall have power to make laws for regulating the sale, letting, disposal, and occupation of the wastelands of the Crown within the Colony, and also for imposing texes and levying Customs duties.

The expense of collecting the Revenue, the Interest on Loans negotiated prior to the Constitution Act coming into operation, and the Loans themselves as they mature, form, under the provisions of that Act, primary charges on the Consolidated Revenue Fund. All loans negotiated since then, together with the interest annually payable thereon, are also, under the Acts authorizing such Loans, made primary charges on that Fund.

All Money Votes or Bills must in the first place be recommended to the Legislative Assembly by Message from the Governor, and no part of the Public Revenue can be issued except on Warr5ants bearing the Governor's signature, and directed to the Treasurer of the Colony.

THE AUDIT ACT

This Act was passed to regulate the receipt, custody, and issue of public moneys, and to provide for the audit of the Public Accounts. Its main provisions are the following:–

That all Collectors, Receivers, and Disbursers of public moneys are to be public Accountants, and as such are required to provide security for the due performance of their duties, and for the due accounting for moneys coming into their hands by virtue of their respective offices.

Collectors of public moneys in Sydney are required to pay their collections into the Treasury or Government Bank weekly, or daily if considered desirable; Collectors in the interior monthly, or at such other times as may specially be appointed.

The Treasurer or his deputy the Receiver is also required to pay his collections daily into the Bank keeping the Public Account.

Moneys can only be drawn from the Public Account in the Bank under the authority of the Governor's Warrant. Before the Governor signs a Warrant he must have the certificate of the Auditor General that the various sums therein asked for by the Treasurer are legally available for issue. On receipt of the governor's warrant the paymaster, under the authority of the Treasurer, issues cheques upon the Public Account in the Bank, for the payment of all duly authorized claims against the government.

Appropriations of Parliament are available for issue during the year for which obtained and, if required, for three months thereafter. If not then expended they lapse, unless contracts or engagement to carry out the Services have been made and entered into before the expiration of the year for which such Services were provided for, in which case they are kept alive as long as necessary. (This provision has since been modified by the insertion of a clause in the annual Appropriation Acts giving the votes of Parliament a currency of two years, as the limit given in the Audit Act was found very inconvenient in practice.)

The Manager of the Bank, keeping the Government Account, has to forward daily to the

Treasurer and Auditor General respectively, a statement of each day's transactions. The Treasurer has likewise to furnish the Auditor General daily with a copy of his Cash Book, together with vouchers and authorities in support of the entries therein shown.

The Treasurer, or any Public Accountant, paying inadvertently or otherwise, a sum of money in excess of Parliamentary authority, or making a double payment, is liable to be surcharged by the Auditor General for the amount so overpaid.

The Treasurer is required to publish in the Government Gazette a Quarterly Statement of his receipts and expenditure, and to prepare also an Annual Statement of the same, within three months of the close of the financial year, for the use of the Auditor General, who must audit and thereafter submit such

Annual Statement, with his report thereon, to Parliament.

The Auditor General, being an officer of Parliament, can only be removed from office by the Governor with the advice of the Executive Council, upon the address of both Houses of the Legislature.

THE TREASURY

The Treasury is the Department entrusted with the collection and disbursement of the

Revenues and other public moneys of the Colony. It is under the control and general management of the Treasurer and Secretary for Finance and Trade, who, being a responsible Minister, ceases to act when the Government of which he is a Member retires from office. The permanent head of the Department is the Under Secretary for Finance and Trade, who is responsible to the Minister for the efficient conduct of its business. The following are the principal officers in the Treasury–that is, those have charge of branches, viz.:–

The Chief Inspector of Public Revenue Collectors' Accounts, and Consulting Accountant,
The Accountant
The Receiver
The Paymaster
The Examiner of Expenditure Accounts
The Clerk of Correspondence
The Registrar of Records.

The Under Secretary, the Receiver, and the Paymaster are under heavy security for the faithful discharge of their respective duties. The subordinate officers of the Pay and Receiving Branches also give security, proportioned to the responsibilities of the positions they occupy; the office hours are from 9 to 4, daily, excepting on Saturdays, when they are from 9 to 1.

REVENUE

The Revenue of the Colony is now classed under the following general heads, viz:–

Taxation
Land Revenue
Receipts for services rendered

Miscellaneous Receipts

The first of these, Taxation, consists of Customs Duties–that is, duties levied on certain goods imported into the colony; and Excise duties on refined Sugar and Molasses, and on Spirits, distilled in the Colony. Duty on Gold exported or sent to the Mint for coinage and certain Trade Licenses.

The Land Revenue, which is collected under the Land Acts of 1861 and 1875, and the Mining Act of 1874, embrace all receipts under the following sub-heads, viz:–

Proceeds of Land sold by Auction.
Proceeds of Sale of Improved Lands. Proceeds of Sales of Land by Selection after Auction (now in abeyance).
Sales of Provisional Pre-emptive Rights.
Deposits on Lands Conditionally Purchased.
Instalments of Lands Conditionally Purchased.
Balances of such Purchases paid up.
Interest on the Balances of conditional Purchases unpaid.
Rent and Assessment on Pastoral Runs. Quit Rents.
Mineral Leases and Mineral Licenses.
Leases of Auriferous lands.
Miners' Rights and Business Licences.
Fees on the Preparation of Enrolment of Title-deeds.
Miscellaneous Land Receipts.

Receipts for services rendered (collected under various Acts of Parliament) include Railway and Telegraph Receipts, Postage, Commission on Money Orders, Mint charges, Fees for escort and conveyance of Gold, Pilotage and Harbour and Light Rates, Fees for the Registration of Cattle Brands, Contributions towards the prevention of Diseases in Sheep, and Fees of Office generally.

The Miscellaneous Receipts are composed of Rents, other than rents of Land, Fines, and Forfeitures, Proceeds of Sale of Government Property, Interest on Bank Deposits, and various minor items, which cannot properly be embraced in any of the three classes above, referred to.

COLLECTORS OF PUBLIC REVENUE

Although the Treasury is the Department into which all Revenue and Public Moneys have ultimately to be paid, there are numerous duly appointed officers, both in Sydney and throughout the Colony, authorized to collect Revenue on behalf of the Treasurer. The principal Collectors in Sydney, such as the Collector of Customs, the Commissioners for Railways, the Postmaster General and the Superintendent of Electric Telegraphs, pay their collections into the Bank keeping the Public Accounts daily; and forward daily vouchers to the Treasury containing full particulars of all such deposits. Other Collectors in Sydney pay their collections once a month, except in the case of Land Agents, who are required to make weekly remittances, in order that the necessary steps may be taken as early as possible for completing the sales and leases of land effected by them. All collectors of Revenue have to give security for the faithful discharge of their duties. These securities are proportioned to the probably amount of collections within a given period.

INSPECTION OF PUBLIC REVENUE COLLECTORS' ACCOUNTS

The Accounts of Collectors of Public Revenue, both in Sydney and the interior, are from time to time, but at irregular intervals, carefully examined by Inspectors attached to the Treasury. These officers' inspections have been found more effective, because local and minute, than the audit of the attested accounts furnished by Collectors periodically to the Auditor General.

EXPENDITURE

With the exception of the amount reserved under the Constitution Act as a Civil List of Her Majesty, the amount required for the payment of interest on the Public Debt, and a few sums appropriated permanently under special Acts for various Services, the Revenue of the Colony is left entirely to the control of the local Legislature. Any expenditure therefore out of the Consolidated Revenue Fund without the express sanction of Parliament is illegal; and should the Auditor General, in the course of this audit of the Treasurer's accounts, discover a payment for which provision had not been legally made, it would become his duty to report the circumstances to Parliament.

All moneys raised by Loan are kept in an account separate and distinct from the Consolidated Revenue Fund, so that the Government can use no portion of such moneys for any purpose foreign to that for which it was obtained, without being immediately reported to Parliament by the Auditor General.

The expenditure of Loan Funds is carried out in precisely the same manner as expenditure out of the Consolidated Revenue Fund. Parliament authority must be obtained both for the Loan to be raised and the services to be paid for out of the proceeds. Heads of Departments and others entrusted with the carrying out of the services provided for by Loan, forward from time to time duly certified claims to the Treasury, where they are paid under warrants of the Governor previously obtained.

No appropriate or balance of the appropriation for a Loan service is cancelled or written off until the service has been completed, or all idea of carrying it out abandoned by the Government. Moneys thus saved on a Loan can only be dealt with by Parliament, that is, they cannot be expended by the Government unless under a fresh appropriation of the Legislature

METHOD OF RAISING LOANS

Although Parliament fixes the amount of every Loan, as well as the rate of interest to be paid thereon, the mode of borrowing is left to the Governor with the advice of the Executive Council. A few of the smaller and earlier Loans were raised in the Colony, at rates of interest varying from 2¾d. To 3¼d. per cent. Per diem. Since, however, Loans of greater magnitude have become necessary, our financial agents there have effected the negotiation of them almost exclusively in England. From the establishment of Responsible Government until recently, the Loans of this Colony have been raised on debentures bearing interest at the rate of 5 per centum per annum, with a currency generally of thirty years. In 1873 the rate of interest was however reduced to 4 per cent, and a Loan for £509, 780 at that rate was the same year authorized to be raised by conscription; that Loan has been negotiated in the Colony at prices ranging from 95 per cent to par.

The Debentures of the last two or three Five per cent. Loans negotiated in London realized prices varying from 95 to 104 per cent, and those of the three and a quarter million Four per Cent. Loan negotiated there this month realized an average price of £98 9s. 3d. The Debentures issued by this Government have consisted almost invariably of three denominations, namely £100, £500, and £1,000, and every Loan is composed of a certain proportion of each denomination.

THE TRUST FUND

This Fund embraces all accounts of a special nature, excepting Loans, which, as already stated, are by law kept separate and distinct from all other accounts. Trust Funds are moneys set apart for particular purposes, either by Parliamentary or Executive authority, and must be reserved for those purposes alone. The various accounts embraced in the Trust Fund are kept in the Treasury, and the money in the bank where the Public Account is kept. Payments out of this fund can only be made under the warrant of the Governor, obtained in the usual manner = that is, the Auditor General must first certify that the amounts asked for by the Treasurer are legally available for issue.

PUBLIC DEBT

In 1855, the year in which Responsible Government was established in this Colony, the public debt was only about two millions. On the 31st December 1878, it stood at £11,688,119 9s 2d. Exclusive of advance to the amount of £1,950,000 made from the Consolidated Revenue Fund, pending the negotiation of authorized loans, so that in twenty-three years there has been added to it a sum of only about nine and a half millions. During that period loans have been paid off finally to the extent of £946,000. The following summary of the services for which this debt has been incurred will show that the money borrowed has to a large extent been applied to public works of a reproductive, permanent, and beneficial character–in short, towards the settlement and progress of the Colony, viz.:–

Expenditure to 31st December 1878:–

Railways	£10,139,464.14.7
Telegraphs	430, 186.13
Immigration	569,930.0.0
The Sewerage and Water Supply of the Metropolis	443,261.14.6
For improving the Navigation of Harbours and Rivers	941,460.11.5
Public Works and Buildings Generally	865,620.9.11
Roads and Bridges generally	396,950.7.9
Public Works, Queensland, when It formed part of New South Wales	49,855.86
TOTAL	£13,836,729.19.8

BANKING ARRANGEMENTS

Local Account

The Bank of New South Wales, which is the oldest, the largest, and the most influential monetary institution in the Colony, has for very many years past satisfactorily conducted the local Banking business of the Government. The agreements under which this business has been conducted have from time to time been modified to meet the state of the Public Funds and the altered circumstances of the money market. The present agreement does not expire until the 30th June 1880. Under it the Bank pays the Government interest at the rate of 3 per cent, per annum on the daily aggregate balance, less a margin of £50,000.

Should the Government require to overdraw its account at any time during the currency of the agreement, it can do so to the extent of £200,000 subject to an interest charge at the rate of 5 per cent per annum.

Under certain conditions detailed in the Banking Agreement, which had the approval of the Legislative Assembly, the Government were empowered to make “Special Deposits” with Banks other than the Bank of New South Wales, at a rate of interest not exceeding 4 per cent, per annum. At the present time there is, under this agreement, a sum of £1,725,000, under Special Deposit with nine of the City Banks.

The Treasury collections are deposited in the Bank daily, and payments therefrom, can only be made by cheques drawn by the Paymaster on the Treasury. Heads of Departments and other officers in Sydney, entrusted with either the collection or expenditure of public moneys, keep their accounts with the Bank of New South Wales. Collectors of Public Revenue in the interior also keep their accounts with the Branches of that Bank, in districts where such are established, and transmit their collections to the Treasury by the drafts of such Branches on the Head Office. For these drafts the Bank charges one-eighth one per cent. The charge against the Government for exchange is made quarterly, and the interest payable on its credit balances is brought to account half-yearly. Statements called “Bank Sheets”, showing the payments made and the money received by the Bank on behalf of the Government, are furnished to the Colonial Treasurer and Auditor General, respectively, daily–to the former to enable his Accountant to check the books of the Receiver and the Paymaster, to the latter to enable him to audit satisfactorily the accounts of the Treasurer.

LONDON ACCOUNT

The London Branch of the Bank of New South Wales has also for a considerable period managed the financial business of the Government in England. The agreement for the conduct of that business expires on the 30th June 1880. Through the Agency of the London Branch of this Bank all the larger Loans of the Government have been negotiated, as well as all payments made for Interest on the Public Debt, and for Railway and other materials purchased by the Agent General on behalf of the Colony.

For negotiating Loans the Bank is paid, under the existing agreement, a commission of one-quarter per cent. On the nominal amount of any Loan not exceeding one million, and one-eighth per cent. On any amount in excess of that sum. One-quarter per cent. Of commission is also allowed on the principal sum of debentures paid off, and on payments involving verification of accounts or transmission to the Colony by documentary evidence or vouchers. For interest on the public debt, which is payable half-yearly in London, a charge of one-half per cent is allowed.

The interest payable to the Government in respect of any cash balance in the hands of the Bank is 1 per cent below the Bank of England rate, for the time being, on the daily balance; and the interest chargeable to the Government for cash advanced by the Bank is 1 per cent above the Bank of England rate, but the charge on such advance can never be less than 5 per cent during the currency of the agreement.

When the proceeds of a loan, or any portion thereof, have to be made available to the Government in Sydney, exchange upon the operation is chargeable at a rate one-quarter per cent, less than the rate then ruling for sixty days bills on London, or, if required by the Bank, notice of the desired transfer must be given, so that the transfer may be regulated in accordance with the scale provided by the agreement.

When funds are required in London by the Government they must be placed there in one of the three undermentioned ways:–

By remitting sovereigns through the Bank at current rates of freight and insurance, and cost of package.

By remitting the bills of the Bank at one quarter per cent less than the exchange of the day.

By placing in the hands of the Bank, as collateral security, Government Debentures for sale, on which the Bank must advance up to a sum of £350,000, if required.

Copies of the London account, supported by vouchers and authorities, &c., are furnished monthly to the Treasurer and Auditor General, respectively. On receipt of these documents the receipts and payments therein shown are at once abstracted and passed through the books of the Treasury in the same manner as if the transactions had taken place in the Colony.

REVENUE AND EXPENDITURE

The Revenue and Expenditure of the Colony is increasing year by year in proportion to the prosperity of the people and the increase of population. This is naturally to be expected for as new lands are taken up and outlying districts occupied, demands upon the Government for all those services which tend to promote the well-being of a community are constantly being made; and although these services when granted create an additional expenditure, there generally follows an augmentation of the revenue, both from the sale and occupation of the waste lands of the Colony, and the larger consumption of dutiable articles.

When responsible Government was established in 1855, the revenue amount to £973,178, the population being then only 277,000. Ten years later–that is, in 1865, and after the Colony of Queensland had been formed out of the Northern Districts of New South Wales–the revenue amounted to £1,755,462, and the population to 411,000. In 1875, exactly twenty years after the introduction of Responsible Government, the population had increased to 606,000, and the revenue to £4,121,996. The population is now estimated at 700,000.

During the last six or seven years the revenue has largely exceeded the expenditure, and notwithstanding that Loans for Public Works and other purposes have been paid off out of the annual surpluses of these years, to the extent of nearly two millions, there was left an actual surplus on the 31st December, 1878, of close upon two millions and a half. One-half of this surplus it is proposed to expend upon public works and buildings of a permanent and national character–still reserving a million and a quarter for future appropriation.

The following statement, taken from the Government Gazette, of 2nd January last, shows in a condensed form the actual revenue and the actual disbursement during the year 1878:–

It will be observed that the expenditure here shown amounts to a larger sum than the Revenue of 1878. It must, however, be understood that this expenditure includes a large amount chargeable to the Revenue of previous years, which owing to the lapse of certain appropriations for public work under the provisions of the Audit Act, could not be incurred until re-votes for such services were obtained.

The Treasury, New South Wales, JAMES THOMSON
8th May 1879

REVENUE, 1878

Taxation			
Customs	£1,148,737.	0.	9
Duty on refined sugar and molasses	40,212	15	4
Duty on spirits distilled in the Colony	4,007	4	5
Stamp Duties (arrears)	9	17	4
Duty on Gold	6,898	14	9
Licenses	109,851	16	0
	1,309,717	8	7
Land Revenue			
Sales	1,915,466	16	0
Interest on Conditional Sales	160,544	11	1
Pastoral Occupation	216,092.	3.	6
Mining Occupation	11,662	11	4
Miscellaneous Receipts	21,946	6	1
	2,325,712	8	0
Receipts for services rendered			
Railway receipts	£860,285	2	10
Telegraph receipts	72,095	3	6
Postage	148,571	15	4
Commission on Money Orders	5,737	12	0
Mint Charges	9,810	0	0
Fees for escort and conveyance of Gold	1,465	1	2
Pilotage and Harbour and Light rates	32,062	5	2
Registration of Brands	850	1	9
Contributions under the Sheep Disease Prevention Act	7,188	12	0

Fees of Office	45,516	10	2
	1,183,582.	3.	11
Miscellaneous Receipts			
Rents, other than rents of land	6,096	17	5
Fines and Forfeitures	9,939	13	8
Interest on Bank Deposits	91,771	15	5
Other items	65,098	19	6
	172,907	6	0
Total Revenue of 1878	£4,991,919	6	6

EXPENDITURE, 1878

Civil List charges	£48,231	16	4
Executive and Legislative Departments	19,133	7	4
Colonial Secretary's Department	4,584	6	11
Volunteer and Military Forces	62,138	18	9
Ordnance Department	22,222	4	0
Police	187,347	11	3
Prisons	72,466	14	1
Audit Department	6,219	18	0
Registrar General's Department	15,750	1	3
Agent General for the Colony (London)	2,850	0	0
Immigration	95,126	16	11
Medical Officers and Lunatic Asylums	64,355	10	6
Charitable and Benevolent Institutions	80,180	2	8
Department of Justice and Public Instruction	4,911	14	3
Public Instruction and Educational Establishments	375,360	5	1
Free Public Library	5,008	7	7
Observatory	2,626	17	4
Museum	2,299	4	6
Attorney General's Department	4,592	15	10
Administration of Justice	124,351	1	1
Treasury	14,585	16	1

Customs	48,587	11	5
Government Printing Department	34,988	15	10
Stores and Stationery	91,003	5	7
Marine Board	38,157	17	10
Administration of the Public Lands	355,807	18	6
Department of Mines	18,269	9	7
Department of public works	7,080	16	5
Railways	698,446	3	3
Public Works	317,677	3	5
Harbours and Rivers Navigation Works	184,237	3	11
Roads and Bridges	525,496	14	1
Post Office	281,119	11	0
Electric Telegraphs	96,181	13	7
Interest on Loans	560,651	10	8
Repayment of Loans	27,400	0	0
Drawbacks and Refund of Revenue	268,387	0	9
Charges on Collections	4,342	15	10
Endowment of Municipalities	82,634	17	10
Sydney Branch of the Royal Mint	16,250	0	0
Pensions–36 Vic. No. 29	8,806	5	8
Departments other than those abovementioned	33,025	16	8
Miscellaneous Services	195,990	1	4
Total Expenditure in 1878	£5,108,881.	2.	11

APPENDIX B

THE FORGOTTEN RECORDS

These are extracts taken from letters by Deputy Assistant Commissary-General. George Thomas William Boyes from Sydney to his wife in England. Lithgow was a friend and colleague of G.T. Boyes, and was to be his lodging partner until Boyes' wife arrived in the colony from England. However, the wife, Elizabeth, remained in England until 1832 before joining her husband in the Colony of VDL. By that time Boyes had been promoted and made the Commissary in VDL. In spite of Boyes looking forward to sharing lodgings with Lithgow, the Governor allocated the house to the office of the Colonial Treasurer, and Balcombe (the Treasurer), and his family lived upstairs, in this office/residence. This letter does not appear in the collected writings of Boyes, which has been described by the curator of the Mitchell Library in Sydney as being a valuable outline of life in the colony in the 1820s and early 1830s. Boyes was a voluminous letter writer, and his family saved the letters for many generations.

On 24th January 1824 Boyes wrote:

We arrived at Hobart town on 27th December (1823) and reached here (Sydney) on the 6th January

1824 per '*Sir Godfrey Webster*'. The situation in Hobart is extremely beautiful and the River Derwent up where we went to the Falls about 25 miles from the town, is the most beautiful thing I have ever seen. The approaches to this place and the country around it is quite uninviting, except the fine clear blue bay–the country about may be described as made up of rocks, not very high (so that there is no sublimity) peeping through and tumbling down from trees of a stunted, ragged and frightful appearance . . . notwithstanding its beauty VDL is not the country for a settler and in my opinion the poor wretches, as well as sick ones, had much better have staid quietly at home.

At Hobart town there was no lodging to be had, prices of everything enormous–butter 4/–to 7/–per pound; eggs 3/–per dozen. Fish as dear as butter–the little fruit available was enormously dear and of wretched quality.

Dined with the Governor, Commissary Moodie and Harbour Master Bromby.

Here at Sydney, it is different–some things are expensive eg House-rent . . . butter 3/-, eggs 1/6 to 2/-Peaches very fine and vegetables scarce. Dined with Governor Sir Thomas Brisbane . . . Lithgow not yet arrived from Isle de France (Mauritius)–I am ready to commence my duties as soon as I am supplied with a house . . . Goodsir and Howard my fellow officers are on The *Guildford* which has not yet arrived, though we left her at Teneriffe for here direct . . . From what I have seen, I think this country will do–have seen some pleasant spots on the banks of the River that would suit us. (Boyes' wife was not to join him until 1832)

On 12th April 1824, he wrote:

. . . We have had several arrivals lately. Judge Francis and family per The *Guildford.* The *Hibernia* anchored on the 5th bringing Mr Radford (Commissary Radford); Mr & Mrs Balcombe and family coming out as Colonial Treasurer (office at corner of O'Connell and Bent Streets, known as Balcombe's house); Sax Bannister, Attorney-General (Ist Attorney-general under constitution of 1824) and two Misses B, the elder a great botanist. There are some good houses here. I have taken one of the best. Three rooms on the ground floor–one 36' x 28' x 18' high–over these, 6 good-sized rooms for Lithgow and myself, fine cellars, dairy etc, pump, coach-house, stables for six horses, veranda on two sides and drying green. Rent 125 pound . . . there is much, indeed a great deal more society than I want. I have all my books and amusements about me.

I will now take you up the country with me to Morton Park (near Appin between Liverpool and Campbelltown). Mr De Arietta (hereafter referred to as D'A) who was employed in the Government printing office, whose establishment was recommended by Lithgow, and who during the greater part of the Peninsular War, accompanied Commissary Wilkinson and occasionally dabbled with merchandise, perhaps as a sought of go-between with his patron and the contractors). An unfortunate speculation laid him low, but the claim of his against the governor appears to have been tactfully settled through negotiations through Morton Pitt MP. Lord Bathurst ordered he be given 2,000 acres to cultivate vine and the olive (about which he knew nothing). In richness of soil and beauty of situation his grant yields nothing in the country but then he began at the wrong end. Instead of feeding sheep, he put in the plough, and his little ready money was swallowed up and his estate mortgaged to full value. His temper, naturally good, became soured by disappointment, and the gay, easy open-hearted man of thirty became, at 48, envious, suspicious, irritable and at times he is quite different, but in short time the bright beam is lost amongst the clouds that darken his brow. To you, I have played with the light and absurd parts of his character, reserving what I have to say on the side for the man who spoke ill of my ill-fortune but friendly protégé.

D'A was born at San Sebastian, spent his boyhood in France, his early manhood in England, out of the last he got the language in which he chooses to converse. He has almost forgotten French and Spanish.

On the 31st January, (1824) D'A had called with his gig and took me away to Liverpool. Our way was cut through the woods and the 'rude' track was bounded by ill-shaped forest trees through which a hot wind prevailed; for the last mile, in the dark, he entertained me with accounts of the most notorious bushrangers; and from time to time anxiously enquired if my pistol was safe. The next morning we proceeded through burning forests, ignited trees crashing down at times, and, here and there, the fire crackled through the grass and apparently surrounded us like seas of flame. We breakfasted with Mr Howe in Upper Minto, after which the land began to open out. I soon found reason to lament the unfeeling spirit that had urged the settlers to give so many noble trees wantonly to the axe and flame. To reproach such people for want of taste would be absurd, since few of them have ever heard of such a principle but a sense of interest might have struck them forcibly that, to leave time on the property they did not intend to cultivate would be the highest economy. John Oxley, the colonial surveyor, has cleared 2,000 acres of every tree and his example has been universally followed. We called on Mr Wild at the government Stock Farm and finally arrived at Morton Park at 4pm.

On 2nd February, (1824) we had walked down to the Nepean River, bathed, made a sketch etc (Boyes had a skill for sketching well, and these sketches form an important 'picture' of the early colony)

On 3rd February, Mr Rumker the astronomer came out in the Governor's suite and stayed at Government house assisting the Governor with his calculations (Brisbane was a proficient astronomer): but an unfortunate eclipse of the moon separated them forever–watching the progress of the earth's shadow over the face of the moon.

'Done' said Sir Thomas (Brisbane) 'Done' said Rumker but not at the same third of time. 'Eight digits' said Sir Thomas; 'Nine digits' said Rumker. His Excellency's accuracy was questioned, and his character perhaps at stake–Rumker though a poor dependent was too proud of his Science to yield on so important a matter as a whole digit, and as Sir Thomas showed no disposition even to split the difference the two great men separated for ever–Rumker is a German–a spare meagre form approaching squalidness–his eyes sunk deep in the head, his whiskers hanging down over his shirt collar–and his black hair reaching his middle, guiltless of a curve. His limbs appeared to be hooked and eyed to his body, and with air, the most distrait he rolled about as if unhinged by intoxication.

A coat, that perhaps once was black, permitted a dirty piece of cotton to be seen at every bend through various formed crevices that time had worn in its texture; his waistcoat had disappeared altogether, and what was left of an old pair of kerseymere trousers was nothing to speak of. Like another Cincinnatus he flew from the court to the ploughed field, and was standing at the door of his hut, just as I have described him; serving out salt pork to his men, when we rode up to the door, the inside of the domicile well corresponded with the external indications. The logs of which the hut had been built, owing to the very dry weather, had retreated from each other, so that he could have an eye to every inch of his farm without moving from his box, for chair he had none. On the table was a broken basin, a blunt-edged knife–black and corroded–a German ephemeris (an account of the daily state or opposition of the planets–a journal of daily transactions) for 1818; a 4 foot telescope on a mahogany case coated with clay was lying on the sod; on the table were lying also, half a melon, one side shrivelled, implying frugality even in the use of this simple luxury; particles of tea and sugar–a bone spoon of colour of rusty bacon . . . (commissary) ration books interspersed with unintelligible characters similar to those in Moore's Almanac. The bed simplicity itself–a discoloured blanket and an old stuff cloak, spread with three bars of ironbark, received the weary limbs of the philosopher when eager for repose.

The next day Rumker walked over to D.A's to dinner, in a hot wind, a little discomposed as to his toilet, and apologised for his appearance. So no more can be said.

The Governor one day insisted on Rumker accompanying him on a shooting party. 'Now' said Rumker 'I have no love for the sport, and besides I do not know how to shoot and besides I have never fired off a gun myself in all my life that I know of. When we were going along we see two magpies sitting upon a tree; they were evidently a man and a wife, when the Governor lifted his gun to his shoulder in order to fire and kill one of the birds; Sir Thomas shoots very well but I got so choked up that I threw down the shot belt, that he had made me bring, and stomped on it like mad. I have never liked him since'.

During the evening Rumker talked much and well upon the fine arts–he spoke of Memnon's head and the horses of Monte Cavallo, and told me he played the piano, whereupon he murdered an air of Cimarosa's and promptly fell fast asleep. The exercise, the wine, and the unusual animation of the evening overpowered his faculties. He rose at daylight and walked home. His recollection is that he had the key of the barn and the men could not commence thrashing until he returned. He was on his away before he had half recovered from his previous excitement.

On the 22nd, upon returning from bathing in the Nepean River, I was summoned to see the gardener who had shot off his hand. I found the poor fellow lying in a cart, just about to start for Liverpool, it then being 9 am and he could not possibly reach the station before 5 PM. He bore his misfortune with what might have done honour to a Heathenish philosopher, merely asking if he had killed the bird and saying that it served him right for presuming to fire off a gun on a Sunday. D'A in the meantime was running about exclaiming 'Oh, my God, what shall I do without a gardener? Oh, what great loss I meet with? Nobody shall tell what I lose. Oh my tobacco, who will take care of my tobacco? Any other time would not be such a great loss to me.

Nothing can make up to me for so great a loss.

Not caring a fig for the poor fellow who had sustained an irreparable loss, and thinking only of himself, because D'As chaise was sitting in the yard and it could have taken the chap to the hospital with ease and safety within 3 hours.

On 29th, we expected Rev'd Mr Reddal to read prayers but he came not. I walked over to Dr. Douglas' grounds (later to become Douglass Park).

On March 4th I was reading the history of Michael Howe and the bushrangers of VDL–a small pamphlet curious only as being the first that issued from the Hobart town Press.

On 5th March, D'A and I talked about (1) Mr Macarthur's horses destroying his corn (2) the cargo of Irish port which O'Callaghan of Cork deceived him about, (3) Mr Morton Pitt, M.P. for Dorsetshire and (4) the richness of the soil of Morton Park and his intended improvements (5) His exploits with bushrangers and what he would have done had there been occasion (6) the kindness and vigour of the late Governor (Macquarie) and the coldness and weakness of the present (Brisbane), and a curse on the colonial secretary for reducing the price of wheat from 10/–to 4/–a bushel (7) The fidelity and good qualities of his dogs contrasted with the sloth, roguery and ingratitude of his servants (8) the promising appearance, mode of curing and probable quality of his tobacco.

Now I have been with him altogether for 47 days, say 5 hours a day, conversing at meals and when walking, and 8 hours when driving for 4 days i.e. 32 hours; 36 days at home–180 hours i.e. a total of 212 hours divided by 8 topics, gives almost 24 hours to each.

After my sufferings Job appears to be tolerable. The more so as D'As whole range of the English language does not exceed 50 words

At this time, the tobacco business engrosses the table chat. The fiery weather keeps me much in the house and I am at his mercy . . . D'A would repeat over and over "I wish Talboy (the overseer) would come. I cannot go on with my tobacco till he comes. When I build my other store there will be room enough for my tobacco. If my tobacco turns out well, I shall build my new house, as you shall see. Ah, my good sir, if Governor Macquarie was here now it would be quite a different thing. It would be better for me I tell you if it was not for him (Brisbane), better if he had no say. D'A puts the plough in the ground and you shall do very well. My God, I clear 400 acres and sow my corn and then comes the colonial secretary and brings the price down to 4/-. Did you ever see better land than mine? It is the richest, most beautiful land of any you shall see. Smell that piece–it has never before been turned over. The bouquet! Did you see that last load of tobacco; it had such fine leaves–as long as that!"

The evenings now are exquisitely beautiful, the moon near the full; the air is balmy, but there is no silence–the fields swarm with crickets, the watch-dogs bark, the shouts of the watchmen are heard in the distance, scaring the horses from the Indian corn. The native dog' bark is short and piercing; the opossum scrambles up the trees and utters his notes of love or terror–some night bird moans his lost love or courts another. The curlew shrieks on hill and in vale, the cuckoo (aye, the cuckoo) in autumn lends its note to break the silence of night, or rather to increase its discords, but my reveries are interrupted by 'What are you thinking about?'

On the 16th I am off to Sydney the day after tomorrow and have bidden adieu to my favourite river and its rocky banks and in considering how many hours I have spent in rambling about the Nepean, I cannot think of my departure with indifference. After heavy rain, it cleared up this afternoon, and the lichens, the mosses, the myrtles and mimosas melted into balmy drops as I passed them. Each shrub too fragrance on my head and perfumed my path. It is a grey sober twilight sort of evening and but for the tinkling of the little bellbird as I climbed the rugged path that led up the precipitous bank, the silence was complete.

In these wild sequestered scenes there is nothing to remind you of England, of animals you meet: with the Wallaby, the Kangaroo rat, the native dog, the opossum, the native cat, all differing from those of our country. The woods swarm with birds whose notes are entirely new to the European ear, and are as various as they are discordant–sometimes when I have been bathing in the Nepean River these feathered savages have jumped up all at once yelling, screaming, shouting and laughing. 50 native birds can make a lot of noise.

The country about Morton Park (this property is now part of the Morton National Park, east of Goulburn, and on the Shoalhaven River) is very beautiful; you ride over a succession of hills that are neither high nor steep, covered with loads of grass and the trees are never thick enough to impede your way–the whole of the ride is very like a park in England; from the summit of the little hills you get occasional peeps over a great extent of country and when mellowed into the distance the external woods lose their monotonous effect.

Port Jackson cannot certainly be called ugly because there are so many covers and islands in it. The variety is pleasing but the banks, not very high, are composed of rugged sand stone in all sorts of grotesque forms and covered with ill-shaped trees, blasted by lightening and storms till they have almost lost their genetic character.

Sydney (in 1824) is a large town possessing some thousands of houses. A great many are handsome and most of these have broad verandas–still there are many of the original houses of the first settlers standing, and as they continually obtrude themselves on your notice, and are of a very mean character, the first impression of the whole is by no means favourable.

The heat has been excessive this year–they have had no rain for 5 or 6 months but it is now very pleasant–temperatures from 65 to 70 degrees.

I find Mr Cunningham, the King's botanist, an excellent creature, of course, by this time I know everybody in the colony that is worth knowing. I see a great many faces among the prisoners and emancipated convicts that are familiar. There are several Jews here, rich, keeping a handsome Tilbury etc. There is among them a fellow by the name of Raphael, rather stout and not tall–two or three Levis, a Lazarus–a Josephson and some others. A Mr Robertson, formerly with Glimaldi and Johnson (Merchants), keeps a shop near the landing place and is doing very well.

On May 24th, (1824) he wrote

The *Brothers,* a convict ship, arrived at Hobart some weeks ago, after it had left England about 6.10.1823 and brought Mr Lithgow. I have been writing to the Governor ever since I arrived and the said Governor (Brisbane) has played me such a dirty trick about an office that I had fully determined to ask permission to return to England when Lithgow arrived. Mr Balcombe, who was sent out, as Colonial Treasurer has not been acting like an English gentleman. He had taken the only eligible house (corner of O'Connell and Bent Streets) for an office over my head after I had come to regular terms with the proprietor, and what is more extraordinary, the Governor, who, between ourselves is a great fool, has lent his name to the proceeding–it certainly was not an affair to take up as an individual, so I contented myself with telling the Colonial Secretary officially what I thought of the transaction. I liked Lithgow at first sight, but I think however there must be something contagious in this atmosphere, for however perfect some of the higher classes, or what the Edinburgh Reverend (Lithgow) calls the 'undetected thieves', might have left their country as to character, they quickly degenerate to beings who could hold no rank in English society. They daily commit or are parties to the most questionable transactions, and yet expect to be, and are, received into the best society of Botany Bay. I am just sent for to go on a board at the stores–Radford and I live together–he has charge of the Military Chest. I expect that as soon as we begin our duties there will be the deuce to pay among them. The whole system has been shockingly conducted. There has been no system worthy of the name. Mrs Wemyss (wife of Commissary Wemyss the predecessor to Commissary Laidley) keeps aloof from all society here. She calls on no one. The people are so bad that her conduct meets with my entire approbation, particularly as I am admitted once or twice a week to her table. The *Brothers* arrived after having left at Hobart Town her valuable cargo of 89 female convicts.

Captain Piper is the Naval Officer here, a situation that has given him 4 or 5,000 pound a year and, I suspect he spends every farthing of it. He lives in a beautiful house just after you enter Port Jackson (Point Piper, Double Bay, Rose Bay) and it is certainly a sweet situation, but it stands alone, for there is nothing like it in the colony. He has laid out immense sums upon it and in making roads to it and no expense has been spared, I am told, to ornament this fairy palace. They say that he has upwards of 100 men employed about him. He does the thing properly, for he sends carriages and four, and boats for those who like the water, and returns his guests to their homes in the same manner. He keeps a band of music and they have quadrilles every evening under the spacious verandas. At the table there is a vast profusion of every luxury that the four quarters of the globe can supply, and you must know that this fifth or pickpocket quarter contributed nothing of itself. I was invited but declined, for there is no honour in dining with Piper, for he invites everybody whom comes here indiscriminately. At the moment his invitation arrived, Sir James Jamieson, who is the richest man in the colony, was asking me to make Regentville my home, whenever I could visit the Nepean, and he also has the finest house in Sydney, and when down in the Town has all his friends about him, and what is better than all, the governor cannot get him to Government house.

I dined with the Wemyss' on Saturday, the party consisting of Major Bates, just arrived from Mauritius, Mr Savage–a Merchant, Lieutenant Henry Dumaresq, Dr Mitchell, Mr Howard (Assistant-Commissary, Radford and myself. Mrs W. although considerably past the usual age is now nursing herself for an expected baby. Nature seems to have entered into the views of the colonisation very completely and when the ladies conduct themselves with propriety, has put no limits to their provocative powers, nor marked any specific age for their cessation. Wives so situated are allowed to knock off 10 years from all future acknowledgements.

On 12th May, (1824) he wrote

Radford and I entertained the following party at dinner: Major Bates, Mr Lithgow, Lt. Dumaresq, Mr Goodsir and Mr Walker (of Rhodes, Sydney and VDL)

On 25th May (1824), he writes:

The *Guildford* sailed for the Derwent where she takes aboard Lt Gov Lovell and returns to England. The *Midas* will be the next ship home. What, with Botany, Chemistry, Mineralogy, Music and Drawing, I have not a moment to spare. The thunderstorms are very violent, and in some seasons frequent. I have heard the thunder roll and seen the lightning flash for 3 hours without an instant's cessation, more resembling the heavy fire of artillery than the war of elements.

The *Adrian,* which brought out the new Lieutenant Governor to VDL has arrived in Sydney, bringing newspapers to the middle of January. Major Morisset (Lieutenant Lawson preceded him), the Commandant at Bathurst, and old friend of Lukens and mine, has paid us a visit, which I hope to return when I can decently absent myself from office for a fortnight. In the meantime I have plenty of subjects for the pencil and have just finished my first view and begun another. Nothing in the shape of drawings has yet left the colony, except a few by Major Taylor of the 48th, and they have very little merit. I have the prints made from them and they are so deficient in perspective. Without local character, they lose all effect.

Last Thursday, Sir John Jamieson gave a Ball and supper–I think about 140 sat down. He has a famous large house and one room contained the whole party–about a dozen carriages conveyed the whole party to the house by about 9 PM. Though all the servants were convicted felons, I heard of but one robbery from Darcy Wentworth, the Chief of Police, who lost a diamond broach of some value. The whole thing with that one exception was conducted in a most orderly way and might be quoted as an example to the most fashionable routs in the English metropolis. The women danced tolerably well, and all preserved. I returned home pretty sick of it by 3 AM but a large proportion kept it up until daylight. Mr Wemyss gives a grand dinner party the day after tomorrow to the Chief Judge, the Attorney General, Colonial Treasurer, the Judge Advocate (John Wylde was the second officer in command of the military), and Lt-Colonel Balfour of the 40th Regiment, Radford and myself and the Colonial Auditor Lithgow. For Thursday, cards have been issued for a Ball and supper being a farewell party to the officers of the *Tees* which ship is about to leave for the East India States and after that, I think, I shall have had quite enough of it.

Generally speaking, I dislike the people here beyond anything I have ever before experienced, and except for our own little circle I do not mean to visit or receive!

On 6th July 1824 he wrote:

Three ships will sail tomorrow for England–the *Midas,* the *Countess Dalhousie* and the *Rambler.* Recently this town has been all gaiety, with balls every week, but I have accepted only one of the three invitations received. I have only attended Sir John Jamieson's. I prefer my fireside and a book.

Last Sunday passed very much to my mind. Mr Berry, a merchant, took me over to his brother's place on the other side of the cove; after walking uphill about 1 ½ mile (to Crows Nest house), we came upon a house built upon a spot cleared of trees. From the veranda there is a view of Botany Bay. It looks over Sydney and the windings of the cove up to Parramatta, then an immense forest of trees planted by hand of Nature till bounded by the Blue Mountains about 30-40 miles off, and then sat down to a fowl as large as a turkey–roast leg of mutton and curry, cauliflower in the highest perfection and turnips–the whitest and best flavoured that I have eaten for years. These vegetables were reared on soil composed of the scrapings of the rocks and dust and small pieces formed by blowing up the great masses, after being first planted out, no attention was paid to them and as to head-glass or frame there was no such contrivance on the ground.

This is certainly a most extraordinary climate–we have hardly anything but fine sunny cloudless skies–but it is now far too hot in the middle of the day to take much exercise. I do not think that Lithgow will remain here long, as the situation does not answer his expectations.

On the 15th September, (1824)

The *Prince Regent* leaves tomorrow with Major Bates returning to Mauritius thereby. I took a trip to Parramatta to pass the day with Captain Hibbert of the 40th in command there. The *Tamar* sailed on the 25th to form a settlement on the north-west coast, some 2 or 3,000 miles from here (Port Essington), and a few days after another expedition sailed for a similar purpose to Moreton bay–Lt. Miller of the 40th has gone as commandant, his wife insisted on going with him; they were in the enviable position of being on a craft of 140 tons so full of bipeds and quadrupeds that the crew have to sleep on the deck, if at all. No medical attendant on hand, and the need to land on a desolate coast.

Two barristers, Wentworth and Wardell have just arrived, together with Bannister the Attorney General. Wentworth is a native of this colony (being born at Norfolk Island), but also the illegitimate son of the greatest landowner here (Darcy Wentworth). They made a motion the other day that the old half bred Attorney who had been doing all the business of the court should be turned out and be no longer allowed to practice as Attorney and Counsel.

The ship *Mangles* arrived on the 25th. I met a Colonel Mills at the Wemyss house. He is a very ridiculous old man who has been a Colonel in the Army. He is the M.P. for Winchelsea and a West Indian Planter.

Lithgow has just been appointed to the Audit of the Colonial Treasury, as well as still being the commissary accountant, and he intends to recommend to the Governor on his return from Morton Bay that I should be sent to take charge of the accounts of VDL and audit the treasury ship of that colony. There is nothing I should so much delight in as to be stationed in the VDL: the country is magnificent, as fine as anything in Scotland without its barrenness. It offers rivers and lakes, mountains and valleys and meadows with a climate much more temperate and steady than England and free from the fierce extremes of this country.

The *Prince Regent* sails tomorrow. What a fuss they are making about the Agricultural Coy (the AAC); no one will benefit from it except the great farmers here, who would never be able to turn their flocks and herds into cash without the money of the wiseacres in England. Depend upon it; whatever they lay out here is gone forever, without the prospect of a return.

24th August 1824–

Every morning I leave home at 9 AM and have a beautiful walk of about 3 miles that winds through a variety of superb shrubs, to all of which you are a stranger, along the shores of the little inlets into Sydney Cove; the mornings are fresh and sunny, and at every turn I discover something new in the prospect, or the same prospect seen under different feelings.

There will be everything in this colony in time except plenty of water and honest men."

APPENDIX C

THE LITHGOW COLLEAGUES

Working as Number Two man (only the Colonial secretary was in a more senior position), and being appointed to so many Committees and Boards, Lithgow worked with most of the notable colonial figures–both political and commercial. It is of value to review the background and circumstances of those special few that influenced Lithgow and the structure of the Colony. It will become apparent, that working in a small colony, everyone knew everyone and marriages between prominent families often kept a dynasty in formation, to the obvious benefit of the colony.

The Main Associates

Ovens–co-authored the analysis and Report (to Darling) on convict work practices. Ovens was a confident of Gov. Darling, and an Engineer
Dumaresq, Henry
J.T. Campbell (Col. Sec)
Alex McLeay (Col. Sec)
William Stewart
George T. Palmer
Samuel Marsden
D.L. Riddell (Colonial Treasurer)
C.D. Ridden, (Colonial Treasurer)
William Cowper
W.G. Broughton (Archdeacon)
E. Deas Thompson (Col. Sec)

Sir Thomas Mitchell
W. Ellyard Jr

Governors

Brisbane,
Darling,
Bourke
Sir George Gipps
Charles A. Fitzroy

Secretaries of State

Earl Bathurst
Under Secretary Hay
Viscount Goderich
Rt Hon. Huskisson
Rt. Hon. E.G. Stanley
Lord Glenelg
Lord John Russell
Earl Grey

Lithgow's committees etc

Board of Trustees of the Clergy & School Lands
Member–Legislative Council
Acting Private Secretary to the Governor
Director–Bank of New South Wales
Magistrate & J.P.
Executive Council nomination 2.12.1835
Coal Board 25.10.1847
Board of General Purposes
Committee of Management of the Orphan School

Events of Interest in Lithgow's career

Bank of New South Wales
Responding to charges by Hume MP (Westminster)
Female Factory
Coal Board
School & Clergy Land Committee
Compilation of 'Blue Books' by Colonial Auditor & lateness thereof.
Activities of the Legislative Council
Dispute between School & Clergy Lands Board & Dr. J. D. Lang
Locating 13,000 pound of colonial funds in London and other problems with the Agent-General in London (Mr Barnard)
Delay in settling Estate of John Ovens
Transmitting Statements of R & E to London & their delay
Pay Dispute on appointment as Auditor
Reduction in number of clerks
Pay arrangements with acting governor Lindesay
Dispute with the British Treasury over the cost of the Police & Goal Services
Negative comments by the Commissioners of Audit
Report on the Gov. Printing Office
Audit on 'Contingent' Account
Loan by Colonial Treasury to 'Military Chest' and 'Commissariat' Chest

UNDERSTANDING THE LITHGOW COLLEAGUES

The society within the early colony meant that there were at least three strata's of society within the settlement and community.

The Government Officials and senior military officers were at one end and in time, some successful free settlers were welcomed; at the other end were the bulk of the population, that is the convicts. In the middle stood the emancipists, ticket-of-leave people, and the growing number of immigrants–those 'poor' and 'unworthy' folk that Britain was so ready to sponsor away from their shores. The three strata's rarely mingled and few graduated from one rung to the next (one exception was Simeon Lord, a merchant and trader who had been groomed by some of the Military officers as a 'front' for their exploitative plans.

Lithgow was obviously in the company of the wealthy, influential and powerful. He was respected as the second most senior public servant, even if the Public Service of the day was only a few hundred men.

Lithgow associated with these men during working hours–politicians in the Legislative Council, Board members of his various activities as well as the settlers, pastoralists and eventually squatters who were politically influential. We can mention a few whose names recur numerous times in the press of the day, alongside the name of Lithgow, or his official correspondees or his associates on these Boards and Committees.

Major John Ovens was an official Governor's secretary, and confident, brought by Brisbane to Sydney when he was appointed Governor in 1821. Together with Lithgow, Ovens wrote a detailed report for Darling on convict work practices, convict operating costs, and productivity reform. Initially, upon his arrival, he had been appointed chief engineer with general supervision of convict gangs. He had been ideally suited and situation to report on the improvement to efficiency, because of his engineering background, whilst Lithgow was the numbers man, who was able to put a 'face' to the report. Ovens accompanied captain Currie on an expedition to the upper Murrumbidgee and Monaro District in 1823. It was Ovens who told Lithgow of the great potential of the Monaro region and it was Lithgow who secured a 'run' in the area for sheep. Brisbane was quite 'gushy' towards Ovens as he would become towards Lithgow a little later and one can wonder about the objectivity of Brisbane when he writes "no public officer here has rendered me the same essential service, the Colony such benefit, or imposed upon the Mother Country such a heavy debt of gratitude" (HRA I; XIII P532). The governor made Ovens his private secretary when he was not finding Frederick Goulburn cooperative. Ovens planned a retirement to his estate at Concord (today a Sydney suburb) to coincide with Brisbane's departure. However he died just six days after Brisbane's governorship ended.

Henry Dumaresq was a brother-in-law of Darling, his military secretary in Mauritius and private secretary to Governor Darling in NSW and

Secretary to the Executive Council. The brother, William Dumaresq, an Engineer, married Alexander McLeay's daughter. A nephew, Charles Darling, appointed an assistant private secretary, completed this family circle of nepotism, and encouraged by this artificial support, Darling saw himself 'as the chosen defender of the King's authority in an immense territory', where he was paranoid in his suspicion of disloyalty, especially by the military garrison

Upon his retirement in 1834 (Darling was recalled in 1831) he became a Director/Governor of the Australian Agricultural Company. Henry had a 13,000-acre estate at Muswellbrook (named St. Heliers) which according to John Dunmore Lang was run as "one of the best-regulated estates in the colony, with incitement to industry (among the convicts employed) and good conduct are rewards, not punishments". (Lang: An historical & statistical account of NSW).

George Thomas Palmer was the son of John Palmer, the distinguished Commissary-General from Phillip to Macquarie and Brisbane. His first posting in NSW was as Superintendent of government livestock. Resigning after a year, he commenced acquiring land and livestock, including a large acreage where Canberra now stands. He was also a shareholder in the Australian Agricultural Company. His association with Lithgow was increased when Palmer was appointed to the management committee of the Female Factory in the late 1820s. Palmer later served in the Legislative council with Lithgow. Lithgow found him to be 'a man of good education, high honour and integrity, active diligent and intelligent'

Samuel Marsden was the most prominent and successful parson in the colony for nearly 30 years and was very influential as a pastoralist, magistrate and government antagonist. Lithgow sat with him on the Bench and on the Female Factory Board

William Cowper was an active clergyman who essentially remained faithful to his calling whilst in the colony. He administered the Diocese during Bishop Broughton's absences and after his death. Lithgow admired Cowper and sat with him on the Church and Schools Board. Cowper reactivated the Benevolent Society of NSW (formed in 1817) and sat on its Management Board along with Lithgow.

William Brodribb is not a name hanging off many lips, but his is a name connected with Lithgow and his story offers another insight into Lithgow. He had been convicted in 1816 'at the Gloucester Assizes of administering unlawful oaths and transported for seven years. Macquarie transferred him to Hobart where he took the position of clerk of the magistrate's bench'. He returned to NSW and after touring the Monaro, became a partner in a cattle station. In 1837 we find that he became the manager 'of a run held by William Lithgow–the Colonial Auditor' (ADB). We learn the general location of the run from the fact that Brodribb "petitioned for a punt over the Murrumbidgee near the homestead and in January 1838, Deputy-Surveyor-General Perry reported that a 'better site could not have been chosen for a town of the first class Gundagai–(ADB). So at least we know that Lithgow put his association with the Pastoral movement to good, practical use–by becoming a pastoralist himself!

Lithgow worked under and with some fine Colonial Secretaries

John Thomas Campbell, (not related to the Robert Campbell clan of successful traders) was the private secretary to Macquarie and was very influential in the Government organisation of the very early colony. "For eleven years Campbell was Macquarie's chief assistant in the administration of the colony, his intimate friend and loyal supporter" (ADB). Macquarie had wanted to reserve the newly vacant post of official Colonial Secretary for Campbell but the Colonial Office in London appointed Goulburn to that position. In 1824 Brisbane appointed Campbell to the Legislative Council (Lithgow was to join shortly thereafter), and then in 1826, Governor Brisbane (Macquarie's successor) appointed Campbell a member of the influential and important Land Board (Lithgow was already a member) and to the Board of general Purposes, of which Lithgow was also already a member and which supposedly advised the Governor on all matters involving colonial affairs. The Sydney *Monitor* wrote that it was his (Campbell's) eloquence and perseverance next to those of Chief Justice Forbes that the freed portion of our community are indebted for that valuable privilege, the right to sit as jurors in the Supreme Court of NSW". (*Monitor* 1 Nov 1817).

"Campbell took a leading part in the founding of the Bank of NSW in 1816-1817. As the first President of its Board of Directors he gave thorough attention daily to every detail of its organisation and operations until it was well established. He was not re-elected in 1821, after an enthusiastic and competent four years" (R.F. Holder–*Bank of NSW–A History)*. Campbell joined Lithgow as a large livestock holder and operator in the Monaro region of southern NSW

Alexander McLeay arrived in the colony in 1826 and was colonial secretary between 1826 and 1836 before becoming active in a community way. He was the first president of the Australian Museum, the Australian Subscription Library and the Botanic Gardens and Agricultural Society. He was Speaker of the Legislative Council between 1843 and 1846. Lithgow was also his colleague on the Land Board. "In 1824 Lord Bathurst had decided to end the friction between Governor Brisbane and Major Goulburn in the administration of NSW by recalling both officers and replacing them with General Darling and an experienced civilian assistant. After some persuasion by Bathurst, McLeay was induced to accept the appointment on June 25th 1825 as Colonial Secretary of NSW at a salary of 2,000." (ADB)

Edward Deas Thomson, although a close colleague and one with whom Lithgow would work closely with for many years, still found time to complain publicly about Lithgow during the time of Governor Fitzroy. Thomson writes (in personal letters) that he strived for high standards and had little sympathy for inefficiency and frequently received too little support from other senior public servants such as Riddell (Treasurer) and Lithgow (Auditor). Thomson also writes that 'the gold rush in 1851 strained the capabilities of the senior echelon in the public service. The additional work brought by the discovery of gold and the spread of population impelled him to apply in June 1851 for a salary increase of 500 pound' (ADB). Fitzroy granted this request. It was during this period that Lithgow decided to retire. He was working long hours, and was under great stress and pressure and was overlooked by Fitzroy in the granting of additional salaries even though the number of clerks was reduced at a time of additional demand for clerical assistance. Even Thomson received an assistant, thus relieving him of some of the burden. Lithgow's circumstances, his partial distrust of Thomson and the offer of a pension of 339.3.4 per annum, made him decide to retire on 30th April 1852. Lithgow had extensive private interests. "From the grant of 2,000 acres and a Sydney Building allotment in 1824 he had built up substantial estates. He held shares in the Bank of NSW and the failed Bank of Australia. His retirement was relatively short-lived as he died in 1864. Thomson had worked in the Royal Navy and in the USA and the West Indies before accepting the position of clerk of the council in NSW. He took up this position in 1829 as clerk to the Executive and Legislative Councils at 600 pound a year, but soon won Governor Darling's approval by his competence and industry. He was also a member of several boards concerned with the control of convicts and claimed to have found particular satisfaction on the Convict Assignment Board, where he suggested the chief regulations introduced in 1835 for the assignment of male convicts. He received special favouritism with Governor Bourke whose daughter Thomson married in 1833. This led to his appointment, over Lithgow's head to the role of Colonial Secretary. This was the start of distancing and distrust between Thomson and Lithgow. McLeay had been close to Lithgow and had been grooming Lithgow as his successor. The new Thomson position also carried with it membership of the Executive Council and the Legislative Council, a body to which Lithgow had already been appointed.

Lithgow should have had much in common with Thomson; Thomson was born in Edinburgh and educated at Edinburgh High School, afterwards going onto the University of Edinburgh, where Lithgow had studied some years previously. Both men had studied political economy and attended lectures by the Scottish writer J.R. McCulloch, whose ideas on free trade became important to both Lithgow and Thomson.

William Elyard was another who claimed close association with Lithgow. He was a senior clerk in the Colonial-Secretary's office and was an important junior link in the McLeay-Darling-Lithgow administrative revolution. He rose to under-secretary position and was Lithgow liaison between McLeay and the audit office.

William Stewart was a soldier and the Lieutenant Governor, highly regarded by Governor Darling. Stewart was employed in various duties by making him a member of the Land Board, the Board of General Purposes and the Board of Inquiry in 1826 into the Female Orphan School. Lithgow also sat on each of these boards and worked closely with Stewart

William Broughton was one of the earliest public servants in the colony, arriving with the First Fleet as a servant to Surgeon White. After first becoming the 'store-keeper' in Parramatta in 1793, he replaced John Palmer as Commissary when Palmer went off to London in support of Governor Bligh in 1809. He became a landowner through large grants and was a significant shareholder and director of the Bank of NSW, and a supporter of the Benevolent Society, which is where Lithgow came into association with him. The ADB claims "among a motley crowd of dissolute officials, Broughton stands out as a loyal, trustworthy public servant who, as Macquarie reported, performed 'honest, faithful, useful and arduous service for thirty years', but because he had no powerful patron in London was consistently passed over in favour of less competent men".

Campbell Robert Riddell was a public servant all of his life and originated from Scotland, where he had joined the colonial service, first in Ceylon and was then transferred to Sydney. Governor Bourke praised Riddell's performance on the Board for assigning Convicts, although this task, combined with Riddell's duties as Colonial Treasurer, did not carry extra pay, much to Riddell's grievance. However Bourke did commend him for his 'promptitude and benevolence in finding employment for female migrants. Riddell, like his predecessor Balcombe, acted 'imprudently, when he placed the holdings of uninvested savings bank deposits in an account of his own, instead of in a Treasury account. Riddell was an executive councillor (a member of Bourke's Executive Council, not as Riddell but as the treasurer. Always aspiring to be Colonial Secretary, Riddell was appointed temporarily in 1854 when Thomson went to England with the draft constitution for self-government. He retired in 1856.

John Thomas Bigge was not an associate of Lithgow, but it was as a result of the reform movement following the Bigge Reports in 1822 and 1823 that Lithgow's positions of Deputy–Commissary of Accounts and Colonial Auditor were established. His reports collectively prompted the insertion in the Act 4 Geo IV, c.96 of clauses to set up limited constitutional government through Legislative Council, to enable extensive legal and financial reforms and to make new provisions for the reception of convicts from England. Bigge's work was valuable and important to the colony's development but his assessments were not without bias. Macarthur's influence gave Bigge the opportunity of criticising Macquarie. Among the Bigge proposals of any substance were the detailing of convict gangs to clear land, the sale of crown lands and preparation of adequate registers of prisoners. Brisbane placed Lithgow in charge of the implementation of these new plans. Bigge's Reports canvassed four principal themes: "general colonial conditions, the convict system, relations between social classes and Macquarie's programme of public works. Much was made of the alleged mismanagement of convicts and Bigge seemed little concerned that the convict system was working better than ever before in the Colony, that Macquarie's methods had produced and maintained 'peace if not harmony' (Macquarie) and that he had curtailed most brutality and violence". (ADB) While Bigge properly exposed inefficiency in district constables, theft from government medical stores, flaws in the ticket-of-leave system for convicts, inadequacies of country education, poor accommodation for female convicts, faulty regulation of liquor traffic and a multitude of similar defects, he failed to account for the very real achievements of government'. (Fletcher: *The British Empire in Australia)*

Lithgow worked with five Governors between 1824 and 1842, and was respected and supported by each of them in turn. They generally spoke highly of this Scotsman who had panache for hard work, lateral thinking and integrity.

Sir Thomas Makdougall Brisbane was the son of ancient Scottish lineage. He also attended (like Lithgow) the University of Edinburgh. Brisbane's policies for the colony were largely based on the Bigge reports and the instructions derived from it, modified by his own impressions. Brisbane found the land grants system in a mess: 340,000 acres of grants by Macquarie had still to be located; land was occupied and transferred without legal title, and boundary disputes were a constant hazard. He instituted a ticket-of-leave system, which enabled land to be immediately occupied without a survey and graziers given security against trespass. In fact, the instructions on the disposal of crown lands, which led to the Land Board and Lithgow's appointment as a commissioner, owed much to Brisbane's advice that he found great satisfaction in noticing the 'very prominent similarity' between them and the practice he had been following in NSW. In 1824, Brisbane had begun selling Crown lands at 5s an acre, and between May and December 1825 more than 500,000 acres were sold. Brisbane received instructions on convict affairs from Bathurst and, as a result, reduced road-gangs and the numbers employed on public works (in Sydney), and organised in their stead, gangs to clear land for settlers in return for payment. Brisbane made other notable policy decisions which

Established an agricultural training college

Established the NSW Agricultural Society, which amongst other activities, financed the importation of livestock

Reduced the assistance to new settlers, making it very difficult to commence farming without adequate capital

Experimented in growing Virginian tobacco, Georgian cotton, Brazilian coffee and NZ flax

Initiated currency reforms by which commissariat payments were set at a fixed value of 5s to the Colonial dollar, or about 1/8th above their intrinsic value. The system was not a success and a sterling standard was adopted

From 1825, all commissariat supplies were called by tender, but this price competition hurt small farmers and with little grain tendered, a minor recession occurred

He gave financial aid to official church groups. His stand against clergymen indulging in private trade hurt relations between Brisbane and Marsden

His attitude towards aborigines was ambivalent, but he gave the London Missionary Society 10,000 acres as an aboriginal reserve

He ended control of the Sydney *Gazette* by government officials

He set up the Legislative Council in 1823 and entered into the transition from Governor autocracy to co-operative advisory consensus

Brisbane did not concern himself with all the details of his administration and even though Lithgow was overworked, as were most senior public servants of the day, and liked Brisbane, he spoke after Brisbane's departure of a mild, unpartial and a firm administration, but J.D. Lang was to comment that Brisbane was 'a man of the best intentions, but disinclined to business, and deficient in energy' Lang: *Historical & Statistical Account of NSW)*

Sir Ralph Darling was a military man who commanded a garrison in Mauritius before being appointed governor in NSW in 1824. The ADB describes his concept of government as "one of military simplicity; strict adherence to regulation, and the unquestioning personal allegiance of his subordinates". He found these qualities in Henry Dumaresq, whose sister he had married, and who he appointed his private secretary, and in Alexander McLeay who he appointed Colonial-secretary and whose daughter married William Dumaresq. In his zeal for efficiency Darling introduced many improvements and reforms into the machinery of government, not the least being an expertly integrated and supervised public service. Another significant reform was his monetary and banking reform, led off by the inquiry into the Balcombe affair in which the Colonial Treasurer, the collector of customs and other officials had long been using government funds for their own profit. Lithgow was appointed by Darling to investigate and report on these misdemeanours. The first Act enabling an Legislative Council to advise the governor, expired and was replaced by a second Act (9 Geo IV, c.83) and this allowed Darling to expand the number of Councillors from seven to fourteen with half of them now being non-official (or appointed from outside government circles). The governor was also required to abide by a majority decisions on his bills in the council. Darling was ordered to establish a Church and School Corporation (of which Lithgow was a member). Darling restructured the Land Board to stop fraud and absentee landlords. Again under pressure from London, Darling gave the Australian Agricultural Company a second choice for its location and a monopoly over coalmines at Newcastle for thirty-one years Darling's land policies caused widespread disruption in the colony and brought crown land sales to a stop. The C & S Corporation (Church and School Corporation) was not to receive any crown land until 1828. Lithgow excused himself from involvement in this land fiasco, even though the Land Board was responsible for implementing the Governor's policy. Fletcher (in *Ralph Darling: A Governor Maligned*) writes that 'Darling was an able administrator, but had little sympathy with popular reform and less with its restless symptoms. His manner was dull, forbidding and humourless; he mistook formality for dignity'. Darling, writing in his own defence stated that "general popularity is not always the companion of integrity–it would have been impossible to satisfy many of the colonists without an abandonment of every principle of justice and duty".

Sir Richard Bourke came to Sydney via Malta and Cape Colony (South Africa), where was acting governor. Bourke was enthusiastically welcomed to the Colony in December 1831 partly because his reputation in Ireland and the Cape had preceded him. His life was shattered by the death of his wife after only 4 months in office and his public disagreements with colonial secretary McLeay and Treasurer Ridden. Lithgow remained loyal to Bourke but remained immersed in his many boards, committees and audits. Bourke sponsored the Church Act, through the Legislative Council (7 Wm IV, no.3), which served to keep the number of churches and clergy of all denominations substantial and to keep pace with the rising population. Lithgow supported this bill, and as a Presbyterian minister he was in favour of State grants to each recognised religion. Bourke also sponsored through the Council, an education bill, proposing a general system of education, wholly controlled and paid for by government, in which visiting clergy were to give religious instruction on a weekly basis. Bourke was active in two other important policy matters, aided by Lithgow–Crown Lands and sponsored Immigration. The Crown Lands Occupation Act (7Wm IV, no.4) provided for annual occupation licences for depasturing livestock on 'unsurveyed runs' beyond the limits of location, where commissioners of crown lands (Lithgow sat on the Land Board), also acting as magistrates, were to carry the rule of law. In 1835 Bourke appointed a select committee (of which Lithgow was a member) to examine the whole subject of immigration. "In colonial eyes the 'bounty' system was the better plan and it became one of the few Bourke measures supported by both political factions in the colony.

Bourke's period of government was one of active economic growth. Between 1831 and 1837: revenue increased from 122855 to354802; exports rose from 324168 to 760054 and population rose from 51000 to 97000; convict population rose from 21000 to 32000. Under the immigration program sponsored by Bourke the proportion of convicts in the general population had decreased.

Bourke's high place in public esteem was shown by the response to the fund commenced by the people to erect his statue (it stands today before the State Library of NSW, in Sydney). Being part sponsored by Lithgow it was filled rapidly and was also contributed to handsomely by Lithgow.

Bourke resigned in December 1837 after his challenge and humiliation by Colonial Treasurer C.D.Riddell.

Sir George Gipps arrived in Sydney in February 1838. His immediate concerns were disagreeable Legislative Council from which he received no support and regular challenge to his submissions, the separation of Victoria from NSW and the end to transportation. The next challenge in which he locked horns with the grazier dominated elected Legislative Council, was the demand by squatters for security of tenure over remote lands occupied by squatters, not wanting to buy the crown land. Gipps wrote to Stanley (Bathurst's successor at the Colonial Office in London "The lands are the unquestionable property of the Crown, and they are held in trust by the government for the benefit of the people of the whole British Empire. The Crown has not simply the right of a landlord over them, but exercises that right under the obligation of a trustee". (K. Buckley: *Historical Studies* 1955). The squatters were furious at Gipp's decision to limit a 'run' to 4,000 sheep or 500 cattle on an area of no more than 20 square miles, and to impose a licence fee of 10 pound. Wentworth, Windeyer, Robert Lowe and Lithgow formed a pastoral association, in 'vehement opposition' (Lang: *Historical & Statistical Account of NSW*). In retrospect the regulations were fair and equitable but the combined opposition by the landowner-squatter alliance damaged Gipps for some time. Gipps was the first of the governors actively in favour of open immigration, and supported the two schemes in operation–the first was free passage paid from government funds, and the second was the bounty scheme by which individual settlers were subsidised from government land revenue to bring out their own nominated immigrant workmen. The depression of 1841-1843 was the undoing of Gipps. Although partially contributed by a severe drought from 1837 to 1842, the main cause was the over-commitment of colonial funds to support the immigration program, followed by the downturn in crown land sales, and Gipps was forced to borrow one million pound in London to meet the colony's obligations. Bounty immigrants arrived in great numbers despite the depression causing reduced demand for labour. Gipps also drew on the military chest and when that chest was empty he withdrew all government funds from the colonial banks and forced them into an illiquid condition. Caroline Chisholm was left to find work for the many female immigrants newly arrived. Gipps concluded that the depression was due entirely to 'speculation' and he withheld consent to measures passed by the Legislative Council to check the evil consequences of the depression. On education Gipps also had little success. Opposition to further change from within the Legislative Council, forced Gipps back to the Bourke plans and a further increase in funding to the state sponsored education program. On Aboriginal policy Gipps proved himself to be 'humane, practical and courageous' (ADB). The Aborigines Committee reported to the House of Commons in 1837 and the suggestion for new policy in Australia was "the reservation of lands so that aboriginals could continue as huntsmen until 'tilling the soil ceased to be distasteful' to them, education of their children, increased expenditure for missionaries and for protectors, and, if necessary, the prosecution of whites". 'Weakened by inadequate finance, the official policy collapsed. How can I check the outrages that are now a frequent occurrence beyond the boundaries of location?' (ADB).

A few days before he left the colony in 1846, fighting ill health, the *Sydney Morning Herald* stated its firm conviction 'from the matured observation of eight years, sir George Gipps has been the worst Governor NSW ever had'. "Gipps was certainly governed by high principles, a strong sense of justice and unostentatious generosity. He was blessed with a logical mind and had a very sharply analytical bent, a sense of detail, and unimpeachable moral character. Like many very intelligent people, he was impatient and somewhat irascible" (ADB)

Sir Charles Augustus Fitzroy was the last of the five governors Lithgow served under in the Colony between 1824 and 1852. He brought to the Colony, in 1845, the 'lustre of aristocratic connections, success in two governments, a shrewd earthy judgement of men and events, robust health and an obvious preference for peace at any not-too-unreasonable price' (A.P. Martin: Life *& Letters of Robert Lowe*). Fitzroy, in trying to develop good relations with the Legislative Council, was able to announce to the Council, that Earl Grey (the new Secretary of State) was 'willing to surrender to the council the right of appropriating the casual revenues of the Crown, a concession much valued'. (ADB). Fitzroy was able to settle the Gipps confrontation with the Council over crown lands by the passage of the Waste Lands Occupation Act of 1846 (9 & 10 Vic, c.104) through the Imperial Parliament. This gave squatters the long leases, renewals, rights of pre-emption and other concessions that they had demanded. Robert Lowe who had switched sides from pro-squatters to anti-squatters led a protest movement, denouncing grey for giving into the squatters. On 31st July 1847, Earl grey wrote to Fitzroy proposing to separate Port Phillip from NSW and introducing representative government to that new colony, and VDL, and South Australia, along the same lines as enjoyed by NSW. The Australian Colonies Government Act of 1849-50 was accepted in NSW with little negative response. Fitzroy was concerned with the lack of unity on the question of constitutional reform would arouse a bitter contest for power. He pointed out to the Colonial Office that 'a large transfer of power from Britain to NSW was advocated by the most loyal, respectable and influential members of the community'. (ADB)

The biggest problem posed to Fitzroy during his term was the discovery of gold. The government (effectively the Governor in executive council) asserted the right of the Crown to control mining and adopted a system of licences that cost each miner 30s per month. The council hoped the fee would be high enough to deter an indiscriminate rush to the diggings. As Governor-General over all colonies, he had wide discretion to advise the lieutenant governors in other colonies on matter of common interest. He was greatly interested in railway construction but missed the opportunity of preventing the break-of-gauge problem between NSW and Victoria. Fitzroy was a populist who prided himself on popularity with all classes. He stood for no inconvenient principles! Sir William Denison succeeded him in 1854 but Lithgow had retired in 1852 and showed little interest in political affairs after his retirement.

If we are what we associate with then we can draw a temporary conclusion about Lithgow, from his colleagues. 'Among the congregation of great, near-great, non-great, and the never-great was a quiet man, a man of modest wealth with little or no pretence'. (Ludlum: *The Matarese Countdown)*

APPENDIX D

THE LITHGOW TIME-LINE OF KEY EVENTS

Lithgow's sources, as has been explained in this text, are few and mostly relate to major economic events in the colony.

Primary sources are from the State Records Office (formerly State Archives), and include Colonial Secretary's letter files from 1824 to 1855.

The SRO also retains copies of the accounting regulations and Treasurer's office reports between 1820 and 1855.

The SRO contains the files of Original Blue Books from 1822 to 1856, although these have now been published on microfiche, and photocopied into bound volumes at the NLA and SLNSW.

Secondary sources include the HRA and the newspapers of the day.

These secondary sources serve a useful purpose in tracking Lithgow's life and creating a time-line of key events, which can then be more closely examined, in its original context.

One of the very first steps in assembling relevant data was to prepare the attached time-line, which was gathered from HRA, The *Sydney Gazette* and *The Australian.*

This document is attached in this study as a means of the reader relating to and understanding these secondary sources and the events they portray.

Month	Year	Source	Notation/event
1	1784	ADB	Born
	1803-06	ADB	University of Edinburgh
	1806-08	ADB	Clerk in British Army commissariat
	1808	ADB	Transferred–Helgoland
	1812	ADB	Transferred–Mauritius
	1823	ADB	Transferred–Colony of NSW
10	1824	Austn	Apptd Asst Comm-general
10	1824	HRA	Appt WL as A-G
11	1824	Austn	Apptd to audit colonial revenue accts
11	1824	Austn	Subscribes to Busby's culture of the vine
1	1825	Austn	Member of Agric Society
1	1825	Austn	Confirmed as Auditor of Accts
4	1825	Austn	Subscribes to benevolent society
6	1825	HRA	Salary as A-G
6	1825	HRA	Reports on convict work gangs with Ovens
8	1825	HRA	Brisbane commends W.L to Lord Bathurst
9	1825	HRA	WL reports on bread contract dispute
9	1825	HRA	Report on bread contract
11	1825	Austn	Made justice of peace
11	1825	Austn	Apptd auditor male& female orphan fund-church /school accounts
11	1825	Austn	Signs civil officers address
12	1825	Austn	Signs address to Gov. Darling
3	1826	HRA	Report on comp by surveyor Busby
4	1826	Austn	Requires claims against Orphan School
5	1826	HRA	Inquiry into B of NSW
5	1826	HRA	C'ttee on colonial coinage

5	1826	Austn	Apptd Dir of Bank of Sydney (BNSW)
6	1826	HRA	Apptd to Land Board
7	1826	HRA	Land Board report
7	1826	HRA	2nd Land Brd Rpt
7	1826	HRA	Sepn of commissary dept in VDL from NSW Gov.
8	1826	Austn	Witness in Oakes case
9	1826	Austn	On agric society C'ttee
12	1826	HRA	Bathurst's approval of WL as director of BNSW
12	1826	HRA	Rpt on gov exps to m'tain convicts
12	1826	HRA	3rd Land Board rpt
1	1827	Austn	Sits on bench in Sydney
1	1827	HRA	List of magistrates
1	1827	S.G.	Retires as director of the Old bank
3	1827	S.G.	Employs John Foley
3	1827	HRA	4th Land Rpt
3	1827	HRA	Rpt on value of convict lbr
3	1827	HRA	rpt on exps of convict mntce
4	1827	HRA	sepn of comm accts from col. auditor
4	1827	HRA	sepn of comm accts from col. auditor
5	1827	HRA	Appointed member of the Harbour Dues Board
5	1827	Austn	Member Harbour Dues brd
5	1827	HRA	Minute of E.C.
6	1827	S.G.	dines with Agricultural Turf Club
6	1827	S.G.	apptd temp priv sec to governor and clerk to exec Cncl
6	1827	Austn	re-elected Dir BNSW
6	1827	Austn	Apptd Acctg Priv Sec to Gov
9	1827	HRA	nomination of WL as dir of BNSW
9	1827	HRA	instn to Treasurer
11	1827	S.G.	considered as collector of customs
11	1827	S.G.	subscribes to monument of Duke of York
11	1827	S.G.	re-elected Dir BNSW
11	1827	S.G.	returns from priv sec to gov

11	1827	Austn	Rtns to Audit Office
2	1828	S.G.	defended by 'Monitor' for delay in publishing Abstract of Colonial Accts
3	1828	S.G.	steward of Agric & Hort Soc of NSW
4	1828	S.G.	fndtn mbr of Austrn Racing Club
4	1828	HRA	approv for sepn of comm accts from A-G
4	1828	S.G.	attends mtg of Agric & Hort Society of NSW
5	1828	HRA	Brd of Female Factory
5	1828	S.G.	subscribes to Benevolent Society
7	1828	HRA	late 'Blue Books'
7	1828	HRA	clerical salaries review & reforms in audit office
8	1828	HRA	instn re quarterly warrants
9	1828	Austn	resigns from Commissary dept
9	1828	Austn	m'br agric society
9	1828	HRA	extra clerical help–question of gov. Darling
11	1828	HRA	return of 'grants of land'
12	1828	HRA	claim for seizure of brandy
12	1828	HRA	rpt on addn assts for the bonded stores
2	1829	HRA	appointed to Legislative Council
2	1829	HRA	rpt #2 of Female Factory
3	1829	Austn	apptd with Thomson to act as Col Tsr
4	1829	HRA	recomm. on Campbell land grant
5	1829	HRA	rpt on 'bonded stores'
7	1829	Austn	apptd to Leg cncl
8	1829	HRA	E.C. rpt on brandy seizure
11	1829	HRA	acctg as Priv. Sec to gov
12	1829	Austn	re-elected Dir BNSW
2	1830	HRA	Trustee rpt by Clergy & School Lands
6	1830	Austn	apptd Mbr S'hldrs c'ttee of BNSW
9	1830	HRA	E.C. rpt on BNSW
9	1830	HRA	rpt on reorg of gov depts

12	1830	HRA	def. the colonial gov against Mr Hume MP
1	1831	Austn	Apptd Trustee Clergy & school Estate
	1831	HRA	rpt from L.C.
5	1831	Austn	Buys shares in Bank of Australia
7	1831	HRA	lateness of Blue Books
8	1831	HRA	Quit rents on crown land
10	1831	HRA	rpt by WL on 1831 expenditures
10	1831	HRA	WL and the will of John Ovens
11	1831	HRA	reply to pamphlet by J.D. Lang
2	1832	HRA	matter of Col-Gen in Ldn (Barnard)
4	1832	Austn	receives land grant in Sydney
6	1832	HRA	lateness of Blue Books
9	1832	HRA	WL and the will of John Ovens
1	1833	HRA	military personnel on 1/2 pay
3	1833	HRA	Goderich approv of WL blue books
8	1833	Austn	Subscribes to Hibernia Bank
9	1833	HRA	matter of Col-Gen in Ldn (Barnard)
9	1833	HRA	reduction in clerks for comm
7	1834	HRA	1833 Blue Books
7	1834	HRA	request of WL for 1832-33 Blue books
9	1834	Austn	Subscribes to Edward Lombe Fund
9	1835	Austn	Explains to Leg Cncl views on Police/gaol expenditure
12	1835	HRA	nomination of WL as EC
2	1836	HRA	matter signed by WL as Acctg priv Sec to gov
3	1836	Austn	On c'ttee of Southern Assocn
5	1836	Austn	Signs address to governor
5	1836	Austn	attends levee
6	1836	Austn	m'br Southern Cattle Assoc
8	1836	Austn	buys house in Elizabeth St–1200 pnd
9	1836	Austn	On Circular Wharf c'ttee
10	1836	HRA	transmitting Blue books 1832

11	1836	Austn	joins new club
12	1836	Austn	signs transportation petition
6	1837	Austn	on immigration c'ttee
2	1838	Austn	attends levee
3	1838	HRA	validation of Bourke's salary
3	1838	HRA	validation of salaries to Dumaresq & Lindesay
3	1838	Austn	apptd Leg Cncl
4	1838	Austn	Title to Riverina land promised
5	1838	Austn	pledges not supply spirits as wages
5	1838	Austn	subscribes to Bourke statue
5	1838	Austn	signs call for immign meeting
9	1838	Austn	granted title to riverina land
12	1838	Austn	subscribes to bourke statue
12	1838	Austn	subscribes to Bourke memorial
3	1839	Austn	on provsn c'ttee of BASNCo
5	1839	Austn	Takes shares in India SSCo
5	1839	HRA	rpt on gov steamer for communication
7	1839	HRA	WL's opinion of 'contingent account'
11	1839	HRA	rpt on lunatic asylum
12	1839	HRA	audit queries unanswered
12	1839	HRA	audit queries unanswered
1	1840	HRA	Blue Books transmitted
8	1840	HRA	blue book delays answered
8	1840	HRA	fin rpt to L.C
6	1841	HRA	blue book submitted
6	1841	HRA	blue book matters
9	1841	HRA	WL sick for weeks
1	1842	HRA	rpt by Labour & Emigration Comms
1	1842	HRA	delays in Blue books
2	1842	HRA	blue books for 1839
3	1842	HRA	blue books for 1839
4	1842	HRA	blue books for 1839
4	1842	HRA	Brit Tsy minute on negotn of bills
4	1842	HRA	Blue books for 1840
4	1842	HRA	request for Barnard's books
6	1842	HRA	Blue books for 1841
8	1842	HRA	rpt on gov ptg off

9	1842	SMH	sells house in Cumberland Cnty-Gipps Ward
10	1842	HRA	Blue books for 1842
10	1842	HRA	t'fr to Military Chest
10	1842	SMH	Ratepayer–Gipps Ward–County of Cumberland
12	1842	HRA	rpt on Comm & water police
4	1843	HRA	WL to Mitchell re pers liability
7	1843	SMH	A-G–apptd Leg Cncl
12	1843	SMH	votes for dissoln of Nth Syd Ferry Coy
1	1844	SMH	Apptd Trustee of NSW Svgs Bank
3	1844	SMH	Robbed in Parramatta Road, Sydney
9	1844	SMH	files claim against J.H. Potts
11	1844	SMH	retires as dir of BNSW
	1852	HRA	retires as Colonial Auditor
	1858	HRA	retires from Legislative Council
6	1864	ADB	dies in St. Leonards

APPENDIX E

MACQUARIE BUILDING PLANS AND COSTING

Extracts from the following document are included in the main text and are repeated in this format to include the author's valuation of each Macquarie period building.

LIST OF GREENWAY BUILDINGS

Costing of Macquarie Construction Programs

Hospital, Sydney
Magazine, Fort Phillip
Design of Government House, Sydney
St. John's Parsonage, Parramatta
Portico, Government House, Parramatta
Macquarie Lighthouse, South Head
Obelisk, Macquarie Place, Sydney
Military Barracks, Sydney
Government Wharf, Windsor
Parramatta Gaol, Parramatta
Hyde Park Convict Barracks
St. Matthew's Church, Windsor
Chief Justice's House, Sydney
Colonial Secretary's House, Macquarie Place, Sydney

Judge Advocate's House, Macquarie Place, Sydney
Chaplain's House, Spring Street, Sydney
Government Stables, Government Domain, Sydney
Fort Macquarie, Bennelong's Point, Sydney
Public Fountain, Macquarie Place, Sydney
St. Luke's Church, Liverpool
St. Luke's Parsonage, Liverpool
Female Factory and Barrack, Parramatta
Female Orphan School, Parramatta
Government House, Sydney
Dawes Point Battery, Dawes Point, Sydney
Turnpike Gate & Lodge, Parramatta Road, Sydney
St. Andrew's Church (Foundations), King Street, Sydney
Supreme court House, King Street, Sydney
Lumber Yard, Bridge Street, Sydney
Male Orphan School, George Street, Sydney
Dockyard, George Street, Sydney
Market House, George Street, Sydney
Court House, Windsor
Charity School, Elizabeth Street, Sydney
Police Office, George Street, Sydney
Granary & Store, George Street, Parramatta
St. Mary's Catholic Chapel, Hyde Park, Sydney
Princess Charlotte Memorial
Liverpool Hospital, Liverpool.
Pigeon House
Governor Brisbane's Bath House, Government Domain, Sydney
St. Matthews Rectory, Windsor
Ultimo House, Ultimo Sydney
House for Sarah Howe, Lower George Street, Sydney
House for George Howe, Charlotte Place, Sydney
Tomb for George Howe, Devonshire Street Cemetery, Sydney
House for Sir John Jamieson, Charlotte Place, Sydney
House for T.W. Middleton, Macquarie /Hunter Streets, Sydney
Work for R.W. Loane
Cottage, Parramatta
Proposed House, George /Argyle Street, Sydney
House for Sir John Wylde, Sydney

Bank of New South Wales, George Street, Sydney
Wharf House, Lower George Street, Sydney
House for Jemima Jenkins
Shop for John Macqueen, Lower George Street, Sydney
Cleveland House, Bedford Street, Surrey Hills
Cottage, Cockle Bay, Sydney
Pair of Houses for Sir John Jamison, George Street, Sydney
Shop for George Williams, George Street, Sydney
House for Robert Campbell Sr, Bunkers Hill, Sydney
Shop for Barnett Levy, George Street, Sydney
Henrietta Villa, Point Piper
House for Thomas Moor, Elizabeth Street, Liverpool
Waterloo Warehouse, George /Market Streets, Sydney
House for William Cox, O'Connell Street, Sydney
Regentville near Penrith
Glenlee, Menangle
House for Robert Crawford, Lower Fort Street, Sydney
House & Store for Robert Campbell Jr, Bligh Street, Sydney
Bungarribee, Eastern Creek
Hobartville, Richmond
Warehouse for John Paul, George Street, Sydney
Springfield, Potts Point, Sydney
Jerusalem Warehouse, George Street, Sydney
Grantham, Potts Point, Sydney-

RECONSTRUCTING THE MACQUARIE ERA

CONSTRUCTION PROGRAM

The Bigge's Report provides a partial list of building work completed by Macquarie. The items, which to Bigge are the most useful buildings on the list, include:

(The numbers refer to references in Greenway's–1822 Map of Sydney)

Sydney Items

The Commissariat (King's) Store at Sydney (8)
St. Phillips Church at Sydney (12)
Improvement of Government House at Sydney (1)
Sydney Gaol (30)
Clearing of grounds contiguous to the Government Houses (1)
A Parsonage House at Sydney (30)
Military Barracks at Sydney–Wynyard Square (13)
Hospital in Sydney–"Rum" Hospital–Macquarie Street (21)
Hyde Park Convict Barracks (20)
Military Hospital in Sydney–Wynyard Square (27)
Improvements to Lumber-Yard at Sydney (28)
Improvements to Dockyard at Sydney (29)
St. James Church (19)
Colonial Secretary's House & Office (4)
Sydney Cove-Governor's Wharf (26)
Water Bailiff–House and landing (31)
Houses for Judge-Advocate (Judge of Supreme Court)–(4)
Court-house at Sydney (18)
School-house at Hyde Park (16)
Market house at George Street, Sydney (15)
Government stables at Sydney (2)
Fountain in Macquarie Place (6)
Obelisk in Macquarie Place (7)
The Turnpike Gate–Lower George Street (22)
Fort (Macquarie) at Bennelong's Point (3)
Battery at Dawes Point (10)
Greenway's House and office (9)
Windmill–(built at Public Expense)–at Garrison barracks (23)
Windmill–(built at Public Expense)–at the Domain. (24)
Magazine at Fort Phillip (11)
St.Andrew's Church foundation (15)
Orphan House in Sydney (25)

Parramatta, Windsor, Liverpool & Outer Sydney Area Items

Carters Barracks and gaol at Windsor
Female Factory at Parramatta
St. Matthews Church at Windsor
Church at Liverpool
Chapel at Castlereagh
A Parsonage House at Parramatta
A Parsonage House at Liverpool
Hospital at Parramatta
Hospital at Windsor (a converted brewery formerly owned by Andrew Thompson)
Hospital at Liverpool
Convict Barracks at Parramatta
Improvement of Government House at Parramatta
An asylum for the aged and infirm near Sydney
Bridge at Rushcutter's Bay–South Head Road
Macquarie Light-house at Sydney South Head
(This list accounts for 46 items on Bigge's 63 reference)
Newcastle Items

Hospital
Gaol
Commandant House
Surgeons Quarter
Workhouse
Blacksmiths Forge
Pier
Windmill
Parsonage House "(Bigge Report)

(We now account for 55 out of the 63)

Greenway Items (drawn but under construction)
Officer Quarters-Hyde Park
Alterations to Judge Advocate's House
Alterations to Lumber Yard building
Alterations to Dawes Battery

Alterations to Liverpool parsonage
Portico, Gov House, Parramatta
Alterations to Orphan School, Sydney
Alterations to Government House, Sydney
Judge Field's House–Sydney
Plans for Mr. Marsden's House at Parramatta
Survey for the new General (Rum) Hospital
Plans for the Windsor Church
Plans for the Liverpool Church
Plans for Judge Field's house
Plans for Parramatta Female Factory
Survey of Parramatta Bridge
Survey of Sydney Gaol
Measuring work by contractors at Sydney Gaol
Plans for Windsor Court-house
Plans for new toll-gate
Plans for Obelisk in Macquarie Place
Plans for fountain in Macquarie Place.
(If we count 'alterations' to buildings, we can account for the whole 63 items stated by Commissi oner Bigge to have been undertaken in the Macquarie Era)

THE AUTHOR'S ESTIMATES OF CONSTRUCTION COSTS FOR THE MACQUARIE BUILDINGS

The Commissariat (King's) Store at Sydney (8)		7500
St. Phillips Church at Sydney (12)		3250
Improvement of Government House at Sydney (1)	600	
Sydney Gaol (30)	6000	
Clearing of grounds contiguous to the Government Houses (1)		200
A Parsonage House at Sydney (30)		350
Military Barracks at Sydney–Wynyard Square (13)		11000
Hospital in Sydney–"Rum" Hospital–Macquarie Street (21)		0
Military Hospital in Sydney–Wynyard Square (27)		6750
Improvements to Lumber-Yard at Sydney (28)		2000
Improvements to Dockyard at Sydney (29)		1000
St. James Church (19)	6240	

Colonial Secretary's House & Office (4)		875
Sydney Cove-Governor's Wharf (26)		3500
Water Bailiff–House and landing (31)		1250
Houses for Judge-Advocate (Judge of Supreme Court (4)		4800
Court-house at Sydney (18)	6450	
School-house at Hyde Park (16)		3500
Market house at George Street, Sydney (15)	300	
Government stables at Sydney (2)	9000	
Fountain in Macquarie Place (6)		500
Obelisk in Macquarie Place (7)		375
The Turnpike Gate–Lower George Street (22)		2750
Fort (Macquarie) at Bennelong's Point (3		21000
Battery at Dawes Point (10)		4675
Greenway's House and office (9)		1695
Windmill–(built at Public Expense)–at Garrison barracks (23)		2250
Windmill–(built at Public Expense)–at the Domain. (24)		2230
Magazine at Fort Phillip (11)	1240	
St.Andrew's Church foundation (15)	2500	
Orphan House in Sydney (25)	2180	
Parramatta, Windsor, Liverpool & Outer Sydney Area		
Carters Barracks and gaol at Windsor		9750
Female Factory at Parramatta		278500
St. Matthews Church at Windsor		5600
Church at Liverpool		5250
Chapel at Castlereagh		4750
A Parsonage House at Parramatta		1250
A Parsonage House at Liverpool	520	
Hospital at Parramatta		6500
Hospital at Windsor (a converted brewery formerly owned by Andrew Thompson)		3365
Hospital at Liverpool		5850
Convict Barracks at Parramatta		21500
Improvement of Government House at Parramatta	1120	
An asylum for the aged and infirm near Sydney		8625
Bridge at Rushcutter's Bay–South Head Road		2275

Macquarie Light-house at Sydney South Head	7050	
(This list accounts for 46 items on Bigge's 63 reference)		
Newcastle Items		
Hospital		6693
Gaol		8824
Commandant House		1356
Surgeons Quarter		1569
Workhouse		5228
Blacksmiths Forge		2135
Pier		3556
Windmill		2150
Parsonage House "(Bigge Report)		1189
(We now account for 55 out of the 63)		
Greenway Items (drawn but under construction)		
Officer Quarters-Hyde Park	10600	
Alterations to Judge Advocate's House	600	
Alterations to Lumber Yard building	2000	
Alterations to Dawes Battery	1200	
Alterations to Liverpool parsonage	520	
TOTALS	55600	344865

Kitchen Estimates 922,857.13.11

Since the actual total for the estimated construction work completed in the Macquarie era is less than $500,000, and it is most unlikely that the total could have reached $922,000, then it is safe to assume that Henry Kitchen, in producing this misleading estimate to Commissioner Bigge was provided with the intention of further blackening the names of both Greenway and Macquarie–both of whom disliked and were disliked by Kitchen. A deliberately malicious and deceptive piece of disinformation by Kitchen.

There is another possible explanation that stretches credulity somewhat but could be justified as a possibility. It is always assumed that convict labour was essentially 'free', and should therefore not count or contribute to the total cost of the finished construction.

If we make a number of assumptions concerning day rates of equivalent pay, and about the productivity level of the convicts in a major construction job, keeping in mind they were supervised by other convicts, then we may be able to say that the 400,000 pound of cost assembled in the Table above is for materials and that the equivalent value of the convict labour makes the difference of the 522,000 to bring the total estimate up to Kitchen's estimates.

The relevant assumptions are (based on Greenways cost estimates on Page 59 above)

The number of days of mechanics labour to complete the Government House Stables was 16,686.5

The average cost per man day was 1 shilling

Labour reflected a 33% content of the total finished cost.

So applying these assumptions to the construction work in the rest of the table, we find that all projects would have taken 2,683,108 days of mechanics labour or approx 8,450 man years. The convict population increased between 1812 and 1820 by 10,800 men and totalled 19,000 men by 1820, and to suppose that 44% of the male convicts were employed in construction work is not unreasonable. At the minimum rate of 1s per day, our labour cost total becomes 134155 pound; thus, at an average of 3 shillings (compared with Coghlan's cost for 'free' mechanics at 5s per day, we would achieve the difference of 480,000 pound. Coghlan estimates that a convict would only produce about 60% of a 'free' labourer.

Our conclusion, if we stretch the point, is that Kitchen's estimate of a construction cost for the period of 900,000 is valid if our materials are valued at 402,000 and our labour accounts (at the average rate of 3 shillings per day) to a further 470,000-pound.

COUNTING THE PENNIES PUBLIC FINANCE IN THE COLONY OF NSW 1788-1855

CHAPTER 1

PREFACE

The purpose of this study is to expand the existing knowledge of how the colonial economy of NSW grew in terms of the use and provision of public finance.

Public Finance, at least in relation to the colonial economy embraces multiple concepts including the appropriation and use of British Treasury funds, the raising of colonial revenues by way of import duties and other taxations and the recording and reporting of these funds, and the contribution to the colonial funding of economic growth and development by the Commissariat. The study of capital formation in the early economy has to-date been based on massive assumptions but not reliably measured until N.G. Butlin commenced his research for the year 1861. Preliminary assessment is now made for the pre-1861 period Capital formation in the form of public and private funds as well as the human capital can, in fact, be broadly assessed for the period 1802 to 1861.

This study runs for the period from the formation of the penal settlement in 1788 to the transfer to self-government in 1856, but obviously references to economic events outside those parameters must be referenced, and these references will also include mutually exclusive topics such as economic drivers for the period and special economic events for the period. Nine economic drivers of varying importance have been identified as have five special economic events which fuelled the growth of identifiable sectors of the colonial economy, such as growth in and from the pastoral industry; the introduction of formal education which contributed to the drop in illiteracy from over 75% to under 25%, over a period of less than a quarter of the 19th century.

Linked with the analysis of capital formation in the colonial economy, is the important question of British Foreign investment into the colony. This too came in multiple ways, including immigration, speculation, direct investment, government borrowing in Britain, availability of loan funds through new financial institutions and, of course, the introduction of the first bank and the subsequent development of a fully fledged banking and financial services industry. The Pastoral houses provided export funding and then rural mortgage loans, and there came about this special link between the land grant companies, the pastoral houses, the pastoral industry, foreign investment and massive speculation in livestock and rural land holdings.

Possibly the second most significant economic driver, after capital formation, was the growth of population. This was sourced from immigration from Britain and natural increase within the colony. The population history of the colony is rather short because of the circumstances of the colony, but is measured in terms of the transportation program (convicts dominated the labour market until the 1830s), the immigration program funded from revenues generated by crown land sales and the land grants program which encouraged settlers (ex-military as well as professional farmers and pastoralists in exchange for land grants and labour–convict–concessions).

The story of public finance in the colony is an exciting one, but sources are limited mainly to the official records (such as HRA, HRNSW, AJCP) and only two economic historians have formerly contributed to the literature–Butlin, S.J. in *Foundations of the Australian Monetary System* (1953) and Butlin. N.G in *Forming a Colonial Economy* (published posthumously in 1994 from earlier notes). Specialty sub-texts have been assembled by other economic historian's e.g. *One million pound & a million acres*–Damaris Bairstow and her story of the AAC Company(2003); Frank Broeze, *Mr Brooks & the Australian Trade* (1993) and Margaret Steven *Merchant Campbell* (1965).George Linge made a large contribution in his *Industrial Awakening (*1994).

This writer has concentrated to-date on the main symbols of the colonial economy by studying *The Economic role of the Commissariat* ***and*** *The Role and growth of the office of Treasurer and Auditor-General in the Colony,* as well as preparing *An Economic History of the Van Diemen's Land Company (1824-1899).* The literature is slowly being added to but this present work is the first to complete a review of the public finance of the colony between 1788 and 1856

Five chapters in the study cover the period 1788 to 1856 whilst they also cover the contents referenced above. A sixth chapter attempts to summarise the results and conclusions from the study.

The Treasurers of the Colony knew only the advantages of balancing the books each year–there was no deficit financing undertaken until after 1856 when overseas borrowing commenced with the financial houses in the City of London, who had accepted the credit worthiness of the Colony and hastened to use this new outlet for surplus funds available for investment by Britain. The use of bank drafts for export commodities had commenced with the large wool exports to Britain and led to the creation of the Union Bank of Australia and the Bank of Australasia[1]. This period also saw the rise of the great pastoral and financing houses–Brooks and Younghusband, Dalgety and Goldsbrough Mort. Shipping fleets grew rapidly after 1792 for transporting convicts and then free immigrants and returning with wool[2], and other commodities. The P & O operators, with their One million pound of paid up capital won the lucrative mail contracts from the British Government and commenced regular monthly trips from London to Australia[3].

The published public accounts reflect an annual cumulative surplus (of revenue over expenditures) each year from 1822 to 1900[4]. What this meant was that the Colonial Treasurers and their advisers had the flexibility of running into temporary deficit, for instance in 1838 (–£164102) and 1839 (–£121464) knowing that the cumulative surplus of £314,517 (as

---

1 Butlin, S.J. *Foundations* P.449

2 Farrer, T. *Free Trade versus Fair Trade (1886)*

3 Farrer *ibid*

4 Ginswick statistics quoted by Butlin, N. G. in *Forming a Colonial Economy*

of 1837) would allow them to do so without having to borrow long-term. In this instance the cumulative surplus was reduced to only £28951[5]. The habits of recording in the various periods varied and opened the way for considerable mistakes and misinterpretation, as will be seen.

For the purposes of this study, there are five significant public finance periods during the 19th Century: the first is the goal and orphan fund period 1802-10, the second is the Police and Orphan Fund period 1810-21, the third covers the 'Blue Book' period 1822-55; the fourth is the post self-government period 1856-89, and the fifth will be the pre-Federation period 1889-99.

Governor Macquarie had appointed Darcy Wentworth and Reverend Samuel Marsden to be Treasurers of the Police and Orphan funds and we find their monthly reports published in the *Sydney Gazette* of the period 1810-1821. From 1822 clerical staff within the Colonial Secretary's office recorded the Blue Book even though William Lithgow as Colonial Auditor-General was held responsible for its compilation, audit and transmittal to London[6]. Prior to self-government public service lines of demarcation between the offices of the Colonial Secretary, the Colonial Accountant and the Colonial Auditor-General were unclear. From 1856, all accounting and reporting functions came under the Treasury, whilst the Colonial Secretary's department was responsible for the more routine 'housekeeping functions of colonial government. The main difference in recording between the Orphan & Gaol Funds and the Blue Books is that the Funds were original records, whereas the Blue books were transcriptions of other records. There was, in fact, nothing in the Blue books that had not been collected in another record.

The Blue Books contains the comprehensive (albeit delayed and information of doubtful accuracy) recording system of the times whilst the Consulting Accountant to the NSW Treasury (James Thomson) introduced a new system after self-government, which was burdensome, intricate, and open to much abuse. It was as if the NSW Treasury, following self-government went out of its way to develop a singularly complex system to justify its

---

5 Butlin, N. G. *ibid*

6 Beckett, G.W. *The first Colonial Auditor-General– William Lithgow, a biography*

continued existence. After self-government, the ledgers were kept in an 'open' condition until all of the funds appropriated to each line item in the budget were spent. This system had become even more complex after the introduction of Appropriation Bills in 1831. The system of keeping accounts 'open' sometimes meant the ledgers could not be closed for upwards of three years, by which time the trail was cold in trying to keep track of annual revenues and expenditures. This problem was corrected in 1885, when a return was made to annual statements based on cash inflow and outflow[7].

Observations on early Reporting Systems

Many of the Marsden and Wentworth funding transactions created major conflict of interest situations. It is interesting to muse how a Reverend gentleman who was paid from the Civil List at the rate of £150 per annum, could afford to operate 4,500 acres of pasture land (about 1/3rd received in grants, and 2/3 rds in purchased freehold land) and build up a flock of 3,500 sheep in a span of less than twenty years. Even allowing that some of the land came about from grants, all the sheep were purchased and although the convict labour assigned to him was unpaid, they had to be kept, with sleeping huts, food and clothing furnished. A close check on the built up of flock numbers shows that the computed rate of natural increase was physically impossible Marsden was obviously adding to his flock by other means. As was noted earlier, Marsden was Treasurer of the orphanage fund. We might also ask why its monthly meat bill ran to over £60 even though it owned and operated a sheep grazing operation, which sheep were regularly sold 'on the hoof' and then bought back as dressed meat[8]. For its annual sale of livestock in 1811-1812, the orphanage received only £127, but from the same source purchased over £700 of dressed meat. The means were easy to share the spoils between those who could help him gain wealth and reach his target of becoming a large landowner and successful grazier. Marsden's orphanage housed only female orphans aged from 5 to 14. On an average month, Marsden paid the butcher over

7 Thomson, James *Financial Statements of the Colony 1856-1886*

8 The Orphanage accounts reflect this policy but Yarwood in his biography of Samuel Marsden also confirms the practice.

£60, being for an average of 2,500 lb of meat (the average price per pound was 6 pence). By the 30th September 1818, Marsden held £3,033 in the orphanage account, and on average disbursed £550 each month from that account. Marsden's chief biographer, Alexander (A. T.) Yarwood makes no reference to any financial irregularities during Marsden's period as Orphan Fund Treasurer, but a careful audit of the quarterly published accounts shows errors in addition, and funds accounted for.

The only 'admonishment' that Macquarie made, if one can imply an act of admonition from a minor regulatory change, was that a lesser percentage of revenue from tariffs and duties was to be directed to the Orphan Fund. Macquarie, in 1817, chose to modify the basis of the Orphanage Fund revenue and deleted an item by redirecting that revenue to the Police Fund. In 1818, Macquarie then directed that £3,000 of the balance in the Orphan Fund be deposited with the new Bank of New South Wales[9].

Macquarie made no objection to the fact that Marsden was misdirecting funds from the Orphan Fund for the repair of St. John's Church, Parramatta, in July 1811 to the extent of £56, nor to paying the Matron of the Orphanage a monthly stipend of £5 when the going rate would have been only £1 per month, nor of paying £4.5.0 for a bonnet for his wife from the fund[10]. Macquarie personally approved each quarterly statement submitted by Samuel Marsden, as Treasurer of the Orphan Fund, when presented to the Lieutenant Governor for 'auditing', obviously without proper 'auditing' procedures being used. The 'auditing' function could not have been taken very seriously because numerous of these approved statements included arithmetic errors[11].

The Orphan Fund, as published in the *Sydney Gazette,* quarterly between 1811 and 1820, showed numerous arithmetic errors, always on account of a shortage, and one may wonder why, with numerous others handling

---

9 HRA 1:10:169 Macquarie letter to Marsden as attached to a despatch to Lord Bathurst

10 The Orphanage accounts show this purchase

11 The writer recreated each quarterly report on a spreadsheet by categories and having identified an arithmetic error, checked with the source documents to verify who, in fact, made the error

the accounts, such as the other Trustees, the Governor's secretary, or the Judge-Advocate, no-one ever picked up these quite substantial errors. During the course of the years 1812-1818, the amount of shortage or error in addition came to a total of £997[12].

Wentworth, as Treasurer of the companion 'Police' Fund, also had his dubious methods. He built up large surpluses of cash and bills receivable rather than spend funds on road and bridge or wharf construction; he did expend large amounts by using military men for 'repairs' to the streets of Sydney and other questionable contracts, which were never commented on publicly by Macquarie, and never checked as to quality or indeed, the work being actually carried out[13]. Macquarie's 'blindness' to any inconsistencies or abuses in the accounts, made it appear that he was only interested in outcomes, regardless of how they were achieved.

Wentworth was also the town Magistrate and Superintendent of Police responsible for fines, both positions being an important source of revenue to the Police Fund. Two items of regular expenditure open to abuse, and which appear to be inordinately high were purchase of firewood and lamp oil and payment for the capture of absconding convicts[14]. The Military personnel were fleecing the Government stores, operating the importation of consumption goods and the barter system in the Colony and were obviously monopolising the ample rewards in cash available if one found favour with Wentworth[15]. These fiscal irregularities persisted until 1822, when the 'Blue Books' were introduced and commenced the following year.

Members of the NSW Legislative Council, after its formation were always considering new means of raising local revenues, as the British Treasury was far from flexible and open in offering funding to the colony for other

---

12 This shortage was identified by this writer

13 Macquarie makes this admission by stating to Bathurst that his time was better spent that following behind Darcy Wentworth.

14 This analysis follows from the spreadsheet by categories referred to in Footnote 20

15 This analysis also follows from the spreadsheet by categories referred to in Footnote 23

than civil list and commissariat expenditure items. The British treasury for those early years had its funds committed almost exclusively to the European and French wars, and the colony was never considered a priority in allocating working funds, and Britain saw an excellent opportunity to cut its own expenditures in the colony and use local revenues and taxation instead. Once local revenues reached the level of £10,000 per annum, being about 10% of the total required from the Treasury to operate the colony, the Treasury relied on this taxation to replace British funds.

Legislative Councillor, Robert Campbell, recommended to the Governor on 25th August 1835 that the British Treasury should consider paying a flat rate of £10 per head for each of the 20,000 convicts in the colony at that time by way of maintenance and support to the local treasury. He suggested that 'because the accumulated balances in the Treasury are evidences not of superabundant revenues but of defective financial arrangements whereby public buildings have fallen into disrepair or become unfit for the required purposes'. Campbell suggested that 'because the large revenue raised is not the result of industry or creation of wealth but proof of the improvident and vicious habits of the community'. He noted that '3/4 ths of the revenue of £157,300 arises from duties on spirits'. This whole proposition was rejected by Governor Sir Richard Bourke, but associate Councillors, John Blaxland wrote a letter also on 23rd August, 1835, suggesting that the British Treasury had saved over £1,000,000 by using New South Wales as a penal colony–he represented that £1,913,462.17.0 had been saved if hulks had been used or £1,008,837.5.6 if prisons had been built. He was basing his numbers on a saving of £30 per head per annum for the 20,207 convicts in the colony at that time.

In response to this disagreement between Bourke and the Councillors, Bourke announced that 'the revenue of last year has been unusually productive. We are able to provide for such objects as tend to improve the morals, augment the wealth and procure the comfort and convenience of all classes of the community. These include supporting Public Schools and places of religious worship, the formation and improvement of roads and the repair and erection of public buildings'[16].

---

16 Votes & Proceedings NSW Legislative Council 1835

Conclusions for Chapter One

This work is the study of colonial Finance in NSW from 1788 to 1855, in order to reach an understanding about both Public Finance and Private Finance–its source and usage in the colony.

Associated with this study will be a reflection on the creation of Capital–private and public, human and financial. This is one area that Timothy Coghlan, Colonial NSW Statistician and author of *Labour & Industry in Australia* (four volumes–1917) and the series *Wealth & Progress of NSW between 1886 and 1902* excels in. In future chapters the formation of capital in the colony will be studied, as will the method and policy of recording and reporting financial affairs in the colony.

Professor S. J. Butlin, the pre-eminent portrayer of Australian Economic History in his work 'Foundations of the Australian Monetary System 1788-1851' (1953 Edition), wrote, "Australian Economic History is the major part of all Australian history;–from the beginning, economic factors have dominated development in a way that should gladden the heart of any Marxist. What is true of any particular strand of economic growth–land settlement, labour relations and labour organisation, immigration, secondary industry–is also true of each major stage in the development of the community as a whole: each is characterised by economic changes which conditioned political, social and cultural change.'[17]

To explore the most important of the economic events in the Colony from 1788 to 1855 is to inexorably intertwine our history, both social and political, with the growth of wealth and the growth of the people from the commencement of the original penal settlement to the age of self-government.[18]

These economic events don't fall naturally into the same level of importance as do tragedies such as floods or wars, earthquakes or unnatural dramas such as social riots. These events were awakened by the wonderful aura of discovery. The exploration over the mountains to open up a new land,

---

17 Butlin, S.J *Foundations* op cit

18 Beckett, G.W. *A Population History*

and unfold the story of the rivers; the discovery of gold, and the unfurling of the workers flag and untold riches; the amazing growth of the pastoral industry; the development of the great 'iron horse' and the opening of the vast inland to settlements; the unfolding of the education system to all young Australians 'free, compulsory and secular' with the relief of seeing illiteracy drop from 75% to under 20% in the decade;

The development of communications, from bush telegraph to the electric telegraph around the world, but mostly the natural advance of democracy leading finally to full self-government.

All these marvellous events had a major impact on the economy of the day. Revenue grew from £72,000 in 1826 to £13,000,000 less than 40 years later, without diminishing the peoples will to work and the acceptance of the government's right to fairly tax its people and create a strong social infrastructure. Revenue per head rose only from £2.08 to £3.79 over the 40 years, whilst the standard of living, by whatever measure, expanded exponentially

Export earnings kept pace with imports, so we did not buy overseas at the expense of the local ability to make new and worldly goods. By 1850 our exports, due to wool and gold, had out run imports, for the first time, but always the numbers grew. Exports grew from £3.08 per head in 1826 to £14.55 per head in 1860. Imports grew from £10.39 to £21.57 in the same period, seldom with imports less than exports during that time.

In 1850, in anticipation of full self-government, the Governors began playing with 'temporary' borrowing in order to meet monetary policy obligations and expectations, and to keep the budget in balance. Gold and wool exports came as immigration burgeoned and railways and other infrastructure capital expenditure came into sight. The impeccable relationship between the Colony and the 'City' of London, allowed attractive and relatively easy borrowing of capital in Britain.

The financial establishment and the workings of the first Commissariats are both to be considered, along with a consolidation and summary of the first Public Accounts in the colony, being the Gaol, Police and Orphan Funds. The first appropriation bill was brought down in 1832, long after the 1823 reforms to appoint an advisory council to the Governor. Both moves were small steps on the path to responsible Government. Full self-government in 1855 continued the slow reform of the treasury system and prompted further parliamentary reforms of financial statements prepared for the New South Wales Legislature. Finally, the Parliament received, in 1856, full control of its financial destiny and was able to increase and diversify sources of revenue and allocate funds for expenditure with only the local population watching over their shoulders.

Each of the five distinct financial periods will be analysed and examined, together with the economic and historical events, which so strongly shaped the life and future of the 'Mother' Colony.

Marjorie Barnard in her study [19]of the Macquarie Administration offers an insight into the economic planning by Macquarie for the colony. 'He was a road-builder and grasped what has remained a first principle in the colony–that roads must pioneer the country. The colonial Office thought otherwise. If those who would benefit by roads and other public works could not pay for them, said Lord Liverpool, it was an indication that they did not need them. Nevertheless Macquarie went ahead with his plans.'

The Colonial Office also opposed the concept of trade within and by the colony. Barnard comments[20] 'since the colony considered itself civilised it must have a monetary convention. That the colonial Office did not think so is an epitome of its whole conception of the colony. In theory it was to remain in a state of balanced simplicity, a penal settlement in which the convicts, at the end of their sentences, became peasant farmers, supporting themselves and the town with their produce, and, if possible, exporting some commodity to England that would reimburse the Home Government for its expenditure. Such people could live by barter. There would be no foreign imports. A little change for officials to jingle in their pockets was all that would be needed'.

---

19 *Macquarie' World,* Marjorie Barnard *(1946)* p. 45

20 *Macquarie' World,* Marjorie Barnard *(1946)* p. 56

CHAPTER 2

TOWARDS SELF-SUFFICIENCY

Early Intentions, Policies & Plans

It was British policy to retain the concept of a prison settlement but only if the colony could pay its own way. Such dual desires were in conflict. Autocracy (as in being necessary to operate a prison) would destroy any freedom of enterprise, which in any other circumstances was essential to the growth of colonial income. Would social and political progress come with economic advances?

Wealth would increase continuously between 1802 and 1850, not due to any industrialisation, but due to an entry into a cycle of investment in pastures and sheep–'the golden age'. Wealth was measured in purely tangible forms–Coghlan in '*The Wealth & Progress of NSW*–1886', computed the wealth of the colony at that time, in terms of the value of rural holdings, the value of residential town developments, the value of government buildings, of roads and other infrastructure, plus the value of all usable plant and equipment. Needless to say, this measurement got unwieldy and did not last as a statistical guide to the success of the colony. Probably Coghlan was being forced to compare the colony of NSW with other colonies in Australia as well as with similar countries overseas, for political purposes. Coghlan produces a table comparing the NSW wealth per head with that of numerous overseas countries, with little point except to comment that measuring standards were different elsewhere.

The cycle rolled forward–opening up new land, adding the grazing of sheep, adding to 'national income' followed by more investment–and the cycle rolls around again. Diversification of the economy soon followed and led to an ever-increasing standard of living, which, in itself sustained further growth.

Capital formation followed, mostly in agriculture but increasingly in manufactures[21]. Such steps usually relied on borrowing externally, but such borrowing must have been accompanied by development of financial institutions.

A society, which cannot by its own savings finance the progress it desires must strive, in the alternative, to make itself credit worthy and will only succeed if it follows market opportunities and adopts comparative advantage.

Because future prospects depend so much on present imports, the colony must look for profitable export industries[22]. It must also offer prospects of gain to people of enterprise.

Let me restate the salient points of the above synopsis.

The main characteristics of the colonial economy in transition[23](before 1832) are

The Colonial Government adopted the policy of free enterprise and free trade, during and following the administration of Lachlan Macquarie.

Out of necessity there was a dominance of agriculture in the economy–this was a social phenomena because of the needs and availability of convict labour.

Social problems with bad treatment of aborigines and convicts curbed the otherwise 'clean' image of a successful economy.

---

21 Butlin–Forming the Colonial economy

22 Based on Hainsworth–The Sydney Traders

23 Beckett, G 'The economics of Colonial NSW' (colonial press 2003)

Lack of catalysts for British private investment prevailed until Macquarie converted the colonial image in the 1810-1820 period with new buildings, cleaning up the slums of the 'Rocks' area, and encouraging new enterprise.

Wealth creation was taking place through capital investment and speculation.

The growing need for financial institutions came with the commencement of borrowing and capital migration.

The need for private borrowing overseas occurred because of the lack of savings, wealth and financial institutions in the economy before 1830.

On the other hand the key factors of the (gradually) maturing colonial economy changed slightly (after 1832)

Transportation and the convict labour program was the catalyst for growth until growth plateaued and transportation became more of an economic burden that could not continue to be tolerated

The importance of the on-going British treasury support payments was that there was a steady flow of funds arriving in the colony, not only as support payments for the convicts, but they also had a flow-on effect through the commissary into the pockets of small farmers, pastoralists and vegetable growers as well as to the numerous cottage industries springing up throughout the settled areas of Sydney, Parramatta, Liverpool, Newcastle and the Hawkesbury.

The role of free immigration and the accompanying capital contributions was essential to the constant demand for labour, enterprising operators and the capital formation within the colony. They brought capital goods, capital ideas and just plain capital to the colony.

The role of land sales[24] was that it provided the colony with the funding boost it required to diversify the colony. Land revenues provided the

---

24 Butlin 'Forming the colonial economy'

direct funding for immigrants, aboriginal support, and a small amount of supplemental discretionary funding for the governor.

The rise of the pastoral industry was crucial for trade, attracting immigrants, British investment and then to the attracting of manufacturers associated with the agricultural industries, including the extraction industries.

The growth of manufactures[25] closely followed the growth of the agricultural sector and attracted another source and variety of capital and direct investment

British capital investment and speculation was encouraged by the creditworthiness of the colonies, by direct investment of landowners from Britain and by migrant flow. British newspapers gave many column inches to events in the colony and there was a constant stream of books being written about life and exploits and successes in the colony.

Population growth[26] was constant and fast and was supported by emancipated convicts, and convicts whose sentences had expired, by free immigrants and even by British ex-Military personnel attracted to the colony from India and post-Napoleonic Europe.

The importance of education cannot be overstated. The illiteracy rate between 1788 and 1802 was high, but Marsden led the movement for schooling young people as well as creating literacy programs for the mature aged worker[27].

Statistics collected for the period come from a variety of sources such as 'The blue books' original records held by the (NSW) State Records Office, from the HRNSW and the HRA. Some of the pre-1822 statistics are questionable but with nothing better, they offer a limited picture of life in the colony. Coghlan was the official collector of statistics for over 30 years and his 'Wealth & Progress' provides a vital contribution to our

---

25 Hainsworth 'The Sydney Traders'

26 Hartwell 'Economic Development of VDL'

27 Abbott–Chapter 3 in Economic Development of Australia

understanding of fiscal events, trends and achievements within the colony as well as a graphic comparison of the six colonies.

Each of these elements contributes to the growth of the colonial economy.

Thus, this is 'how' the economy grew[28], the 'why' is another matter. The why was, in reality, to further the goals of British colonial policy–to create a strategic base for defence and foreign policy rationales, as an investment outlet, as a source of trade, both with raw materials being exported to Britain and British goods being imported–a Navigation Act scenario, and mostly, in practice as a transference of some of the worst social ills in Britain to a colony' out of sight'. Wrapping all these aspects together was the goal of self-sufficiency and self-support.

As in any modern economy, the colonial economy had practical and physical limitations[29].

The trade and economic cycles in the colony were influenced by events overseas, as well as local.

Droughts and floods, insect plagues and livestock disease.

Grazing land had limited availability until explorers found a way across the Blue Mountains in 1816.

The Depressions of 1827 and 1841-1843 were man made and largely the result of British speculators, but the negative effects were largely offset by the boom times which attracted the investors and speculators, improved the trading between the two countries and improved the overall standard of living at a rate far greater than if there had been no cycles.

To offset these limitations[30], there were a number of positive aspects within the economy

---

28 Beckett 'The Economics of Colonial NSW' Chapter 3–Policies & Planning

29 Based on Beckett, G 'The Public Finance of Colonial NSW' (colonial press 2002)

30 Based on Butlin, S.J. 'Foundations of the Australian Monetary System 1788-1851'

There was a continuous and growing flow of convicts between 1820 and 1842. In all over 160,000 convicted souls found their way to the colonies in Australia.

Ever increasing physical and fiscal resources were provided by Britain to the colonial economy.

There followed the creation of basic capital accumulation by individuals.

Sustained higher living standards were underpinned by British fiscal support.

The growing population was underpinned by the progressive freeing of prisoners, as well as by sponsored immigration, which in turn brought a constant social change.

Other commentators and writers comment on the source of growth in the colonial economy. Abbott and Nairn[31] introduce a number of specialist economic historians in their edited version of 'The economic Growth of Australia 1788-1820', Hartwell[32] writes of the Economic Development of VDL 1820-1859, and Fitzpatrick[33] offers another opinion in 'The British Empire in Australia'.

Butlin, N.G[34] suggests his own formula of economic growth factors in 'Forming the Colonial Economy'.

However, Abbott in his Introduction[35] points out the dearth of any written treatment of the early phases of Australian economic development in publication between 1939(Fitzpatrick) and Shaw's Convicts and Colonies[36] in 1966. Abbott & Nairn try to fill that gap through a collection of short papers, usually an abbreviated version of the author's full account

---

31 Abbott & Nairn (eds) Economic Development of Australia

32 Hartwell 'Economic Development of VDL'

33 Fitzpatrick 'The British Empire in Australia'

34 Butlin, N.G. 'Forming the Colonial Economy'

35 Abbott & Nairn 'The Economic Growth of Australia'

36 Shaw, A.G.L. 'Convicts & Colonies'

elsewhere in print. They believe (as stated in their Introduction) that the 'economic advantages to the colony included the resources made available by Britain, although the convicts provided merely the means, not the end of settlement'[37]. They also insist that the economic and strategic motives ascribed to Britain in the settlement of the colony must include the 'examination of the decision to transport convicts to Botany Bay in terms of British colonial policy before 1786, and of the prevailing social and economic conditions in Britain and their possible relation to crime[38]'.

Having considered the how of the equation seeking to determine the contribution to growth of the colonial economy, now we need to consider the reasons why.

The economic growth of the colony was but one of the considerations necessary to meet the defence, foreign policy, economic and social goals of the British settlement plan. An undeveloped colony did not gain the British any credibility in meeting their goals, and it was the transfer of the convicts to this alternative penal settlement that provided the workhorses of development to meet their full objectives. In addition, at least in Governor Phillip's settlement implementation plan, the convicts would be used to develop the infrastructure whilst at the same time encouraging the extraction and utilisation of available raw materials ready for shipping back to Britain.

We will now consider the key factors set down above, within the space constraints of this exercise. Each one would be the subject of a broad study in chapter length[39], under a number of category headings viz. Colonial Economic Statistics; Capital Formation in the Colonial Economy; Sequencing the Growth (an Abbott concept); The Patterns of Growth and The Cottage Industries.

---

37 Introduction to Economic Development of Australia 1788-1821

38 Abbott & Nairn (eds) 'The economic Growth of Australia 1788-1821'

39 Refer Beckett who includes chapter length discussions in 'The Economics of Colonial NSW'

A. Statistics

The statistical[40] summaries[41] show numerous highlights of the colonial economy and can be listed as follows:

The population growth[42] was regular and challenging, although the surplus of males over females was disparate and potentially detrimental. We should be mindful of the number of children and their specific needs. The nexus between total population and those 'on the store' was broken and reduced year by year. This progress affected the role, influence and operation of the commissary. Two other observations on the population growth can be made. Firstly, the growth rates in the Town of Sydney followed similar trends to those later found in Parramatta, Liverpool and Windsor. This means that selected decentralisation locations were attractive to new settlers and met the needs of these settlers. Secondly, as the earliest settlement outgrew its natural boundaries (of the Blue Mountains, the Hawkesbury to the north and the Nepean to the south), the new expansion settlements of Bathurst (ten (10) small land grants were initially made 1815-1818) and Newcastle (twenty-three (23) small agricultural grants were made in 1821) supported Lord Bathurst's policy of large-scale land grants to be a catalyst to growth.

The number of convicts[43] arriving in New South Wales made a big difference to the colony in transition

The volume of treasury bills[44] drawn by the colony, especially in those first important 30 years, reflected two facts–the amazingly low cost to the British Treasury of operating the colony (that Treasury goal was being achieved) and of just where the 'capital formation' in those early years was coming from.

---

40 Sourced from Beckett, G 'Handbook of Colonial Statistics' (colonial press–2003)

41 Reproduced in the appendix to this study

42 Source HRA, *passim*

43 Shaw, A.G.L. *Convicts & the Colonies* pp363-8

44 Bigge, J.T.–Appendix to Report III (1823)

The return of livestock[45] shows the successful pasturing of sheep and cattle and the quality of management, climate and husbandry proffered this burgeoning industry.

Trade statistics[46] (imports) shows the source of such imports and the need for securing the Asian trade routes, for the majority of imports arrived from India and China and only in 1821 were the majority of imports from Britain.

From as early as 1810, private farming[47], based on evidence to the Bigge enquiry as contained in his subsequent report, was dominant, successful and essential to the needs of the colony. The accuracy of some of the statistics is questionable but they are the only statistics available. The total acres appear to be well balanced between grazing (sheep, cattle and hogs all grew rapidly with little sign of breeding loss or slaughter for food) and grain, with wheat and maize sharing the farming land.

By reviewing the prices obtained at the London auctions of NSW Wool between 1818 and 1821[48], we can understand Bathurst's goal of growing 'fine' wool, which he thought would have averaged 12s per pound rather than the 2s 10p it actually achieved.

Wool shipments[49] soared between 1807 and 1821 and grew from 13,616lb to 175,433lb annually during that time.

An early 1821 map of Sydney[50] shows the location of the emerging manufactures of the colony. The second slaughterhouse had opened, a sixth mill was opened and we find the locations of boat-building, tanneries, salt works, furniture, candles, earthenware, tea and tobacco and a brewery, all serving the colony. Manufacturing was not the largest employer but in terms of import replacement goods, was the most important employer.

---

45 Source: Select Committee of the House of Commons on Transportation 1838

46 Wentworth, W. C. 'History of NSW '

47 Bigge evidence

48 Macarthur Papers Vol 69

49 ibid

50 NLA Map Collection–Sydney Map published 1822

Agriculture won the export stakes and supported the colonial local revenue base by allowing imports to match exports, and supporting a duty and tariff on all imports. This local discretionary revenue started off small and convenient, but grew rapidly into a major government source of revenues to cover every expenditure apart from the direct costs of the convict system.

A listing of major Public Works[51] helps us understand the benefits to the colony of the free settlers, the convicts, the contractors and the entrepreneurs. In summary, the period between 1817 and 1821 witnessed the development of 6 main roads, of major government buildings, of churches, of military barracks and growing infrastructure. Mostly the period witnessed the success of the Macquarie administration and his major contribution to the colonial economic growth.

This writer's assembling of raw colonial economic statistics[52] (refer appendix) suggests a positive balance of payments growth during the 1826-1834 period with growth, but sometimes negative balance of payments at other times. Imports took a dip in the depression years of 1827 and 1828 but grew dramatically until the next depression of 1842-1844. Local revenues, which the British treasury relied upon to replace contributions from Britain, also grew as a reflection of the burgeoning colonial economy. If we use 1826 as a base year then growth to 1834 became a cumulative factor of 280% over those 8 years or a remarkable 4% per annum.

All in all, the statistics acquaint the reader with a fairly comprehensive picture of 'how' (much) the colony was growing, especially during those important formative years. The colonial establishment had laid the basis for a successful colony and for supporting the future rounds of convict transfers.

---

51 Cathcart, L–Public Works of NSW

52 Beckett 'Handbook of Colonial Statistics (colonial press 2003)

CHAPTER 3

LOCAL TAXATION

A reader may ask, why 1800 and why 1810. As we saw in the first chapter of this study on the rise of public finance and public accounting in the colony, 1802 was the first attempt to record either income or expenditure in the colony. The British Treasury had for the years between 1788 and 1801 recorded all of the expenditure in equipping and moving the first and second fleet, and for the provisioning and victualling the colony for this same period. However, with the necessary, but loose, mechanism of drawing Bills on the Treasury for most purchases, there is a great deal of doubt in the mind of Butlin, Shann and even Clark, that the published figures of the period are accurate.

For this study we are relying on the source documents–the hand-written documents prepared by Reverend Samuel Marsden and Asst Surgeon Darcy Wentworth, 'audited' by the Lieutenant Governors each quarter and then published for all settlers to read in the *Sydney Gazette*.

In a splendid work, edited by James Thomson in 1881, the resources of the Sydney Morning Herald were used (since the Hansard transcription service had not yet commenced in the New South Wales Legislative Chambers) to assemble the Treasurers statements between 1855 (the First Parliament) and November 1881 (the Tenth Parliament).

Thomson wrote in the Preface "Some years ago it was considered desirable that all the Financial Statements made since the inauguration of Responsible Government should be collated and printed for future reference, and for distribution amongst the Public Libraries, Schools of Arts and other literary institutions of the colony. The task of editing these Statements was entrusted to me, I presume, of the experience, which I had acquired, during a long course of years, of the financial affairs of the colony, and the practical knowledge which I possessed of its public accounts generally. Until recently (when Hansard commenced a reporting service in 1880) no authorised copy of any of the Financial Statements (by the Colonial Treasurers) was in existence, so that in the discharge of the duty imposed upon me I had to carefully revise the reports that were given of them in the *Sydney Morning herald*, which I found extremely accurate. In revising these statements I had to compare the Herald's figures with the published printed documents,–a labour which necessarily involved much trouble and occupied a considerable amount of time.

I have placed, as an Appendix to the Financial Statements, a memorandum explanatory of the financial system of New South Wales and an account of the rise, progress and present condition of the public revenue, as it is considered they may be found useful to those who take an interest in the financial affairs of the colony. I prepared these two papers in 1876 and 1879 for the information of the Imperial Government, who had it in contemplation at the time to publish some kind of official work on the defences, financial resources, and general condition of the several Australian colonies."

Why 1810? This was the year during which Lachlan Macquarie arrived in the colony, as the successor to William Bligh, whose failure to govern for all residents led to a slackness and sickness in the colony, which would take many pains from Macquarie to make better and allow the deep wounds to heal. Macquarie reformed the Commissary operation firstly, then 'reformed' the public finance and the public reporting of the colony, but tightening up the currency movement, creating a bank to assist both the traders and the colonial merchants, and 'regularising' the accounting mechanism of the 'Orphan Fund' and the 'Police Fund'.

The period between 1802 and 1810 was highlighted by a change of governor (King to Bligh) in 1806. This date marked a social decline in the colony, with Macarthur turning into a bitter enemy of the governor, followed by a re-alignment of the NSW Corps allegiances away from the governor and towards the rampant self-serving individually profitable trading activities of the military officers.

The colonial economy had been running in freefall. Little government support, a touch of entrepreneurial activity and a few governor declarations that urged the emancipists onto a self-supporting 30 acres and off the general stores. By the end of the King era, he could account for only 180,246 pounds in 'value' of assets as a 'credit against expenses'.

The value of grain and supplies in the commissary stores of about 62,000 pound

The value of buildings completed by King, could only account for 6,500 pound

The value of public livestock owned by the governor would amount to 112,000 pound

The contribution of King to the colonial economy was little (especially when compared to Macquarie). He was not even the able administrator that Phillip had encountered in the time prior to 1792, and other than a few social welfare titbits, King managed to let the colony run without much interference by government. Many more persons were dependent on the government store in 1806 than when King accepted his appointment in 1800. Hunter had led the social decay during his years of 1795 and 1800, but much of his era was spent undoing the damage completed by the interim administrators (between Phillip and Hunter)–Captain Grose (upgraded from Lieutenant Governor for two years, and then Captain Paterson, acting as Lieutenant governor for the next year. These three years allowed the military officers to become dominant in the colony and run things on their own terms–the assignment of the convicts; the run-away trade in spirits; the use of spirits as the means of exchange; the absolute domination of the military in buying shiploads of goods for re-sale. It took the shipment of Macquarie's own regiment to the colony and the withdrawal of the NSW Corps to finally put a stop to the military occupation of spirits and trade. Bligh saw the problem but appeared powerless to intervene.

H.V.Evatt describes these years well in his 'Rum Rebellion'. In a forward to the 1938 edition, Hartley Grattan (a Carnegie Scholar 1937-38), and an American who became enamoured with Australian History wrote" the law can become a weapon in the social struggle and the courts a battleground of opposing class interests on which justice is weighed in favour of one side. This is inn response to Justice Evatt's assertion that 'the Courts were the true forum of the little colony . . . . there was no legislature, no avowed political association or party, no theatre and no independent press' but the major social issues are generally apt to be subverted to the interest of the dominant class in the community." This class struggle pitted Bligh against Macarthur even though the English Government's economic plan for the colony envisaged the strong establishment of a small-holding peasantry in the country, the bulk of the peasants in any future of the colony then visible would be limited to time expired and emancipated convicts. Grattan suggests this economic plan was merely the projection on virgin Australia of an economic pattern being disrupted by the industrial revolution, which plan was destroyed after Phillip's departure from Sydney by the military officers.

The military, in the period between Phillip and Hunter, manipulated their own plan into full operation. They wanted a trading monopoly which was a combined with land holding on an extensive scale along with the ruthless exploitation of convict labour. Rum became the established medium of exchange and it was monopolised to raise its price, whilst consumption was pushed to the limit, thus allowing the monopolists to make huge profits. The defence of the system became the Rum Rebellion' of 1808-09. The struggle over the rum traffic was merely symptomatic of a deeper issue. The small landholders only existed to be exploited until economically exhausted and then removed through inevitable bankruptcy.

Grattan records in his Forward that "since the officers held, in their hands, the military power, as well as such minimum civil as had been developed, whilst the Courts held the supreme economic power, the combined power made them masters of the community. They directed it in a fashion that benefited themselves, but allowed for no progress" The 'brains' of the system was John Macarthur though he was far from being the sole initiator, beneficiary or protagonist. These monopolists broke three governors–Hunter, King, through complete lack of scruple and set a patter for any successor, even though Bligh had been instruction to break up the monopoly and return the small landholders to the place in the community originally planned for them. Setting about his orders, Bligh quickly fell foul of Macarthur and his associates

Macarthur came through this relatively unscathed, especially in latter-day public opinion, and his legacy, as muted through John Thomas Bigge in 1822 was to create a third economic program of foreseeing a broad acre pastoral industry, utilising the free labour of the convicts, but repaying the costs of the colony afforded by the British Treasury through the export of raw wool and the resulting strengthening of the woollen industry in England.

A review of significant events will show that the 'Rum Rebellion' was not the only big event that affected the colony.

When Phillip arrived in the colony in 1788 and established the penal settlement, he came with the authority to raise taxes. This was part of his instructions dated 2nd April 1787.

"Our will and pleasure is that all public monies which shall be raised be issued out of warrant from you and disposed of by you for the support of the government and for such other purpose as shall be entirely directed and not otherwise".

Phillip had been instructed to create a local commissary (he was provided with a commissary officer) in order to acquire, stock and furnish supplies within the colony to victual convicts, the military and the 40 military wives and families that had arrived with the Fleet. The commissary thus became the heart of the local economy for at least the first 20 years of settlement. The commissary was responsible for planning the rations required for the number of persons to be provisioned, based on the governor's decision on individual rations. The role of the commissary was to purchase supplies from visiting ships or, when available, local suppliers and pay a bill of exchange drawn on the British Treasury. This system provided the supplies needed but promoted great inaccuracies in the recording area, and thus, according to N.G. Butlin, the figures from the British Treasury for the tooling and victualling of the colony during the first few years are questionable and likely inaccurate. Phillip had been authorised to draw a bill at the Cape on route with the First Fleet, in order to purchase fresh supplies for the remainder of the voyage. It would have taken many months for this bill to be presented in London, and so, even if accurate, it is unlikely that the expenditures via bills presented would have reflected the correct time period.

There were many items that became short in the first few years and since there were no local persons to provide a source of supply, the governor stepped in and provided the labour within a government-inspired operation. The governor created his own vegetable patch and orchard in the 'governor's domain' and on 'Garden Island'. The governor organised a 'government farm' for watching over the livestock that had arrived and to grow grain that appeared to do well in the colony. It was to take a convict experienced in English style farming to cross grain strains and achieve a suitable local strain of wheat, barley, corn and maize. Clothing had become a major difficulty, with convicts going around in an advanced state of undress and shoeless. The answer was to establish a clothing factory in which the female convicts could be utilised. This answer would also segregate the male sand female convicts as already the fear of growing numbers of illegitimate children running around the colony occupied the governor's mind. Children meant education, as well as extra mouths to feed and this was a penal colony with growing numbers of convicts expected. Phillip's planning for the colony had not included social or political matters. He had not anticipated free settlers, other than military or civil officers needing to retire and wanting to remain in the colony. Phillip himself had planned only to return to England at the end of his official term.

There were many opportunities for small business in the colony. For a start, very quickly it became apparent that the tools and equipment supplied with the First fleet were neither entirely suitable or in sufficient quantity. The felling axes were of little use against the standard trees in need of clearing around Sydney Cove and the Rose Hill settlements, and naturally, each new 30-acre farmer required a set of tools if he was to clear his land and become a farmer supplying produce to the commissary. But the second most important need was that of transportation. Since there were no working horses there was no need for carts, but there was an urgent need for boats for fishing and movement of people and goods between Sydney and Rose Hill. It took until 1790 for the first locally made boat to be ready to cover the Sydney-Rose Hill (Parramatta) link.

The first mill assembled on Observatory Hill could only grind 6 bushels of wheat each day. Mills were to play an important role in the colony and from just one operating mill in 1795, the number grew rapidly so that by 1848, there were 220 operating mills of which 79 were steam powered, and the remainder were horse, wind or human driven. Mills accounted for over 50% of total industry by the middle of the 19th century.

New industry was to be the mainstay of the fledgling colonial economy. The growth of industry was slow but creative and ranged from road making and road repairs to boat building, whale and seal hunting to a broad range of farming–vineyards, brooms, clothing and linen (from locally grown flax).

Other developments that created work for convicts and a trading and export opportunity were the discovery of coal. Newcastle became a convict centre as well as the main provider of coal for export to South America, England and Calcutta. The discovery of seals in Bass Strait gave encouragement to a large sealing industry, which led to a dramatic growth of the local boat-building industry. Exporting commenced in 1800 with the first shipment of sandalwood, wheat and pork. Obviously trading was expected to grow and become quite important to the colony, because Governor King built the first Customs House on the edge of Sydney Cove.

Funding for the first twelve years of the colony had come from the British Treasury but keeping in mind that the colony was instructed to become self-sufficient as quickly as possible, and also that the governor had been given taxing powers, King decided to impose tariffs on spirits, wine and beer in 1800 to complete the new Sydney Gaol that could not be completed by subscription as originally planned by Hunter.

Thus, by 1800, the colony was finding a sense of direction. King was not the right man for the times and there was more neglect during the Bligh times until Macquarie arrived with enthusiasm and a resolve to build the colony into the giant economy that was expected by the British Treasury.

One of the last acts of Phillip before he left the colony for his home in Britain was to proclaim the hours of work to be adopted by the convict labourers.

Phillip set "from sunup to sundown, with a break of 2 ½ ours during the day". When food was particularly in short supply, Phillip had expected that the finishing hour would be 3 o'clock in the afternoon, which would allow time, before dark, to tend to a vegetable patch or such food sources (livestock) that was being set aside for nutrition apart from foodstuffs supplied by the Commissary.

Hunter era was unremarkable for any positive gains in the colony. He claimed at one time that the Combination act in Britain of 1799 would restrict economic activity in the colony, but this piece of legislation intended by Westminster to stop formation of unions and prohibit strikes, was of little, if any, interest to colonial settlers, who went on their own way building homes, farming, trading, protecting what little they had and being subjugated to the military officers. The only relief or release would come from orderly organisation of the convict work gangs but since the military decided it was not their role to supervise convicts the work supervision was left to independent supervisors, but mostly to other convicts. The system did not work well, at least until Macquarie came to the colony.

Both Hunter and King arrived in the colony with instructions from the British Government to break the trade monopoly by the military, but reform was slow to gain any foothold at all. Even King sought relief from the military activists. King decided to rebuild the government herd of livestock, which was a noble enough plan and designed to provide food in the event of another severe drought and food shortage, but in order to implement his plan, he purchased cattle from the very military officers who were rorting the system and King paid far in excess of their real worth. Lackadaisical supervision of both cattle and convicts saw the cattle escape and until near the end of the Macquarie years, build into a substantial herd worth a goodly sum to the settlers when finally recaptured.

King did introduce a ticket of leave system for the convicts who were in good stead with the military, their direct supervisors, the commissary, and the law. It was King's way of removing convicts who could be trusted to be good colonial citizens from the commissary ration list.

King's other contribution was to foreshadow the usefulness to the colony of a local vineyard, and upon receiving two Napoleonic War prisoners in 1801 put them to work in establishing a wine industry for the colony.

The Hunter River area received a boost when it was found that locally grown flax could be used to produce linen. It was not the best quality but the governor thought it could be of great interest to the English government. In this way King recognised the conflict he was in the middle of. He was the British representative in the colony, was paid (rather handsomely as it turns out) by the British Government from the Civil List, but was usually respected and befriended by the settlers to whom he felt a moral and ethical, if not a legal responsibility. In the event of a conflict between the colony and the crown whose side would he choose?

The flax exercise should have been beneficial to both sides, but King knew in his heart that the local product was not of a high quality and would not be accepted by the British public or the British manufacturers. Likewise in declaring in 1801 that all coal and mineral reserves in the colony were the property of the Crown, he knew that only lackadaisical convict labour would be used to extract, load and work the coal removed from the Newcastle coal–fields. King was a free enterprise man under his gubernatorial cloak and invited Robert Campbell (from India) to set up a warehouse and trading post in the colony.

Campbell brought immediate gain and benefit to the colony by shipping a load of colonial coal from Newcastle to Calcutta.

The British encouraged free enterprise in other ways. The English government was going through one of its phases of privatisation. After the second fleet was thought to be much more expensive that Matra had projected, the Colonial Office decided to ship via contractors future prisoners to the penal colony, for a fixed fee. Competition brought a high price for the privately transported prisoners. Savings were encouraged by the contracts on the ship's captains by cutting food (both quantity and quality), limiting appropriate clothing, eliminating exercise and generally creating deplorable conditions for the prisoners, not least being the overcrowding. As a result the death rate of prisoners between England and Botany Bay was nearly 50% in the third fleet. The Government was only mildly offended by the charges of unlawfulness by Wilberforce and his ilk. But the resolve was to make failure to deliver healthy humans instead of human misery hurt the contractor's pocket. Surgeons were included on each shipping manifest with a bonus of 10/6 for each convict landed in healthy condition and a bonus of 50 pound to the ship's captain for assisting the surgeon to land healthy convicts. The problem may not have been solved but was made much better by these incentives.

With the sealing industry showing great promise, the whaling industry was given new strength mostly by the arrival of American whalers into Sydney Harbour. The local industry got underway in 1802 with 7 ships operating from Port Jackson. The Bass Strait area was using half of the 22 ships operating by 1803. The others were successfully operating in New Zealand and South Australian waters.

The colony by this time was moving through turbulent times. The settlements were mostly rural in nature and relied mainly on produce grown with the assistance of assigned convicts. By governor regulation these assigned persons were to be fed, housed, clothed and generally maintained by the 'master'. This was not an inexpensive program for the masters, especially where smallholdings were involved. King ordered that the commissary purchase all produce from these landholders and set a minimum price at which wheat and other grains would be purchased. In this way the landowners could be seen to receive adequate compensation to meet their obligations to their convict workers. As the colony grew demand for 'luxury' items as well as a broader range of staples also grew and this attracted a growing number of 'speculative' ships into the port of Sydney. A price war developed between the traders, the military and those wanting to participate in the purchasing of imported goods. Governor King, having set the original tariff collections on only spirits, wine and beer, decided to impose a 5% ad valorem duty on all imports in 1802. This immediately created a steady revenue stream that needed accounting for. King assumed that this was discretionary income available to him to dispense, as he considered fair and not as an offset to what the British Treasury was providing to the colony.

King had identified a growing social problem as the one where street children were in large numbers, and decided to do something about it. King formed the female Orphan Committee, with the object of housing, feeding, clothing and educating these children until they could be put into service in the colony. The committee included the Reverend Samuel Marsden who had really been instrumental in recognising the problem and finding a partial solution. King appointed Marsden the Treasurer of the committee and decided to use certain Treasury funds to buy the house of the departing Lieutenant Kent, who made it known that he (Kent) had the finest residence in Sydney. Kent was leaving the colony to return to England and take up another posting and he negotiated with the governor for the government to buy his house at 'valuation'. The valuation was based on a replacement cost, whether or not another house like Kent's would ever be built again, and the valuation came to 1,700 pound. Kent received his money via a bill drawn on the British Treasury, which King prayed would be accepted by the Treasury. The bill was negotiated and the Female Orphanage got a residence for about 80 waifs off the streets, although a revenue-raising plan came about when Marsden accepted destitute children from single fathers for a lump sum of 5 pound. It was not as though Marsden or the Orphan Committee were short of revenue. With the growth tax imposed by King, the amount of revenue raised by the Harbour Master from imported goods, especially the alcohol trade, Marsden was constantly looking for ways to spend his money.

King sent Lt-Governor David Collins off to open a settlement at Port Phillip but Collins decided that the Mornington Peninsula was not an ideal place to commence a colony and crossed the strait and selected Hobart instead. Van Dieman's Land had been settled first in 1803, just as the *Sydney Gazette* newspaper was being founded by King as a means of keeping the settlers informed. He would make many proclamations to the free settlers as well as advertising that certain convicts had gone bush. The scourge of the importation of spirits could not be handled but King decided that 32,000 litres of rum brought to the colony from Bengal by Campbell should be returned and he accepted no counsel to the contrary although Marsden led a group to announce how great noble and strong the governor was becoming. It was at this time, with minimum imports transferring from the colony into Britain that the British Government decided to impose a tariff on all colonial imports. Sealskins had yielded either to the colony or to the British merchants over 100,000 skins between 1800 and 1806. This could be considered an ecological disaster or a trading triumph, depending on one's viewpoint, but then the British Government cashed in on the colonial 'success' by imposing this levy on all imports.

In the colony, prices were heavily influenced by local conditions including droughts and floods, and English economic conditions all affected events in the colony. The drought of 1804 for instance affected the wheat crop and thus the price of wheat within the colony. King decided to increase to price the Commissary would purchase private farm grain but even so the shortages were reflected in the price of bread. A settler could buy a loaf of bread for 4p or barter it with 2 ½ pound of wheat.

By 1805 Macarthur could see the writing on the wall for his days as a military officer and accepted his grant of land available to all military who intended to settle in the colony and opened his estate at the Cowpastures, probably the best grazing land within the 1805 limits of the colony.

King's next contribution to the social needs of the convicts was to proclaim a 56-hour workweek for all assignees in return for bed and breakfast, tobacco and tea. The convict rations from the commissary would meet their needs for lunch and dinner.

The first free settlers were wealthy Britains who were enticed into relocating by the offer of free land grants, convict labour to work the land and an allocation of government livestock. The Blaxland brothers responded to this enticement in 1805. In that same year the first colonial built whaler was launched so that greater local participation could be realised.

Pressure on the colony was coming not only from outside the territory but inside as well. We have accounted for King's sudden interest in the growing orphan numbers in Sydney town, but the cause of the problem raises concerns as to the type of society the colony could develop into. Two measures offer some indication of the underlying movement.

In 1805, there were 1400 women in the colony but there were only 360 married couples

Of the 1800 children, under 18, over half were illegitimate

The crime rate in the colony was by 1807, 8 times the rate in England.

The 1806 drought made the wheat crop fail, and the grain became scarce. The price of wheat rose from 1/1/–to 3/14/–per bushel and the price of bread rose 12 fold from 4p to 4/–per loaf. The new governor, sent to replace Phillip Gidley King arrived in Sydney. Tales of the Bounty mutiny and its remarkable voyage of skill and endurance had foreshadowed William Bligh's arrival across the Pacific.

Having outlined the many events, which both curtailed and encouraged the colonial economy, it is time to review the impact on the financial situation brought about by these economic conditions.

N.G. Butlin reports in *Forming a Colonial Economy*

"British decision makers were far from consistent in their attitudes to fiscal obligations to and from the colonists. All governors to 1821 left with at least his fiscal reputation tarnished. Intermittent and at times irascible and condemnatory intervention in colonial expenditures reflected, in part, British ignorance and suspicion. In fact, complex colonial fiscs operated almost from the beginning of the settlement. By 1830, local revenues were offsetting expenditures for everything except convict and defence functions.

"The transfer of prisoners was, from a colonial Australia view, a capital transfer, even if, from a British perspective, the human capital involve had a negative vale. Britain was determined to constrain the British contribution to the colonial operations and to narrow the range of support. It sought ways of ever reducing, to the British taxpayer, the per capita costs of prisoners landed in the colony and to limit the total budgetary costs of sustaining colonies. One way, they decided to achieve this was through auditing public accounts and criticising local behaviour. Other ways was the adoption of a policy of private development of the country, and make the country no longer dependent essentially on convict transfers. A second they decided would be to encourage the emergence of a freed society from a freed population. Thus part of the funds could be diverted from the convict population to the funding of public activity.

"The question remains is the extent to which the colonists could be encouraged to enter the colony and how much of the burden could they bear".

A study of the types of public and private British Investment in the colony is the subject of another exercise, but it can be said here that a wonderful model could be constructed of the formation of a colonial economy.

Consider the inputs: British investment of capital and goods, the transfer of industry–the branch office in the colony, the use of the colony as a source of raw materials–the colonial garden, ripe for the picking. British ships transferring people and goods.

Consider the restraints of population to adopt and utilise the investment

Consider the ultimate limitations of human personality–the convicts forced to labour, when their colleagues back 'home' were lounging in a prison cell. Why should they work in exchange for a limited freedom?

If all this sounds far fetched let us consider the role of free trade and its benefits to Britain.

This is a piece by Sir T. H. Farrer (Bart) from his 1887 book '*Free Trade versus Fair Trade*'. The notation on the front-piece of the book shows the Cobden Club emblem with the words 'free trade, peace, goodwill among nations'. We will discuss Cobden a little later when we review the work of the Federation Senator Edward Pulsford–another outspoken supporter and devotee of the Cobden philosophy, and free trade and open immigration.

"The amount of English capital constantly employed abroad in private trade and in permanent investments, including Stock Exchange securities, private advances, property owned abroad by Englishmen, British shipping,

British-owned cargoes, and other British earnings abroad, has been estimated by competent statisticians as being between 1,500 and 2,000 million pounds, and is constantly increasing. Taking the lower figure, the interest or profit upon it, at 5 per cent, would be 75 million pounds, and at the higher figure it would be 100 million pound."

Farrer then equates this income figure to the spread of imports over exports and finds that the two compare. But then he argues there is the question of freights. "A very large proportion of the trade of the United Kingdom is carried in English ships, and these ships carry a large proportion of the trade of other countries not coming to England. This shipping is, in fact, an export of highly-skilled English labour and capital which does not appear in the export returns of the 19th century, and considering that it includes not only the interest on capital but also wages, provisions, coal, port expenses, repairs, depreciation and insurance; and that the value of English shipping employed in the foreign trade is estimated at more than 100 million pound per annum, the amount to be added to our exports on account of English shipping, must be very large". But he goes further, "add to this the value of ships built for foreigners amounting to over 70,000 ton per annum, worth together several millions, and all these outgoings, with the profits, must either return to this country in the shape of imports, or be invested abroad–I believe 50 million pound is too low an estimate of the amount of unseen exports. In addition there are the commissions and other charges to agents in this country, connected with the carriage of goods from country to country, but each of these items do not appear in the statistics of exports. I can only assume that we are investing large amounts of our savings in the colonies, such as Australia".

The Farrer argument in favour of 'free trade' then turns to the 'fair trade' objections to foreign investments.

Farrer writes "When we point to the indebtedness of foreign colonies to England as one reason for the excess of imports, they tell us that we have been paying for our imports by the return to us of foreign securities; and at the same time they complain bitterly that, instead of spending our money at home, our rich men are constantly investing their money abroad, and thus robbing English labour of its rights here"

But we know that is not the whole story.

If England investors remit capital to the colonies, it is not only in the form of cash (which would come from savings) but it is more often in the form of capital goods. England sends iron; the shipbuilders who make the ships that carry the goods, and the sailors who navigate them. When they reach the colonies, what happens then. They return with grain, or coal, or wool, or timber, and that makes those commodities cheaper in England. The investor receives the interest or profits on that capital invested which would generally be greater than what could have been earned if the capital had been invested in England. Now that return can be spent on luxury goods, invested locally or re-invested overseas to commence the whole cycle again. That return will be employed in setting to work English labour, earn a return and so on.

It remains true that on the whole, based on the Farrer argument, the transfer of English capital from an English industry that does not pay to a colonial industry which does pay, is no loss to England generally, and causes no diminution in the employment of English labour. There are at least two drawbacks to colonial investment by a maritime power; one, in the event of a war, the returns would be open to greater risk, and two; the investors can more easily evade taxation by the English Government.

Obviously since 1886, when Farrer constructed this argument, the world has changed, investment opportunities have changed, England has fallen from its pinnacle as a world power and international commercial leader and the improved collection of statistics now recognises movements of goods and investments on both current account and capital account. But the concept helped put the Australian colony on the map and attracted enormous amounts of private capital into the colony to make it grow and prosper.

Farrer concludes his argument with this observation.

"The desire to make profitable investments, however valuable economically, is not the only motive which governs rich men; it's the love of natural beauty; interest in farming and the outdoor life; personal and local attachments; all of which are quite sure to maintain a much larger expenditure on English land than would be dictated by a desire for gain. Let these other motives have their way, as these investors still contribute to the welfare of the toilers and spinners who produce the goods, and make a good return that in the end makes England wealthier"

If Farrer really believes his wholesome argument, then the theory of developing a colony economy as espoused by the British Government took on great validity, and if it had been followed through fully, the colony may have developed faster and been self-sufficient long before 1830, but on the other hand, it may or would have emulated the British economy much more than it did.

A closer examination should be made of the original intention of 'local' revenue raising. Phillip's instructions had included the right to raise local 'taxation', however Butlin, in *Forming a Colonial Economy* writes that

"At least as early as 1892, Phillip had sought approval for introducing indirect taxation. The British officials approved the raising of charges but not as 'revenue' for disposition by the governor. It took until 1896 for such charges to be put into operation, when Hunter imposed a charge on access to imports, not a duty on the goods themselves".

Hunter's action, writes Butlin appears devious when put into the context that the British reserved the sole right to raise revenue from duties, tolls, and licences.

Again, in the context of the British policy to make the colony self-sufficient and self-regulated, it does not make sense to have firstly included in the official instructions to Phillip the right, if not the obligation to raise local revenues, to then impose restrictions on the governor by limiting the area, range and amount of taxes, but by 1800 King was raising duties and tariffs, with any restriction on amount, disposition or accounting. Butlin may, himself, have misinterpreted the role and intent of the local efforts and the British policy.

Far from being able to privatise development in the colony and rely on private development, the British Government had to take account of the recommendations of the Select Parliamentary Committee on

Transportation, which reported in 1810 on the need, and benefits of continuing with transportation of prisoners to the colony. This policy would continue to provide workers and population for the colonial economy, since by the time the Committee reported, less than 33% of the population were convicts at this date.

On the other hand, four statistics provided to the Committee should have persuaded the Committee to terminate transportation

The cost of convict maintenance rose to a high of 120 pound per convict per annum. This had risen from the previous average of less than 32 pound

Marsden took the first wool for weaving to England and received a very positive reception

The Commissary was able to buy fresh beef and mutton from farmers for rations, and replace salted imports

The port duties in 1810 had risen to 8,000 pound annually and were making a good contribution towards local discretionary revenue for the governors.

The colony was finally finding its feet. A solid base had been set, one from which Macquarie could build and use a building program with investment opportunities relying on free enterprise. The economy was on the move.

The financial statements for the colony during this period come to us via the *Sydney Gazette* each quarter. The newspaper published the quarterly statements of the Orphan Fund and the Police Fund (the successor by name change) to the Hunter-sponsored Gaol Fund.

The Macquarie years are the most special period–they were dynamic in every respect–economically, socially and politically. After the years of torment during the Bligh era, Macquarie was like a breath of fresh air, arriving in the colony. His role was an important one, and he brought with him, not only a new regiment which would further assist in ridding the colony of the vestiges of the 'Rum Corp' and all it stood for, but the hopes and aspirations of the British Government for Macquarie to complete the transition and transformation of the heavily subsidised colonial operations but the possibility of the colony feeding the British manufacturers with resources of raw materials and grow into a recipient of British manufacture. Wakefield foresaw the British Treasury reaping rich harvests from the sale of pastoral land, whilst the free traders saw the colony as an opportunity for being the outlet for British machinery and in so many ways, the branch office for British manufacturers.

A.T. Yarwood states that Marsden's name once again came to the fore during the early Macquarie years. He writes in 'Marsden of Parramatta'

"During the first few years the relations between Marsden and Macquarie deteriorated steadily, for Macquarie identified him as the leader of wealthy colonists who opposed his policies of self-interested and unworthy motives. Involved in the dispute was Macquarie's vision of the colony as a place where convicts had the chance, on proven good behaviour of regaining freedom and aspiring to social recognition and even official positions.

We will set down some of the major economic highlights of the Macquarie era–those very special 11 years between 1810 and 1821. Obviously the one highlight not to be overlooked is the massive contribution to the economy and the future of the colony made by his building program.

Macquarie told Bigge, in a very understated way that he decided the colony could justify a major building program because it would lift the tenor of the colony, lift the spirits of the residents, set the tone for future generations, use local materials (timber, bricks and tiles, lime and, mortar–all of these items were made by convict labour) and use an ex-convict as designer / supervisor (Francis Greenway). The equivalent value of the labour, using 3/–per day as a base rate is 500,000 pound, whilst the value of materials is approx 420,000 pound. Although Bigge agreed that it was a good use of convict labour, and the results cost very little in cash terms to the British Treasury, the benefits were enormous to the morale and the social well-being of the settlers–they were given a boost that might not have come in ordinary circumstances for another few generations, in fact not until the discovery of gold sand the resulting gold rush.

Macquarie began his administration with a goodly amount of economic passion. He talked about establishing a bank. He discussed with his senior officials the expansion of private enterprise and expansion of local industry. Immigration of free settlers was not high on his list of things to do, since he considered the economy needed lots of attention. In this area Macquarie made good progress. The naval boatyard was carrying out building and repair work. The sealing and whaling industry had established a viable export business and was bringing a regular supply of goods and supplies into the colony with every foreign boat that arrived. Blaxland advertised his locally grown salt for sale at 2p per pound. Thus, in addition to the milling operations, boat building, clothing and boot manufactures; the colony could boast a salt manufacturer.

It is only when things are starting to go right that the Government wanted to make change. The second committee on Transportation recommended in 1812 that fewer ticket-of-leave convicts be created. This would affect the commissary operations as well as expanding the cost of maintaining convicts on government rather than assigning them to private 'masters' and taking their clothing, feeding and housing costs off the government. 1812 also saw a second credit/liquidity crisis due to credit withdrawal by British investors.

The next major event with long-term ramifications was the crossing of the Mountain range (the Blue Mountains) that was boxing in the pastoral and farming prospects of the colony. In 1813, Blaxland, Lawson and W.C. Wentworth proudly advised Governor Macquarie that they had found a way across the mountains and witnessed the open panorama on the other side.

Locally, another drought in 1813 created a scarcity of corn and wheat and drove prices higher. Wool was catching on both at home and abroad. The significance of the crossing of the mountain range west of Sydney can be seen in the record quantity of wool being grown and thus the number of sheep running in the colony. In 1814 the Female factory at Parramatta used over 35,000 pound of wool, rising to 40,000 pound by 1818. In the same year the colony exported 30,000 pound of wool to Britain. Macquarie sent Surveyor-General Oxley and Mitchell to mark the route taken across the mountain and explore the open land on the west side of the range. After the 'explorers' returned Macquarie determined to establish Bathurst as the first plains settlement. Wool exported to England was not only a boon to the colony; it raised revenue for Britain as well. Britain decided to impose a duty on wool. Before 1819, the rate of duty was 6p per pound, during 1819 the rate was halved to 3p. During 1819 a new industry was introduced to the colony. In spite of the tariff, the woollen mills could not buy enough colonial wool and asked the British Government to do whatever it could to lift production.

Local industry demonstrated the capacity for innovation which resulted in productivity gains as reflected in total output increases without accompanying increases in labour input. This gain in productivity led to a mini 'business' boom. New settlements were still in demand and a penal settlement was established at Port Macquarie on the north-coast of New South Wales. For every door that opens another closes. Having supported the concept and operation of private enterprise and having encouraged new industry as well as a favourable setting for progress in the colony, Macquarie was confronted with his adversary Commissioner Bigge recommending the privatising of the coalfields. Consolidation in the pastoral expansion meant that in 1821, 80 owners controlled 60% of all land in the colony. Another sign of the times arose from the coal-mines being placed into private hands. The first free labour was used in the coal-mines in 1821. Settlement was now taking place along the south-coast of the New South Wales colony.

The paper used for the *Sydney Gazette* was now locally produced

The credit squeeze of 1812 was the first time economic hardship or stress had reached the colony since 1788 and was the first occasion that the withdrawal of British investment scrambled the comparative gains being made steadily in the colony. Of course, Macquarie tried to counter the effects of the credit squeeze by encouraging trade, creating the atmosphere for entrepreneurs and encouraged local business to establish and grow. This was an unusual credit squeeze and an even more unusual impact on the new and fledgling economy. Since there was little employment, as we know it today, there was little unemployment created as a result of the downturn. The main impact in the colonial economy was in the level of confidence. After the Bligh years and the constant warring between the governor and the military, Macquarie went out of his way to keep the military in its place. Having come to the colony as head of his own regiment he expected and received strong and loyal support and little distraction from the military officers. As a way of reversing the troubled mindset of the population away from the turbulent Bligh years, Macquarie commenced his four-fold program of

A building program of fine buildings that would make the people proud

A local revenue raising program that would provide a significant amount of discretionary revenue to support his local and almost all unapproved activities

A social revolution whereby convicts who had served their time and returned to the regular community were welcomed into society and seated at his table. Simeon Lord was even appointed a Magistrate by Macquarie much to the consternation of leading citizens including Rev'd Samuel Marsden

Encouraging free enterprise and new businesses: privately capitalised and operated.

The withholding and withdrawal of investment capital had only marginal impact. Mostly the traders lessened their level of speculation, which slowed the introduction of new supplies and stocks of new goods into the colony. The export trade still continued but prices sat their destination were lower and in spite of lower wholesale prices demand was reduced in Britain. For once the Keynesian laws of supply and demand did not work.

Governor Brisbane arrived in 1821 to replace Macquarie who had returned to Britain and his home in Scotland.

These are the years leading up to the great recession of 1842. The foundations of the causes of the recession lay in the British influence on and over the colonial economy.

Naturally 50 years from the founding of the first penal settlement produced more than just one recession, although the term of the day referred to the economic collapse as being a depression. Gipps, as governor of the senior colony, found it difficult to ascribe more than partial blame on the British situation, but modern economic historians including Brian Fitzpatrick, Noel Butlin and A.G.L. Shaw place much if not most of the blame on the withdrawal of British Investment from the colony. The depression of 1842 was a follow-on event from the hiccup of 1827. The credit squeeze of 1812 was the first time economic hardship or stress had reached the colony since 1788 and was the first occasion that the withdrawal of British investment scrambled the comparative gains being made steadily in the colony. Of course, Macquarie tried to counter the effects of the credit squeeze by encouraging trade, creating the atmosphere for entrepreneurs and encouraged local business to establish and grow.

Brisbane's arrival in the colony in 1821, marked the end of the successful Macquarie years, and reduced the growth of activity in the colony to a more normal level.

One of the first steps taken by Brisbane was to approve of and encourage the spread of settlement along the south coast from Sydney. The coast to the north of Sydney had been successfully settled for some time, sponsored by the coal fields around Newcastle, the fertile soils of the Hunter River region and the convict settlement in Port Macquarie.

New investors were showing interest in the colony following the publication in England of the three Bigge Reports. One such investment company was being formed in Scotland to exploit trading opportunities between Scotland and the colony. The Australia Company was formed in 1822 in Scotland to take advantage of the coming investment opportunities in the colony. By 1830 over 33% of all landowners in NSW were Scots born.

To further assist the growth of the settlements, Brisbane built a road from Windsor to Maitland and opened up more of the Hunter River district.

The organisation of the convict labour was consistently a problem in the colony, and although Macquarie had taken a personal interest in the convicts by receiving the convict ships into Sydney Harbour and by directing the assignment of convict labour to public projects, Brisbane chose to transfer responsibility for convicts from the Superintendent of Convicts to the Colonial Secretary.

Brisbane suppressed the first recorded discovery of gold from the Bathurst District in 1823. He was concerned his convicts would be tempted to escape the assignment provided and head for the hills of gold. Thus it took a further 30 years for the official find to be publicly announced.

Upon leaving the colony, Commissioner Bigge recommended to the British Treasury that extra import duties be placed on all colonial products except wool, timber and tanning bark. On these goods he recommended lower duties.

1823 also saw the formation of the NSW Legislative Council authorised by the New South Wales Judicature Act (UK legislation) which also extended the role of the Supreme Court in the colony.

In 1824, William Charles Wentworth commenced *The Weekly Australian Newspaper.* The challenge thrown before Brisbane in the newspaper columns brought about the first threat of censorship to the new publication. This followed Brisbane heavy censorship of the *Sydney Gazette* and forbidden to report on local politics.

A giant boost to the development of the colony and the spread of settlement and the attraction of new investment from abroad came with the formation of the Australian Agricultural Company in 1824. The establishment of the AAC is described in more detail later on.

Another new and promising industry was established, when, in 1824, sugar was produced from local sugar cane.

Brisbane opened the Morton Bay settlement in 1824 and moved to further explore the Brisbane River.

Brisbane was recalled without having achieved much of what he was sent out to do. The post–Macquarie years had witnessed the decline of growth and the decline of British interest in the colony.

General Sir Ralph Darling arrived as Governor in 1825 (Brian Fletcher has written a comprehensive biography of Darling's life–*Ralph Darling–A Governor Maligned*)

The first of Darling's proclamations restored the supervision of convict labour to the Assignment Board.

When the question of legitimacy of import duties imposed under former governors was raised Darling moved to ratify their legality through the new Legislative Council

The AAC utilised their exclusive access to the coal-fields of Newcastle and even though the company was the recipient of both a grant of land (one million acres) and an assignment of many convicts, the company decided to modernise coal hand and laid a tramway in Newcastle to carry and move coal from the fields to the wharf.

We noted a first liquidity crisis in 1812 when British investors withdrew credit from the colony. A second liquidity crisis took place in 1827 and was due to a decline in export prices in Britain and cuts in foreign investment.

Darling introduced the concept of pastoral and commercial land leasing in 1828 just as a significant boost in convict numbers arriving inn the colony was creating further investment opportunities and demand for labour. The arriving convicts were mostly assigned to pastoralists and farmers. This boost in transported convicts increased the convict element of the overall population from 29.8 to 46.4

'Bay whaling' was commenced at Twofold Bay on the south coast of the colony in 1828, whilst VDL boasted 5 bay whaling stations.

The only way Darling could try to control squatters and pastoralists was to impose 'limits of location', and by 1829 the limits of location was limited to 219 counties in New South Wales.

Extending the settlements embraced the new colony of South Australia and Edward Gibbon Wakefield published his plan for land reform and the colonising of Australasia.

Labour organisation was underway in Sydney now that the restrictive UK labour laws on association and organisation of workers had been repealed. The Sydney Shipwright's Association was formed as a trade society in 1829. Later, in 1833, the Cabinet Maker's society was formed to maintain piece rates for workers.

New industry attracted many interested entrepreneurs. With over 3 million lb of tea being imported annually from China, tea plantations were first experimented with in northern NSW.

Darling's last acts as governor saw the implementation of the Rippon Regulations which approved crown land sales at 5/–per acre; the Molesworth Committee's recommendation that transportation be suspended, and the funding of immigration into the colony from the Land Fund

Upon the return of Darling to England, Sir Richard Bourke was appointed governor of the colony in 1831.

The colonial governors were still under heavy influence from Britain with Bourke being faced with action being required on the recommendations of the Committee on secondary punishments. Due to the growing crime rate in the colony (it was 8 times the rate in Britain) the UK House of Commons committee recommended more convict discipline and harsher treatment. The crime rate, especially amongst convicts had reached startling levels. In 1835 there were 28,000 convicts and over 22,000 summary convictions against convicts.

Bourke didn't agree with this action but was aware that if free migrants and investment were to be attracted to the colony then the people of Sydney and Parramatta were not to be scandalised by convict misbehaviour, a high crime rate and chain gangs of convicts being paraded through the streets of the principal town.

Due to growing land sales revenue and a strong interest in migration from Britain to the colony, an Immigration Commission was established in London and funded by the Land Fund. Land sales were not the only growth revenue increasing. In 1833 the import duties into the colony exceeded 100,000 (108,466) pound for the first time With the ad valorem duty being set at 5%, this revenue indicated that over 2 million pound of goods were being imported into the colony. With the total population set at 60,794, this level of imports meant that every man, woman and child, civil servant and convict, was importing nearly 33 pound of goods per year. With exports matching imports in value, trade had reached a remarkable level of 65 pound per head per annum in less than 45 years from the original settlement.

The recommendation to cease transportation to the colony was generally welcomed by the town people, but pastoralists bemoaned the fact that they would lose future access to assigned free labour. It was decided that all prisoners convicted to less than 7 years punishment would in future be handled within Britain.

The pastoralists had plenty to be concerned about. The convicts constituted most of their labour, and few free workers were available in the colony to replace them. All this at the same time that wool exports from the colony reached record levels in Britain and replaced whale products as the colony's main export.

They were not welcomed but the first Chinese labourers arrived in the colony in 1837. Plenty of local opposition stopped any large scale transfers of Asian workers to the colonies.

Workers were an important ingredient missing in the colony and that is why the Land Fund was being used to sponsor free settlers into the colony, but they could not arrive fast enough.

The census of 1839 (Sir George Gipps arrived as the new governor in 1838) showed that NSW had 2 distilleries, 7 breweries, 12 tanneries, 3 brass foundries, 77 flour mills, whilst single factories were producing hats, salt, sugar, tobacco and other goods. Bread had become a good barometer of changing prices and cost of living in the colony and in drought or in times of shortage, wheat would rise in cost, and the price of bread would react accordingly. In 1839, the reverse was happening. Good conditions led to a favourable harvest and a good crop so wheat prices fell from 1/2/–per bushel to 2/9 and bread dropped from 4/–per loaf to 1/3p.

By the end of this third period, the colony was making giant strides in growing and acting like a town that was there to stay. Food was plentiful. Jobs were available for everyone wanting to work. The Military was loyal top the Governor and the Legislative Assembly appeared to be acting responsibly. In 1832 the first Appropriation Bills had been provided to the Legislators and it was shown that the colony was in good shape financially. Social problems were being addressed, convict transportation had ceased and less than 1,000 convicts were still under maintenance.

Investment from overseas was being attracted to the colony and there were lots of opportunities for investors and new settlers. There was a cloud on the horizon in 1842 but until that time the colony was under good management.

CHAPTER 4

PUBLIC EXPENDITURE IN THE COLONY

If the statistical summary shows how progress was made in the colonial economy then a brief study of the mechanics of 'capital formation' will evidence the fiscal factors underpinning that progress.

Capital formation in the colony during these early years can be focused on the massive building and construction program. In the new colony, there was a demand for convict and military barracks, housing and government buildings, storehouses for the commissary, docks, wharfs, draining programs, fresh water, and so on. The support services required a supply of bricks, tiles, timber, furniture, roads, boats, agriculture and farming for food production. *The core of government practical economic management between 1788 and 1830 was The Lumber Yard*[53], *which included The Dockyard, the Stone Quarries, the Female Factory, and various timber harvesting, land clearing and road making enterprises.*

The capital for these government enterprises had been provided by the British Treasury, and certainly in greater quantities than originally estimated. Matra, in his 1776 submission to the British Government estimated an outlay of £3,500 for the first year and from then on self-sufficiency

---

[53] Refer Beckett' The Public Finance of NSW' where a full discussion is made of the Commissary and convict management including the various enterprises of the commissary operations.

and no further cost to the British Treasury.[54] This estimate was not only optimistic but did not allow for adequate infrastructure once the colony was settled. Matra's plan was for a small convict contingent by the shore of the deep water mooring, with a fresh water stream close by, level ground for building log barracks and store buildings. No weather disturbances, no wild animals, no deleterious convicts, and a plentiful supply of wild animals and fruit and vegetables, good soils, and no interference from any natives. Matra's dream world was far from realistic and practical but his projections suited the senior government and parliamentary officials who approved a small impractical budget for the expedition.

The basic economic problem within the growing economy, and thus one of the early limitations to solid or speedy growth, was the provision of savings to sustain the army of unskilled and semi-skilled workers engaged in this construction and development work–this in turn, hindered private construction for other than settlers who had ready money to invest in such work, and thus most early residences were supplied and furnished by the government. However, in the absence of an adequate local supply, the greatest part of these 'investment' funds was to be drawn from outside Australia, in the form of imported British capital. This flow of British capital helps our understanding of the aggregate capital formation in the colony. British capital was important in inducing the smooth expansion during the first four decades of the colony, and it was a key factor in the subsequent economic declines in 1827 and in 1842-1844. For most of this period, prices and wages rose slowly if not persistently and inflation was imported on the back of speculative activities.

Obviously public authorities played an important role in capital formation[55] and the public sector seems to have contributed a declining portion of the aggregate from 100% to approx 50% during these first four decades. Four components dominated overall aggregate capital formation. These are ranked in terms of volume: Infrastructure such as roads, buildings, barracks etc; agriculture such as government farms, grain growing and livestock grazing; residential construction, and finally

---

54 HRNSW–Copy of Matra's letter to the British Colonial Secretary detailing the costs of establishing the new colony

55 Based on Hartwell 'Economic Growth of VDL'

manufacturing. In broad terms, we can see that manufacturing investment in workshops and offices matched each other, and it is interesting to note that manufacturing investment did contribute to what was perceived as a dominant agricultural, pastoral and farming economy. It is also noteworthy that the British Government continued to pay for and thus contribute the convict and transportation system, the colonial defence and the 'civil list' for the colonial use.

C. The Role of the State[56]

If capital formation reflected the engine of growth and the statistics reflected the multifarious facets of growth, then the State became the conduit for growth[57]. Competent government policies, capable administration and sound conditions for enterprise were the essential ingredients for colonial economic growth, and even the dichotomy within the colony of 'free enterprise' or 'government enterprise' could not slow the clamour for better living conditions, jobs and a controlled haven for entrepreneurs.

Fitzpatrick in *The British Empire in Australia* reminds us of the transition in 1834 from the point 'where the earliest community was primarily a state-supported establishment to the next point (after 1834) when imported capital applied to wool growing and associated or derivative industries rapidly endowed the community with the character of British private enterprise instead of public enterprise, and appointed the pastoral sector as a field for investment into a profitable colonial territory'[58]. The Forbes Act (by the Legislative Council) in 1834 offered inducements to British capitalists to invest in New South Wales, and as a result the colony of NSW, with three million people, had received twice as much British capital as the Dominion of Canada, with a population of nearly 4.5 million. There are obviously two distinct stages of state intervention in reaching out to overseas investors. Before 1834 the role of the state was to provide British capitalists with free land and labour in the colony,

---

56 Based on Fitzpatrick 'The British Empire in Australia

57 Based on Beckett–Chapter 5–'William Lithgow' where capital formation and the role of government is discussed

58 Fitzpatrick 'The British Empire in Australia

then came the development of sheep-raising of fine wool, and the sequel was, having facilitated the importation of capital for investment, its role was to provide services which would facilitate the earning of dividends on the capital invested. However, even though initial dividends were sent 'home' in ever-increasing quantities, the time came when local people and institutions were the recipients of these dividends and great enterprises were part owned within the colony.

The state had, according to Fitzpatrick[59], four main functions:

Firstly, to take the responsibility for adjusting claims when the economic system reached crisis, as in 1827 and 1842, although Governor Gibbs acted reluctantly and belatedly in the latter crisis.

Secondly, the state is to administer essential services, in the operation of which private investors could not derive normal profits.

Thirdly, the state must nurture enterprise, including well-capitalised undertakings, by means of tariffs, bounties and other concessions.

Fourthly the State is to take responsibility for restoring to private capital, power, which has been taken away from it.

Fitzpatrick can be challenged on, at least, this last point. It surely cannot be the role of the state to supplant, supplement or fiscally support private capital lost within the colonial economy. If private investment criteria is invalid or faulty, then within a free enterprise economy, even one adopting an extended use of government enterprise, private capital must be supported by or subjected to market forces and not 'restored' by the state.

The introduction of the railways, just outside our time-line is such an example. The British were strongly urging private operators to install and operate in-town rail services. The *Sydney Railway Company* was empowered by the Legislative Council to build a private line with the support of 'government guarantees', with the right of the government to resume operations with minimal compensation to shareholders if

59 ibid Page 347

the enterprise collapsed. The enterprise did collapse, was taken over by government planners, financially restored to health and the railway system moved on to be become a successful government enterprise[60]. The role of the State, in this typical case, was not to guarantee speculators, but to protect the suppliers and contractors who placed their trust and faith in the free enterprise system. Fitzpatrick is confusing a touch of Marxist policy with a shackled government enterprise.

We can deduce that the state had an important role in the development[61] of the colonial economy and filled this role with supportive mechanisms and policies–especially guidance for financial institutions following overseas borrowing, overseas investment and land speculation.

D. Sequencing Economic Growth[62]

I come now to a brief study of 'in what sequence' did the economy grow, and as N.G. Butlin, in the Preface to *Investment in Australian Economic Development* writes "I have found no guidance on this question from the few essays which examine the early economy in identifying the sequence of economic growth in terms of both aggregate behaviour and the performance of major investment components".

One must fear to tread where Butlin finds weakness or gaps. This essay may still not fully satisfy the larger Butlin type questions but the immediate concern is about the 'hows' and the 'whys' of the colonial economic growth between 1788 and 1850 and as such there is an obligation, albeit ritualistic, to outline the main sectors of investment contributing to that growth. Since this study may cover many areas, methodology and circumstances of sequential development may not matter as much as first thought.

Some facts should perhaps be stated first as the basis for future conclusions:

---

60 Beckett 'The Public Finance of the Colony of NSW' (colonial press 2002)

61 See also Butlin, N.G. 'Forming the Colonial Economy' for a discussion of these factors leading to changes in financial institutions

62 Based on Butlin, N.G. 'Investment in Australian Economic Development

Government enterprise towered above private enterprise[63] at least between 1788 and 1821 because the government had the sole access to capital, land and labour, and government enterprise met the needs of the colony and its community of free settlers.

Government enterprise was based on two facts–survival and self-sufficiency of the colony. From Phillip's livestock and building materials imported with the first fleet (including his 'portable' government house), government had undertaken to be the planner, the contractor, the financier and the provider of all labour and material resources in this new penal colony. That essentially was the nature of a penal settlement[64]. Then King decided he wanted a little 'spending money' outside the purview of the British Treasury, and this was a development unknown in normal prison or penal colonies but became the first step in the transition to a semi-autocratic free settlement. If this is an anachronism, then substitute 'planned economy' into any government encouragement of free enterprise. Then add Governor Macquarie, who as a free spirit, developer extraordinaire and ego driven creator of entrepreneurship[65]. Macquarie's contribution is in itself extraordinary. He applied, wisely, firm private enterprise principals to planning and development and set his sights on bettering the colonists' standard of living, changing the reliance on government hand-outs (the colony had to stand on its own feet, which is subtly different to being entirely self-sufficient, but is a good first step to self-sufficiency) and encouraging entrepreneurship in the colony. In Macquarie's mind, the role of his administration was to reduce British Treasury support payments, increase discretionary local revenues, build desirable government buildings and infrastructure, and create the atmosphere for manufacturing in the colony.

Obviously agriculture was the main objective of economic planning. It could use most of the convicts arriving in the colony[66]; it was minimalist in skills requirements, and relied more on natural events than most other colonial activities, but was mainly the most important of labour intensive

---

63 A concept of Marjorie Barnard in 'Macquarie's World'

64 Based on Ellis Chapter 11 'Lachlan Macquarie'

65 Concept from Barnard 'Macquarie's World'

66 Refer Shaw 'Convicts & Colonies'

undertakings. Agricultural operations would be extended to government farming, land clearing, timber harvesting and much of the work of the Lumber Yard. Its success was essential to maintaining the colony and making it self-sufficient As was pointed out above, agriculture contributed to more capital formation in the colony than did manufacturing but the rise of manufacturing mostly during and following the Macquarie administration created balance within the economy and created a support structure internally and an import replacement opportunity

The growth of government enterprises such as the government farms, the Lumber Yard,[67] which in turn included the stone quarries, and the timber forests, the Female Factory and the Dockyard, encouraged rather than damaged any move to free enterprise operations. The earliest private enterprises, other than pastoral establishments, were government contractors. Little capital was required, only limited skills (other than a nose for making money) were necessary, and there was plenty of work available and not a lot of competition.

British private capital was uncertain and untried in the colonial context; investment within Britain or in the tropical colonies was considered more profitable and safer; of the hundreds of companies floated in the United Kingdom between 1820 and 1850, only five important companies were formed for investment in Australia. The Land Grant Companies–these were the three (3), plus two banks, within the Australian context–The Australian Agricultural Company (AA Coy), The Van Diemen's Land Company[68] (VDL Coy), The South Australia Coy (SA Coy), Bank of Australasia and The Union Bank of Australia–filled a role as catalyst for attracting new investment and even offered some official sanctioning and support parameters for colonial investing[69].

A question should be posed, at this point, as assistance for understanding the sequence of development. Was the colonial NSW economy in

---

67 Refer Beckett 'The Economics of Colonial NSW'

68 Refer Beckett, G. 'The economic circumstances of the Van Diemen's Land Company (colonial press 2003)

69 Hartwell refers to similar factors in 'The VDL Government' Historical Studies ANZ, Nov 1950

1830 a capitalist economy[70]? It was, as we learnt earlier, an economy in transition before and after that date. In so far as capitalism implies a rational, and acquisitive society, then NSW had been capitalist (urged along by Macquarie) ever since it had broken the bonds of being the self-contained prison promulgated in 1788. Capitalist techniques, as opposed to traditional techniques of economic planning, assisted with the transition from a penal to a free economic society. The transition included the organisation of production by the capitalistic entrepreneur for profit, by the combining of labour and materials into a marketable product. The capitalist enterprise portrayed itself in the banks, the insurance companies, merchant houses and the large-scale pastoral farms–all institutions, which were rationally organised for the pursuit of profits. The most important means of production–land–had fallen by the 1830s into relatively few hands–trade and finance were highly concentrated, most of the population were without ownership of property, and worked for a wage determined by the market. West, in *A History of Tasmania*[71], offers us a quotable insight into the settlement progression "The dignity and independence of landed wealth is ever the chief allurement of the emigrant. Whatever his rank, he dreams of the day when he shall dwell in a mansion planned by himself, survey a wide and verdant landscape called after his name and sit beneath the vineyard planted by his own hands"

Another brief quote may also be in order. Hartwell, writing in *The Economic Development of VDL 1820-1850* thinks "it is impossible to study the trade cycles without reference to general economic development, and the existing economic histories of Australia did not answer the kind of questions I was asking"[72]. His point is that he offered, in his work, a specialist account of economic development, as will this account try to be in relation to the growth of the colonial economy in New South Wales.

70 Butlin, N.G. in 'Forming the Colonial Economy states that the colonial economy was 'capitalistic' This portion of the essay is examining this claim

71 West,' History of Tasmania–edited by Shaw in one volume

72 Hartwell 'Economic History of VDL' P.251

E. Patterns of Economic Growth[73]

Although Butlin raised an interesting question on sequences of growth, any reference to sequences can also be raised in terms of 'patterns'.

The highlights of any 'pattern' can be traced to the foundation of the colony. This will also serve to identify some of the 'whys' in the essay topic.

The colony was founded for the multiple purposes of creating an intermediate stopping point for British ships travelling to India and China, of provisioning them, offering some form of back loading for the return trip to Britain, after unloading goods at this Port of Botany Bay. It was also considered to be of strategic value in limiting the expansion of Portuguese and Dutch interests in the sub-Asian region. Bonus reasons were considered to be that the East Coast region could be a source of raw materials for British industry[74], which was at that time coming to the implementation stage of the industrial revolution, and that any future colony would utilise British shipping and be an outlet for future investment and finally but almost as an after-thought any colony in so isolated a region could be a suitable location for a penal settlement.

Thus the growth in the colony followed first the formation of capital, then the importation preferences of capital, then the needs of the colony and finally the desires and preferences of the entrepreneurs and traders. This cycle continued right up to the discovery of gold, but it was not the traditional boom and bust cycle. It was a trade and investment cycle of designating an investment opportunity, bringing together the capital required, filling the opportunity and recommencing the cycle by starting all over.

The pattern changed somewhat in the mid-1830s (the colony was by now almost a mature 50 years of age) when the pattern of growth suddenly had a new spoke–local wealth, local ownership, locally retained dividends and the need for reinvestment. This change in pattern broke into the

---

73 A Beckett concept developed in The Economics of Colonial NSW

74 Proposed by Sir Joseph Banks (HRNSW–Vol 1)

overseas raising of capital, and the overseas distribution of dividends and the overseas domination of manufacturing in the colony.

Local traders were gaining prominence in sealing, whaling, exporting and importing, merchant financing and the commencement of local auctioneering. Traditionally the Sydney markets had favoured enterprising practitioners who had surplus livestock or cottage industry manufactures, and these pursuits often led to more than the public markets as their distribution point. Simeon Lord, the master trader, bought a hat manufacturer in Botany whose rise had been exactly along those lines, cottage industry production, public markets distribution, rented premises, paid labourers, advertising, then buy-out and take-over.

Government policy fitted largely into this pattern and we have covered already the encouragement of business enterprise, however, the main role of government was to create the climate and the environment for entrepreneurs, borrowers, lenders and a satisfactory circumstance for making a profit and the return of capital. This came by way of successful business ventures, in both the agricultural and industrial enterprises. Because the skill levels within the colony were only gradually expanding and refining, there was official encouragement of British industry expanding with branch operations. Agricultural enterprise was encouraged by offers of land grants and then the cheap sale of land, and later the provision of either cleared land or convict labour.

Abbott[75] discusses the 'constituents' of the New South Wales colonial economy, and lists six. Agriculture; The Pastoral industry; Manufacturing; Trade within the colony; Exports other than wool; Government Works and Services.

Let me turn to some 'constraints' on the growth of the colonial economy; these include[76] Government policy; land, labour and capital.

There was an implied constraint to local colonial growth imposed by the Westminster parliament. The last of the series of Navigation Acts was

---

75 Abbott & Nairn 'The Economic Growth of Australia

76 Abbott & Nairn 'The Economic Growth of Australia

in 1696 but stood unchanged until after the recognition of American Independence in 1783[77]. In general, until the legislation was passed,

British colonists had been free to trade with any country and to use ships of any nationality, and accept the cheapest freights. Following the passage of the legislation and the numerous amendments, they were obliged to use only British (including colonial) ships, to send all their exports direct to Britain and to import all their overseas goods direct from Britain. In this way, writes Abbott in *Economic Growth of Australia 1788-1821*, the colonists were virtually insulated from direct contact with the world economy.

Growth of Public Service 1800-1825

It is not unexpected that the public service for colonial NSW from 1800 revolved around the growth of the settlement, firstly as a penal colony and then changed as its role required transition into a market-driven economy.

The Governor's establishment changed little before Brisbane and Darling came Ion the scene. Its staffing was hierarchal and was based on the head of state being the governor, his deputy (Lt-Governor), and his heads of nominal departments. Darling referred to this group as his 'kitchen cabinet' or Board of General Purposes, but whatever the name, the role and participants remained the same–the chief judge, the chief surveyor or surveyor-general, the commissary-general, the chief surgeon, the chief chaplain and soon the Auditor-general (appointed 1825 under Darling)

Each governor had appointed a private secretary, and in 1822, this position was re-classified with its role expanded, and its own establishment created. Sub elements included the Colonial Treasurer and the Colonial Auditor-General and their expanding staff. The combined duties included issuing land grants, issuing land titles, collecting and accounting for all revenues, recording expenditures, completing feasibility studies for the

77 Discussed in Hainsworth 'The Sydney Traders'

expanding government services and handling all official correspondence into and from the colony.

Typical of the growing bureaucracy was the roads department. As treasurer of the Police Fund, Darcy Wentworth had been responsible for repairing roads, the Superintendent of Convicts was responsible for their formation and the Police Fund and its treasurer were responsible for payment of all associated costs. The British Treasury did not see the need for significant expenditure on road making, so the making and repairing fell to be supported by local revenues and convict labour. Macquarie increased this expenditure enormously when he designed and constructed the Great North Road (to the Hawkesbury), the Great West Road (to Parramatta and Bathurst) and the Great South road (to Goulburn). Within the colony, such road making was essential if new lands and settlements were to be opened up, and livestock moved around the colony. To raise revenue for the colony and to maintain the new roads, tolls were imposed on users of the road system, and these tolls eventually funded ferries and bridges, where rivers and streams had to be crossed.

This review of the growth of Public service is designed to embrace not on the coming 'Public Service 'system with its teams of public servants, but also the role of serving the public with official services. Obviously what springs to mind is the necessity for hospitals, coal for heating, fresh food, transport and communications, livestock, ferry services (initially between Sydney Cove and Parramatta), building materials, and most importantly, labour for hire.

Macquarie expanded this role by initialising a local manufacturing industry, essentially serving as an import replacement opportunity. He encouraged local entrepreneurs, who turned their hand to consumer imports, dressmaking, hats and apparel, shoes and furniture making.

Macquarie also co-ordinated the burgeoning government convict numbers into specialty trade teams for expanding government services.

The timber-cutters, carpenters, sawyers, bricklayers and blacksmiths were moulded into the full-service mini-manufacturing operation named the Lumber Yard. The boat-builders, boat unloaders and wharf-workers and ferrymen were moulded into the Dockyards, the brick and tile makers were pulled into the Brick Yard, whilst new activities included carriage making, cooper workers, whilst the commissariat grew with its own range of livestock herdsmen, slaughter men, storemen and clerical assistants. The commissariat also managed until 1817, the large government farm operations, used for the growing of government grain, vegetables, and fruit, for the colony as a whole.

The interest in the commissariat operating a more general store was too overwhelming and would have failed if the Treasury had not rejected the concept. The initial approach was along the lines of a catalogue service, whereby consumers ordered and paid in advance, and the commissariat placed the import request and added a sufficient margin to cover shipping, handling and clerical services.

Policing services were commenced under Macquarie band these numbers grew rapidly as the settlement grew in Sydney and outlying areas. Macquarie also appointed the first government printer, who used imported presses to publish official government regulations and orders.

The analysis of Accounts extracted from the 'Blue Books' of 1822 through 1828 allows a number of conclusions to be drawn.

The initial claim by the author that the cost to the British Treasury of establishing and operating the Colony, was NOT the millions of pounds claimed by other historians, is born out by examination. The accounting records as maintained by Governor Macquarie from 1822 leads to a statement of 'net revenue and expenses' which purports to offset all revenues against all expenses, and includes as revenue certain convict maintenance charges. Even in 1822 the Colony was showing a small operating surplus. This surplus grew through 1828 until, other than for transportation of convicts to the Colony, the charges on account of the British Treasury were under One Hundred Thousand pounds for protecting, feeding and housing nearly 5,000 fully maintained convicts. Against this cost, the charge for housing, feeding and guarding this same number of prisoners in Britain would have been substantially higher, since in addition to the 5,000 gully maintained convicts there were a further 20,000 being paid for by free settlers and used as supervised labour. Britain surely had found a cheap source of penal servitude for at least 25,000 of its former prisoners, and found a very worthwhile alternative to the American Colonies as a destination for its prisoners.

Revenue from Crown Land sales and rents was used to offset Civil (Crown) salaries and expenses.

It is probably incorrect, at this stage, to say that it cost Britain nothing or at best, very little, to establish and maintain the Colony, but it can be said that from 1842 the costs were limited to maintaining fewer and fewer convicts. But from these convicts great value in terms of agricultural produce, coal and other minerals extraction was derived. Just in terms of coal for lighting, heating, the cost to the government of purchasing these items commercially would have been substantial. The 'Blue Book', however, reflects the use of the coal as a cost rather than a gain as would be the accounting standard today.

A final conclusion could be given that there are much more known records available for this period (the first One Hundred Years) than the author originally thought. The reproduction of the 'Blue Book' by the State Archives Office is a major step forward in understanding the economic challenges faced by settlers and convicts in the early Colony. The sourcing of material from the Blue Book unveils the financial statements and conditions of these early years. It is still considered that finance records of the period 1788 to 1822 are not re-constructible, but the author feels that a deep search through the microfilms forming the Joint Copying Project will provide information on the two Colonial operating funds of the period–the 'Police Fund and the Orphan Fund'. This is a challenge for another time.

An interesting observation is found in_'The Constitutional History of Australia' by W. G. McMinn (1979).

P 33 records "Subject to the need for a vice-regal message, accepting that any locally (Australian Colony) initiated legislation of a money bill nature requires The

Sovereign's ratification, the New South Wales Legislative Council was to have a general right to appropriate revenue from taxation, except for an amount of 81,600 pounds, the expenditure of which was to be in accordance with 'three schedules' to the Act; 33,000 pound for the salaries of those on the civil list eg Governor et al, the superintendent of Port Phillip and its judges and for the expenses of administering justice; 18,600 pound for the chief civil officers and their departments, for pensions and expenses of the council; and 30,000 pound for the maintenance of public worship. Land and casual revenues were also reserved.

The Sale of Waste Land Act raised the minimum reserve price of crown land to one pound per acre, except that large remote areas might be sold at a lower price, and established a formula for the use of the land revenue; fifty percent was to be spent on immigration, the rest was to be expended by the Governor in accordance with British Government directives from time to time. The Governor was to continue to have power to issue depasturing licences and to make regulations for the use and occupancy of unsold lands, but the existence of the Sale of Waste Lands Act placed an important restriction on the colony by implying a prohibition against the Legislative Council legislating on these matters. The first directive on how the Governor was to spend a portion of the fund, enjoined the Governor to spend a proportion on Aboriginal protection and another on the roads; he was left free to hand any surplus over to the Council for appropriation; but it was made clear that the whole of the fifty percent was to be considered as an emergency reserve if the Council proved difficult". McMinn sheds some further light on the Crown Lands mystery by there still remains the question of how, year after year, were these funds fully used or were they just included as a contribution to general revenue. It would appear that somewhere there is a firm directive from the British Treasury that the revenues from Crown Lands sale was to be used to 'offset' British costs of maintaining the Colony. The 'Blue Book' is evidence that as general revenues, these funds were already being used to pay for the costs of feeding, clothing, housing convicts, and we know they were specifically used to pay for 'sponsored immigrants', aboriginal 'protection', and now roads. The costs of the military establishment were charged against general revenues so in the quite large 'pot', nearly all Colonial expenditures were subsidised or offset by revenues from the Sale of Crown Land. Britain put its hand in the till only, it seems, to pay for the shipping and supplies costs of getting their prisoners to the Colony. After 1828, we know that convict production–both agricultural and mineral–went a long way to paying their expenses, so perhaps the British Treasury did in fact get off very lightly indeed, especially fort the benefits it derived.

The vexing question of Crown Lands revenues still remains. It is apparent from the 'Blue Book' notations that this revenue was 'reserved' for specific allocation by the Crown and remained in the Colony as an offset against British Government fiscal obligations (eg Civil List salaries)until self-government in 1855. A relevant quotation from the 1887 Financial Statements of the Colonial Treasurer of New South Wales, follows:

"Prior to the passing of the Constitution Act, the Territorial Revenues of the Colony belonged to the Crown, but upon that coming into operation in 1855, they were placed at the disposal of the local Parliament, and together with the taxes, imposts, rates and duties were formed into one fund, under the title of the Consolidated Revenue Fund. In lieu of the Crown Revenues thus given up to the Colony, an annual Civil List of 64,300 pound was made payable to Her Majesty out of the Consolidated Revenues of the Colony." What this means is that the British Treasury allowed the offset of all direct British payments made on account of the Colony against revenues raised by the sale, rent or lease of Crown lands.

Bigge in his first report to Lord Bathurst recommended that 'the number of convicts employed by the Government on public works should be reduced, both in the interests of economy and because it was argued that these men, especially if working in Sydney, were usually idle, and prone to misbehaviour in town. As far as possible, Bigge's recommended, convicts should be assigned to public service in the interior. He did, however, approve of sending convict offenders to penal settlements for further punishment, and he suggested that the settlements be expanded.

After the departure of Macquarie, administration of convicts became more efficient. The number of convict clerks in government service was gradually reduced, although the Marine and Survey Departments, the hospitals and domestic service for government officials became a reward for good conduct, although convicts were often placed in government service for breaches of discipline or failure to work effectively for private masters. In some areas, government service tended to be arduous.

The majority of convicts were 'assigned' to private employment and provided the bulk of the work force of the colony. Those 'assigned' were taken off commissary support and were entitled to be clothed and fed by their master in proscribed quantities of food and garb.

CHAPTER 5

FOREIGN INVESTMENT TO THE RESCUE

EXPLAINING THE COLONIAL ECONOMIC DRIVERS

1788-1856

In order to understand the growth of the colonial economy, we must understand the economic drivers that underpinned, sustained and supported the colonial economy. There are at least six, if not seven, such economic drivers. They include the factors of (a) population growth, the (b) economic development within the colony, the (c) funding sources such as British Treasury appropriations and the (d) revenues raised from within the local economy (for example, taxes and duties on imports) and (e) foreign investment (both public and private). The traditional concept of growth within the colonial economy comes from (f) the rise of the pastoral industry. A seventh driver would be the all-important Land Board, which played such an important role within the colonial economy The Land Board played an important role in co-ordinating crown land policy, controlling land sales, squatting licenses and speculators, re-setting boundaries of location, establishing set aside lands for future townships and for church and school estates, carrying out the survey of millions of acres of land transferred by grant and sale, and offering terms sales for crown lands and being responsible for the collection of repayments, rents, license fees, quit-rents and depasturing fees. In addition the land board was vested with road reserves for hundreds of miles of unmade roads but important rights-of-way that would well into the future protect access to remote pastoral and farming properties. The main thrust of published material about the Land Board is in conjunction with crown land sales policy, but the Board had a much larger role and the overall Board policies sand performances are what are to be reviewed here.

Although an important factor it is no more important that our other five motivators of the colonial economy between 1802 and 1856. Why have I selected these two specific dates? 1802 was when Governor King first imposed an illegal, but justified and well-intentioned impost on the local free community to build a local gaol to replace one burnt to the ground through a lightening strike but which the British would not replace. The local residents thought a more solid and durable prison was a worthwhile community investment. At the other end, the year of 1856 signalled the first real representative and responsible government in the colony, and although it was not the end of the colonial era, it was certainly the end of Britain 's financial support of sand for the colony and as such the colony was expected to stand on its own two feet.

These six factors will be discussed as mechanisms for 'growing the colonial economy between 1802 and 1856'

One consideration that must not be forgotten is the externally enforced pace of colonial expansion, particularly through the organised rather than the market-induced inflow of both convicts and assisted migrants. What this means is that instead of market forces requiring additional labour and human resources, extra labour and resources were imposed on the colony and there was an obligatory process of putting these people to work, in many cases by creating a public works program and pushing development ahead at an artificial pace rather than at a time and rate suited to the local economy. In much the same way, the 'assignment' system in the 1810-1830 period forced landowners to create clearing and development programs in order to utilise the labour available rather than only develop land as demand required.

1. Population growth including immigration of convicts & free settlers

The reason the colonial society did not change very much in the 1820s is that relatively few immigrants arrived. During 1823, Lord Bathurst, Colonial Secretary, sent instructions to Governor Brisbane (Macquarie's successor) altering the administration of the colony of NSW in most of the ways Commissioner Bigge had recommended in his reports.[78] One result of the Bigge Reports was that Macquarie was officially recalled to Britain even though he had canvassed his retirement before Bigge's arrival in 1819. Macquarie was distressed by the Bigge Reports and took very personally the recommendations made for change. Although there were many implied criticisms Macquarie considered that the public perception was that he had not acted properly in his role as Governor. Macquarie set to and compared the circumstances of the colony at the time of his arrival in 1810, with the great achievements he had made through 1821. In hindsight, Macquarie had accomplished much, mostly by means of arrogantly pursuing a series of policies without the pre-approval of the Secretary or the Government in London.

The arrival of only a few immigrants was because Bigge and the Colonial Office believed that only men of capital would emigrate. Labourers and the poor of England should not be encouraged and, as these people rarely had money to pay for the long passage to Sydney, few of them arrived.[79] Although the numbers were small, few of them came unassisted. In 1821 320 free immigrants arrived and this increased each year; 903 in 1826; 1005 in 1829, but slipping to 772 in 1830. Mostly they were family groups with some financial security.

---

78 Commissioner J.T. Bigge had been sent by Bathurst to Enquire into the State and Operations of the colony of NSW in 1819; the House of Commons had demanded an inquiry into the colony and had threatened to hold one of its own; Bathurst pre-empted a difficult government situation by appointing Bigge with a very broad and wide-ranging terms of Enquiry. Bigge held two years of investigations in the colony and reported to the Commons in 1823 with the printing of three Reports.

79 Australian History–The occupation of a Continent *Bessant* (Ed)

In 1828, the first census (as opposed to musters) of white persons in NSW was taken. 20,930 persons were classified as free and 15,668 were classified as convicts. However, of the free persons, many had arrived as convicts or were born of convicts. In fact, 70% of the population in 1828 had convict associations. However, by 1828, one quarter of the NSW population was native born; 3,500 were over 12 years of age

There was another side to this migration of unregulated souls. Shaw writes" The cost of assistance, the unsuitability of many emigrants, their ill-health, and the numbers of children and paupers that were sent–all these gave the colonists a source of grievance".[80] A large part of the problem was that the English wanted emigration–but those they wished to see emigrate were not welcomed in the colony. A growing opinion in the colony was that free migrants could not work with convicts; the convicts by themselves were too few and with growing expense; therefore transportation must stop and immigration be encouraged. However, immigrants of a good quality were not those the English wanted to send; its preference was for the paupers and the disruptive in the society. To stop transportation would be "attended with the most serious consequences unless there be previous means taken too ensure the introduction of a full supply of free labour". [81] In the next five years, the number of free immigrants increased so much that transportation could be stopped with little political backlash. Between 1835 and 1840, the colony was quite prosperous (it was a case of boom and bust–the great depression came in 1841); sales of crown land were large, and consequently the funds available for assisting immigrants were plentiful.[82]

80 Shaw, A.G.L. *The economic development of Australia* p.44

81 HRA Bourke to Colonial Secretary *Governor's despatches* 1835

82 The British Treasury had agreed to put 50% of land sale proceeds into assisting immigrants with shipping costs; a further 15% into assisting Aborigines' and the balance was for discretionary use by the crown. These percentages changed in 1840 when all sale proceeds were spent on immigration but the land fund still ran out of funds in 1842 and no further assistance was made to immigrants other than by the colonial government borrowing funds in the London market through its own credit.

In 1838, land revenue was over £150,000 and assisted migrants numbered 7,400; in 1839, land revenue was £200,000 and assisted migrants 10,000; in 1840 revenue was over £500,000 and assisted migrants 22,500.

Between 1832 and 1842, over 50,000 assisted and 15,000 unassisted migrants arrived in NSW; or they might have arrived as convicts, and over 3,000 arrived that way each year. Thus between 1830 and 1840 the population of the whole of Australia increased from 70,000 to 190,000, with 130,000 of those in 1840 being in NSW. Of these 87000 were men and 43000 were women; 30,000 had been born in the colony; 50,000 were free settlers, 20,000 were emancipists and 30,000 were convicts.[83]

2. Foreign Private Investment

We need to make the distinction between foreign public investment, and foreign private investment. The British Treasury appropriated specific funds for infrastructure programs in the colony, such as public buildings, churches, gaols, roads etc.

One reason that local colonial taxes and duties were imposed on the colony was to give the governor the funding source for discretionary expenditures in order to improve his administration. There were many instances of expenditures which could not be covered by the British funds, such as a bounty to recapture runaway convicts, building fences around the cemeteries and whitewashing the walls of public buildings (for instance barracks) in the settlement. The British Treasury would have considered such items of expense as being unnecessary. Road repair and maintenance was intended to be covered from toll receipts but they were never sufficient to make necessary repairs. Governors Hunter and Bligh did little to improve public and community buildings, roads and bridges and by the time Macquarie arrived in the colony in 1810, there was a major backlog of building work and maintenance to be undertaken. Macquarie expanded the local revenue tax base in order to give himself more flexibility in pursuing improved conditions for the settlers and the population at large.

83 Shaw *ibid*

Although Macquarie did not specifically seek new free immigrants for the colony, word of mouth circulated that the colony was in a growth stage and worthy of being considered for either immigration or investment. Usually one accompanied the other. The first private investment came with the immigrants. Free settlers would either cash up in England or transfer their possessions to the colony, and this small level of private investment was the start of a major item of capital transfers to the colony.

However, private capital formation took many forms; the early settlers, bought or built houses, they built or bought furnishings, they had carriages and often employed water conservation.

As the system of land grants was expanded and farming was encouraged the spread of settlement required a combination of public and private investment.

The government had to provide roads and townships, and the settlers had to provide pastoral investment. This pastoral capital formation consisted of five main types of assets:

Buildings–residence, outbuildings, wool shed or grain storage
Fences–stockyards, posts and rails
Water conservation–dams, tanks, wells
Plant–cultivators, tools
Stocks–food, clothing, household items, materials for animal care and general repairs–livestock

Stephen Roberts offers an interesting insight into the colony of 1835.[84]

"It did not need much prescience to foresee the whole of the country united by settlement–so much had it outgrown the coastal stage of Sydney town. It was a new Australia–a land of free settlement and progressive occupation–that was there, and the old convict days were ending.

Both human and monetary capital were pouring into the various colonies and transforming the nature of their population and problems. Convicts

---

84 Roberts, S.H *The Squatting Age in Australia 1835-1847 (published 1935)*

no longer set the tone; even autocratic governors belonged to a day that was passing, and instead, the country was in the grip of a strangely buoyant, and equally optimistic, race of free men".

As part of our private capital formation, we must remember the growth of human capital and the needs for specific labour. Capital requires labour with a specific role. The establishment and expansion of farming meant more than shepherding and ploughing. There was a considerable demand for building skills, for construction and maintenance of equipment such as drays and carts, harness making and repair, tool-making etc. It became important, in order to support and sustain capital growth and economic development to be able to employ labour with multi-skills. This was a new phenomenon for the colony, especially since Britain did not develop these types of broad skills and self-motivation in its criminal class. The Rev. J.D. Lang sought a temporary answer by specifically recruiting 'mechanics' in Scotland as immigrant for the colony.

3. British Public Funding transfers

Public Capital formation is obviously different to private capital formation. I have given an example of rural-based private capital formation elsewhere in this study and will do so again here, in order to demonstrate both types of capital investment.

Private capital formation took many forms; the early settlers, bought or built houses, they built or bought furnishings, they had carriages and often employed water conservation techniques, which included tanks or earthen dams.

As the system of land grants was expanded and farming was encouraged the spread of settlement required a combination of public and private investment.

The government had to provide roads and townships, and the settlers had to provide pastoral investment. This pastoral (rural-based) capital formation usually consisted of five main types of assets:

Buildings–residence, outbuildings, wool shed or grain storage
Fences–stockyards, posts and rails
Water conservation–dams, tanks, wells
Plant–cultivators, tools
Stocks–food, clothing, household items, materials for animal care and general repairs–livestock

Public capital on the other hand was a socio-economic based government asset, and included:

Roads, bridges, crossings, drainage, excavation and embanking, retaining walls

Hospital, storehouses, military barracks, convict barracks, Court-house, police posts, government office buildings

Market house, burial ground, Church, tollhouse, military magazines.

Obviously the list can go on and on.

MAJOR PUBLIC WORKS IN NSW 1817-1821

Roads
Sydney to Botany Bay
Sydney to South Head
Parramatta to Richmond
Liverpool to Bringelly, the Nepean and Appin
Buildings
Sydney
A military hospital; military barracks; convict barracks; carters barracks; Hyde Park
Toll-house; residences for the Supreme Court Judge, the Chaplain and the
Superintendent of Police; an asylum; a fort and powder magazines; stables for
Government House; a market house; a market wharf; a burial ground; St. James
Church
Parramatta
All Saint's church spire; a hospital; a parsonage; military and convict barracks; a
Factory; stables and coach-house at Government House; a reservoir
Windsor

St. Matthew's Church; military barracks; convict barracks
Liverpool
St. Luke's church; a gaol; a wharf; convict barracks

4. Economic Development

K. Dallas in an article on *Transportation and Colonial Income* writes, "The history of economic development in Australia is concerned with the transplanting of British economic life into a unique and novel environment. All colonial societies resemble each other in the problems of transplanting, but only in Australia was there no indigenous communal life vigorous enough to influence the course of future development"[85]

Dallas in the same article declares, "The economic effects of the transportation system are usually misunderstood. The real development of Australia begins with the pastoral industry and the export of wool in the 1820s. Until then, penal settlements were a base fore whalers, and made the pastoral possibilities known to English capitalist sheep farmers earlier than they would otherwise have known."[86]

Since this is such a major point on which much disagreement exists, an analysis of its merits is required. No less an authority than N.G. Butlin, J.Ginswick and Pamela Statham disagree, and they record in their introduction to 'The economy before 1850 "the history books are preoccupied with the pastoral expansion in NSW. It is reasonably certain from the musters that a great many complex activities developed and Sydney soon became not merely a port town but a community providing many craft products and services to the expanding settlement".[87]

The next section of this study outlines the remarkable contribution of Governor Macquarie between 1810 and 1821, most of the physical development taking place before the arrival of Commissioner J.T. Bigge in 1819. The table of infrastructure and public building development below

---

85 Dallas, Keith *Transportation & Colonial Income* Historical Studies ANZ Vol 3 October 1944-February 1949

86 Dallas *ibid*

87 The Australians: Statistics Chapter 7 'The economy before 1850'

confirms that the greatest period of economic development in the colonial economy took place under the Macquarie Administration and did not wait until the spread of settlement and the rise in the pastoral industry (which brought with it so many economic problems) in the late 1820s and 1830s.

IMPACT OF THE COLONIAL ISOLATION DURING THE 1800S

The question of isolation was of positive benefit to the British authorities because the concept of creating a '*dumping ground for human garbage*' was synonymous with finding a '*penal wasteland that was out of sight and out of mind*'.

However the disadvantages to the Colonial authorities were numerous

There was the tyranny of distance–the huge risks, of frightening transportation by sailing ship to a land hitherto unknown, uncharted and unexplored, promising huge risks and great loss of life.

Food preservation during the voyage and in the Colony was a challenge with no refrigeration or ice. The only preservatives being salt and pickling.

Communications between Sydney and London made exchange of correspondence, obtaining decisions and permission tiresomely long. It often occurred that the Colonial Governor wrote to a Colonial Secretary, who during the twelve months of round trip, had been replaced with another person.

Laws and justice, in the Colony, were to be based on British law, but in reality, local laws became a mix of common sense and personal philosophies eg Lt Governor Collins, as Advocate-General in the Colony desperately needed law books to practice, but they were never sent. Bligh, as Governor, ruled virtually as a despot and tyrannical dictator, knowing that a sea trip of seven months was between him and any admonishment or complaints being heard.

Factors Affecting British Investment in the Colony

A number of factors affected the level of capital investment into the colony–many were ill informed and relied on delayed newspaper reports on activity in the various settlements. a. The offer of assisted migration b. The failing economic conditions in Britain c. Economic expansion for the pastoral industry due to successful exploration in the colony d. The settlement at Port Phillip and the eventual separation of Victoria from New South Wales would promote great investment opportunities e. The rise of the squattocracy f. The crash of 1827-28 in the colony shakes British Investors g. The Bigge's' Report of 1823 breathed new life into capital formation especially with Macarthur sponsoring the float of the Australian Agricultural Company h. Further along, the good credit rating of the colonies (and there being no defaults on loans) encouraged larger investments and loans into the colonies

I. Shortage of Labour in the colony and the offer of land grants to new settlers became a useful carrot to attract small settlers bringing their own capital by way of cash or goods or livestock with them. j. Two other steps had important consequences, one in the colony and the other in Britain. In 1827 Governor Darling began to issue grazing licenses to pastoralists, and the terms were set at 2/6d per hundred acres, with liability to quit on one month's notice. From this movement grew, writes Mad wick in Immigration into Eastern Australia, the squatting movement and the great pastoral expansion, and the idea of the earlier Governors that the colony of New South Wales should be a colony of farmers was thus abandoned. The concurrent event was the floating of the Australian Agricultural Company in London. Development by the AAC and by the free settlers brought increasing prosperity. Exports tripled between 1826 and 1831. k. There is a connection between availability of factors of production and the level of investment. In the early days of the colony, labour was present–bad labour, convict labour, but still labour. The governors had demanded settlers with capital to employ that labour and develop the land. They proposed to limit land grants in proportion to the means of the settler. Governor Darling declared (HRA ser 1, vol 8) that 'when I am satisfied of the character, respectability and means of the applicant settler in a rural area, he will receive the necessary authority to select a grant of land, proportionate in extent to the means he possesses.

Under Macquarie the colony had boomed with new buildings, new settlements, new investment and lots of convicts. Under Brisbane the needs for economic consolidation and new infrastructure would be addressed, together with an appeal for free settlers.

Some significant events took place during the Brisbane guardianship

The British were intent on accessing every available trading opportunity with the colony, and formed in Scotland *The Australia Company*

A road was built to connect the Windsor settlement to the new settlement at Maitland. This decision opened up the Hunter River district to new farming opportunities

The responsibility for convicts was transferred from the Superintendent of Convicts to the Colonial Secretary, although this move was to be reversed within the next decade

The first documented discovery of gold was made. It was hushed in the colony lest convicts run off to find their fortunes

In Bigge's third and final report, he recommended extra colonial import duties and less British duty on imported timber and tanning bark

The most significant event of all was the confidence placed in Bigge's favourable opinion of the potential of the colonial economy by the London Investment community and the resulting subscription of one million pound for the Australian Agricultural Company. The subscription was accompanied by a grant of one million acres of land around Port Stephens and the allocation of 5,000 convicts, but also brought inflation to livestock prices and availability throughout the colony.

J.F. Campbell wrote about the first decade of the Australian Agricultural Company 1824-1834 in the proceedings of the 1923 RAHS.

"Soon after Commissioner Bigge's report of 1823 became available for public information, several enterprising men concerted with a view to acquire sheep-runs in the interior of this colony, for the production of fine wool.

The success which attended the efforts of John Macarthur and a few other New South Wales pastoralists, in the breeding and rearing of fine woolled sheep and stock generally, as verified by Bigge, gave the incentive and led to the inauguration of proceedings which resulted in the formation of the Australian Agricultural Company.

The first formal meeting of the promoters took place at Lincoln's Inn, London, (at the offices of John Macarthur, junior).

Earl Bathurst, advised Governor Brisbane in 1824 that . . . .

His Majesty has been pleased to approve the formation of the Company, from the impression that it affords every reasonable prospect of securing to that part of His Majesty's dominions the essential advantage of the immediate introduction of large capital, and of agricultural skill, as well as the ultimate benefit of the increase of fine wool as a valuable commodity for export.

The chief proposals of the company are:

The company was to be incorporated by Act of Parliament or Letters Patent.

The capital of the company was to be 1 million pound sterling divided into 10,000 shares of 100 pound each

A grant of land of one million acres to be made to the company

That no rival joint stock company to be established in the colony for the next twenty years

That agents of the company would select the situation or the land grants.

The shepherds and labourers would consist of 1,400 convicts, thereby lessening the maintenance of such convicts by an estimated 30,800 pound or 22 pound/per head/ per annum.

The Royal Charter of 1824 forming the company provided for payment of quit-rents over a period of twenty years, or the redemption of the same by paying the capital sum of 20 times the amount of the rent so to be redeemed. These quit-rents were to be waived if the full number of convicts were maintained for a period of five years. No land was to be sold during the five-year period from the date of the grant".

Being important that the investment be seen to have the support of strong leaders in Britain, and democratic governance, the company operated with· One Governor;· 25 directors; and 365 stockholders (proprietors). The old English structure was retained, that of, Governor and his Court, with the directors being the members of the Court whilst the Governor was the Chairman of the Board or Court

Leading stockholders included

- Robert Campbell
- Chief Justice Forbes
- Son of Governor King
- Rev'd Samuel Marsden
- John Macarthur

Each Macarthur son, John jr, Hannibal, James, Charles, Scott & William John Oxley The Colonial-Surveyor (Oxley)had recommended the area of Port Stephens as an eligible spot for the land grant. The local directors inspected and approved the site but John Macarthur was extremely critical of the selection, the management plan and the extravagance of the first buildings.

This venture was the first major investment into the colony and set the scene for later developments. In 1825 the Van Diemen's Land Company was chartered by the British Parliament and granted land on the northwest corner of the territory.

Both the A.A. Coy and the VDL Coy still operate today after nearly 180 years of continuous operation, a record beaten only by the operation of the Hudson Bay Company in Canada.

Sir Timothy Coghlan was the colonial statistician whilst he was involved in preparing the series 'The Wealth and Progress of New South Wales 1900-01'. He was later appointed as Agent-General in London before compiling the 4-volume set of 'Labour and Industry in Australia'.

Circumstances in Britain contributed greatly to the climate of 'greener pastures' over the seas.

Conditions were never more favourable for emigration than they were during the 1830s. The decade had opened with rioting in the agricultural districts in the south of England. This was followed by the upheavals of the Reform Bill of 1832, the Factory Act of 1833 and the Corn Laws, which kept wages low and unemployment high. The Poor Law of 1834 withdrew assistance from the poor and re-introduced the workhouse. The Irish rebellion was creating both upheaval and poverty

These conditions were met by the enthusiastic reports coming from Australia of the progress being made in agriculture, commerce and the pastoral industry. The assistance granted to emigrants as a result of Edward Gibbon Wakefield's reforms made possible the emigration of people who had previously been prevented by the expense. It is almost certain that free passage would not have been a sufficient enticement if conditions in Britain had not been unfavourable. It is significant that years of small migration coincided with good conditions in England accompanied by unfavourable reports from the colony.

4. Creating Opportunities in the Colony

Availability of land and labour to yield profit on invested capital is the constant decisive condition and test of material prosperity in any community, and becomes the keystone of an economy as well as defining its national identity.

British Government policy for the Australian colonies was formulated and modified from time to time. Policies for the export of British capital and the supply of labour (both convict and free) were adjusted according to British industrial and demographic and other social situations, as well as the capability and capacity of the various colonial settlements top contribute to solving British problems.

By the 1820s there was official encouragement of British Investment in Australia by adopting policies for large land grants to persons of capital and for the sale of land and assignment of convict labour to those investors. Then followed the reversal of the policy of setting up ex-convicts on small 30 acre plots as small proprietors. The hardship demanded by this policy usually meant these convicts and families remained on the commissary list for support (food and clothing) at a continuing cost to the government. It was much cheaper to assign these convicts to men of property and capital who would support them fully–clothe, house and feed them.

We can ask, what led directly to the crash of 1827? a. Firstly, the float of the Australian Agricultural Company raised a large amount of capital, mostly from the City of London investment community, and this contributed to speculation and 'sheep and cattle mania instantly seized on all ranks and classes of the inhabitants' (written by Rev'd John Dunmore Lang) 'and brought many families to poverty and ruin'. b. When capital imports cease, the wherewithal to speculate vanished; speculation perforce stopped; inflated prices fell to a more normal level, and wrote E.O. Shann in Economic History of Australia 'because those formerly too optimistic were now too despairing, and people had to sell goods at any price in order to get money; men who had bought at high prices were ruined, and perforce their creditors fell with them'. c. In 1842, it was the same. The influx of capital from oversees, pastoral extension, and large-scale immigration, caused much speculation. The banks, competing for business, advanced too much credit. Loans were made on the security of land and livestock, which later became almost worthless; too much discounting was done for merchants (Gipps, HRA Vol 23) In the huge central district on the western slopes, along the Murrumbidgee and the Riverina, the squatters triumphed, as was inevitable. He had the financial resources to buy his run–especially after the long period of drought. Four million acres of crown land was sold for nearly 2.5 million pound. The confidence of British investors was waning. A crisis in the Argentine and the near failure of the large clearinghouse of Baring's made them cautious. Stories of rural and industrial strife in the colony were not inducements to invest: and wood and metal prices were still falling Loan applications being raised in London were under-subscribed, at the same time, the banks were increasingly reluctant to lend money for land development, which was so often unsound.

5. Assisted Migration

The dual policy of selling land to people with sufficient capital to cultivate it, and keeping a careful check on the number of free grants was adopted after 1825. 'Yet the Colonial Office', says Madgwick, 'failed to administer land policy with any certainty (R.B. Madgwick 'Immigration into Eastern Australia'). There was no uniform policy adopted to encourage economic development in a systematic and rational way. The Wakefield system found new supporters. The principle had been established that the sale of land was preferred to the old system of grants. The dual system of sales and grants had failed to encourage local (colonial) purchases. They were willing to accept grants or even 'squat' rather than purchase land. Sales to absentee landlords and investors stepped up, and as can be seen from the following table, provided extensive revenue to the British Government to promote free and sponsored migration.

6. Successful exploration promotes new interest in the Colony

A period of rapid expansion followed the change in economic policy. Wool exports by 1831 were 15 times as great as they had been only 10 years earlier (in 1821). The increase in the number of sheep led to a rapid opening of new territories for grazing. It was the search for new land with economic value that underpinned most of the explorations. Settlers and sheep-men quickly followed exploration, and growth fanned out in all directions from Sydney town.

However, exploration was not the only catalyst for growth. a. The growing determination to exclude other powers from the continent stimulated official interest in long-distance exploration by sea and by land and in the opening of new settlements. For instance, J.M. Ward in his work 'The Triumph of the Pastoral Economy 1821-1851' writes that Melville and Bathurst Islands, were annexed and settled between 1824 and 1827, whilst Westernport and Albany were settled in order to clinch British claims to the whole of Australia b. When Governor Brisbane opened the settlement at Moreton Bay in 1824, it was to establish a place for punishment of unruly convicts and a step towards further economic development, and of extending the settlements for the sake of attracting new investment

7. Colonial Failures fuel loss of Confidence

The collapse of British Investment can be traced to one or two causes, or indeed both.

I. The British crisis of 1839 reflected the availability of capital for expansion by the Australian banks of that day–The Bank of Australasia and the Union Bank. These banks, three mortgage companies and the Royal Bank went into a slump due to shortage of available funds and deferred the raising of new funds until after the crisis. Stringency in the English Capital market had a serious impact on the capital raising opportunities in the colonies.

II. The second possibility is that the sharp decline was initiated by bad news of returns in the colonies, and that its role accentuated a slump with the dire consequences experienced in 1842-43. Recovery was delayed and made more difficult as there was 'no surplus labour in the colony'

It would be dangerous to imply or decide that every slump in Australia could be explained as being caused by economic evens. British investment was independent then, as it is now, and so the more valid explanation of the downturn in British investment in this period is that negative reports from the colonies disappointed and discouraged investors with capital to place.

Most facts about public finance in New South Wales lead to the conclusion that it was disappointed expectations that caused the turn down in the transfer of funds. At this same time Governor Gipps (Sir George Gipps) was being pushed by bankers and merchants to withdraw government deposits from the banks and thus this action caused a contraction in lending by the banks which in turn caused a slow down of colonial economic activity. The attached statistics of land sales, registered mortgages and liens on wool and livestock reflects the strong downturn in the agricultural economy, which naturally flowed on to the economy as a whole.

CHAPTER 6

THE NEED FOR MANUFACTURING

Hainsworth in his Chapter Twelve 'Dawn of Industry' from *The Sydney Traders*[88] guides us in a review of the growth of manufactures before 1825.

'Thanks to the initiative of Sydney traders, manufacturing and processing industries emerged very early and helped to transform NSW from penal settlement to colony'.

The traders supplemented government activity, often by carrying out similar activities, and sometimes launched various types of manufacturing in which the government was not concerned. It was natural that the government should play a dominant role at this early stage, for it had the responsibility of clothing, housing, feeding and working the convicts, both male and female. The government role was as the chief employer of the convicts, the chief provider of capital and of course, the chief consumer of their output. In a limited way, the government was prepared to foster industrial enterprise, though this encouragement was haphazard, capricious and oftentimes playing favourites. The government, itself, launched brewing, salt-making, milling and basic textiles, and operated a number of crude industrial processes before allowing them to be taken

---

[88] Hainsworth, D.R. The Sydney Traders

over by enterprising colonists on favourable terms. Privatisation was not a deliberate policy, one more so of convenience.

Sealing[89] by 1800 was dominating the trading calendar. The official return for that year showed over 118,000 skins had passed through Sydney with Simeon Lord and his fellow ex-convicts, Kable and Underwood handling over 72,000 from just one source–Antipodes Island. By 1815, the *Sydney Gazette* was reporting the sealing industry was in decline. The intense harvesting of the seals had lowered their natural numbers, but the British Government was influenced by the 'whale lobby' to raise discriminatory duties against colonial oil, seal and whale. Spermaceti oil was to bear a duty of 15s 9d per ton for British ships but £24 18s 9d if obtained by colonial ships. Duties of £8 8s a ton were imposed on Black Whale oil from the Derwent estuary. Thus through these discriminatory tariffs, colonial oil was virtually barred from London.

Cottage industries were not only the preserve of the small home-based manufacturers. Coghlan[90] points out 'those who had the enterprise and industry to devote land to gardening were amply repaid'. The broad acre crops raised were chiefly wheat and maize, with a little oats and barley, some potatoes and other vegetables.

Excellent opportunities, for fresh fruit and vegetables, were provided by the weather, the climate and the generally good soil around Sydney, but gardening was not undertaken other than by the few conscious of home grown vegetables. They were able, says Coghlan, 'to grow almost all ordinary English vegetables, all the English fruits and some fruits, such as grapes, grew in abundance. Macquarie described his garden at Parramatta as 'full of vines and fruit trees and abounding in the most excellent vegetables'

Stock-raising was given impetus when, in 1805, the two Blaxland brothers arrived in the colony, bringing a considerable amount of capital and more than a little acquaintance with husbandry of cattle. In 1810, horned cattle numbers stood at 12,442. Ten years later, when Macquarie left, the herds

---

89 Based on Hainsworth 'The Sydney Traders Ch12 'The Dawn of Industry'

90 Coghlan, T.A. 'Labour & Industry in Australia' (Page 117–Vol I)

numbered 102,939, so that the annual increase was at the rate of 20.5%. The numbers were carefully guarded and there was no undue slaughtering, and salt beef was still being imported in 1814. Even so, the records show that beef was cheap with a herd selling at £8 per head. Horses, says Coghlan, 'throve[91] in the settlement from the beginning although their numbers increased very slowly. In 1800 there were only 203 horses, but by 1810 the numbers had grown to 1134 and by 1821, the numbers totalled 4564.

Coghlan recognises the importance of the timber industry and writes "the export of timber became fairly considerable and in 1803, Governor King spoke of it as the only staple of the colony"–the inland forests could not be exploited because of the lack of any means of transport, and as a result 'numerous saw-pits were established on the inlets of Port Jackson, along the banks of the Hawkesbury, and later at Newcastle on the Hunter, where convicts were engaged cutting timber as well as in mining coal"

Occasionally cargoes were shipped to India, and in 1809 timber to the value of £1500 was sent to that country in part payment for a return shipment of rice. "The presence of so much valuable timber would in ordinary circumstances have led to the establishment of shipbuilding yards. Vessels were built for sealing purposes as early as 1791, but the presence of craft capable of going to sea was considered a menace to the safe-keeping of the convicts and the governor directed no boats were to be built of greater length than 14 feet". Hunter removed this restriction in 1798, and in fact encouraged the shipbuilding industry by permitting a vessel of 'thirty tons to be built to procure seal skins and oil in Bass Straits'.[92] Campbell then built a vessel of 130 tons launched in 1805[93].

There was considerable activity mostly through the *Dockyard* (attached to the Commissary) in boat-repairs, refurbishing and provisioning, but the stoppage of the fishery in 1810 was a serious blow to the industry.

---

91 This is an editor's change–the Coghlan text states 'shrove'

92 Coghlan, Labour & Industry Vol 1 Page 121-2

93 Steven, Margaret 'Merchant Campbell 1769-1846'

Immigration to the colony was mostly by way of assigned servants between 1821 and 1826, but the difficulty experienced in collecting the payments for the servants made the whole notion difficult. Coghlan tells "in the matter of indentured service many employers, principally those in the country districts were willing to advance £8-10 towards the cost of each immigrant labourer obtained by them and in February 1832 Governor Bourke despatched a list of 803 labourers who might be sent out on these terms. It was on immigration at the cost of land revenue that the colonial authorities placed their confidence. They offered to set aside £10,000 from the land fund for emigration purposes; of this sum they desired that about two-thirds be devoted to promoting the emigration of unmarried women, as the proportion of men in the colony was excessive and that one-third should be used in loans for the emigration of mechanics".

After 1836, it was decided that the whole of the rapidly increasing land revenue of NSW should be devoted to immigration[94] and in 1837 over 3090 immigrants were brought to the colony of whom 2688 were sponsored through the Emigration Commissioners in London and 405 were under the bounty scheme by colonial employers.

The need for manufacturing in the colony was created by local demand for tools, materials and supplies, in large demand for meeting general construction and housing needs. Manufacturing in the colony was catered by the private sector and the government sector. The private sector was sponsored by a handful of entrepreneurs or skilled settlers, who wanted to satisfy local demand for their product by creating a 'cottage industry', due to generally limited demand and a constantly changing market. The public/government sector became involved through the commissariat operations in order to put convicts to productive work, reverse the long lead time for purchasing urgent materials from Britain, and more fully utilise the 'free' local resources such as timber and convict labour. Barnard observes[95] 'The colony was never wholly penal, like France neither's Devil Island, nor was it intended to be. It was, in due course, to be balanced by freed men, their children, and such other settlers, soldiers, seamen and the like who cared to take the reward for their services in land, of which

---

94 Coghlan 'Labour & Industry in Australia–Vol I Page 178

95 Barnard, Marjorie *A History of Australia* 1962 (Page 304)

the Crown had a superfluity. Actually, NSW suffered very little from being a penal settlement and was fortunate in that her first unpromising colonizing material was early swamped by infusions of new blood, that wool, land grants and then gold attracted free colonists. There were no foreign elements to arouse Imperial suspicion, no subject race to put what might have been considered a necessary brake on progress'. This statement by Barnard is a rewriting of history, but would be an ideal policy, if it were true. The settlement was designed to be a penal one, and every move made was designed to be about the convicts–their work, protecting them from themselves, feeding, clothing and maintaining them, providing them with tools, equipment and supplies. Laissez-faire might have been in vogue in London during the Phillip Administration but the settlement struggled whilst awaiting food and other supplies, and convicts were held tightly accountable for all their activities. Until 1823, the entire responsibility for the settlement rested on the Governor. Upon him was bestowed a power to control lawlessness, which he effectively exercised.

The diversity of manufacturing within the colony by 1821, at the end of the Macquarie Administration was far more impressive than could reasonably be expected from a former penal colony transforming itself into a free market economy. Macquarie's enthusiasm for free enterprise and 'cost saving' led to great production sponsored by the commissariat. Convict labour was considered to be without 'cost' and therefore without 'value', as was local raw materials, so much of the output of the commissariat business enterprises left without recognition of value, which well-suited Macquarie's purposes. Ass early as 1812, he had been sternly warned by Colonial Secretary Liverpool [96] that 'the burden of the colony of NSW upon the Mother Country has been so much increased since the period of your assumption of the government of it, that it becomes necessary that you should transmit a more satisfactory explanation of the grounds upon which the unusual expenditure has been sanctioned by you'. Liverpool admitted he had misgivings of this attack when he continued his letter to Macquarie in terms of 'I can't point out what expenses have been unnecessarily incurred, and the only ground I have for forming a judgement is by comparison of the total amount of bills by your predecessors and yourself'. Naturally enough, absolute total were progressively higher, but

[96] HRA 1:7:476 Liverpool to Macquarie 4th May,1812

in terms of bills drawn per head of convict on the store' the comparisons declined. Macquarie was actively creating an investment for the future, and at some future point the colony could easily be self-supporting and outside the need for treasury appropriations. However, in philosophical terms, why should the local revenues be used to support any form of a penal colony for Britain. Surely the free settlers could grow in conjunction with the transfer of convicts to the colony; whilst Britain supported the convicts and the colony supported its own operations. One of Macquarie's goals in having the government business enterprises so active in the colony was to quickly achieve this self-sufficiency and be out from the clutches of Whitehall. Macquarie's thinking was only half right. He was so preoccupied with the economic and fiscal arrangements in the colony that he lost sight of the overall plan. Local revenues were first raised in 1802 and were designed for 'discretionary' expenditure by the governor of the day. The reason for this loose arrangement was that the Treasury appropriated funds for specific purposes such as convict maintenance, and civil establishment salaries, but did not see the need for maintenance works, repairs, infrastructure development and the like, so the money for these essentials had to come from local sources and be reserved for deployment by the government. Whitehall soon caught onto this stream of revenue and although the Treasury officials new it was illegal revenue, they restricted its use by withholding British funds to the amount of revenue raised within the colony. Thus in Macquarie's administration, private enterprise figured as a means of both import replacement and cost saving for the colony. Manufacturing filled the joint roles of availability of key/essential merchandise and of putting convicts to productive work.

Barnard records[97] that even the 'boys–some as young as eleven–were kept in Sydney at Carter's Barracks near Brickfield Hill and were working as a carpenter, shoemaker, stone-cutter, blacksmith, and other trades to which the boys were apprenticed. The product of their labour went into the public store, and a pool of much needed mechanics was created'. This observation is rather unique, is unsourced and does not have the ring of accuracy about it. Barnard is implying that these trades were carried out at the Barracks, which means that materials and tools were brought daily to the barracks. With carts and bodies for hauling purposes being

---

[97] Barnard, M *A History of Australia* Page 237

in very short supply, it seems unlikely that large lumps of stone or tree trunks would be hauled from Upper George Street (the Lumber Yard was at the corner of George and Bridge) all the way to Brickfields Hill for young boys to play with. The carter barracks were used for confinement and punishment, and there was little space for practicing wood craft or stone masonry. It is much more likely that the boys were released on a weekly basis, under supervision, and taken to the raw materials source–for instance the stone-yard and the Timber Yard, which were both on George Street North. This is a rare unsourced apparent contradiction by Barnard. She is probably incorrect when she states the apprentices' output went to the public store–it probably went to the Lumber Yard store–from where all building materials, supplies and tools were inventoried. The public store kept only dry goods, fresh foods or grain.

The extent of private sector manufacturing ranged from clothing, castings and carts to soap, silver-smithing, tanneries and tin-smithing. In addition government manufacturing covered an equally broad range–from nails to timber framing, bricks tiles and stone blocks, forged items and boot making.

The broad intent, because of the small local population, which by itself would not have supported such a sector, was two-fold–to replace imports and the timeframe of a year or two between ordering and receipt of goods, and to create an export market of sorts.

According to Jackson[98], the population in the colony during 1820 was only 34,000 and too small to create sufficient demand for private sector output and to establish economic development.

The early entrepreneurs and their activities raise numerous questions which to-date has not been studied in the literature. Hainsworth records[99] 'Simeon Lord cannot be described as a typical emancipist trader for his operations were too large and diverse, but he was a member of a numerous group. Another was Henry Kable, whose commercial beginnings are still more shadowy–an illiterate man transported in the first fleet, Kable was

---

98 R.V. Jackson *Australian Economic Development in the 19th Century*

99 H.R. Hainsworth *Sydney Traders* P.41

for several years a constable of Sydney and probably profitably plied with liquor the drunks he locked up'. What Hainsworth is by implication questioning, is how these two (of many) eventually became such successful traders? What was their source of start up monies? How did these emancipist traders get started? Hainsworth, later in his study concludes 'the capital they mobilised for shipbuilding and sealing in 1800 must have come from trading'[100] Other examples of early unexplained success include John Palmer and his associates, who as the third Commissary on 5/–per day, became the wealthiest man in the colony during the King Administration, and that was before his sister, Sophia, married the largest merchant in the colony, Robert Campbell. Palmer and his trading colleagues prospered in a colony whose commercial life was supposed to be monopolised by an officer clique.[101] Although the officer class is usually described by historians as having caste a large shadow in the early 1790s under Hunter, they could not stop an undertow of small dealers and emerging traders growing up around them. Rather the officers brought this about by allowing the retail trade to fall into the hands of 'ambitious and able (if uneducated) men with no gentility to lose'[102] In many cases because the wholesale market was officer controlled and these emancipist retailers wanted to continue to expand and grow, they moved into 'cottage' manufacturing–often working with the commissariat to supply finished goods or raw materials for further processing by the Lumber Yard or Female Factory (e.g. Tanned leather, scoured wool, and crushed grain). For many emerging entrepreneurs, this was the way they commenced their manufacturing activities–trader, marketer and then manufacturer. According to Hainsworth[103], Simeon Lord was typical of the early merchant traders. When a shortage of circulating notes occurred, Lord (amongst others) requested his creditor customers to liquidate their debts to him by any means possible. The result was that Lord accepted grain, (which he then put into the store on his own account), most of which he had bartered from his retail customers, payroll bills from military officers with whom he was dealing on a wholesale basis, individual 'notes or bills' payable, which were freely circulating and classed

[100] Hainsworth refers his readers, on this point, to his inserts in the ADB for Lord, Kable and Underwood Volumes 1 & 2

[101] ADB Volume 2–John Palmer (Hainsworth)

[102] Hainsworth *The Sydney Traders* Page 42

[103] Hainsworth *Sydney Traders* Page 83

as petty banking. Lord would consolidate these bills and exchange them for one large bill drawn by the Commissariat on the Treasury in London. This bill he would then release to his suppliers–usually visiting ship's captains, or transfer to his Indian or Macao (Hong Kong) suppliers. So obviously the greatest limitation to entrepreneurial activity in the colony was 'the medium of exchange: the lack of a mint and a Treasury, or even a private bank of issue. However with all its faults the system worked. It was the only system they had and the traders made the best use of it'.[104]

Thus private sector output was limited by government demand for food and materials.

The Jackson theory is that the sale of goods to the government store (commissariat) provided a major source of foreign exchange to the private sector because sale proceeds were made available in the form of Treasury Bills drawn on London.

Organisation of Government Business Enterprises

Under the guise of controlling the activities and rehabilitation of convicts, Macquarie decided that placing all convicts on assignment, thereby removing any financial obligation for their maintenance, a percentage could be put to work on behalf of the government. This would be accomplished in two ways. Firstly, direct convict labour, rather than the preferred contractor program, would be used for infrastructure development and the other public works program, specifically government building.

So there became a great concentration of convicts in Sydney, employed in two big workshops, the lumber-yard and the timber-yard. Both were located on George Street, together with the stone-yard (across from the lumber-yard) and the three-storey Commissary Store, wharf and Dockyard, fronting the western side of Sydney Cove. The convicts worked on a task, or piece system. In the Lumber Yard, surrounded by an 8 foot high brick wall, for security purposes, forges were used for making nail, hinges, wheel irons and other metal products. Other 'sections' were set

---

104 Abbott & Nairn (*Growth)* Chapters 8 & 9

aside around the outside walls of the factory, for boot-making, cabinet and furniture-making, coopers for barrel making, course wool and cotton for slops and hat making. In the centre of the large factory the two saw pits were manned by up to 25 men, who cut the timber taken from the kiln after its drying process. In the timber yards, beams and floor-boards were sawn and prepared from the timber drawn from the lumber-yard. The brick and tile yard was built around a huge kiln (22 feet long by 18 feet high producing 24,000 bricks at one raking. The Stone-yard not only produced large building blocks from stone but also flagstones, hearth-stones and mantelpieces. Within the lumber-yard, was stored all the tools required within the various business enterprises as well as on each work site. Each item was recorded going out and coming in. Equally carefully, all materials–both raw material and finished product–were recorded at the clerk's office located at the main gate. The Superintendent of Convicts, Major Ovens had set a piece work productivity rate. For instance, the shoemaker's gang of about eight me, were supposed to produce a pair of shoes each day, each man from leather tanned at the government factory at Cawdor; likewise, the brass-foundry and the tailors' gang each had their own production goals; the carpenter's gang which was usually of fifty men, was made up of cabinet-makers, turners and shinglers; the bricklayers' gang was generally between five and ten men who were expected to lay 4,500 bricks each week; the Sawyers gang was usually twenty-five men. Other gangs based in the lumber yard were also sent out to garden, cut grass, dig foundations, and carry grain. The lumber yard was responsible for over 2,000 men in all.

The government business enterprises were a comprehensive and massive undertaking, and Macquarie took pride in their output and accomplishments.

Manufacturing is only part of the story included in any study of economic development of the period. Economic development drove public finance in the same way that population growth, pastoral growth and growth of decentralisation and land utilisation impacted on the source and use of public funds. Other factors to be considered include:

The commissariat established multiple stores and supplied foodstuffs and materials (at government expense) not only for convicts but for civilian and military personnel as well. In the early years, well over 50% of the entire population would have been victualled by the commissariat

The commissariat also established, work centres for convicts:

The Lumber Yard,
The Timber Yard
The Dockyard
The Stone Quarry
The Boat Yard
Timber-Cutting Camps
Land Clearing Camps
The Government Farms
The Government stores

These centres employed until 1820 over 50% of the convict population.

The output of these centres was directed at Agricultural output; Livestock supply;

Import Replacement manufactures; Materials required in the Construction and building industries; Materials required in the Public Works and Infrastructure Construction program, and Transport and storage requirements of the government.

Colin White[105] in has concluded that the colonial government controlled the local economic mechanism. There were three main elements to the mechanism:

(1)The government provided the social infrastructure to mitigate risk to individuals, and further, (2) guaranteed a market, at fixed prices, for output of the private sector. This government action also provided (3) grants of free land, inexpensive credit and cheap labour with the return of any redundant labour to government service when needed.

---

105 *Mastering Risk–Environment, Markets and Politics in Australian Economic History* Page 52

Public Works

Public Investment in public works infrastructure was a major challenge. Britain essentially saw the settlement as little more than a tent town. These inhabitants were prisoners, under guard, transported 'out of sight and out of mind' and had no need of money or coins, public buildings or fancy housing or amenities. Early governors from Phillip to Bligh kept to the minimum work and therefore expense, and by the time of Macquarie's arrival, there was a deferred maintenance and construction schedule that dumped all of the expense and workload on his Administration. Commissioner Bigge recorded for his Enquiry that 76 buildings had been completed under Macquarie, some of which were extravagant for example the Governor's *Stables*, The Rum Hospital, and the toll booths on the Parramatta Road. Bigge directed they be revamped and put to alternate (less extravagant use). Bigge made no comment on the provision of water, sewer or drainage measures made for a town with a growing population. Macquarie had drained the marshes in the present Centennial Park as the water supply for the town–and outlawed the use of the Tank Stream for animal grazing, washing, and waste sewer.

Governor Darling, as part of his structuring of a public service for the colony, established in 1826 the first Office of Inspector of Roads and Bridges, with charge over the Engineer's office. From April 1827, his title was changed to Surveyor of Roads and Bridges, and the office remained active until 1830, when in an economy drive, Sir George Murray, Secretary of State for the Colony and War Departments passed these responsibilities to the Surveyor-General. In 1832 the Colonial Architect's Department was established in order to be responsible for the planning, repair and construction of public buildings. In 1833, in another economy drive, this department was also transferred to the Surveyor-General. Later the duties of colonial engineer for superintendence over roads, bridges, wharves and quays were added to those of the Colonial Architect and all planning came under the Surveyor-General. It was this concentration of work load in such few hands that led to an increasing public investment in public works.

Another effort by Governor Darling to centralise planning and control into a new public service bureaucracy, was the establishment of the Clergy and School Lands Department in 1826. The corporation was to receive a seventh in value and extent of all the lands in each county in the colony. Out of this land the corporation was to be responsible for the payment of salaries of clergy, schoolmasters, and for the building and maintenance of churches, school and minister's residences.

Governor Darling had centralised the planning for all public works into one department–the Land's Department which in turn employed the Surveyor-General and provided for the Lands Board. This balance assisted in prioritising and funding all public works and thus brought order to the former Macquarie chaos of building as he saw fit. A by-product of this new policy was that all convicts were now on assignment and 'off the stores', and a competitive contracting arrangement was used for tendering for all public works.

An Economic Model of the Colonial Economy GDP

The pre-1861 period has long been considered[106] too risky to assemble data for creating an economic model of the times. However certain elements of such a model can be identified and used for, in the least, a good indicative assessment of the economic growth between 1788 and 1860.

A practical example of an economic model which could be adapted for the period was found in McTaggart, Findlay and Parkin *Macroeconomics.*

106 N.G. Butlin and T.A. Coghlan write of the inaccurate statistics and other data for this period.

THE PRODUCTION APPROACH

1820

	£
Agriculture, Fishery & Forestry	
Mining	
Water, lighting & heating	
Construction	
Wholesale Trade	
Retail Trade	
Hotels, Cafes	
Transport & Storage	
Communication services	
finance & insurance	
Gov't admin & defence	
education	
health & social services	
cultural & recreation	
taxes on products	
Total	£

The rise of manufacturing was a significant part of the economic growth in the early colony. Of all the sectors, agriculture (including whaling, sealing and wool) gave the most significant results in terms of manpower used, capital invested, export returns, and GDP. In second place would be the development of local natural resources followed closely by manufacturing outcomes. These observations can be made from individual statistics of employment, exports, convict work organisation and data about immigrants and their assets. However, the more reliable statistics will come from the assembly of a model using either the production approach, or the aggregate income/expenditure approach. Both methods will be attempted and compared, but as can be seen an understanding and assessment of manufacturing is essential to either methodology.

Hainsworth in the prologue to *The Sydney Traders* writes 'To study the 'entrepreneur' is to study the central figure in modern economic history–the central figure in economics'. The years 1788 to 1821 are the seed-time of Australian government'.[107]

Although it is difficult to connect the growth of economic development in percentage of contribution terms for any one sector, we know that the more important sectors must be

1. Growth of population
2. Government immigration policy
3. Foreign capital
4. The need for Import replacement
5. The need for foreign exchange through exports.

In each of these the commissariat had a role and an important government need.

The government had to grow the economy at the lowest practical cost, but offer official services which would attract growth, trade and population. This it achieved, at least through 1821, by using the commissariat as the quasi-treasury, the manager of government business enterprises, and the employer of government-sponsored convict labour.

The point here is that the economic model had to incorporate each of these 'input' factors and reflect them. Here in brief is the methodology used.

The commissariat influence over foreign exchange, imports and exports, and government-sponsored manufacturing and even over attracting foreign investment capital is without comparison, but measurable. The economic model for the period does not nor cannot parallel Butlin's measurement of post-1861 GDP, but does use basic ingredients like:

1. Computing working free population
2. Computing working convict population
3. Assuming a productivity adjustment for lower than expected convict output
4. Valuing productive labour at Coghlan suggested rates

---

[107] Hainsworth *Sydney Traders* prologue page 14

5. Interpolating labour product to total output.
6. Comparing annual total production per head of population and per head of 'worker'
7. Estimating total output by industry and comparing this to underlying assumptions about labour output.
8. Extending the estimated GDP from 1800 to 1860 to ensure the recessions of 1810-1816, 1828-29 and 1842-45 as shown in the GDP figures were responsive to these downturns.
9. Comparing the growth of local revenues from 1801 and of trade, for the same period reflected changes to estimated GDP.
10. Announcing the adopted GDP figures for the period 1800-1860 and seeing how they blended in with the Butlin figures.

The results are assembled on a spreadsheet for each year, but a summary has been produced as an extract in order to evidence gains for each ten-year interval, and to show that the Beckett compilations and the Butlin compilations fit in with each other.

TABLE ESTIMATES OF GDP BETWEEN 1800 AND 1900

Year	GDP per head of popln	GDP per head of workforce
1801	13.61	35.1
1811	28.06	49.95
1821	33.54	59.70
1831	35.68	63.51
1841	39.66	70.60
1851	40.13	76.43
1861	46	85
1871	47	118
1877	57	139
1881	63	151
1889	67	158
1891	66	155
1900	57	132

Source: Beckett *Handbook of Colonial Statistics for period 1800-1860*
Butlin, N.G. *Investment in Australian Economic Development 1861-1900*

Certain conclusions can be reached about this table:

1. GDP in the colony grew in each ten year period because the components of that GDP grew eg population, manufacturing enterprises, convict numbers, exports and immigration. As the colony went through its transition from penal to free, especially a free market-based economy, so government investment in services and infrastructure also grew. Personal investment in housing increased and the individual wealth as well as the collective wealth of the colony grew. The down turn in 1900 was due to the recession in the mid-1890s, when many banks failed, unemployment increased and the previous land boom of the 1870-80s crashed, leaving many families and businesses in tough times.

However certain questions remain: This model relates to restricted sectors of the colonial economy, but only touches indirectly on important sectors such as the pastoral industry, the whaling and seal industry. These sectors are indirectly reflective of a growing export market. A more detailed model with declared sub-elements would express the importance of these natural resource or primary production industries including timber, shipping, coal, minerals as well as wool and wool by-products

There were some distractions from within the colony to Macquarie's aggressive enterprise policies. In a wave of perversion, William Charles Wentworth led an anti-Macquarie movement against local manufacturing in favour of importations.

In January of 1819, Macquarie gave permission for a group of clergy, merchants, settlers, and other gentlemen to convene a meeting in the court-room of the new General Hospital, to prepare a petition. The petition was for a redress of grievances and essentially was to try and expand rather than restrict imports into the colony. Macquarie by trying to match exports with imports (in value terms), was restricting the type of imports authorised.

Macquarie, in a despatch to Bathurst of 22nd March, 1819 notates[108] the resolution

---

108 HRA1:10:52 Macquarie to Bathurst 22nd March, 1819

'1. That a regular demand exists in the colony for British manufactures of nearly all descriptions, greater than the established mercantile houses here have supplied or are likely to supply regularly.
2. Restrictions prevent merchants from employing ships of less three hundred and fifty tons burthen (under the *Navigation Acts)*
3. That this meeting requests Gov Macquarie to try and expand shipping between Britain and Australia for transporting Manufactures and colonial produce.'

The sentiments were laudable but the request baseless. The commissariat with its huge buying opportunities could have achieved the desired result. Merchants' collaborating into a buying group could have achieved the same result but the obvious solution was to encourage the local production of all imported items at a lower cost.

Macquarie made no recommendations to Bathurst, which meant that he had strictly fulfilled his role to the petitioners, and had left Bathurst with the opinion that the colonial manufacturers and merchants were ill-prepared to fight British exports

In over 300 pages of text, John Ritchie[109] reviews the submissions made in the colony to Commissioner Bigge, but does not recite any submission made by merchants or manufacturers. However in the Bigge reports, we find details of evidence submitted by Simeon Lord about his manufacturing activities. At his factory at Botany Bay, he employed between 15 and 20 convicts in the making of:

Blankets	Stockings
Wool hats	Trousers
Kangaroo hats	Glass tumblers
Seal hats,	Kettles
Possum skin hats,	Thread
Boot leather	Shirts

109 Ritchie, John *Punishment and Profit- The Bigge Commission in to NSW'*

Between 1810 and 1820 the number of sheep trebled in the colony, and many producers were finding it more profitable to sell carcasses instead of fleeces

Local manufactured items did not entirely replace imports. Items were still imported from India and China.

From India came
Sugar
Spirits
Soap
Cotton goods

From China came
Sugar candy
Silks
Wearing apparel

Colonial Exports included
Sandalwood
Pearl shells
Bache de mar
Whale oil and meat
Seal Oil

Trade exchange, on a barter basis, was made with a number of the Pacific Islands of 'coarse cotton' and ironware, for coconut and salt pork.

Among other evidence to the Bigge Enquiry were numerous complaints by manufacturers on the limited supply of materials, the high cost of buying from government business enterprises–for instance the cloth produced by workers at the government female factory was 2/5 1/4 d per yard, whereas at Mr Kenyon's private establishment it was only 11d. The Manager of the Robert Campbell merchant business complained to Commissioner Bigge about the duties on whale and seal oil from the colony, arriving in England. He also criticised the port regulations which required captains to give 10 day's notice of intention to sail–he claimed this resulted in high wharfage charges.

Ritchie (*Punishment & Profit)* concludes that although Bigge wanted to encourage trade and certain manufacturing, he was reconciled to the fact that their promotion would not provide an adequate or proper solution to the question of convict employment, punishment and reform. [110]

Observations on Industry & Commerce in NSW

By 1820 Simeon Lord had turned the profits of fishing in the south seas and trade in the Pacific Islands into a manufactory at Botany Bay where he employed convicts and from 15 to 20 colonial youths making blankets, stockings, wool hats, kangaroo hats, seal hats, possum skin hats, all of them shoddy but cheaper than English imports of hats, boots, leather, trousers, shirts, thread, kettles and glass tumblers. [111]

The heavy influx of immigrants during the Darling Administration brought its own difficulties, especially when drought and depression closed down on the colony at the end of the 1830s. This period led onto the sever economic depression of 1842, which had been fuelled by a reduction of foreign investment, a cessation of the British speculators and absentee landlords, as well as local factors, partly sponsored by Sir George Gipps, the successor to Darling as Governor. Between 1831 and 1841, imports had increased by 518 percent to a total of over two and a half million pounds and exports by 1257 percent to a total of two million pounds.[112]

The severe drought of 1825-8 was unfairly blamed on Darling, as was the epidemic of 'hooping cough' which killed Darling's own son and of smallpox which afflicted the colony.

Between December 1831 and December 1832 325,549 gallons of spirits and 109,406 gallons of wine were imported and at least another 11,000 gallons of gin were distilled locally–all for a population of only 15,000.

---

[110] Evidence of sundry manufacturers to Commissioner Bigge Enquiry)

[111] An quote extracted from Clark, A History of Australia sourced by Clark from 'An account of Mr Lord's manufactures, submitted to Commissioner Bigge, 1st February 1821

[112] Barnard, Marjorie *Sydney–A story of a City'* P.18

As for prices, milk was 8 pence per quart, potatoes were fifteen shillings a hundredweight, beef had declined to one penny halfpenny a pound[113], mutton twopence halfpenny, veal five-pence, pork four-penny halfpenny. Fowls cost from 1/9d to 2/3d per pair, whilst butter varied from season to season between 1/–and 3/–per pound,; cheese sold at 4 pence per pound, Cape wine was 8d to ½ per pint and port was 1/45 to 2/–per quart. Respectable lodgings were a pound per week. And a horse could be hired for 10/–a day, and a gig for 15/–per day. Housing costs had risen to 530 pound for a six-roomed cottage

The depression that lasted from the late 1830s to 1842 but created a slow down in the colony until gold was discovered in 1852, caused an estimated 1638 bankruptcies. There was a glut of livestock such that sheep were selling for 6d per head. Land sales ceased and there was an oversupply of labour for the first time in 50 years. Almost a final blow to the struggling economy came with the discovery of gold in California, with estimates of 5757 houses being empty out of the 7100 houses in Sydney town.[114]

The economy in the period up to 1800 was based upon the limited trade monopolised by military men like John Macarthur as well as a steady expansion of government-financed agriculture to feed the growing number of convicts. This expansion could only continue until the colony became self-sufficient in food. Then an alternative product, of sufficient value to be exported would be required to generate the hard currency that in turn would pay for the increasing imports demanded by the growing economy. Only by developing such a staple export could the colony become economically viable and thereby partially believe the treasury of the burden of supporting it. With such a staple export attracting additional population, the colonists would also have some hope of eventually claiming the continent's wide interior.

By 1802, Governor King could report to London that seal skins were the way ahead in terms of exports. More than 100,000 skins were landed in and shipped from Sydney between 1800 and 1806, In 1804, 11 Sydney-based

---

113 Beef during the Macquarie Administration was bought by the Commissariat at 5 pence per pound

114 Barnard Marjorie *ibid*

ships were engaged in the Bass Strait sealing trade, in addition to the large number of ships in pursuit of whaling.

By the early 1800s there were four main types of economic activity in the colony. Agriculture and grazing was making the colony almost self-sufficient in this product, and large landowners were undermining the governor's attempts to encourage yeomen farmers. Many of these large landowners also engaged in mercantile activities. A growing number of emancipated convicts became traders on their own account, with speculation in trade marked by gluts and scarcities. Many merchants also operated their own vessels, engaging in sealing and whaling. The number of whalers operating out of Sydney rose from 5 in 1827 to 76 in 1835. Between 1826 and 1835 the value of fishery products passing through Sydney reached £950,000. In 1849, there were 37 boats based in Hobart employing 1000 seamen.[115]

Sealing and Whaling were followed by exports of wool. Although only 29 sheep had arrived with the First Fleet, successive convict fleets added to the flocks and herds and the numbers quickly expanded by natural increase. By 1805, there were 500 horses, 4000 cattle, 5000 goats, 23000 pigs and 20000 sheep. The efforts of these large landowners, including John Macarthur resulted in a dramatic change in the export statistics, with the weight of wool being exported rising from just 167 pounds in 1811 to 175,433 pounds in 1821.[116]

By 1835, the supremacy of pastoralism was beyond dispute, with exports of fine wool dominating the trade figures. The success of the pastoral industry was at the expense of the British government's efforts to slow the invasion of the interior. The success was the result of a combination of factors–cheap land taken from the Aborigines; cheap labour in the form of convict and even cheap Aborigine labour from those able to supervise large flocks over extensive unfenced grasslands in the interior.[117]

---

115 Day, David *Claiming a Continent–A new History of Australia.* Pages 49,50,51

116 Day, David *Ibid pages 52,53*

117 Day, David *ibid* page 74

Not surprisingly the Europeans found the same attractive places to settle, as the aborigines also found most desirable–water sources and native grasslands.

By 1850 over 4000 pastoralists with their 20 million sheep occupied 400 million hectares (1000 million acres) of inland Australia.

The growth of population contributed greatly to the rise of manufacturing and the general economic growth in the economy. NSW grew from 76845 Europeans in 1836 to 187243 in 1851. Growth in Port Phillip and South Australia was even more dramatic. By m1841 more than half the male population of NSW was colonial-born or immigrant rather than convict, while convicts and emancipists comprised just over 1/3rd of the total population. However males still outnumbered females roughly two to one.

One aspect of trade is generally overlooked when it comes to identifying special and important exports. Wool exports began to sour in the early 1820s, and most historians claim wool dominates agricultural exports and that opinion clouds the real truth.

In fact from 1788 to 1828, if a reliable set of export statistics is compiled, it will be surprising if Australian-owned whaling and sealing vessels are found to be less productive than sheep in those first 49 years. The figures do exist for the next six years from 1828 and for Australia as a whole; whaling narrowly exceeds wool for that period, whilst as late as 1833 whaling is New South Wales' main export industry. However, after that time, 'wool races away, yielding in the last three years of the 1830s almost double the export value of Australia's whale products[118]

A secondary importance of this industry is that each vessel whilst in port is estimated to have spent an average of £300, not counting the sovereigns the crew spent in the inns and elsewhere.[119] Then there was the work for the dockyards. Shipbuilding was probably the largest and most dynamic colonial manufacture before 1850, and Tasmania alone built 400 vessels from small cutters to ships of 500 tons burthen that joined the

---

118 Blainey, Geoffrey *The tyranny of Distance* Page 115

119 Coughlin, T.A. *Labour & Industry in Australia* Volume 1, Page 367

England-Australia run. Blainey also observes that the reluctance to put whaling into accurate perspective in importance to the colonial economy stems from apathy towards maritime history. He claims that 'except for ship-lovers, the sea and ships are still virtually banished from written history'.[120]

Bigge referred in his third report in 1823[121] to the high level of efficiency amongst the convicts assigned to 'task work' for the government manufactures. Commissioner Bigge discovered at the close of the Macquarie period that the significance of the Government Store as a market for colonial produce and a source of foreign exchange were greater than ever. The heavy increase in the number of convicts transported after the end of the Napoleonic wars had correspondingly increased the government's demand for foodstuffs. Thus Bigge reported, had retarded the growth of export industries by encouraging the growth of agriculture–farming as opposed to grazing. 'It is possible, given other circumstances the settlers might have turned their attention to the production of other objects than those that solely depended upon the demands of the Government'[122]

Bigge also refers to the high level of skills used in the Government Business Centre–the Lumber Yard–and to the benefit the colony derived from the local public sector manufacturing.

Summary

Of the nine economic drivers within the colonial economy, the role of manufacturing had the far reaching and desirable results.

The Macquarie Administration decided to centralise and highly regulate the labour and output of the more than 50% of the convicts, who having arrived in the colony were assigned to private or government work. For those assigned to government labour, the broad range of activities required

---

120 Blainey *ibid* Page 116-7

121 Commissioner Bigge's Estimate of the value of convict labour in Sydney for 1822

122 Bigge, J.T. *Report on the Agriculture and Trade of NSW* 1823 Page 22

a smarter government store than had hitherto been the case. The store was to have on hand sufficient tools and materials to keep these people fully utilised in their allotted task. Those convicts assigned to land and road clearing needed grubbing tools and axes. They required hauling equipment, and food supplies. Those allocated to public building projects and public infrastructure required tools, bricks, blocks, tiles and a large array of sawn timbers.

The Governor ordered the commissariat to create a central facility for assembling and distributing these materials. Most items could have been ordered in from Britain or elsewhere in Europe. The lengthy purchasing and requisition procedures required a lead time of between fifteen months and two years. Thus Macquarie's charge to the Commissariat to employ convict labour in the manufacturing locally of as many imported items as possible created an import replacement program that created employment, led to private sector entrepreneurs, and generated a program of transition in local manufacturing from the public to the private sector.

Commissioner Bigge reported on the extent of the trades utilised in the Lumber Yard and it makes an impressive list[123]. The trades carried on in this government business enterprise [in this case, the Lumber Yard] are also reported on by Major Ovens, the former Superintendent of Convicts[124]

'In the Lumber Yard are assembled all the indoor tradesmen who work in the shops such as blacksmiths, carpenters, sawyers, shoemakers, tailors etc. The workmen, carrying on their occupations under the immediate eye of the Chief Engineer are probably kept in a better state of discipline than those, who working more remote, are dependent on the good behaviour of an overseer for any work they may perform. Whatever is produced from the labour of these persons[125], which is not applied to any public work or

123 Bigge, J.T. *Report on the Agriculture and Trade of NSW* 1823 Page 22

124 Report by Major Ovens to Governor Brisbane on reorganisation for the Lumber Yard HRA 1:11:655-7

125 Sawn timber for framing, roof battens, flooring, window frames, doors, nails, bolts, bellows, barrels, furniture - from Beckett *The Operations of the Commissariat of NSW 1788-1856*

fore any supply of authorised requisitions, is placed in a large store and kept to furnish the exigencies of future occasions'.

Growth in the colonial economy came in numerous guises, such as technological progress in industry and agriculture, transport and communication; the growth of population, and the accumulation of capital; the discovery of raw materials, and the spread of economic freedom.

The rise of a manufacturing sector relied on most of these areas, especially technological gains, supply of capital, immigration of skilled trades and Macquarie's sympathetic encouragement of entrepreneurs. Although not as vital as the agricultural sector, the manufacturing sector provided substantial employment, innovation, skills training, and the basis for potential decentralisation. Most importantly, during the Macquarie Administration, the manufacturing sector supported Macquarie's transition from a penal to free market economy. As the colonial economy stabilised, it became attractive for a large number of British based industries wanting to open branch offices in the colonies to invest in small scale activities, often transferring skilled labour from Britain to underpin their colonial operations.

Local industry also helped develop local resources, both human and capital. Both coal and timber became important exports for the colony, whilst the list of other natural resources being developed for both local use and exporting grew longer and longer.

New industry required new talents and skills. So a number of adjunct industries came into being–engineering design, equipment manufacturing and equipment maintenance. Not all new equipment was imported and particularly in agricultural equipment suitable for local conditions, local manufacture and assembly was the norm rather than the exception.

Employment in the sector grew to an important level, with the number of factories in NSW increasing from 37 in 1829 to 174 in 1850[126].

---

126 Butlin, Ginswick & Statham *The Economy before 1850* (Australians: Historical statistics–p.108)

Exports increased during the same period from £79,000 per annum to over £8,000,000[127]. Boatbuilding peaked in 1843 at 46 vessels for the year, although the average size halved between 1841 and 1843. There were 102 vessels registered in the colony in 1841 disbursing 12,153 tons. By 1843, this number had declined to 77 and continued to decline until the 1900s.[128]

Even as late as 1827, the Colonial Office was still very suspicious about the expenses of the convict establishment. Lord Bathurst wrote of 'the difficulty I feel in reconciling the scarcity of assignable convicts . . . . with the enormous and increasing expense with which this country is still charged'[129] Every effort to trim convict maintenance expenses or expand the assignment system impacted on the Commissariat business operations. The Superintendent of Convicts would agree to the training of apprentices, only to find them sent of 'on assignment' whilst the best workers in the Lumber Yard were always in demand by private manufacturers, and government building workers, were constantly in demand by the private contractors.

[127] Butlin et al *ibid* - P. 109

[128] Sourced by Beckett from original data in *Australians: Historical Statistics*, Coghlan and Butlin

[129] HRA 1:8:221

CHAPTER 7

GROWING THE COLONIAL ECONOMY–GDP 1800-1860

Special Theories on the Pattern of Economic Growth in the Colony 1788-1860

The Aborigines (pre-British occupation of 1788) were careful custodians of the land who had utilised the land in accordance with tradition and expectations of affinity and as a food source. The aborigines sought to preserve a practice long in existence that did not overdevelop or over use the land or its resources but which produced all the needs of its limited population

If there is any worthwhile validity in comparing farming systems between the pre–and post 1788 practices, then they are comparable to the extent that both systems supported, at various times differently, their population. Native grasses vs. improved pastures, and domesticated livestock vs. native livestock. Both yielded sufficient 'value' from the land to support individual needs; both could co-exist but the 'invaders' wanted unrestricted access to the land; their ways were only to 'clear fell' the country, thus transforming the land from its natural cycle to an unnatural cycle of waste of natural resources, removal of underlying 'natural support' system of replenishment, and of over-utilising the natural burden of the land.

Post-1788, and until 1802, economic growth was limited to subsistence farming, and a settling in system, whereby the more intellectual civil servants and colonists took time to understand the land, its abilities and limitations. This prefacing to development was essential in order to lay the foundation for a longer-term successful future. Then, as now, there were two types of thinking and planning–rush ahead and do whatever it takes to succeed in the short-term, or move cautiously with an intent and some knowledge to succeed long-term. The governors mostly were of the latter mindset but were equally aware of the limitations imposed on the colony by irregular supplies of food arriving from the 'home country' and the growing quantities needed, as well as the directions made by the British Colonial Office to be self-sufficient, self-supportive and live within a shrinking budget. The most outstanding example of this 'conflict' was the livestock brought with the first fleet, was left untouched even though the colony was starving. On the other hand, the conflict with the aboriginals resulted in a failure to utilise the native wildlife or the sea-life adequately or appropriately as a transition arrangement and evidence of planned co-existence. This first period was like 'treading water' rather than making progress.

The second period (1802-1821) was a period of consolidation, planning and moving ahead at great speed. Although the last of the naval governors–King and Bligh–were pre-occupied with internal conflict and curbing civil unrest, the period was unrestrained in terms of individuals pursuing self-interest–not in an entrepreneurial way, but as a means of doing 'for ourselves' what the administration should be doing. This was a period of transition when the systems were being developed and being 'bedded in'. It was a period of learning, of exploring, of making 'ends meet' with limited resources, great ingenuity and more than a modicum of luck. The economic growth was reflected in the survival of the people; the ill-treatment of the native peoples; the spread of settlement and the resulting open plains and broad acres which unshackled the limitations on grain production and livestock grazing previously experienced; the transformation of the economy from the 'barter' economy pre-Macquarie to an economy with a monetary system; the transformation of the economy from a mindset of 'penal colony' to that of a colony with a future; the organised and structured building and construction boom. The period came to an end with the 'reflections' of a bureaucrat (John Thomas Bigge), who became a tool of the influential and a pawn of the blinkered few who could not see a future for the colony. The greatest gains during this period came from the unlikeliest of sources–the development of a road system, the intelligent harnessing of convict labour, but the greatest gain of all came from the imposition, collection and utilisation of the colony's discretionary revenues. These revenues collected from a 'tax' or duty imposed on imports, gave the governors access to discretionary expenditures which otherwise would not have been funded. Subtle improvements in the quality of life, which the British Government would not have supported. The Colonial Office in London drew on the policy of people in the colony not having a standard of living higher, whilst in the colony, than they would have enjoyed at 'home' and certainly not the convicts. It was this local revenue, for many years outside the influence of Whitehall, which made the difference to the people in the colony. Macquarie refined the collection of these revenues and people could physically see the change in the colony, and their spirits rose accordingly, and there was less unhappiness, more positive thinking and expression and an overall more productive economy with greater growth and positive movement.

The third period was short 1821-1827. It was as if the Bigge Report, based on his assessment between 1819 and 1822, but his findings were not published until 1823, placed a yoke around the neck of the collective colony and struggled to restrain the urge to move ahead, whilst going through a radical restructure of the way ahead. A different type of governor was installed and they were made very aware of the 'new' post Bigge approach to developing the colony–more convicts would arrive; expenditure for their support would be minimised, and local revenues would be used to run the colony on a daily basis. Both Brisbane and Darling acted responsibility, advanced the political changes for the local administration with its advisory bodies, and encouraged an open, free and 'creative' colony–entrepreneurs were welcome, but then so were speculators, and that was what brought this period to a close–a depression of 1827.

The fourth period was longer, 1827-1842, with growth of manufactures and the primary industries (led by wool) growing at an equally fast rate. The pastoral /wool industry brought most of the capital, created most of the export trade and showed the greatest capital creation and returns on capital. The manufacturing industries attracted the free settlers and provided an employment base for the growing army of emancipists. Its greatest benefit lay not in its meagre exports, but in its successful import replacement. This period witnessed large population growth, large livestock numbers, large quantities of exports (always matched by continuing import needs) and growing wealth creation. As with the third period, it closed with a major depression, man-made, with imported downturns from Britain, withdrawal of speculators and then investors, a slowing of migrants arriving

The fifth period was 1842-1850. If my assumption is valid that 'periods' were defined not by people, such as the arrival of a new governor, but by events, then there is a natural period break in 1850. The discovery of gold, the rebalancing of export composition from wool and grain to gold, and the dramatic surge in local revenues led to marvellous change in the colonial economy. A migrant inflow, previously unspeculated upon by Governors, was the first step, and the second was the spectacular benefits of the coming of rail.

The sixth period was 1851-1856. This period was defined by political instability leading up to independence and the fight between the British Treasury that could see the burgeoning local revenues, worth protecting and fighting for, and the local Legislative Council, that could sense independence through self-government coupled with the growing local revenues which could be otherwise lost to the colony, if self-government without conditions was not achieved.

BIBLIOGRAPHY

Alexander, Michael. "Mrs. Fraser on the Fatal Shore:
Appleyard, R.T. "Australian Financiers–Biographical Essays"
Austin, A.G. (ed.) "Australian Educations 1788-1900"
Australians–A Historical Library–in eleven volumes.
Barcan, Alan. "A History of Australian Education"
Barnard Eldershaw, M. "A House is Built"
Barnard Eldershaw, M. "Phillip of Australia"
Barnard, Marjorie. "A History of Australia"
Barnard, Marjorie. "Sydney, The Story of a City"
Bate, Frank, R.M. "Samuel Bate–Singular Character"
Bessant (ed.) "Australian History–The Occupation of a Continent"
Blaikie, George. "Remember Smith's Weekly?"
Blainey, Geoffrey. "A Land Half Won"
Blainey, Geoffrey. "All for Australia"
Blainey, Geoffrey. "Triumph of the Nomads"
Blainey, Geoffrey. "The Tyranny of Distance"
Brett, Bernard. "Captain Cook"
Bridges, Peter. "Foundations of Identity–Building Early Sydney 1788-1822"
Broadbent, James. "Francis Greenway Architect"
Brodsky, Isadore. "Sydney Takes the Stage"
Brodsky, Isadore. "Sydney's Little World of Woolloomooloo"
Broeze, Frank. "Mr Brooks and the Australian Trade"
Buckland, Jill. "Mort's Cottage" (1838-1988)
Butlin "War Economy 1939-1942"

Butlin & Schedvin "War Economy 1942-1945"
Butlin, N.G. "Forming a Colonial Economy–Australia 1810-1850"
Butlin, N.G. "Working Papers in Economic History"
Butlin, S.F. "Foundations of the Australian Monetary System 1788-1851"
Cannon, M 'The Land Boomers'
Cannon, Michael "The Land Boomers"
Cannon, Michael "Australia–Spirit of a Nation–A Bicentenary Album."
Cannon, Michael. "Life in the Country–Australia in the Victorian Age Vol 2"
Carter, H.B. "His Majesty's Spanish Flock 1788"
Casey, R.G. "Australian Father and Son"
Chambers, John H. "Australia–A Traveller's History"
Clark, C.M.H. "A Short History of Australia" 1969
Clark, C.M.H. "A History of Australia"–V1-6
Clark, C.M.H. "A Short History of Australia" 1963
Clark, C.M.H. "Occasional Writings & Speeches"
Clark, C.M.H. "Select Documents in Australian History 1788-1850
Clark, C.M.H. "Select Documents in Australian History 1851-1900.
Clark, C.M.H. "Sources of Australian History"
Cleverley, John F. "The First Generation–School & Society in Early Australia"
Cobley, John. "Sydney Cove 1788"
Cobley, John. "Sydney Cove 1789-1790"
Cobley, John. "Sydney Cove 1791-1792"
Cobley, John. "Sydney Cove 1793-1795"
Cobley, John. "The Crimes of the First Fleet Convicts"
Coghlan, T.A. "Labour and Industry in Australia"(4 volumes)
Coghlan, Timothy. "The Wealth & Progress of N.S.W. 1900-1901"
Collins C.R. "Sage of Settlement"
Collins, David. "An Account of the English Colony in N.S.W." (Vols 1 & 2)
Coltheart, Lenore. "Significate Sites–History and public works in New South Wales"
Connah, Graham "The Archeology of Australia's History"
Copland, D.B. "The Australian Tariff–An Economic Enquiry"
Copland, D.B. "The Australian Tariff" 1929.
Crisp, L.F. "The Parliamentary Government of the Commonwealth of Australia"
Crisp, L.F. "Ben Chifley"

Crowley, Frank "Colonial Australia 1841-1874"
Crowley, Frank (ed.) "A New History of Australia"
Crowley, Frank. "Australia's Western Third–A History of W.A."
Crowley, Frank. "Colonial Australia 1788-1840" Vols I-III
Crowley, Frank. "Colonial Australia 1875-1900"
Davidson, Rodney. "Australian National Trusts–Historic Houses"
Davison, Graeme. "The Use and Abuse of Australian History"
de Vries-Evans, Susanna. "Historic Sydney as Seen by its Early Artists"
Deakin, Alfred. "And be One People"
Deane, Phyllis "The First Industrial Revolution"
Diamond. L. "The Seahorse & The Wanderer (Ben Boyd)"
Dickey, Brian. "No Charity There"
Dickey, Brian. "Politics in New South Wales 1856-1900"
Dufty, David "Historians at Work–recreating the past"
Dunbabin, Thomas "The making of Australasia"
Dunn, Michael. "Australia and the Empire–from 1788 to the present"
Dyster, Barrie (ed.) "Beyond Convict Workers"
Eggleston, F.W. (ed.) "The Peopling of Australia"
Ellis, M. H. "Francis Greenway"
Ellis, M. H. "John Macarthur"
Ellis, M. H. "Lachlan Macquarie"
Emanuel, Cedric. "Historic Buildings of Sydney Sketchbook"
Emanuel, Cedric. "Historic Sydney Sketchbook"
Emanuel, Cedric. "The Rocks–Sydney's Most Historic Area"
Emanuel, Cedric. "Sydney Harbour Sketchbook"
Emmanurel, Cedric "Historic Towns of NSW"
Evatt, H.V. "William Holman–Australian Labour Leader"
Evatt, H.V. "Rum Rebellion"
Farrer, T. H. "Free Trade vs Fair Trade"
Fitzpatrick, Brian. "The Australian People 1788-1945"
Fitzpatrick, Brian. "The British Empire in Australia–An Economic History 1834-1939.
Flannery, Tim. "The Birth of Sydney"
Flannery, Tim. "Watkin Tench 1788"
Fletcher, Brian H. "Ralph Darling–A Governor Maligned"
Flower, Cedric "Treasures of Australia"
Fogarty, Br. Ronald. "Catholic Education in Australia 1806-1950"
Fowles, Joseph. "Sydney in 1848"

Frances, R. "The Politics of Work"
Fraser, J.F. "Australia" (1910)
Gamble, Allan. "Botany Bay Sketchbook"
Gamble, Allan. "Setting for a Campus"
Gamble, Allan. "St Mary's Basilica–Sydney"
Gamble, Allan. "University of Sydney Sketchbook"
Garran, Andrew (ed.) "Australia–The First Hundred Years"
Gordon, Harry "The Eyewitness History of Australia"
Gould, Nat. "Town and Bush"
Grattan, C. Hartley. "Introducing Australia"
Greenwood, Gordon. "Australia–A Social and Political History"
Harris, Max. "The Land that Waited"
Haskell, Arnold, L. "The Australians–The Strategic Position"
Hazell, E.G. Some Came Free
Herman, Morton. "Historic Building of Parramatta"
Herman, Morton. "The Blackets–An Era of Australian Architecture"
Historic Records of Australia–Series I, II, III (Vols 1-33)
Historical Records of N.S.W. 1762–1811 (9 vols.)
Historical Records of Victoria–Vol 7.
Horne, Donald. "Billy Hughes"
Howe, Robert. "The Sydney Gazette 1803-1842"
Hughes, Robert. "The Fatal Shore"
Illustrated History of Australia
Inglis, K. S. "The Australian Colonists"
Ingpen, Robert. "Pioneer Settlement in Australia"
Jervis, J 'The cradle City of Australia–Parramatta'
Jose, Arthur W. "History of Australasia"
Joy, William "The Explorers"
Joy, William "The Exiles"
Joy, William 'The Liberators'
Karskens, Grace. "The Rocks–Life in Early Sydney"
Keesing, Nancy. "John Lang and the Forger's Wife"
Kerr & Falkus "From Sydney Cove to Duntroon"
Kiddle, Margaret. "Caroline Chisholm"
King, Jonathan. "The First Fleet"
King, Jonathon "In the Beginning . . . ."
Kingsmill, A.G. "Witness to History"

Kingston, Beverley. "The Oxford History of Australia–Glad, Confident Morning 1860-1900"
Klugman, K. "The Australian Presence in the Pacific"
Kociumbas, Jan. "The Oxford History of Australia–Possessions 1770-1860"
La Meslee, Edmond Marin "The New Australia–1883"
Lacour-Gayet, Robert. "A Concise History of Australia"
Laidlaw, Ronald. "Mastering Australian History"
Lane, P.H. "An Introduction to the Australian Constitution"
Langley, Michael. "Sturt of the Murray"
Larcombe, F.A., "The Origin of Local Government in NBSW 1831-1906"
Lawson, Will. "When Cobb & Co was King"
Lines, John D. "Australia on Paper–History of Mapping"
Lourandos, Harry. "A Continent of Hunter Gatherers"
Loveday & Martin "Parliament Factions and Parties"–1856-1889
Lyne, Charles. "The Industries of New South Wales"
Macintosh, Neil K. "Richard Johnson–Chaplain to the Colony"
Mackaness, George 'Australian Historical Monographs'
Macmillan, David S. "The Debtor's War"
McIntyre, W. David. "Colonies into Commonwealth"
McNiven, Ian (Ed) "Constructions of Colonialism"
Melbourne, A.C.V. "Early Constitutional Development in Australia"
Melbourne, A.C.V. "William Charles Wentworth"
Menzies, R.G. "Post War Reconstruction in Australia"
Moorhouse, Geoffrey. "Sydney"
Mudie, James "The Felonry of NSW"
Mulvaney, J. "A Good Foundation–Reflections on the Heritage of the First Government House, Sydney"
Murdoch, Walter. "Alfred Deakin"
Oats, W. N. "Backhouse & Walker–A Quaker View of the Australian Colonies 1832-1838"
O'Donnell, Dan. "James Hannell 1813-1876 Currency Lad"
Palmer, Vance. "National Portraints"
Palmer: "The Great Days of Wool"
Park, Ruth. "The Companion Guide to Sydney"
Philips, David (ed.) "A Nation of Rogues?"

Quick & Garran, "The Annotated Constitution of the Australian Commonwealth"
Reynolds, Henry. "The Law of the Land"
Reynolds, John. "Edmund Barton"
Richards, Thomas. "An Epitome of the Official History of New South Wales 1788-1883"
Robson, L.L. "The Convict Settlers of Australia.
Ross, Lloyd "John Curtin for Labor & Australia"
Russell, Eric. "Thomas Moore & The King's Dock Yard 1796-1816"
Scott, Geoffrey. "Sydney's Highways of History"
Serle, G "The Rush to be Rich"
Shann, Edward. "An Economic History of Australia"
Shaw, A.G.L. "The Story of Australia"
Shaw, A.G.L. "Great Britain and the Colonies 1815-1865"
Shaw, A.G.L. "The Economic Development of Australia"
Sherer, John. "The Gold-Finder of Australia"
Simpson, Margaret 'Old Sydney Buildings
Smith, Robin (ed.) "Australia's Historic Heritage–The birth of a nation"
Souter, Gavin. "Lion and Kangaroo–Australia: 1901-1919"
Souter, Ngaire. "Around the Quay"
Steven, Margaret. "First Impressions–the British Discovery of Australia"
Steven, Margaret. "Merchant Campbell 1769-1846"
Stone, R.D.J. "Makers of Fortune"
Sullivan, Martin. "Men & Women of Port Phillip"
Somers, Anne "Damn Whores & God's Police"
Tennant, Kylie. "Australia: Her Story
Terry, F.C. "New South Wales Illustrated"
The Australian Encyclopedia–in six volumes.
The Macquarie Book of Events
Thomson, James. "The Financial Statements of N.S.W. 1855-1881"
Toohey, John. "Captain Bligh's Portable Nightmare"
Travers, Robert 'Rogues' March'
Turnbull, L. H. "Sydney–Biography of a City"
Twopenny, Richard. "Town Life in Australia"
Van Sommers, Tess. "Sydney Sketchbook"
Various: "Treasures of Australia"
Various: Australia–Spirit of a Nation"
Wadham, Samuel. "Land Utilization in Australia"

Walker, Mike. "Australia–A History"
Wannan, Bill. "Very Strange Tales–The Turbulent Times of Samuel Marsden"
Ward, Russel "Australia since the coming of Man"
Ward, Russel (ed.) "The New Australia–Edmond Marin La Meslee" (1883)
Ward, Russel. "Australia"
White, Unk. "Sydney Harbour Sketchbook"
White, Unk. "The Rocks Sydney"
Williams E. N. (ed.) "The Eighteenth Century Constitution"
Wood, G. Arnold. "The Discovery of Australia"
Wood., F.L.W. "A Concise History of Australia"
Yarwood, A.T. "Samuel Marsden–The Great Survivor"
Yarwood, A.T. "Marsden of Parramatta"

INDEX